#7

THE TOWNS OF MEDIEVAL WALES

THE NORTH WEST VIEW OF CAERNARVON CASTLE.

Caernarfon

The Edwardian Castle-Borough, begun in 1283, as it appeared to
Samuel and Nathaniel Buck in 1742.

The TOWNS of MEDIEVAL WALES

A Study of Their History, Archaeology and Early Topography

Ian Soulsby

Formerly Director of the Welsh Urban Archaeology Research Unit,
University College, Cardiff

Phillimore

1983

Published by
PHILLIMORE & CO. LTD.
Chichester, Sussex, England

ISBN 0 85033 437 3

We gratefully acknowledge
The British Academy
and
The Twenty-Seven Foundation
for their generous assistance in
the publication of this book

Printed and bound in Great Britain by
THE CAMELOT PRESS
Southampton, England

CONTENTS

LIST OF FIGURES

Frontispiece: Caernarfon—The Edwardian Castle-Borough

ACKNOWLEDGEMENTS

This book has its origins in the work of the Urban Archaeology Research Unit at University College, Cardiff, 1973-78. Reflecting the increasing importance attached to the study of urban history and archaeology, the Unit was created to conduct research into the historic towns of Wales with a view to safeguarding those archaeological deposits threatened by redevelopment. My overwhelming debt, therefore, is to the Inspectorate of Ancient Monuments who provided the necessary funds, and also to the Manpower Services Commission, whose additional support enabled the initial project to be completed. My thanks are offered also to Professor Michael G. Jarrett who guided the work of the Unit in its early stages, and I am particularly grateful to him for the extended use of the facilities of the Department of Archaeology which allowed this book to be completed.

In preparing this study I have benefited considerably from the advice, freely given and readily accepted, of many friends and colleagues. My thanks in particular are extended to Chris Delaney and Dilwyn Jones, former members of the Urban Research Unit, while Susan Wrathmell proved to be a valuable aid throughout the final stages. I am also grateful to her for the preparation of Figure 2 and Table II. The final manuscript was read for me by Dr D. Huw Owen, and I would like to record my gratitude to him for his many suggestions and above all, for his encouragement. Further assistance was forthcoming from Professor Gwynedd O. Pierce, particularly with regard to place-name forms, while I would also like to take this opportunity of declaring my debt to the many private householders, farmers and clergymen who, almost without exception, readily allowed access to their properties so that the necessary field-work could be satisfactorily carried out.

This book would have been the poorer, in addition, had it not been for the unfailing assistance of the staffs of the various Welsh County Record Offices; the National Library, Aberystwyth; and the Public Record Office. I am especially grateful to the library staff of University College, Cardiff, and in particular to Dr Glyn Ashton and Mr Gwilym Hughes, who met all of my many requests with unfailing cheer and alacrity. Mr Hughes also generously permitted the loan of the valuable topographical prints which appear as illustrations in these pages. For Figures 35 and 104 I am indebted to the Aerial Photographs Division of the Department of the Environment. In the preparation of all the plates I am grateful to John Morgan, who also transformed my own amateur photographs into a more presentable form. The many town maps which appear in this book are the commendable work of Chris Mitchell and Albert Pawlak, while in the processing of all illustrations I have benefited considerably from the technical expertise of my friends David Evans and Howard Mason.

Finally, I would like to express my gratitude to my mother who has always given me great encouragement. She will be proud of this book, as, indeed, my father would have been had he been alive to see its publication.

PREFACE

This book is concerned with the circumstances and chronology of medieval town foundation and development in Wales and with the principal topographical features which existed within each urban community. While considerable use has been made of documentary sources this study does not purport to be a definitive history of towns, but is rather an attempt to combine the results of field-work with historical and archaeological evidence, written with the aim of securing the place of Wales in the increasingly popular field of urban history.

In preparing the Gazetteer, which constitutes the principal part of this book, I have consciously avoided a typological approach in determining the choice of sites. Beyond the holding of regular markets and evidence of nucleation no satisfactory definition of the criteria for medieval urban status has been advanced, and some of the more conceptual approaches to the subject are hopelessly inappropriate in a country where towns rarely assumed more than modest proportions.[1] Instead I have relied on the lists of chartered and prescriptive boroughs provided by E. A. Lewis in 1912 and Maurice Beresford in 1967 together with the historic towns named by the Council for British Archaeology in 1972.[2] To these I have added several other sites which appear to have been similar in form, content and function. To consider the town map of early Wales as consisting merely of boroughs, several of which disappeared within a few decades of their foundation, to the exclusion of other important, although unincorporated communities the like of Wrexham and Dolgellau, would clearly be a gross misrepresentation.

In a work of this kind it is inevitable that future research and excavation will cast doubts on some of my assumptions and calculations. The lesser towns, particularly, have hitherto been little studied, and it will be apparent from these pages that the archaeologist has not yet applied himself with sufficient force to the subject of urban history in Wales.[3] If some of my conclusions are to be modified or even rejected, I will readily seek comfort in the knowledge that this book may have done something towards stimulating a greater awareness of the need for a more intensive programme of urban excavation, before it is too late.

In the use of place-names I have conformed to modern practice and adopted the forms advanced by Elwyn Davies, *A Gazetteer of Welsh Place-Names,* third edition, Cardiff, 1967. As far as possible I have followed present usage, although some anglicised forms have been retained in those cases where the Welsh form has yet to gain the ascendancy, e.g., Llantwit Major instead of Llantilltud Fawr; Caerphilly rather than Caerffili.

1. *See, for example,* Schledermann, H., 'The idea of the town; typology, definitions and approaches to the study of medieval towns in northern Europe', *World Archaeology,* ii (1970), 115-27.

2. Lewis, E. A., *The Medieval Boroughs of Snowdonia,* London, 1912; Beresford, M., *New Towns of the Middle Ages,* London, 1967; Heighway, C. (ed.), *The Erosion of History,* C. B. A., London, 1972. I have excluded the single case of Whitecastle in Gwent (SO 380168) for which I have found no evidence to suggest that there was ever a town in the area of the castle.

3. For a recent review of the situation *see* Delaney, C., 'The Present State of Welsh Urban Archaeology', in Barley, M. (ed.), *The History and Archaeology of the European Town,* London, 1977, pp. 35-46.

ABBREVIATIONS

Annales Cambriae	Ab Ithel, J. B. (ed.), *Annales Cambraie* (R.S.), London, 1860.
Ann. Margam	*Annales de Margam,* in Vol. IV of *Annales Monastici* (R.S.), London, 1866.
Archaeology in Wales	The Newsletter of Group 2 (Wales), the Council for British Archaeology.
Arch. Camb.	*Archaeologia Cambrensis;* the Journal of the Cambrian Archaeological Association.
Atlas of Wales	John Speed's *Theatre of Great Britaine, 1610,* Part II, Wales (1676 edn.).
B.B.C.S.	*Bulletin of the Board of Celtic Studies.*
B.C.S.	The Board of Celtic Studies.
Beresford, *New Towns*	Beresford, M., *New Towns of the Middle Ages,* London, 1967.
Black Book	Willis-Bund, J. W. (ed.), *The Black Book of St David's,* Cymm. Rec. Ser., V, London, 1902.
Bowen, *Britannia Depicta*	Emmanuel Bowen, *Britannia Depicta or Ogilby Improved,* 4th edn., London, 1753.
Brut y Tywsogion	Jones, T. (ed.), *Brut y Tywysogion* (Chronicle of the Princes), Peniarth MS. 20, B.C.S., Hist. and Law Ser., XI, Cardiff, 1952.
Brycheiniog	The Journal of the Brecknock Society. P.R.O. Chancery Records.
Cal. Anct. Corresp.	Edwards, J. G. (ed.), *Calendar of Ancient Correspondence Relating to Wales,* B.C.S., Hist. and Law Ser., Cardiff, 1935.
Cal. Anct. Petitions	Rees, W. (ed.), *Calendar of Ancient Petitions Relating to Wales,* B.C.S. Hist. and Law Ser., XXVIII, Cardiff, 1975.
Cal. Ch. Rolls	*Calendar of Charter Rolls* (P.R.O.).
Cal. Cl. Rolls	*Calendar of Close Rolls* (P.R.O.).
Cal. Lib. Rolls	*Calender of Liberate Rolls* (P.R.O.)
Cal. Pat. Rolls	*Calendar of Patent Rolls* (P.R.O.).
Cal. Welsh Rolls	In *Calendar of Chancery Rolls: Various, 1277-1325* (P.R.O.).
Camden, *Britannia*	William Camden's *Britain, or a Chronological Description of the most flourishing kingdoms, England, Scotland and Ireland,* trans. Philemon Holland, London, 1610.
Carm. Antiq.	*The Carmarthenshire Antiquary:* the Journal of the Carmarthenshire Antiquarian Society.
Carter, *Towns of Wales*	Carter, H., *The Towns of Wales,* Cardiff, 1966.
C.B.A.	The Council for British Archaeology.
Ceredigion	The Journal of the Cardiganshire Antiquarian Society.
C.I.P.M.	*Calendar of Inquisitions Post Mortem* (P.R.O.).
Clark, *Cartae*	*Cartae et alia Munimenta quae ad dominium de Glamorgancia pertinent,* ed. G. N. Clark, 2nd edn., 6 vols., Cardiff, 1910.
D.B.	*Domesday Book* (Record Commissioners), 4 vols., London, 1783-1816.
D.L.	P.R.O., Duchy of Lancaster Records.
E	P.R.O., Exchequer Records.
E.H.R.	*The English Historical Review.*
Fenton, *Tours in Wales*	*Richard Fenton's Tours in Wales, 1804-14,* ed. J. Fisher, *Arch. Camb.* supplement, 1917.
Glam. County Hist.	*The Glamorgan County History,* III, The Middle Ages, ed. T. B. Pugh, Cardiff, 1971.

H.M.S.O.	Her Majesty's Stationery Office.
Hogg and King, 'Early Castles'	Hogg, A. H. A. and King, D. J. C., 'Early Castles in Wales and the Marches', *Arch. Camb.*, CXII (1963), 77–124
Hogg and King, 'Masonry Castles'	Hogg, A. H. A. and King, D. J. C., 'Masonry Castles in Wales and the Marches', *Arch. Camb.*,CXVI (1967), 71–132.
Itinerary	Smith, L. T. (ed.), *Leland's Itinerary in Wales*, London, 1906.
J. F. H. S.	*Journal of the Flintshire Historical Society.*
J.M.H.R.S.	*Journal of the Merioneth Historical and Record Society.*
King's Works	Colvin, J., *et. al.*, *History of the King's works*, 2 vols., H.M.S.O., 1963.
Knowles and Hadcock, *Medieval Religious Houses*	Knowles, D. and Hadcock, R. N., *Medieval Religious Houses in England and Wales*, 2nd edn., London, 1971.
Lewis, *Topograpical Dictionary*	Lewis, S., *Topographical Dictionary of Wales*, London, 1833.
Liber Landavensis	Evans, J. G. (ed.), *Liber Landavensis: The Book of Llan Dav*, Oxford, 1893.
Littere Wallie	Edwards, J. G. (ed.), *Littere Wallie*, B.C.S., Hist and Law Ser., V, Cardiff, 1940.
Lloyd, *Owen Glendower*	Lloyd, J. E., *Owen Glendower*, Oxford, 1931.
Mon. Angl.	Caley, J. and Ellis, H. (eds.), *Dugdale's Monasticon Anglicanum*, 6 vols. in 8 parts, London, 1817–30.
Mon. Antiq.	*The Monmouthshire Antiquary*: proceedings of the Monmouthshire and Caerleon Antiquarian Society.
Mont. Coll.	*The Montgomeryshire Collections*: the Journal of the Powysland Club.
Morgannwg	The Journal of the Glamorgan History Society.
Morris, *Welsh Wars*	Morris, J. E., *The Welsh Wars of Edward I*, Oxford, 1901.
MSS. Relating to Wales	Owen, E. (ed.), *Manuscripts Relating to Wales in the British Museum*, Cymm. Rec. Ser., IV, 1908.
Nash-Williams, *Roman Frontier in Wales*	Nash-Williams, V. E., *The Roman Frontier in Wales*, 2nd edn., revised under the direction of M. G. Jarrett, Cardiff, 1969.
Owen, *Cal. Pembs. Records*	Owen, H. (ed.), *Calendar of Public Records relating to Pembrokeshire*, Cymm. Rec. Ser., VII, London, 1914.
Owen, *Description of Pembroke-shire*	Owen, H. (ed.), *The Description of Pembrokeshire*, George Owen, Cymm. Rec. Ser., I, London, 1892–36.
P.R.O.	Public Record Office.
R.C.A.M.W.M.	*Report of the Royal Commission on Ancient Monuments in Wales and Monmouthshire*, county inventories.
R.S.	Rolls Series.
Rec. Caern.	Ellis, H. (ed.), *Registrum Vulgariter nuncupatum, 'The Record of Caernarvon'* (Record Commissioners), London, 1838.
Round, *C.D.F.*	Round, J. H. (ed.), *Calendar of Documents Preserved in France Illustrative of the History of Great Britain and Ireland* (P.R.O.), London, 1899.
S.C.	P.R.O. Special Collections 6, Minister's accounts; Special Collections 8, Ancient petitions; Special Collections 11–12, Rentals and Surveys.
T.A.A.S.	*Transactions of the Anglesey Antiquarian Society.*
T.C.H.S.	*Transactions of the Caernarfonshire Historical Society.*
T.D.H.S.	*Transactions of the Denbighshire Historical Society.*
T.R.S.	*Transactions of the Radnorshire Society*
Turner, *Town Defences*	Turner, H., *Town Defences in England and Wales*, London,1971.
V.C.H.	*The Victoria History of the Counties of England.*
W.H.R.	*The Welsh History Review.*
Y Cymmrodor	The Journal of the Honourable Society of the Cymmrodorion.

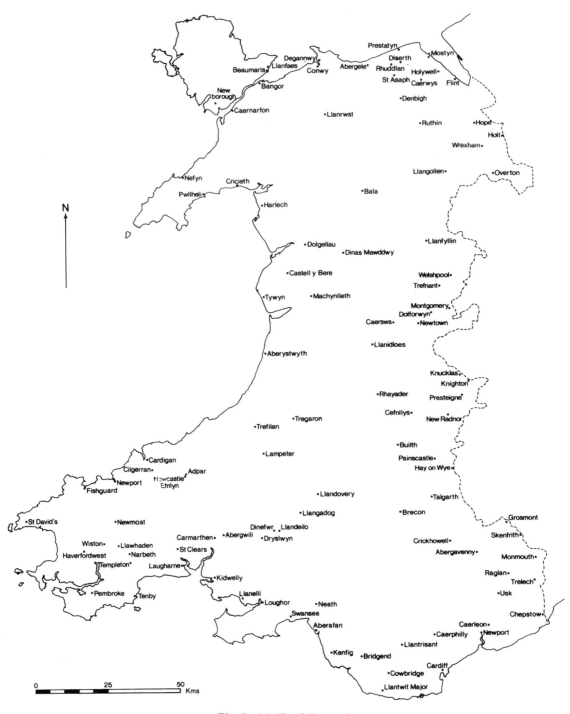

Fig. 1. Medieval Towns in Wales

Chapter One

THE ORIGINS AND EARLY DEVELOPMENT OF WELSH TOWNS

The Urban Genesis

THE INTRODUCTION OF TOWNS and urban life into Wales is traditionally associated with the 'English' conquest and for both the historian and patriotic Welshman alike, names such as Caernarfon, Flint, Rhuddlan and Beaumaris are synonymous with the loss of Welsh independence which followed the death of Llywelyn ap Gruffudd in 1282. Their founder, Edward I, continuing the work of his father, Henry III, and their royal predecessors, and pursuing the policy of town plantation already begun in Gascony, consolidated his hold over the Welsh with a network of impressive castles and dependent English boroughs.[1] It was in this way that the majority of Welsh towns came into being and their contrived foundation rapidly transformed the economic and demographic map of the country. Those granted borough privileges came to dominate and monopolise local trade, since all commercial activities had to be conducted within the liberties of the borough. No Welshman was allowed, at least initially, to hold burgages, plots of land within the borough. To him such places were alien, bastions of English military superiority and commercial monopoly, and it was no surprise that the towns were among the earliest targets for attack during periods of rebellion.

The list of these so-called 'planned' or 'planted' towns is a long one and includes many of the more familiar names on the modern urban map. The coastal towns of the north already mentioned, together with Aberystwyth, Pembroke, Swansea, Cardiff and Newport (Gwent), were all Norman and Edwardian creations populated by immigrant English, and to a lesser extent by French and Flemish settlers. Not all the towns of Wales were foreign plantations however, and not all were military foundations; several which emerged in the late 13th and 14th centuries such as Nefyn, Dolgellau and Wrexham lacked both castle and town defences and were predominantly Welsh in their population. These were organic settlements, transformed into full towns from small native *trefi* and illustrating the trend towards urbanisation which was already apparent in Welsh society.

Writing in the late 12th century at a time when many English boroughs had already been planted, Giraldus Cambrensis noted that the Welsh had possessed no towns of their own before the Norman Conquest.[2] His phrase has been much quoted and often discussed, but for the most part it remains a fair assessment of the situation as it existed in the 1180s. Towns as such there may not have been, but time after time we find communities of varying extent and importance already

1

established on sites subsequently utilised for urban development by the Normans
and their successors. Usually centred around a Celtic church or occasionally an
earlier Roman fort, these small settlements were often allowed to remain alongside
the later planted borough, while others, such as those which fell under the control
of the bishops of St David's, were simply reorganised and reassessed along burghal
lines. By the date of the final conquest of Gwynedd more substantial Welsh
communities had appeared which·show indications of nucleation, like Llanfaes
in Anglesey and Nefyn and Pwllheli in Llŷn. Fashioned and developed by the
native princes these were certainly towns and were immediately recognised as such
by the victorious English administrators. For the most part, however, there remains
considerable support for the traditional view that urban life was not a characteristic
of Welsh society as it existed before the era of plantation. On the other hand, the
various sites chosen by the conquerors for their castles and boroughs were influenced
by the presence of established vills and other potentially nucleating features—a
church, holy well; the remains of a Roman fort; a Welsh 'maerdref' or market centre;
or a small *tref* established at a fording point or along a coastal creek. Before
proceeding with a closer examination of town plantation and development it would
be therefore of value to look more carefully at the role of these pre-urban nuclei
and to do so chronologically up to the Norman arrival.

The Roman Background

Although the Romans established a detailed network of forts, marching camps
and civil settlements throughout Wales, their locale and distribution had little
influence on subsequent settlement history. 'There is no direct connection', wrote
E. A. Lewis, 'between the "old towns" of Roman Wales and the "new towns" or
"boroughs" of the Middle Ages.[3] Such a view is not to deny an element of
continuity, most noticeable in the south-east, but for the most part this had more
to do with the general physical advantages of site than with anything else. At
Cardiff the first Norman motte was thrown up within the defences of a Roman fort,
and there are similar overlaps at Abergavenny, Carmarthen, Usk, Caersws, and
probably also at Cowbridge and Monmouth. Only at Caerleon and Loughor,
however, can it be said that the lay-out of the Roman settlement had any direct
influence on the plan of the later medieval town.[4] In both cases the established
street-pattern was readopted and the existing gates repaired and utilised, although
at Caerleon, where the Roman remains were observed by Giraldus,[5] the early motte
was sited beyond the surviving defences. Elsewhere, as at Caernarfon, Neath,
Prestatyn, Caerphilly, Llandovery, and Brecon, the medieval towns grew up some
distance removed from the old forts and the link between the two was confined
to the natural advantages of the general area in which they were sited. Undeniably
the presence of a ready supply of building materials which a Roman fort provided
together with an established road network exerted their influence over the medieval
town planner, but for the most part the link between the two was confined to a
mutual appreciation of the physical landscape. In particular the attraction of rivers
and their tidal points for defence, communication and commerce was decisive in
both periods for the control of Wales.

The Celtic Background

If Giraldus is to be believed, no towns were established in Wales in the centuries between the Roman withdrawal *c.* 410 and the *adventus Normannorum* in the late 1060s, although this is not to exclude varying degrees of settlement on sites which were later utilised for town foundation. Indeed, examination of the Gazetteer will show that many medieval towns and boroughs reveal an element of earlier occupation, varying from an early church with a scattering of dwellings beyond its walls to established, larger communities like the one which developed beyond the Roman fort at Carmarthen. An important, but often impossible task is to ascribe a date for the creation of such settlements; was it during the centuries immediately following the Roman period or was it considerably later, a trend influenced by the towns already established by the Normans? The ecclesiastical boroughs under the control of the bishopric of St David's illustrate the difficulties inherent in this problem. Entries in the *Black Book of St David's,* the record of the bishopric's territorial possessions for 1326, list burgages at Adpar and Llangadog in Dyfed, both today small, rural villages.[6] In contrast to the inhabitants of St David's and Llawhaden,[7] however, two of the bishopric's other boroughs, the burgesses were overwhelmingly Welsh and the communities appear to have been well established at the time of the survey. Both had been granted the right to hold a weekly market in 1281,[8] but there are no indications of plantation, and we appear to be dealing with Welsh communities which were simply reassessed according to the fashion of the day. What we would like to know but are unfortunately unable to determine, is the degree of settlement here before the commercial advantages secured in 1281; were these grants to already significant communities or was nucleation a later development encouraged by the appearance of a regular market? Similar questions, for the most part unanswerable, can be asked for a number of urban sites which have a suggestion of an earlier Celtic background. To what extent had the presence of St Cadog's church at Llangadog attracted permanent settlement in the centuries before the lands passed under the control of St David's? Likewise, what was the degree of Welsh settlement beyond the gates of long-established religious cells at Llandeilo, Bangor, Tywyn, Llangollen, St Asaph, Llantwit Major, Tregaron, Llanrwst, Cilgerran, Llanelli, Welshpool, Talgarth, Raglan, and Cricieth? In all these instances, and with the possible additions of Newcastle (Bridgend), Abergele, Kenfig, and Skenfrith, an existing Celtic church was incorporated within the immediate area of a medieval town. Their role in the urbanising process is perhaps suggested by the frequent holding of the medieval markets within the actual churchyards themselves, as at Llanelli,[9] while in some cases (Rhayader and Wrexham) market day itself was a Sunday in order to take advantage of the large gatherings.[10] There are other indications of established Welsh communities which pre-dated later towns. The examples of Llanfaes, Nefyn and Pwllheli, urban centres fostered by the princes of Gwynedd, will be considered later in a fuller discussion of specifically Welsh towns, but elsewhere native settlement can also be detected. At Monmouth the construction of the Norman motte necessitated the levelling of a Celtic church with the familiar dedication to St Cadog, together with the removal of the Welsh community across the river to form the medieval suburb of

Overmonnow.[11] In the north, at Ruthin, the borough laid out in the 1280s, and populated predominantly by Englishmen was sited around an established *tref* which constituted the administrative centre for the commot of Dyffryn Clwyd. A survey of the town carried out in 1324 recorded a total of 70 burgesses, of whom one-third were Welsh, and noticeably concentrated in Well (Welsh?) Street.[12] Similarly a plan of the borough of Welshpool in 1629 names the area on the north bank of the Lledan Brook in the area of St Mary's church as the 'Welshe towne', possibly referring to the pre-urban community which grew up around the early church (the predecessor of St Mary's?) which is reputed to have been founded by St Cynfelyn.[13]

These examples, together with several others which will become apparent as this study progresses, illustrate the role of pre-urban nuclei in the later selection of town sites. Such communities formed the basis from which the organic Welsh towns developed while they were also partly instrumental in determining the distribution and location of the 'English' boroughs. A site which had been traditionally frequented by the surrounding populace for spiritual and commercial reasons and which was already regarded as a focal point was ideally sited for purposes of town plantation.

The Anglo-Saxons

In striking contrast to the situation in England, urban development in Wales owes little to the Anglo-Saxons. Their settlements were transient affairs confined to the border areas where control constantly alternated between English and Welsh. Anglo-Saxon communities established in the 9th and 10th centuries seem likely to have disappeared under Welsh pressure by the time of the Norman arrival. While several towns along this Marcher region bear Old English names like Chepstow, Wrexham and Presteigne, there are no grounds for assuming any noteworthy degree of settlement or influence on later urban trends. The Domesday Survey of 1086 extended to Knighton, Overton, Hope, Caerleon, and Prestatyn, but the entries reveal few suggestions of town life.[14] Knighton, in fact, appears as a waste manor with no mention of a vill, and later surveys show the borough to be 60 per cent. Welsh, which indicates a retreat on the part of the English settlers.[15] There was no town at Hope before the 13th century, while the vills recorded at Caerleon and Prestatyn were Welsh settlements which had only recently fallen under Norman control. Indeed, the only instance of significant Anglo-Saxon urban settlement in Wales appears to have been in the north at Rhuddlan where the later borough laid out on the banks of the Clwyd by Edward I in 1277 was sited immediately north-west of a large, defended enclosure which appears to have been the *burgh* of *Cledemutha* ('Clwyd-mouth') founded in 921 by Edward the Elder. Yet again however, this community had been dispersed by the time of the Norman advance and control had reverted to the Welsh who had erected their own stronghold within the *burgh* defences.[16] So in this solitary example of an Anglo-Saxon attempt at urban foundation in Wales there is no direct evidence of continuity, although the example of Rhuddlan provides a further instance of the Norman preference for extablished sites.

This examination of the background to town development and of the existing, potentially nucleating features of the landscape serves as a useful introduction to the more substantial developments achieved by the Normans and their successors. As we have emphasised, it was from beyond the borders of Wales that the real impetus came for urban foundation with towns conceived as essential features of the conquest and military and administrative consolidation. Some of these creations, like Bere in Meirionnydd, were short-lived affairs destroyed by the Welsh within a few years of their existence, but the majority were more durable settlements which survived the turmoil of numerous sackings and burnings. While in more modern times several of these early boroughs experienced a marked decline—Trelech, New Moat, Dryslwyn, and Dinefwr are but a few of the many examples—others, like Cardiff, Swansea, and Newport, continue to dominate the urban map of Wales.

The introduction of English boroughs also had its influence on settlement patterns in the regions which remained under the authority of the native princes. In Gwynedd and Powys they were not slow to realise the financial benefits which town plantation brought to the founder and during the second half of the 13th century there were several Welsh attempts at plantation as well as the enlargement of existing communities. The purpose of the following analysis is to provide a chronological and typological survey of these various settlements and their wider relationship to the history of Wales during the medieval period. While it is proposed to adopt a chronological approach to the investigation this will inevitably raise several difficulties which need to be isolated. The fundamental point which emerges is that it is rarely possible to provide a specific date for the foundation of a particular town unless it be a planted borough whose charter not only has survived but which can be dated accurately. With the majority the first documentary reference is often to an attack and a town may have existed for a lengthy period before it was plundered by the Welsh. Nor is the first mention of the castle (where one was raised) always an indication of a town existing in its shadow. At Aberafan the Norman motte was built *c.* 1106 and the church first appears in the latter part of the century, but there is no definite evidence of the town until it was incorporated in 1283-1314.[17] A fuller appreciation of this point will become clear from Table I which indicates the number of early mottes around which towns developed and where possible the chronological relationship between their construction and the earliest references to the civil settlement. The second problem which arises from this analysis concerns classification. While it is proposed to classify the 105 Gazetteer entries into 'English' and 'Welsh' towns a degree of duplication is inevitable since in some cases the grounds for rigid demarcation are slight. Bearing in mind these considerations, the discussion will follow the following divisions: (1) the Norman period, extending the analysis to *c.* 1150; (2) the following period until the accession of Henry III, i.e., 1150-1216; (3) the reign of Henry III, 1216-72; (4) the reign of Edward I, 1272-1307; (5) later foundations; and (6) an examination of the Welsh towns.

(See Table I on page 6.)

TABLE I

Illustrating the number of early castles erected within the area of later towns
and the chronological relationship between the two

TOWN	CASTLE Earliest reference	TOWN Earliest reference
Aberafan	c. 1100	1283–1314
Abergavenny	c. 1090	c. 1090
Bangor	c. 1100	1201
Brecon	1093	c. 1100
Bridgend (Newcastle)	c. 1106	c. 1106
Builth	1168	1217
Caerleon	c. 1070	1171
Caernarfon	c. 1090	1188
Cardiff	1081	1120–47
Cardigan	c. 1110	1158–65
Carmarthen..	1094	1109
Chepstow	1070	1075
Cilgerran	1166	1204
Crickhowell	?	1281
Grosmont	1137	1250
Haverfordwest	c. 1110	c. 1110
Hay-on-Wye	1121	1216
Kenfig	1080	1135–54
Kidwelly	c. 1110	c. 1110
Knighton	1182	1292–3
Lampeter	1136	1285
Laugharne	c. 1170	1247
Llandovery	1116	1185
Llanelli	1190	c. 1300
Llanidloes	?	1263
Llawhaden	1188	1281
Loughor	1151	1247
Monmouth	c. 1070	c. 1100
Neath	1185	1231
New Moat	?	c. 1200
Newport (Gwent)..	c. 1090	1172
Pembroke	1093	1100
Prestatyn	c. 1164	c. 1150
Raglan	c. 1100	1354
Rhuddlan	1073	1086
St Clear's	1188	1282–8
St David's	1081?	1115
Skenfrith	c. 1070	?
Swansea	1116	1153–84
Templeton	1116?	1283
Tenby	c. 1100	1260
Usk	1138	1262
Wiston	c. 1130	1220

(1) The Normans

The Norman contribution to the development of urban life in Wales was considerable. For the first time since the Roman period large areas of the country were overrun and control achieved by the systematic construction of motte-and-bailey castles at key strategic locations. In their shadow small civil communities were established, defended initially with earthen banks and ditches, and populated with Norman, English and Flemish settlers whom the Marcher lords lured away from the relative safety of their other lands across the border and on the Continent. In the early years these towns were frontier communities with a military as well as an economic role to play. Not only was every burgess expected to till his lands in order to provide food for the garrison as well as his own family, but he was also required to play a part in the defence of the whole community and take up arms when the need arose. The towns also had a psychological part to play in subduing the Welsh who continued to wrestle for the control of their country. The physical impact of the castle on the landscape was formidable enough, but by granting markets to the infant boroughs and making them the sole places where commercial transactions could take place they became the compulsory focal point of the dependent district.

The Norman advance into Wales was conducted along lowland routes from the three strategic border centres of Chester, Shrewsbury, and Hereford. The earliest town plantations, therefore, were those along the Marches and the coastal plains together with some of the Pembrokeshire boroughs where conquest was partly achieved by sea.[18] By 1075 the town of Chepstow was already being valued at £16,[19] while the Domesday Survey of 1086 recorded nascent communities alongside the mottes at Prestatyn and Rhuddlan in the north.[20] The castles of Monmouth[21] and Caerleon[22] had also been erected by this time, and it seems likely that work had also begun on laying out the boroughs by the end of the century. The evidence suggests a similar date for Cardiff, Brecon, Pembroke and Tenby, and as the Normans progressed westwards further settlements were initiated in the early years of the following century. Pembroke received its first charter from Henry I in 1100,[23] and Carmarthen in 1109.[24] Swansea was not incorporated until 1153-84,[25] but Henry de Newburgh had raised the motte during the first decade,[26] when work was also begun at Haverfordwest, Neath, Kidwelly, and Kenfig, the latter borough already being enclosed with a timber palisade by 1135-54.[27]

There are also indications that small urban communities were established at a number of other points along the course of the Norman advance although here the evidence is less specific. The mottes at Caernarfon and Cardigan both date from the 1090s, and their construction may have been accompanied by the laying out of civilian settlements,[28] although the venture at Caernarfon must have been short-lived as the area had reverted to the Welsh by 1115.[29] At Newcastle (Bridgend) the first fortifications were raised c. 1106, and perhaps a start was made on the borough which was sited around the existing church of St Illtyd.[30] In Gwent the examples of Abergavenny, Caerleon, Chepstow and Monmouth point to an early date for the first community at Newport, although the initial motte was later abandoned in favour of a new site, and also at Usk where both the castle and

Fig. 2. The Towns of Norman Wales

Prestatyn

Rhuddlan

Caernarfon

■ Definite foundations

□ Probable foundations

Presteigne □

Cardigan □

Hay on Wye □

Fishguard □

■ Brecon

□ St David's

Wiston □

■ Haverfordwest

Carmarthen ■

Abergavenny ■   Monn

Kidwelly ■

Tenby ■

Usk □

Pembroke ■

■ Neath

Swansea ■

Caerleon ■

Newport □

Ch

Kenfig

Bridgend □

Cardiff □

N

0   25   50
Kms

priory are mentioned in the first half of the 12th century.[31] Work on the borough of St David's seems a likely feature of this period, resulting, perhaps, from the charter of privileges granted to the bishops by Henry I in 1115.[32] Likewise an early settlement may have been conceived at Fishguard, where the church bears the familiar Norman dedication to St Mary, as does that at Hay, where the castle had been built by 1121.[33] At Presteigne the beginnings of the town are visible in the Herefordshire Domesday which refers to the period 1128-39,[34] while, finally, at Wiston the laying-out of a small borough may have accompanied the construction of the motte which has been completed by 1130.[35]

During the following centuries the majority of these early foundations were modified and enlarged, their castles rebuilt and their defences strengthened. Many were so thoroughly devastated by the Welsh during the campaigns of the 13th century that their subsequent rebuilding removed nearly all traces of the early settlement except for the churches and castles. The remaining topographical evidence, however, coupled with the results of modern archaeological investigation, is sufficient to provide an insight into the form of the Norman towns in Wales. In contrast to their later Edwardian counterparts these were small ventures and unsophisticated in their appearance. A small church, a triangular market-place, a few streets lined with burgages and the whole defended with an earthen bank and an outer ditch, were the essential characteristics. Enough is known of the early towns at Abergavenny, Cardiff, and Rhuddlan to illustrate the relationship between the Norman community and the enlarged 13th-century boroughs. Work at Abergavenny was begun c. 1090 by Hamelin de Ballon, who sited his town within the the area of the Roman fort of Gobannium.[36] A motte was erected at the southern apex and a bank and ditch constructed around the nascent community. Recent excavations have detected sections of these defences which were found to lie well within the later circuit of masonry walls built in the late 13th and early 14th centuries.[37] The Norman borough, in fact, appears to have been no more than half the size of its Edwardian counterpart.

Archaeological investigation has also produced evidence of a similar situation at Rhuddlan, although in this case the borough planned by Edward I in 1277 occupied an adjoining site to the Norman town and did not incorporate it within the walls. As early as 1073 Robert, cousin of Hugh of Avranches, Earl of Chester, had replaced an existing Welsh stronghold with a motte-and-bailey and the civilian settlement was well established by 1086 when the Domesday Survey recorded the presence of a mill, church, mint, and 18 burgesses.[38] This was evidently a small community, and although it lay within the lengthy defences of what was probably Edward the Elder's *burgh* of 'Cledemutha' none of the existing banks were utilised. Excavations conducted in 1969-71 located traces of the Norman walls to the north of the motte, together with the church and graveyard within them. On the east side natural protection was afforded by the River Clwyd and although the full circuit of the defences was not revealed, enough was detected to show that they enclosed a small area which was no more than a quarter that of the *burgh*.[39]

In South Wales the pattern was repeated at Cardiff, Carmarthen and Haverfordwest. The first motte at Cardiff, the work of Robert fitz Hamon, again sited within

a former Roman fort, had been completed by 1081. Work laying out the borough
to the south commenced soon afterwards and the first charter dates from 1120–47.[40]
This was a small town which formed only a part of the later walled borough
mapped by John Speed in 1610.[41] Its defences were also built of stone, and sections
of the wall were uncovered during building operations in 1901. It appears to have
followed the line of Church Street some 150m. south of the castle wall and almost
parallel with it.[42] Speed also indicates a possible corner tower by St John's church
with a length of walling leading south along Trinity Street to enclose the churchyard.
The traditional street-pattern within this area has a distinct appearance of regularity
which distinguishes it from the remainder of the later walled town, suggesting that
the Norman borough consisted only of High Street with Castle Street and its
extension, Duke Street, as the principal east-west axis.

In the case of Carmarthen the Normans were again attracted by the presence of
an existing settlement and their new castle-borough was sited near a Welsh
community which in turn had developed by the Roman town of *Moridinum*.[43]
This area fell under the control of William fitz Baldwin in the mid-1090s, and the
borough had been laid out by 1109 when the inhabitants received their first
charter from Henry I.[44] Initially it was defended by earthen banks supplemented
by water-courses which provided natural barriers to the south, west and north. In
1223 stone walls were constructed around the same circuit, but these enclosed a
much smaller area than that defended in 1415 when the walls were extended
eastwards.[45] The Norman borough, in fact, consisted only of Guildhall Square,
Quay Street, and Bridge Street, while the original town church (the since-demolished
St Mary's) also lay within this area.[46]

Likewise at Haverfordwest the initial plantation, known as the 'Castleton',
constituted only a small proportion of the borough which was enclosed in the
second half of the 13th century. This settlement was contemporary with the
construction of the first castle by Gilbert de Clare *c.* 1110 and was established
immediately to the west of St Martin's church. It was defended by a short circuit
of masonry walls with three gates while the southern limits of the town were
determined by the course of a stream known as 'Schitrikislake' which flowed
eastwards into the Cleddau.[47] These defences also lined the northern bank of the
stream so when in 1264 the burgesses received a murage grant to enclose a greater
area of the expanding borough it was found necessary to build another gate along
its course to provide access to the 'new town'.[48] This enlargement of the town
wall was achieved simply by extending the east and west walls of the 'Castleton'
due south with the addition of a second south wall completing the circuit. This
expansion saw the incorporation of a second church within the walled area (St
Mary's), as also took place at Cardiff. The appearance of such second churches, in
fact, is often a valuable pointer to similar developments elsewhere. At Pembroke
the earliest church, again bearing the familiar Norman dedication to St Mary, lies
a short distance beyond the outer wall of the castle, while at the eastern end of the
virtually impregnable limestone ridge on which the borough was sited stands
St Michael's, which dates from the later 13th century.[49] Here again there is a
suggestion that the initial settlement begun by Arnulf de Montgomery in the 1090s

was subsequently enlarged with an eastward extension of the early defences. The view is strengthened by the presence of two medieval market-places within the borough, one by St Mary's church which would correspond to the Norman commercial centre, and another at the eastern end of the peninsula near the East Gate, which would have served the inhabitants of the larger, late medieval town. Certainly from the parallels afforded by Rhuddlan, Cardiff, Abergavenny, Carmarthen and Haverfordwest the initial settlement is unlikely to have extended along the full length of the peninsula.

(2) 1150-1216

Urban activity continued throughout this period, but political considerations in England dictated that it be on a reduced scale to that achieved by the Normans and confined to a smaller geographical area. Henry II, succeeding to the throne in 1154 following the strife which characterised Stephen's reign, had enough to do with his own barons, the Church, and events in France and rebellious Ireland for Welsh affairs to assume more than a secondary role. The king had also been checked in battle by Owain Gwynedd in 1157 and the result did much for the Welsh cause. The prince of Gwynedd retained and strengthened his grip in the north-east, while in the south-west Rhys ap Gruffudd secured control of the greater part of Deheubarth, including all of Ceredigion, except for the sole royal outpost of Cardigan.[50] For the most part, therefore, town foundation was confined to the well-established areas of English authority and in particular to the lordships of Pembroke, Glamorgan and Gwent.

In 1173 the castle at Usk was enlarged,[51] and the work may have been accompanied by an extension of the Norman borough, while at Neath and Brecon the initial settlements were abandoned in favour of establishing new communities across the river. At Aberafan and Grosmont both the castle and church are first documented in the latter part of the century and the boroughs may also have been conceived.[52] In mid-Wales the evidence is more specific and the towns of Llandovery, Llandeilo and Builth are first recorded in 1185, 1213 and 1217 respectively,[53] while further north Caersws, which has the regularity of a planted borough, also appears to date from these years.[54]

Attempts at town foundation were also made within the English territories of the west. A castle at Llanelli had been erected by 1190, and perhaps a small borough laid out as at St Clear's where both the motte and the Cluniac priory date from the second half of the century.[55] Further west at Newport in Cemaes the castle had been completed in 1197 when a charter was granted to the new English borough,[56] while a town at Cilgerran is recorded in 1204, although this was a small community housing only 22 taxpayers in 1292.[57] This period also saw the emergence of two organic towns which had developed around the long-established religious houses at Bangor and St Asaph. In 1143 St Asaph was created the *caput* of an independent bishopric, and as at St David's this attracted a degree of lay settlement which was subsequently mapped by John Speed in 1610. The same cartographer also recorded the existence of a small community beyond the walls of the new Cathedral church at Bangor built in 1120–39 under the direction of Bishop David and the town *per se* is mentioned in 1211.[58]

As these examples illustrate this period saw no significant developments in town foundation and the few planned ventures were small, relatively insignificant, and occasionally short-lived affairs. Any early borough at Llanelli must have been abandoned after 1215 when the castle fell to the Welsh under Rhys Ieuanc.[59] It was not until the reigns of Henry III and his son Edward I that Wales experienced a degree of urban activity comparable with that carried out under the direction of the Norman kings.

(3) The Reign of Henry III (1216–72)

This period is characterised by the rule of the two Llywelyns, Llywelyn ab Iorwerth and Llywelyn ap Gruffudd, both intent on creating a strong Welsh feudal state; and by the opposing activities of the king and his Marcher barons, particularly the de Clares in Glamorgan and the Mortimers in Maelienydd (Radnor). The policy of town foundation was revitalised and the reign witnessed the birth of several new urban communities as well as the expansion of a number of established boroughs. The new plantations were firmly concentrated in the south and along the eastern border. Montgomery received its first charter in 1227, while three years later Henry III was at Painscastle where a borough was planned and the inhabitants granted a weekly market and yearly fair.[60] During the 1240s the Mortimers raised the castles of Cefnllys and Knucklas together with small dependent boroughs,[61] while New Radnor and Knighton were also border communities established during these years. The burgesses of New Radnor received a murage grant in 1257 and those of Knighton in 1260, and by the end of the century the latter housed 71 taxpayers.[62]

This high level of activity was also repeated in the south. In Gwent the castle at Trelech is first recorded in 1231 and it seems highly likely that work was also begun on laying out the borough which emerged as one of the largest medieval towns in Wales.[63] At Cowbridge the new community received its first charter in 1254 from Richard de Clare, and within eight years the burgess total had reached 58,[64] while in the uplands of Glamorgan Llantrisant Castle had been built by 1246 on a hilltop alongside a Celtic church, while the new castle at Caerphilly was begun in 1271 when 80 burgage plots were also laid out.[65] These middle years of the century likewise saw the emergence of a town alongside the ancient ecclesiastical centre at Llantwit Major,[66] together with the beginnings of urban communities at Laugharne and Loughor. In 1247 Guy de Brien secured the holding of an annual fair at Loughor, while Laugharne was granted a market and fairs in 1247, and the borough was incorporated in 1278–82.[67]

In North Wales, however, the power of the house of Gwynedd restricted such a proliferation of Enlgish townships and the principal urban developments at Nefyn, Pwllheli and Llanfaes were the work of the Welsh themselves. Only at Degannwy and Diserth were attempts made to establish new English boroughs. Both foundations date from Henry III's campaign against Dafydd ap Llywelyn who had succeeded Llywelyn Fawr in 1240. The castle at Diserth was begun in 1241 and the first burgages taken up in 1248, while the same year saw the creation of the borough of Degannwy where an existing castle had been refortified in 1245.[68]

Other than the appearance of new planned English settlements the reign of Henry III was also a period of expansion for established towns, and one which saw much castle rebuilding and the replacement of early town defences with more formidable masonry walls. The burgesses of Haverfordwest received a grant of murage in 1264 when the original 'Castleton' became dwarfed by a new town to the south.[69] A similar grant had been secured by the men of Hay in 1237, their action prompted, no doubt, by a Welsh attack in 1232 when their borough was put to flames.[70] A circuit of stone walls was built around the town, and the old motte was abandoned with the erection further north of a new masonry castle. At Presteigne the small community was granted a market and yearly fair in 1225,[71] while at Skenfrith the enlargement of the castle under the direction of Hubert de Burgh (1201–39) may also have seen an extension of the civil settlement.[72] Finally, in the south the town of Caerleon, 'reduced to ashes' by Llywelyn ab Iorwerth in 1231,[73] had to be planned anew, while under the guidance of the de Clares the burgess total rose to an impressive 400 at Cardiff.[74]

(4) The Reign of Edward I (1272–1307)

The early years of the reign were disastrous for the house of Gwynedd and for the cause of Welsh independence. Llywelyn ap Gruffudd, from a commanding position in 1267 when by the Treaty of Montgomery Henry III had acknowledged him Prince of Wales, had seen his forces routed by Edward I's army in 1277 and by the end of 1282 he was dead. By the Statute of Rhuddlan of March 1284 provisions were made for the future governance of Wales and her status as a self-governing realm had come abruptly to an end.[75] Such, at least, is the retrospective conclusion, although Edward I, still faced with the prospect of periodic rebellion, must have been less convinced of the durability of his successes. Military triumph had to be matched with administrative consolidation, and accordingly the king was obliged to embark upon an extensive programme of castle and town foundation just as the Normans had attempted 200 years earlier. The results amount to a watershed in the history of Welsh urban development. Not only did Edward himself conceive an impressive network of fortified boroughs encircling the land of Gwynedd, but his example encouraged similar activities on the part of the Marcher barons with a whole host of new plantations as well as the extension and refortification of established communities. The combined result was the appearance of some 30 planned towns *de novo* while there is evidence that a more than equal number experienced significant expansion.

Associated with the successful military campaign in 1277 was the inception of the formidable string of castle-boroughs in the north and north-west. Work was begun at Flint and Rhuddlan, while in the same year at Aberystwyth Edmund, Earl of Lancaster, elected to abandon the old motte and construct a new stronghold and English borough at the mouth of the Rheidol.[76] Both Flint and Rhuddlan received their charters in 1284, an important year which also saw the incorporation of Bere, Caernarfon, Conwy, Cricieth and Harlech, together with the already established community at Cardigan and the grant of markets and fairs to the Welsh vill of Llangollen.[77] The following year borough status was conferred on Holt which quickly expanded to boast 159 burgesses in 1315.[78] Also in the north Denbigh had been incorporated by Henry de Lacy in 1285 when the town already contained 63 burgages.[79] This level of activity was continued into the 1290s with charters to Caerwys in 1290, Overton in 1292, when the town housed 56 taxpayers, and the appearance of English communities at Hope and Mostyn.[80] Prompted by the uprising of Madog in 1294 work was also begun on laying out the castle and borough of Beaumaris in the following year, a development which necessitated the total removal of the nearby Welsh inhabitants of Llanfaes across Anglesey to the appropriately-named Newborough.[81]

Although the evidence points to an intensive level of urban activity in the north the creation of new English towns also had its appeal to the Marcher lords of the south and east. In 1280 Roger Mortimer secured the privileges of a weekly market and annual fairs at Newtown. Crickhowell emerged in the following year, and Rhayader is first documented in 1304, although the town may well have been laid out a decade or two earlier.[82] New foundations were few in the old kingdom of Deheubarth with the appearance only of Newtown in 1298, an English community established near the ancient Welsh seat of Dinefwr, and at Newcastle Emlyn in 1303.[83]

In the south-west, however, town development was more marked. Narberth first appears in the 1280s, while the first burgesses at Templeton appear in 1283 and at Llawhaden in 1292.[84] The latter formed part of the estates of the bishopric of St David's and is illustrative of a wider trend which saw the incorporation of several other ecclesiastical boroughs in the region. Some, like Llawhaden itself, were planned settlements with a predominantly English population; according to a survey of the bishopric's lands in 1326 the town contained 174½ burgages.[85] In the same year there were 42 at New Moat and 130 at St David's, where the early town had seen significant expansion following the grant of markets and fairs in 1281.[86] Elsewhere, the bishopric's remaining boroughs were essentially Welsh *trefi* reorganised along burghal lines and remaining predominantly Welsh in their population. At Llandeilo there were 30 burgesses in 1326, although this had already been regarded as a town in 1213.[87] The survey also noted 96 burgages at Adpar and a further 33 at Llangadog, both overwhelmingly Welsh communities.[88] Finally, at Abergwili, near Carmarthen, where Bishop Bek had built a new collegiate church in 1287, there were 25 burgages, although in this instance the holders were an interesting and fairly even combination of the two races.[89]

The range and extent of the new towns which appeared during Edward I's reign was also matched by the development and expansion of the established English boroughs, as well as by the emergence of many Welsh towns, a trend which will be discussed at a later stage. At Cardigan the burgage total increased from 128 in 1274 to 172 in 1308,[90] while at Knighton the 71 taxpayers recorded in 1292–3 had almost doubled to 126 by 1304.[91] Similar growth took place at Usk where the burgage total of 141 in 1262 had risen to 294 in 1306, and at the Welsh town of Nefyn where under English direction the 50 households recorded in 1284 had expanded to a community of 93 taxpayers in 1293.[95] Other Welsh vills were similarly expanded, but with the addition of English settlers. At Llantrisant a native *tref* whose total rents amounted to 13s. 4d. in 1262 had become an English borough of 145½ burgages by 1306-7,[94] while at Dryslwyn the vill was enlarged in 1287-89 when a new ditch was dug and by the end of the century the town housed 43 burgages.[95] At Ruthin the original *tref* had become a predominantly English borough of 70 burgesses by 1324.[96] There were also developments at Tregaron following the award of a market and fairs in 1292.[97]

From these examples it is evident that the population of many already established towns doubled during Edward I's reign. Cowbridge provides a further illustration of this expansion with the burgess total rising from 135 to 1282 to 278 in 1306.[98] Likewise at Llandovery, under the direction of John Giffard, the 37 burgages recorded in 1299 had increased to 81 by 1317.[99] Occasionally, such a degree of growth was achieved even more rapidly. Tenby, devasted by the Welsh in 1260, was reconstructed in the 1280s by William de Valence, who issued a new charter, and by 1307 a thriving new borough of 241 burgages had been created.[100] At New Radnor developments which usually spanned several decades were achieved in three years with the burgess total soaring from 97 in 1301 to 189 by 1304.[101] Such rapid growth also appears to have taken place at Trelech, now a small, rural community situated between Monmouth and Chepstow. No date is known for the foundation of the town, but it is unlikely to have been earlier than 1231 when the castle is first mentioned, while the absence of any burgage totals before 1288 points to a date in the second half of the 13th century. In that year, however, Trelech contained 378 burgages, a total surpassed only by Cardiff, and later by Denbigh.[102]

(5) Later Foundations

By 1300 the forces of town plantation had largely been spent, in Gascony and England as well as in Wales, and apart from the emergence of several organic Welsh communities there was little further attempt to continue the proliferation of English boroughs.[103] By the end of Edward I's reign in 1307 the English hold over Wales had been secured with a more than adequate network of castles and dependent towns. There were also sound economic reasons for a reduction in the level of activity. The commercial prosperity of each urban enterprise depended not only on the natural advantages of site, particularly of access to rivers and roads, but on its being sufficiently removed from the nearest neighbour and rival. Too many in so small a country would have resulted in an economy overburdened with towns, each serving only to undermine each other's status and prosperity. While there are instances of some Welsh towns being uncomfortably close to each other, such as Adpar and Newcastle Emlyn, Degannwy and Conwy, substantial water-courses separated them and minimised economic interference. Where there were no such barriers the lesser town was deliberately removed, as in the case of Llanfaes whose continued existence would have threatened the prosperity of Beaumaris.

Likewise in 1278 the burgesses of Montgomery successfully petitioned Edward I for the closure of Gruffudd ap Gwenwynwyn's market at nearby Welshpool, which was proving detrimental to their own, and secured its removal to Trefnant.[104] After 1330, then, urban activity was confined largely to development of the established communities, some of which expanded considerably, while others proved to be complete failures. Newborough in Anglesey, laid out in 1303, was the last of Edward I's ventures in Wales, and although there is the occasional borough first documented after the king's death, it seems most likely that they were earlier foundations. At Abergele, for example, the first burgesses appear in 1311, those at Talgarth in 1309, and at Raglan in 1354, but in all three cases there are suggestions of an earlier, native background.[105]. The solitary example of a medieval town planned after 1307 was Bala in Meirionnydd, laid out c. 1310 by Roger Mortimer and conceived as a deliberate attempt to curb the rampant lawlessness threatening the commot of Penllyn.[106] Thereafter urban plantation disappears from the Welsh landscape, to emerge much later and in different circumstances when the vitality of the Industrial Revolution saw the appearance of another wave of 'new towns'—Aberaeron, Tremadoc, Morriston, and their like.

(6) The Welsh Towns

It is a reflection of the English contribution to the formulation of the town map of medieval Wales, that consideration of the specifically native foundations should occupy the final position in this discussion of urban origins. In terms both of total number and individual importance it was the planned, alien settlements which dominated, not the smaller, often undefended Welsh communities which were largely confined to the upland region where only the hardiest of Englishmen were willing to take up burgages. It is always difficult to enumerate the English towns from surviving documentary evidence which is often inadequate and fragmentary, particularly so in the case of the lesser plantations. Although few foundation charters survive, an examination of their early extents and of the racial composition of the listed tenants affords a valuable indication of urban origins. Examination of the topography also has a contribution to make, and a town with little recorded history can sometimes be identified as a plantation by the regularity of its early street-pattern. Bearing in mind, then, the limitations inherent in a statistical analysis, which relates to an age so far removed, a final assessment of the English role in town foundation can be made. Of the 105 medieval 'towns' to be considered in the Gazetteer, there are good reasons for assuming that 75 (71) per cent. were planned alien settlements, either royal boroughs or the work of some local seigneur. These figures exclude Newborough in Anglesey which, although an Edwardian foundation, was overwhelmingly Welsh in its population and character; and Abergwili, where the inhabitants were an even combination of the two races. Yet the English contribution did not end with their own plantations, since it had an indirect influence on settlement trends elsewhere. Local lords, Welsh as well as English, were not slow to identify the commercial benefits which accrued from markets and fairs and the encouragement of nucleation.

The result was the appearance in the 13th century of a number of native towns, most of which developed from an older *tref* or *maerdref*; and which were economic rather than military ventures. Likewise the Welsh aristocracy itself was not averse to the idea of planned settlements and the English model was readily accepted by the lords of Powys who laid out their own boroughs along the eastern March. The aim of the following discussion is to isolate and analyse these two types of Welsh town and to identify the circumstances behind their development.

The relationship between the long-established centres of Welsh religious life and the siting of the later planned English boroughs has already been emphasised in our discussion of pre-urban nuclei. Likewise the examples of Bangor, Llantwit Major, St Asaph and the boroughs under the control of the bishopric of St David's illustrate the attraction of early churches and their role in the development of the native towns. A further instance is provided by Tywyn in Meirionnydd where by 1293 the 'clas' or mother-church of St Cadfan had become the focal point of a small town with its own weekly market.[107] A similar background can often be identified in the case of other Welsh communities which in the 13th and 14th centuries underwent the morphological transition from *tref* to town. By 1334 Llanrwst had assumed the status of 'a *burgus* and housed 21 burgages, the majority in Welsh hands,[108] while at Llangollen the small vill centred on St Collen's church was enlarged after 1284 when Edward I granted the inhabitants a weekly market and two yearly fairs.[109] Tregaron also had its origins as a small settlement in the shadow of St Caron's church, and like Llangollen it illustrates the importance of the English impetus in its development to full urban status. In 1290 the vill and surrounding lordship were conferred on Geoffrey Clement who secured similar commercial privileges and under his direction and that of his descendants who controlled the area until the mid-15th century Tregaron rose to become, as Leland observed in the 1530s, 'the chief town of the lordship of Pennarth'.[110] The trend is further illustrated by the examples of Dolgellau and Wrexham, the latter in 1315 ranking as a town of 44 taxpayers settled in the area of St Giles' church, all but eight being Welshmen.[111]

While the presence of an early religious centre was important in the development of some Welsh towns, others originated from the administrative network of pre-conquest Wales. The example of Ruthin where the English borough incorporated the commotal centre of Dyffryn Clwyd has already been cited, while on a lesser scale the English borough at Dryslwyn was laid out in the area of an established Welsh town where the existing castle was refortified.[112] At Trefilan in Ceredigion, however, the since decayed town attached to the castle built by Maelgwyn ap Rhys in the early years of the 13th century remained a Welsh settlement, as did that at Dinefwr, for long the seat of the princes of Deheubarth.[113] This proved also to be the case with the manorial boroughs of Llŷn, Nefyn and Pwllheli, *maerdrefi* or princely seats which developed under the direction of the house of Gwynedd, but whose subsequent expansion under Edward I's officials was achieved without an influx of English settlers. These were organic settlements which had assumed the status of *burgi* long before they were incorporated by Edward, the Black Prince in 1355.[114] Surveys carried out in 1284 following Edward I's succession to the territories of Llywelyn ap Gruffudd indicate the urban character of both communities. Nefyn, lying along the pilgrim route to Bardsey Island, contained 50 households, a church, priory, and a princely residence; it held its own markets and carried out a degree of maritime trade as well as being the centre of a viable herring fishery.[115] Pwllheli was the smaller of the two with 21 householders, but the princes also had a seat there and the town boasted its own markets and fairs.[116]

This transition from *maerdref* to town took encouragement from the examples of the prospering English boroughs and it was a trend made possible by the development of a money economy in the northern districts of Gwynedd. Investigation into the growth of commutation in the region, the substitution of cash payments for customary renders in kind, has shown the changeover to have been well advanced by the late 13th century. Money was circulating more freely, and its presence encouraged the development of market centres where commerical and administrative business could be carried out.[117] A similar background lies behind the growth of Llanfaes in Anglesey where the urban population came to exceed that of Nefyn and Pwllheli combined. The town developed at the northern entrance to the Menai Straits where Llywelyn ab Iorwerth had founded a friary in 1237-45.[118] The position was ideally suited for commerce, not only with the rest of Anglesey but with mainland Wales and Liverpool, and its revenues accounted for 70 per cent. of Llywelyn ap Gruffudd's total return from trading activities within his whole dominion. By the time of his death Llanfaes had become a thriving community of some 120 households.[119] Unlike the manorial boroughs of Llŷn, however, the town was not permitted to remain, although this may not have been the case were it not for Madog's revolt of 1294-5. The rebellion convinced Edward I that his castle-borough at Caernarfon could not alone dominate the Menai Straits, particularly since it left the whole of Anglesey without an English stronghold. The king accordingly planned a new borough, the modern Beaumaris, and appreciating the natural advantages of Llanfaes' position both in strategic and trading terms, he chose to sight the new venture alongside the Welsh town which was subsequently demolished and the inhabitants transferred across the island to the vill of Rhosfair where the town of Newborough was laid out to accommodate them.[120]

These activities of the princes of Gwynedd in encouraging the development of nucleated urban communities were paralleled along the eastern March and in Ystrad Tywi where native leaders were also influenced by the success of the Anglo-Norman boroughs. In 1285 Rhys ap Maredudd secured the holding of a weekly market and annual fair at Lampeter and by 1317 a small Welsh borough of 26 burgesses had come into existence in the area of an old motte and the existing church of St Peter.[121] In Powys such developments were more striking as the local Welsh leaders embarked upon a more elaborate programme of town foundation. Their first attempt, the borough of Welshpool, proved ultimately to be the most successful. Gruffudd ap Gwenwynwyn granted the new community its foundation charter in 1241-45, and by 1292 'La Pole' as it was then known had grown into a community of 106 taxpayers, a figure which more than doubled in the following 30 years.[122]

In striking contrast, the second attempt at plantation proved abortive. In 1273 Llywelyn ap Gruffudd began work on a castle at Dolforwyn, near Montgomery, where he also laid out a small dependent borough. The enterprise was immediately opposed by the Mortimers who saw it as a threat to their own foundations and they successfully petitioned Edward I, who accordingly ordered Llywelyn to abandon the scheme. The royal demand was ignored, however, and in 1277 Roger Mortimer besieged the castle when it seems likely that the civil settlement was dispersed.[123] There are no subsequent references to the borough which completely failed to assume any urban characteristics. The success of the Welshpool venture, however, encouraged the lords of Powys to plan further boroughs on the Anglo-Norman model, and in 1280 Owain de la Pole was granted a weekly market and two yearly fairs to be held in the small vill which had developed around the church of St Idloes overlooking the Severn.[124] Growth was initially slow, and by 1292 this new town of Llanidloes housed only 13 taxpayers, although by 1309 the figure had risen to sixty-six.[125] The pattern was repeated at Machynlleth where Owain secured similar commercial privileges in 1291 and by the end of the century the town had developed into a community of 61 taxpayers,[126] their tenements lining two principal streets with the unmistakeable appearance of a planned settlement. A further town was laid out at Llanfyllin in 1293–95, but this was a smaller venture, consisting initially of only 30 burgages.

In general these native urban foundations were lesser affairs than the English boroughs on which they were modelled. Only at Welshpool and the ill-fated Llanfaes did the number of households exceed 100, while the majority were much smaller concerns, often with less than half that number of taxpayers. Moreover, with the possible exception of Dolforwyn, the Welsh communities were exclusively administrative and commercial concerns, and often lay undefended, in contrast to the formidable walls which surrounded Conwy, Caernarfon and many other English boroughs. They illustrate in their unsophistication one of the most important consequences of the Anglo-Norman conquest, the proliferation of nucleated urban communities whose existence as trading centres gave further encouragement to the growth of a predominantly money economy and a more sophisticated commercial life. Ultimately the emergence of the native Welsh towns served to lessen the alien character of the strictly English plantations in which, by the middle of the 14th century, Welshmen were also electing to take up burgages and play a fuller part in the development of urban life.[128]

The Early Development of Welsh Towns

The foregoing discussions of town origins and early growth has highlighted the important differences which distinguished the urban map of medieval Wales from its modern counterpart. While the familiar centres of Cardiff, Newport, Abergavenny and Denbigh figured prominently, so also did the now insignificant communities of Holt and Trelech, while Dryslwyn and Llawhaden were larger than Cricieth and Harlech. Other towns such as Bere, Diserth and Cefnllys were planned boroughs which have long since disappeared, while the site of the once prosperous Kenfig now lies covered by formidable sand dunes whose consistent advance forced the burgesses to withdraw in the 15th century. Such examples of urban decay in Wales are legion, illustrating the inability of many planted communities to prosper once their military importance had declined and their castles ceased to be maintained. In 1300, however, this trend was in its infancy and most towns were steadily developing into more sophisticated urban communities. The relative wealth of statistical information relating to the burgess and other taxpaying inhabitants from this period makes it easier to reconstruct the town hierarchy as it existed in the later years of Edward I's reign, a task almost impossible for the remainder of the medieval period when the farming out of many boroughs reduced the frequency of contemporary extents. In proposing such an attempt it is important to appreciate its limitations. In the first place not all towns were boroughs, and while periodic surveys frequently reveal the numbers of burgages in the latter there are few such records for the unincorporated towns. In all there are nearly 30 urban communities for which no such statistics are available. Where burgage totals have survived, moreover, they are not always a reliable indicator of the whole population even when they are multiplied by five, the number adopted as the size of the average medieval household. In 1306, for example, there were 278 burgesses at Cowbridge,[129] while at Holt in 1315 there were 159, although Holt also housed a further 204 other tenants, while none are listed at Cowbridge.[130] Yet not every town dweller would have been a burgage holder or even a lesser taxpayer; there must always have been a poorer, landless element who paid no rents or dues, and were therefore omitted from contemporary records. Burgage totals themselves are not always a reliable indicator of the resident burgess population either, since some burgesses frequently held more than one burgage. Conwy in 1295 housed 112 burgages, but only 99 burgesses;[131] Llawhaden's 174½ burgages in 1326 were in the hands of 126 burgesses;[132] while the 162 plots at Knighton in 1304 supported 126 burgesses.[133] In many instances, however, only the burgage totals are known, and it has been necessary to reduce them accordingly by 25 per cent. since the proportion of burgages to burgesses in the instances where both sets of figures are available is in the region of four to three.

A final limitation on our analysis has its roots firmly in the political history of medieval Wales. The years for which town surveys are most frequent, the period 1250–1330, was also one of war and conquest in which the Anglo-Norman boroughs were regularly devastated by the Welsh long after Edward I's victory over Llywelyn the Last. Thus the size of a town as suggested by statistical returns in a given year may have altered drastically within a decade, as illustrated by the example of Caerphilly where Welsh attacks reduced the burgage total from 116 to 1281 to 44 in 1306.[134] In spite of these difficulties a reconstruction of the urban hierarchy remains a valuable exercise, not only because it provides an indication of each town's size and relationship to the other, but because it ultimately highlights the profound impact of subsequent episodes, notably the Black Death and the rebellion of Owain Glyndŵr.

The number of taxpayers in each town as recorded in the late 13th and early 14th centuries is indicated in the form of a histogram (Table II).[135] The dominance

TABLE II

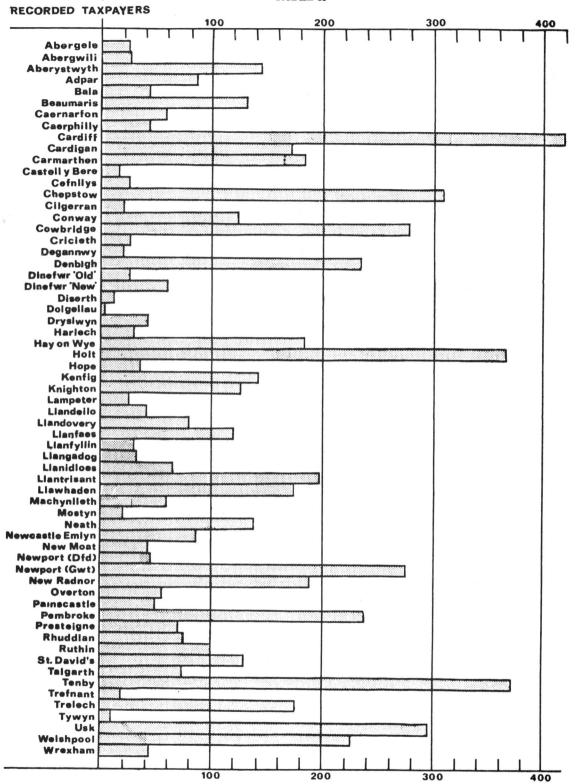

The Urban Hierarchy at the end of the 13th century

The histogram records the relative size of towns according to surviving totals of taxpayers and burgages/burgesses. Where several sets of figures are available for a particular town those dated nearest to 1300 have been used. The Table is incomplete since lack of information has necessitated the omission of 43 communities.

of Cardiff, with 420 burgages in 1295, is clear, but also expanding rapidly were Holt with 363 tenants in 1315; Haverfordwest with 360 burgages in 1324; Tenby with 352 in 1329–30; and Trelech already with 378 plots in 1288. At the lower end of the scale stood a group of minor communities such as Pwllheli with 21 households in 1284; Cilgerran with 21 taxpayers in 1292; Mostyn 20; Trefnant 18; and Diserth with only twelve. Tywyn and Dolgellau had yet to assume any urban character with only nine and three taxpayers each, while other small settlements included Cefnllys, Degannwy, Lampeter, and Abergele. One of the most interesting features to emerge from the histogram is the moderate character of the Edwardian boroughs of the north where the civil communities clearly bore little relation to the magnitude of their respective fortifications. Castell-y-Bere is exceptional with only 16 taxpayers in 1292, but Harlech and Cricieth were also unable to develop, and their burgage totals failed to exceed thirty. Of the remainder Caernarfon and Rhuddlan were relatively modest with 59 and 75 plots occupied in the 1290s at a time when other boroughs like Hay housed nearly two hundred. At Conwy and Beaumaris the burgage totals exceeded 100, and their populations at the end of the century were probably in the region of 600–700, but this was exceeded even by the native borough of Welshpool which contained 173 burgesses in 1309. As we have already seen, however, burgage totals failed to correspond with burgess numbers, the latter tending to be smaller as individuals came into the possession of more than one plot, or others lay empty as a result of a Welsh attack. The finest illustration of this point is provided by the case of Trelech, where the high burgage total recorded in 1288 had fallen to 271 in 1306, and they were in the hands of only 113 burgesses. Overall, however, the burgage-burgess relationship of four to three holds good and it allows a closer insight into the relative populations of towns as they stood *c.* 1300. Table III lists the 77 towns for which figures are known according to the numbers of burgesses and taxpayers in each. The entries in each of the four groups are in declining order of seniority and where only the burgage total is known the burgess population has been calculated at 75 per cent. of the whole. In the case of towns for which several early surveys exist, the one carried out nearest to 1300 has been used.

With 20 towns housing less than 30 recorded tenants, and altogether 50 towns with under 100, it becomes clear that smaller urban communities were more common. At the higher level 19 contained 100–200 taxpayers, but there were only eight with more than 200, while Holt and not Cardiff emerges as the English borough with the largest enumerated population. In all the 77 towns contained almost 6,800 tenants at an average of nearly ninety per town. By extending this figure to the remaining 28 urban settlements for which we possess no early returns (and the group is representative of Welsh towns as whole), it becomes possible to arrive at an estimate for the whole country of 9,300 taxpayers. From this total we can tentatively calculate the whole urban population by adopting the enumerator of five. While this number may appear to be slightly high since it represents the average household and women in their own right were occasionally burgage and tenement holders as well as their husbands, it no more than compensates for the unrecorded, sometimes semi-permanent elements which were present in most

TABLE III

The Urban Hierarchy, *c.* 1300

BURGESS/TAXPAYER TOTALS

1	2	3	4
Under 30	30–100	100–200	Over 200
Llandovery	Conwy	Abergavenny	Holt
Abergwili	New Radnor	Denbigh	Cardiff
Narberth	Adpar	Tenby	Cowbridge
Llanfyllin	Nefyn	Newport (Dyfed)	Haverfordwest
Cilgerran	Llanfaes	Pembroke	Chepstow
Pwllheli	Flint	Carmarthen	Usk
Lampeter	Rhuddlan	Hay	Newport (Gwent)
Harlech	Ruthin	Cardigan	Monmouth
Mostyn	Presteigne	St David's	
Cefnllys	Llanidloes	Knighton	
Degannwy	Machynlleth	Llawhaden	
Dinefwr (Old)	Newborough	Grosmont	
Abergele	Overton	Trelech	
Cricieth	Talgarth	Llantrisant	
Trefnant	Newcastle Emlyn	Aberystwyth	
Bere	Bangor	Kenfig	
Llanrwst	Raglan	Welshpool	
Diserth	Painscastle	Neath	
Tywyn	Kidwelly	Beaumaris	
Dolgellau	Caernarfon		
	Wrexham		
	New Moat		
	Llangadog		
	Llandeilo		
	Bala		
	Hope		
	Dinas Mawddwy		
	Caerphilly		
	Dinefwr (New)		
	Drylswyn		

TOTALS

	1	2	3	4
Towns	20	30	19	8
Tenants, approx.	370	1,800	2,500	2,100

medieval towns. The result is an estimated total figure of 46,500, surprisingly high when the total population of Wales in 1300 has been variously calculated at between 200,000 and 300,000 people.[136] By this early date, then, it would appear that between 15½ per cent. and 23 per cent. of the inhabitants were already town dwellers.

What proportion of this total were Welshmen is more difficult to estimate, particularly since the racial composition of several towns was mixed while others were exclusively English or Welsh. Englishmen found their way into the Welsh towns in small numbers, like the eight at Wrexham in 1315,[137] one, perhaps two, at Lampeter in 1317,[138] and a handful recorded at Nefyn in 1293.[139] On the whole, however, the smaller and generally more remote native communities proved less attractive to the English than did their own towns and boroughs to the Welsh who by 1300 were already making noticeable inroads. The English outpost of Abergele housed two Welshmen in 1311, while the substantial Welsh community at Ruthin was incorporated into the new borough.[140] The native element at Aberystwyth was also high,[141] and the Welsh were also taking up burgesses in Beaumaris where by the mid-14th century the English element had become a minority.[142] Neither did the other Edwardian boroughs remain exclusively English. At Harlech and Bere one-third of the taxpayers were Welsh as early as 1292,[143] while at Conwy in 1284 one of the three chaplains serving the church of St Mary was required to be 'an honest Welsh chaplain by reason of the difference of the language'.[144] Hope was an evenly mixed community, while 60 per cent. of the taxpayers recorded at Knighton in 1292 were Welsh.[145] Overall, there is sufficient evidence to suggest that by 1300 the native element in the English boroughs was already in the region of seven per cent., and the English constituted about three per cent. of the population of the specifically Welsh towns. Adjusting our respective totals accordingly, about 8,000 Welshmen, or 17 per cent. of the total urban population, were already town dwellers, a figure which must surely dispel the lingering myth that they found little attraction to such a way of life.

Late and Post-Medieval Decline

From their high point in the early years of the 14th century the majority of Welsh towns experienced a lengthy period of marked decline characterised by serious reductions in population, and, in extreme cases, the complete disappearance of several minor communities. Others decayed to such an extent that regular markets ceased to be held, many buildings were abandoned and decayed, and the towns became small 'rural townships' devoid of any real urban features or functions. The reasons underlying such developments are not hard to find; the effects of the Black Death in the middle and later years of the 14th century followed by the rebellion of Owain Glyndŵr were so disastrous that some towns failed to recover while the population of others fell by more than half. Another important reason for the decline was the abandonment of many castles during these years which had particularly adverse effects on the smaller towns and boroughs. At Harlech in the 1290s, for example, the men of the castle garrison outnumbered the taxpayers in the small borough, and the same was true of Cefnllys, Diserth, Bere, Dolforwyn, Knucklas and Cricieth. Except for temporary refortification during the Glyndŵr revolt itself, however, many of the lesser castles had served their usefulness by the end of the 14th century. Only the more important structures with an essential administrative role to perform continued in use, while the majority were allowed to decay, and with them the dependent civil communities.

The Black Death or the 'Great Pestilence' first reached Wales early in 1349 and within a year it was affecting the whole country. This initial outbreak was followed by the 'Second Pestilence' which broke out in the winter of 1361-2, and there were further, albeit milder, epidemics like that of 1369 throughout the remainder of the century.[146] Estimates of the total death toll in Wales are hard to come by. J. C. Russell put forward the view that in Britain as a whole the plague of 1348-50 killed off about 20 per cent. of the population, while the additional losses resulting from the later outbreaks may have reduced the total by half by the end of the century.[147] For urban Wales the evidence is fragmentary but nevertheless conclusive; towns were decimated almost overnight, and at the end few were more than shadows of their former selves. At Ruthin in the single month of June 1349 some 77 inhabitants died.[148] The effects were generally so severe that the burgesses of Rhuddlan were granted a reduction of 25 per cent. in the farm of their borough, while at Montgomery one-third had to be remitted.[149] As a result of the epidemic of 1369 30 per cent. of the burgages at Trelech lay empty for lack of tenants,[150] while between 1348 and 1368 burgage rents at Abergavenny fell by half.[151] Everywhere reduced rents and revenues became commonplace, while the following decades were characterised by declining markets and urban decay.

The long-term effects of the plague on Welsh towns are difficult to determine since it must be considered along with the Glyndŵr rebellion and the general urban decline of the 15th century. Some of the larger boroughs, in fact, recovered very quickly and stand in striking contrast to the general pattern. At Denbigh the number of burgages saw an increase from 235 in 1305 to nearly 500 by 1373,[152] and at Haverfordwest the total rose from 360 in 1324 to 422 in 1376.[153] In general, however, these were exceptions, and the full effects of the plague are probably best illustrated by the examples already cited together with that of Cefnllys where half the burgages lay empty in 1383.[154] Such a decline followed so quickly by a national rebellion was to see the end of several such lesser communities.

The Glyndŵr rebellion, the last Welsh uprising to assume the character of a national revolt, broke out in September 1400, reached its peak during the years up to 1406, but remained a force until 1410 with its leader eventually dying in obscurity c. 1417.[155] Significantly the earliest target for the rebels was the borough of Ruthin,[156] and throughout the years of major disturbance other boroughs and towns were regularly attacked 'for that they stood for the King of England'.[157] Some, like Tenby in 1405, successfully withstood the efforts of the besiegers, but the majority were put to the torch and thoroughly devastated.[158] In all, the accounts of contemporary chroniclers and the evidence from subsequent financial returns indicate that more than 40 towns fell victim to the rebels and the actual final total may well have been considerably higher. Even those which escaped were adversely affected by the ravages of the surrounding countryside, which brought about a further decline in their already decaying commercial life. Evidence from individual towns indicates the thoroughness of the destruction. Rhuddlan, already suffering from the ravages of the 'Pestilence', was 'completely burnt and totally destroyed by the rebels', and 60 burgages still stood unrepaired 35 years later. Flint was similarly devastated and the borough also had to be abandoned, since the townsfolk 'dared not dwell outside the castle'.[159] At Harlech 46 houses were destroyed, virtually the whole town;[160] while Newport (Gwent), attacked in 1402, stood as the head of a lordship valued at nil in the following year.[161] The attack on the borough of Overton in 1403 forced the English burgesses to abandon the town and the majority failed to return so that a century later there were 'but . . . twenty houses'.[162] Not only the English towns suffered at the hands of Glyndŵr's supporters, however; no rents were received at Pwllheli in 1408 'because of the rebellion'[163] while at nearby Nefyn, burnt in 1400, it was said in 1413 that no one wished to live there.[164]

The long-lasting effects of the Glyndŵr revolt on the urban economy can be readily illustrated. Kidwelly in 1444 was 'waste and desolate',[165] while the burgesses of Newcastle Emlyn still stood £36 in arrears because their borough had been 'devastated by the Welsh'.[166] At the end of the century 60 burgages at Llantrisant remained unoccupied for lack of takers,[167] while even at Cardiff tenements still lay empty, destroyed 'in the time of the Rebellion of Wales in bygone years'.[168] Holt, where in 1315 there had been 363 tenants alone, had seen its total population fall to about three hundred, while by the 1530s[169] much of the walled area at Chepstow no longer housed burgages but had been 'converted into little medowes and gardens'.[170] Some towns, as we have already indicated, even disappeared altogether. Cefnllys, Bere, Diserth and Dolforwyn were already declining before the Black Death and the rebellion, but the end of others can be directly attributed to these momentous episodes. Dinefwr, attacked in 1403, was 'ruinous' a century later, and now nothing but earthworks remain to indicate the site of the English borough.[171] Likewise Dryslwyn disappears from the records after its attack in 1403,[172] and little more is heard of the communities at Wiston, New Moat, and Trefilan.

In general the malaise which characterised most Welsh towns in the 15th century continued into the 16th and 17th centuries. While evidence relating to urban populations has its limitations for this period the combined testimony of contemporary observers points conclusively to widespread urban decay. John Leland, who compiled his *Itinerary* in the years 1536-39, visited most of the country's towns and passed comment on the situation of some 58 of them, while additional observations are forthcoming from the pens of Elizabethan writers such as George Owen, Camden, and Speed.[173] Subjective as their comments are, they remain a valuable supplement to the meagre documentary evidence relating to Welsh towns in the post-medieval period.

Inevitably there were exceptions to this general decline, and some of the larger English boroughs, in particular, recovered very quickly from the ravages of the plagues and Glyndŵr', and even experienced some modest expansion. Estimates of urban populations in the years 1545-63 have been made for a number of towns by Leonard Owen,[174] and at the head of the hierarchy stood Carmarthen, described by Camden as 'the chief Citie of the country', with 2,150 souls.[175] It was followed by Brecon with 1,750, while close behind were Wrexham and Haverfordwest with populations in the region of 1,500.[176] Kidwelly, despite the old town being 'near desolate', had seen new growth across the River Gwendraeth and now housed 1,100 people,[177] while in Cardiff there were more than 1,000 inhabitants.[178] Swansea,

Denbigh and Caernarfon were only moderately smaller,[179] and in Monmouth in 1610 there were 266 burgesses.[180] Ruthin too, was prospering, being 'full of inhabitants and well replenished with buildings',[181] while Leland also wrote favourably of Builth, Abergavenny, Cowbridge, Presteigne, and Welshpool as good market towns.[182]

Elsewhere, however, the picture is more depressing. Cardigan and Aberyswyth were boroughs of only 55–80 houses,[183] while Caerphilly had declined so much that its burghal status and privileges had almost been forgotten.[184] In Pembrokeshire Tenby had yet to recover fully, and was still 'a little town', while according to George Owen Pembroke itself was 'very ruinous and much decayed' with an estimated population of about six hundred and thirty.[185] Apart from Haverfordwest the county's other towns were generally in a sorry state. Owen wrote that markets had ceased to be held at Fishguard, Cilgerran, Wiston, and Llawhaden 'by reason of the povertie of the townes',[186] while in 1594 Newport contained only 50 burgages as against the 233 recorded there in 1434.[187] St David's was a town of little more than 50 houses.[188]

Some of the smaller communities, it is true, were proving capable of holding their own. Machynlleth in 1545 supported 51 taxpayers, only 10 less than the late-13th-century figure,[189] while Newborough, which housed 58 taxpayers in 1352, had become a town of '93 houses and 12 crofts' in 1547.[190] Beaumaris in the middle years of the century was a borough of some 555 inhabitants, which compares favourably with the 132 burgages originally taken up (x 5),[191] while Llanidloes' population of 324 also stands comparison with the 66 burgesses recorded there in 1309.[192] Generally, however, the lesser towns fared badly throughout the late-medieval and early-modern periods and most had to wait until the 19th century before experiencing any marked improvement. Leland noted over thirty towns which were in a sorry state, while Speed's town maps of 1610 illustrate the shrunken, rural character of such places as Harlech, Flint, Radnor, and Montgomery.[193] Bala had also become only 'a little poore market',[194] while at Pwllheli, Bangor, Caersws and Llandovery the markets had either ceased altogether or were only occasionally held.[195] Aberafan had been reduced to 'a poore village', Raglan was 'bare', Kenfig had been engulfed by 'the Sandes that the Severn Se ther castith up', while Newport (Gwent), Hope, Hay, and Cricieth were all 'clene decayed'.[196] Others, such as Tregaron, Narbeth, Llanelli and Llangollen, were no longer even regarded as towns but merely as 'vilages'.[197]

Epilogue

From the evidence of subsequent observers such as Emmanuel Bowen and Edward Lhuyd and topographical artists like Gastineau and the brothers Buck it is clear that the general decline of town life and institutions continued into the 18th and early 19th centuries.[198] There were exceptions, of course, principally the larger commercial centres which managed to sustain their economic prosperity, while others near the coast or the rich mineral deposits of Flintshire and Glamorgan, were beginning to expand with the first stirrings of the Industrial Revolution.

Neath, according to Leland only a 'little town' had two centuries later grown into a 'large town . . . trading much in coales',[199] while the early development of the woollen industry had seen Welshpool transformed into 'a considerable Town with a good market'.[200] Yet the evidence of the first official census of 1801, together with the Tithe Maps of the 1840s revealed many towns and boroughs to be decayed; rural communities with only earthworks and castle mounds to suggest their former importance. The economic developments of the 19th century were to see many of these communities regain something of their former importance, although others were to be by-passed almost completely by the spread of industrialisation. The history of Welsh towns during these later centuries is, however, well beyond the scope of this present study, although it will undoubtedly be a story well worth telling.

(Notes at end of Chapter Two, pp. 51–56)

Chapter Two

THE SITE AND TOPOGRAPHY OF THE EARLY TOWN

The Siting of Towns

THE SUCCESS OF ANY URBAN VENTURE, whether it be a planned town or an expanding organic community, depended not only on the expertise and vitality of its inhabitants, but on the wealth and resources of the surrounding countryside. Here the location of the early town was all-important, and for the most part the advantages or disadvantages of site determined levels of prosperity, and in extreme cases even the survival of communities beyond the Middle Ages. Several of the most favourable sites for town development had, in fact, been used long before the first Norman adventurers began to penetrate the Welsh Marches. As we have already seen, Abergavenny, Loughor, Caernarfon, Neath, Caerleon, Usk, Caersws and Carmarthen were all boroughs planned on or near sites previously favoured by the Romans whose surviving road network may also have been instrumental in the appearance and early development of Newtown, Holt, Bala, Dolgellau, Newcastle (Bridgend), Chepstow, Cowbridge, and perhaps also St Asaph.[1] Primarily, however, and the observation applies in these instances as well as with the remaining towns, the determining factor in the selection of site was the presence of water, the fundamental requisite for military and commercial success. All but 10, in fact, of Wales' medieval towns lay either along the coast or the course of a river.

A total of 24 towns occupied coastal sites and the number reflects the importance attached to communication by sea which was readily preferred to lengthy journeys by land over inadequate roads and by cumbersome modes of transport. Significantly, of this group all but Bangor, Tywyn, Pwllheli, Nefyn, and the short-lived Llanfaes were English foundations whose garrisons and burgesses could be supplied by ships in times of Welsh attack. Access to the sea in these cases also proved beneficial to the urban economy. Most coastal towns became involved in varying degrees of maritime trade, while the inhabitants were further able to enrich their coffers as well as their diets by engaging in commercial fishing. Nefyn, Tenby, Conwy, Pwllheli and Aberystwyth, in particular, boasted a successful herring industry throughout the medieval period. The early quay, a feature also of Cardiff, Swansea, Caernarfon, Chepstow and Newport (Gwent) was as important for the economic life of the town as was the castle for its defence.

Other services, of course, were also provided by these coastal communities. The major ports supplied the more inland towns with a variety of imported goods as well as handling the home-produced surplus for export. They were also valuable disembarkation points for troops *en route* to the more distant English boroughs.

As an integral part of the medieval communications network the coastal towns also operated ferry services linking rivers and estuaries which were difficult to circumvent by road and too wide for the bridge builder. Conwy and Degannwy were so linked, while a regular ferry, operating initially from Llanfaes, crossed the Menai Straits and linked Anglesey with mainland Wales.[2] In the south, also, a ferry connected Loughor with Llanelli,[3] while another, mentioned in 1306, operated across the Tawe from Swansea.[4]

In strategic terms, the predominantly English coastal towns played a vital part in the conquest, settlement and administration of Wales. By necessity, however, the majority of urban communities lay inland and were sited along the principal valley routes from which control could be exercised over the surrounding areas. The Welsh towns, also, were predominantly concentrated well away from the sea since the coastal plains had been the first areas to fall to the Norman conquerors. Some of these inland foundations like Denbigh, Llantrisant, and probably also Castell y Bere, Dolforwyn, Cefnllys and Diserth, were laid out on the summit of hills and their position illustrates the purely military circumstances of their foundation. The great majority, however (over 70 in all), were sited along river courses which offered a multitude of advantages. In the first place rivers provided natural lines of defence and often removed the necessity of constructing a full circuit of town walls.

Chepstow, laid out within a meander of the substantial River Wye, had only to be protected to the south and west, while at Llanidloes the presence of the Severn flowing past the western side of the borough meant that only a partial circuit of walls had to be built. More favourable still, of course, was the presence of two or more rivers whose confluence points often provided ideal locations for town foundations. About fifteen of the inland towns were sited at such points and these were predominantly Anglo-Norman castle-boroughs. The group includes Monmouth, laid out where the Monnow flows into the Wye; Brecon, at the confluence of the Usk and Honddu; and Bala, sited at the northern end of Llyn Tegid where the Dee and Tryweryn join.

It was not only the major rivers which were utilised in this way, however, and even minor streams were often valuable, as the example of Llandovery illustrates. Here the initial Norman borough was bounded on the west by the Tywi, then following its old course, while the eastern limits of the town were determined by the lesser Nant Bawddwr which flowed southwards into the Afon Gwydderig, a tributary of the Tywi. Accordingly the community was defended by water on three sides, and a ditch had only to be dug to the north.[5] As the borough expanded, moreover, the new development took place to the east across the Bawddwr, but here again natural protection on this western side was provided by the Afon Brân which flowed parallel to the Bawddwr and likewise into the Gwydderig. There are numerous other examples of such minor water-courses being incorporated into the town defences. At Caerphilly the triangular enclosure formed by the confluence of the Nant Gledyr and Porset Brook seems likely to have been the site of the early borough, while the boundaries of the substantial community at Trelech were determined by the rectangle formed by the Penarth Brook, the

River Olwy, and two minor streams. Other similar instances include St Clear's; Llanfyllin; Dinas Mawddwy; Cilgerran; Abergwili; Carmarthen, where the borough was laid out within a meander of the Mill Stream as it flowed down to the Tywi; and Abergavenny, a town sited at the confluence of two tributaries of the Gavenny which itself flowed past the southern limits of the walled borough.

As well as a vital asset in considerations of defence, an adequate supply of water was also a prerequisite for commercial success. It supplied the power for the town mill; facilitated the development of early industry; allowed the construction of weirs, and thus the supply of fish and eels; and supported the townsfolks' agricultural activities in times of low rainfall. Equally important, particularly for the English boroughs, rivers provided valuable lines of communication with other towns and ultimately with the coast. Thus several urban settlements, although well inland, were strategically sited at the highest tidal points where they could be supplied by ships, an important consideration in times of Welsh unrest. Neath, Cilgerran, Carmarthen, Haverfordwest, Rhuddlan, St Clear's, and even Holt, were planned boroughs all belonging to this category, while of the organic towns the Conwy was still navigable as far as Llanrwst, while even Dolgellau, despite being 12 miles inland, could still be reached by small vessels sailing up the Maw. Like the coastal communities their inhabitants could also involve themselves in a degree of water-borne trade and many also had a quay as an important feature of the townscape.

Town Plans and the Urban Framework

In their plan, lay-out and physical appearance the early Welsh towns were far from a homogeneous group. The regularity which characterised the planned Anglo-Norman foundations was for the most part absent from the native towns whose irregular and often haphazard street-patterns reflected the more gradual and unsupervised nature of their growth and development. Tywyn, Dolgellau, Llantwit Major, and their like, stand in marked contrast to the uniformity which characterised such Edwardian boroughs as Rhuddlan, Caernarfon and Flint. It is quite clear, in fact, that much thought lay behind the process of town foundation, and that great efforts were made by the English urban planners to achieve uniformity in plan and arrangement. The almost professional nature of such activity was illustrated in January 1297 at Harwich when Edward I gathered around him a number of experts in the field to discuss the whole business of urban planning.[6] Not all Welsh towns, however, can be conveniently categorised into 'planned English' or 'irregular Welsh' communities, and not enough is known of the original format of such places as Trefilan and New Moat which had ceased to possess any urban characteristics as early as the 15th century. Others, indeed, may have been almost indistinguishable from the castle complex, lacking even the appearance of a distinct settlement. At Knucklas, Bere, Dolforwyn, Cefnllys and Old Dinefwr the burgesses may well have resided within the bailey alongside the storehouses and quarters of the military garrison. Such was certainly the case at Dryslwyn where in 1360 all but 14 of the 48 burgages lay within the castle defences.[7] Similarly at Kidwelly the initial settlement was sited within the outer earthworks of the Norman motte, while the unusually large bailey at Kenfig, extending over eight acres, also housed part of the early town.[8] Foundations such as these, however, were not representative of the alien boroughs as a whole, although they may well illustrate a first stage in the development of the older, Norman foundations which in their early years were probably the smallest of communities living alongside the castle garrison. In contrast to the organic towns, the English boroughs by the close of the 13th century reflected the increasingly sophisticated techniques of urban form and planning which had already been tested and approved in England and Gascony. Wherever the terrain allowed, and it should be remembered that most Welsh sites were chosen for their military rather than urban potential, streets and burgages were laid out in a regular manner, a pattern which was in turn continued as the community expanded beyond the initial area of settlement.

Of the various classifications which can be applied to the early towns the largest single group were those which followed the traditional grid plan whereby several principal streets crossed each other at right angles forming a number of equal-sized quarters or *insulae,* the whole enclosed with either masonry or earthen defences.[9] Over thirty towns can be placed in this category although in size and arrangement there are significant degrees of variation. The achievement of precise regularity was often hampered by the limitations of site whereby natural features such as marshland, rising ground or a meandering river affected the arrangements in a particular area of the town. At Montgomery, for example, attempts at a grid pattern proved successful only in the southern area of the walled borough because of the rising ground which led to the formidable ridge on which the castle was sited. Similarly at Cowbridge it proved impossible to lay out the town in the form of a truly regular rectangle on account of the River Thaw, whose course necessitated a sharp deflection in the south-eastern section of the enclosing wall.

Moreover, it should also be remembered that few towns were instant creations, and in most cases it was only after several decades of existence that they reached anything like the size of their medieval extent. Typical of most Anglo-Norman boroughs was Usk which expanded from 141 burgages in 1262 to 294 by 1306,[10] and while the later growth evidently did not take place unsupervised it is clear that the attention to detail which characterised the principal Edwardian foundations was not applied. Indeed, it was only in these cases where castle and borough were conceived and laid out as a single entity with uniform burgages that the nearest to a true grid system was achieved. Although, therefore, its basic form can be detected at Abergavenny, the two Newports, Cardigan, New Radnor, Overton, Swansea, and elsewhere, the finest representations remain the examples of Flint, Caernarfon, Rhuddlan, Newborough, Beaumaris, and the much-decayed Holt.

While the grid pattern was often adopted as the basic format for several new towns in many other cases it was unnecessary to arrange the burgages in such a regular manner. Most of the alien boroughs were, after all, only moderate concerns which hardly warranted such complex planning. Two opposing lines of tenements flanking a length of roadway or the highway which led from the castle gates was often sufficient, and with some 30 towns laid out this way it proved

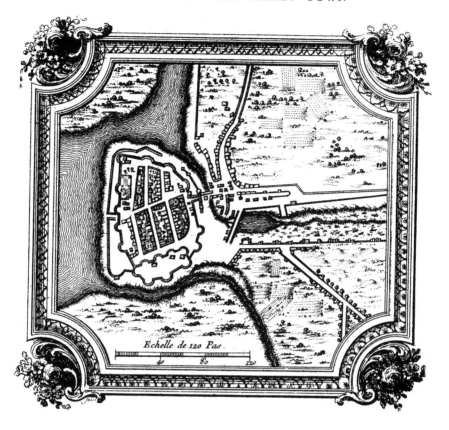

Fig. 3. Caernarfon

An early French print of the Edwardian borough. The open space east
of the castle represents the site of the market-place, while the large
mill-pool filled in during the last century, is also clearly visible.

to be as common as the grid settlements. Pembroke, confined to a narrow peninsula,
could not have been planned in any other way, but other notable examples of the
single street borough include Cilgerran, Abergwili, Bala, Llawhaden, and the native
foundations of Newtown and Welshpool. Such communities could be relatively
easily defended by the construction of a bank and ditch following the rear line of
the burgages with the addition of only short stretches and a gate at each end of the
highway. As well as being a convenient form for many planned English boroughs,
such a linear plan also proved to be the most natural arrangement of several organic
Welsh communities which had developed along the line of a single road—Llangollen;
Lampeter; Llangadog; and Dinas Mawddwy are among the finest examples.

Simple variations on the single street plan were also frequently adopted,
particulary where a town was laid out at a crossroads with the junction as the site
of the market-place. At Caersws, Ruthin, Caerwys and Hope the early boroughs
took the form of a cross with the two principal streets bisecting each other at

right angles. Elsewhere the single street was supplemented with the addition of a secondary cross-limb which resulted in a 'T' shape; Brecon and Cardiff are valuable examples of this plan which was also adopted by the princes of Powys in the laying out of Llanfyllin and Machynlleth. Of the remaining towns a few, like Llantrisant and the initial walled area of Denbigh, were sited on the summit of a substantial hill and followed a circular plan, but the great majority were irregular in form and often lacked a castle and even enclosing defences. In the main these were native settlements where the transition from *tref* to full town had been a gradual process unattended by supervision of plan and arrangement. Tywyn, Dolgellau, Llantwit Major, Llandeilo, and the manorial boroughs of Llŷn—Nefyn and Pwllheli—were typical of this group where growth was haphazard and often had to be fashioned around existing features such as a *llan*, with its large, circular churchyard, or an established market-place which already occupied the flattest and most advantageous area of the town.

Whatever the plan or racial and political background of the towns of medieval Wales, as a group they illustrate in their topography the various features which were common—and essential—to all such early urban communities. Towns, for the most part, had to be defended and castles and walls were as essential as churches and market-places. Both the urban and neighbouring inhabitants had also to be governed and administered with the resulting appearance of town halls, gaols and market houses; while the sick and infirm required hospices and almshouses. The early urban topography, in short, was rich in its variety and it is to these features, their frequency and distribution, that our attention will now be directed.

Mottes and Castles

Since most of the early Welsh towns were Anglo-Norman plantations it comes as no surprise that the castle was adopted as a dominant and vital feature of the urban topography. Indeed, such adoption was almost universal; of the 105 towns included in this study a stronghold of some description, either a motte-and-bailey, a ringwork, or a more elaborate masonry structure, was present within the immediate area of at least 82 of them.[11] As the qualification implies, moreover, this is perhaps a conservative total which by necessity fails to take into account the possible existence of other mottes with no documentary history which may have long since been levelled or ploughed out. At Pwllheli, for example, the survival of the names 'Cadlys' and 'Pen y Mownt' point to the presence of a fortification there, but there is no other substantiating evidence.[12] Significantly the case of Pwllheli together with Adpar, Dolforwyn, Llanidloes, Trefilan and Welshpool, alone constitute the native element in this group, while conversely the only predominantly English communities where a castle was not an integral feature of the townscape were those of Caersws, Abergele, Hope, Fishguard, Mostyn, Newborough, St Asaph, and Cowbridge, the latter hardly undefended since it was walled and lay only a short distance from St Quentin's castle. Clearly, then, the castle was regarded as a vital feature of the alien boroughs, but not of the Welsh towns where its building usually preceded and was generally unconnected with the development of the town.

The castles of Wales have been the subject of an extensive literature and it is unnecessary here to attempt more than a broad outline of the various types and their distribution throughout the early towns and boroughs.[13] They varied from the simple motte-and-bailey to the complex and elaborate masonry structures which towered over the communities at Raglan and Caernarfon. The motte was the standard early form which retained its basic appearance in several of the minor towns where there was little justification for the construction of costly stone castles. The mottes, also, however, varied in their size and sophistication. At Trelech, Adpar, and Templeton, the surviving mounds are small, and although they now stand much lower than they once did it is evident from modest circumferences at the base that these were far from being substantial structures. In striking contrast, however, stand the remains at New Radnor and Wiston where both the formidable mottes and their large baileys illustrate this form of stronghold at its most elaborate.

In its infancy the Norman motte was topped with a simple wooden tower which was often later replaced by a stone keep, although limited excavation in this field makes it near impossible to estimate how many keeps there were in Wales. The finest example of the stone keep is that at Cardiff, although other examples have been noted at Crickhowell, Caerleon, Llantrisant, Loughor, and Prestatyn. By and large, however, the simple motte-and-bailey gave way in the late 12th and 13th centuries to more elaborate structures which in their varying states of preservation still remain a feature of many Welsh towns. Usually these castles were erected on the same site as the old motte since this already occupied the most advantageous position, while the subsequent growth of the town around it often left the later castle builder with little room to manoeuvre. Occasionally, however, a new site was selected as at Knighton where the borough developed to the north-west of the original motte, Bryn y Castell, where work on a new castle was begun by William de Braose in 1191-2.[14] Again, at both Rhuddlan and Newport (Gwent) the original Norman mottes were abandoned in favour of more suitable positions, while at Hay-on-Wye the initial stronghold was also replaced by a new castle which was incorporated within the defences of the borough whose walls were erected in the 1230s.[15] In the main, however, these were exceptions to the standard procedure which normally involved the partial levelling of the motte and the construction of a new and more elaborate structure, as illustrated by the examples of Neath, Pembroke, Caernarfon, Monmouth, and Llandovery.

Although these later masonry castles were often successors to earlier structures this was not always the case and several of the Edwardian strongholds, in particular, were erected where there had been no earlier occupation, either military or civil. The castles of Flint, Beaumaris, Conwy, and Aberystwyth were constructed on virgin sites, at least in terms of Anglo-Norman settlement, and were planned as integral parts of their respective boroughs which were laid out and defended as part of a single grand operation. Such works are justifiably regarded as representing the high point of 13th-century castle building, but for the medieval town dweller their counterparts at Llantrisant, Kidwelly, Newcastle Emlyn, St Clear's, and their like, all of which extended over an area equivalent to at least one-third of that covered by the town, must have appeared just as imposing—and reassuring.

Town Defences

As impressive and substantial as were many of Wales' medieval castles, these strongholds provided no actual protection for the civil communities which existed alongside them, except, of course, for the small group of minor towns which were largely confined to the already defended castle baileys. The Anglo-Norman boroughs in particular lay constantly under the threat of Welsh attack, and their survival depended heavily on the provision of an adequate circuit of man-made defences.

Town defences in Wales varied considerably in their form and sophistication according to the size and importance of the particular settlement, the expertise of its inhabitants, and the resources available to them.[16] Many of the lesser towns, in fact, including several English boroughs, such as Hope and Newcastle (Bridgend), do not appear to have been defended at all, and the townsfolk had to abandon their homes and seek the safety of the castle in times of attack. In general the absence of artificial defences was a feature of the native towns which lacked any strategic or military functions, although there were occasional exceptions, as at Bangor, where Edward I is reported to have erected some defences in 1284, although we know nothing more of them or, indeed, of their location.[17] Of this whole group only Owain de la Pole's foundation of Llanidloes appears to have been enclosed with a full circuit of banks and ditches.[18] In general though, all towns, both Welsh and English, made full use of natural features which often reduced the need for no more than the minimum of human effort. At St Clear's and Newcastle Emlyn the boroughs were laid out within promontory sites protected on three sides by water which necessitated only the digging of a single ditch on the landward side; while other towns sited within a pronounced river meander, such as Newtown and Chepstow, again required only a single line of defence to complete the circuit.

The earliest and often the only form of artificial defences consisted of a wide ditch together with an inner bank built from the earth thrown up during its digging. Sometimes the bank was topped with a timber palisade, but this was not a standard addition and excavations at Rhuddlan, for example, have shown that one was never erected there.[19] In the absence of adequate documentary evidence coupled with the effects of centuries of erosion, farming activities and redevelopment, it is impossible to provide anything more than an estimate of the number of Welsh towns defended in this manner. Several of these early banks, moreover, were subsequently replaced with stone walls which removed all visible traces of the earlier defences, and but for a few noteworthy examples, such as Montgomery, Abergavenny, Flint, and Llanidloes there has been little systematic archaeological investigation in this field.[20] To an extent, however, the absence of excavation can be overcome by recourse to other methods of enquiry which include the study of early prints and maps, topographical writings, and field-work involving a close examination of the local landscape. Early forms of street names, too, have their value not only in determining the former presence of defences, but in plotting their course; at Kidwelly the presence of Ditch Street (now New Street) is self-explanatory but other common clues include Frog Street, often a reference to the inhabitants of the town ditch, and Dark Street, which was sometimes conferred on the street nearest to and under the shadow of the town defences. Elsewhere, of course, the remains of these banks and ditches can still be seen quite clearly, while traces of others, as at Trelech, can be detected by aerial photography. Such vestiges are visible from the ground at Llanidloes, New Radnor, Usk, Kidwelly, Rhayader, Flint, and Rhuddlan, while sections of the Roman earthen defences subsequently utilised by the medieval town planners are also evident at Caerleon and Loughor. A full list of these towns for which we have evidence of these early defences is provided by Table IV, but it must be stressed that this can be no more than a provisional effort which will no doubt be modified in the light of future excavation. It excludes, moreover, the cases of Bala, Degannwy, Crickhowell, and Overton, where the burgesses were given license to enclose their towns, but there is no evidence to suggest that the work was ever carried out.[21]

TABLE IV

Bank and Ditch Defences

Abergavenny	Kidwelly	Newport (Gwent)
Bangor?	Knighton	New Radnor
Beaumaris?	Laugharne	Rhayader
Brecon?	Llandovery	Rhuddlan
Caerleon	Loughor	Ruthin
Caernarfon	Monmouth	St Clear's
Dryslwyn	Montgomery?	Swansea
Flint	Neath?	Trelech
Kenfig	Newcastle Emlyn	Usk

During the course of the 13th and early 14th centuries it became common practice to replace the early defences with a more elaborate circuit of stone walls. The traditional view that this work involved the erection of the wall along the same line as the earthen bank is not, however, supported by events in Wales since the evidence from Cardiff, Abergavenny, Rhuddlan, and Haverfordwest indicates that the early Anglo-Norman settlements were much smaller than their later walled counterparts.[22] It is hard to imagine, as well, that the early borough of Chepstow covered anything more than a fraction of the huge 113 acres enclosed in the late 13th century. Rather the process appears to have involved the extension of the initial defences to incorporate areas of later growth, as took place at Carmarthen in 1415 when the walls were lengthened to enclose a substantial built-up area which developed beyong the East Gate.[23] Nor, indeed, should this substitution of stone for earth be taken as an indication of the inadequacy of the early method of defence which, significantly, was considered quite sufficient by Edward I to protect his new boroughs of Flint and Rhuddlan. Indeed, excavations at these sites have revealed the formidable nature of the early method; at Flint the town ditch was shown to have been 2.7m. deep and 13.7m. wide,[24] while Rhuddlan was enclosed with a broad, flat-bottomed ditch some 2.4m. in depth which stood between two mighty banks of which the outer was as much as 17m. wide.[25]

Evidently the transition from earth to masonry defences was much more than a simple process of improvement. To an extent, perhaps, it reflected the increasing use of stone as a building material, but at the same time the cost of quarrying and transportation must have imposed a considerable burden on many of the lesser towns which can hardly have been met from the profits of murage, the toll levied on certain goods sold in the town whose revenue was intended for the construction of the walls. Of greater significance, perhaps, were considerations of prestige which saw stone walls as symbols of prosperity, urban independence, civic pride, and English superiority. Indeed, the mighty defences planned at Caernarfon and Conwy must have represented a definite psychological victory over the surrounding Welsh, while at the same time stimulating other burgesses to embark on similar schemes elsewhere. It may well have been for such reasons, also, that other communities unable to replace the entire length of the early defences with walls chose to rebuild their gateways in stone, as took place at Laugharne, Radnor, Ruthin, and Newport (Gwent).

From the architectural viewpoint, and in particular the extent of the remains at Denbigh, Conwy, Tenby, and Caernarfon, it is evident that such walls were substantial works which were sufficient to protect the town. That Pembroke, for one, was never taken by the Welsh throughout the medieval period was hardly unconnected with the impregnability of its defences. In general the accepted width of these walls was in the region of 6ft. (1.8m.),[26] although there were local variations, and parts of the wall at Aberystwyth were nearly 9ft. (2.7m.) wide.[27] Also, as with the early banks, additional protection was often provided in the form of an outer ditch like the one at Tenby which was 30ft. (9.1m.) wide.[28] For the most part these ditches have long been filled in and built upon, although their line can sometimes be detected by a slope or a marked change in level as in the case of Kidwelly where the course of the western ditch is indicated by the sloping tombstones in the graveyard of the Siloam Baptist chapel which was built upon it. No longer remaining, either, are most of the impressive town gates which originally provided access to the walled boroughs. Many, nevertheless, outlived the rest of the defences since they frequently fulfilled additional functions; the upper storeys were sometimes inhabited or were used as a town hall, while the basements were utilised, as was that at Kidwelly, for the borough gaol or 'lock-up'.[29] These gates, as Speed's town maps of 1610 show, were often still standing in the early 17th century, while some such as the North Gate of Cardigan remained until the mid-19th century.[30] With the steady increase in urban traffic, however, many were finally demolished during the latter part of the century and today examples of these gates, or portions of them, remain only at Caernarfon, Denbigh, Cowbridge, Conwy, Pembroke, Chepstow, Kidwelly, Tenby, and Monmouth.

As proved to be the case with the list of towns defended with a bank and ditch it is only possible to arrive at a provisional total of the walled towns in Wales. Stone, although less vulnerable to the elements than earth, was a valuable building material, and once the walls had ceased to be maintained they were commonly robbed for new building projects, sometimes to the extent, as in the case of Montgomery, of removing nearly all traces of their former presence.

However, there is sufficient evidence to indicate that at least 21 towns, significantly all Anglo-Norman boroughs, were walled in stone and surviving remains, which vary from almost the full circuit at Conwy to the small fragment adjoining the south-east corner of the castle at Cardiff, can still be seen at 10 of them.

TABLE V

Towns walled in stone \

Abergavenny	Carmarthen	Kidwelly
Aberystwyth	*Chepstow	Monmouth
Beaumaris	*Conwy	*Montgomery
*Brecon	*Cowbridge	*Pembroke
*Caernarfon	*Denbigh	Ruthin?
*Cardiff	Haverfordwest	Swansea
Cardigan	Hay-on-Wye	*Tenby

*The asterisk denotes those towns where sections of the walls survive.

Burgages and Burgesses

Within the medieval borough the standard unit of land was the burgage, the tenure of which gave the holder the privileges and status of a burgess. The plots usually fronted the market-place or one of the other principal streets and assumed a characteristic shape, long and narrow with a tenement at the front and the remainder used either as a garden or to house workshops and yards connected with the particular trade of the tenant. Occasionally these burgages were known by other names, such as the *placeae* (places) recorded at Newborough and Degannwy in 1304-6,[31] but they probably amounted to the same and were almost all let at a fixed, almost standard rental of 1s. a year.[32] Even in the unincorporated towns where the tenants were simply listed as 'taxpayers' rather than burgesses the picture was very similar, to the extent that by the end of the medieval period the term 'burgage' was being increasingly used to describe a unit of land within a town regardless of the legal position of the community itself.[33]

In many of Wales' smaller towns which have not experienced periods of marked redevelopment and where rebuilding has not assumed greater proportions than simple infilling, much of the original burgage pattern remains, sometimes in a remarkable state of preservation. Included among the noteworthy instances are Bala, Holt, Cilgerran, Kidwelly, and Newborough, while even in several of the larger towns such as Aberystwyth, Cardigan, Pembroke and Newport (Gwent) much of the former pattern survives. It is clear from both the documentary and topographical evidence, however, that the burgage in Wales was not of uniform size with standard dimensions, but varied considerably not only from town to town, but even within towns. The officials who supervised the laying out of the new planned boroughs undoubtedly strove for uniformity wherever possible, but the limitations of site often frustrated these attempts: at Newport (Dyfed), for example, the burgages in the central chequer where houses fronted both sides, were inevitably shorter than those on the opposite sides of the two principal streets where the plots could continue unrestricted down to the two parallel flowing streams which formed the natural boundaries of the borough. Some idea of this variation is forthcoming from documentary sources. At Caernarfon and Cricieth the burgage was 80ft. long by 60ft. wide (24m. by 18m.); at Beaumaris it was equally as long though only 40ft. wide (12m.),[34] while a plot which changed hands at Flint in 1300 was said to be 'in length six-score feet and in width four-score feet' (36½m. by 24m.).[35] Even in the planned Edwardian boroughs, then, there was noticeable variation in burgage size. At Caernarfon the plots in the north-east and south-east chequers bounded by the town wall would have been substantially shorter than the 80ft. (24m.) quoted, little more than 50ft.(15m.). Elsewhere further statistical evidence confirms this irregularity. At Llantrisant in 1631 it was stated that a burgage there was tradition-ally quite small, only 24ft. long by 20ft. wide (7m. by 6m.),[36] a restriction evidently determined by the hilltop location and the need to accommodate as many plots as possible on a site where half of the available area was already taken up by the castle and an existing Celtic church. By examining the surviving pattern within those towns where there has been little subsequent coalescing or redevelop-ment this diversity is confirmed; at Cilgerran the burgages are particularly well preserved, especially off the south side of the High Street, where they attain an average length of nearly 200ft. (61m.) and a width of 26ft. (7.6m.), dimensions also found at Bala, although at Newborough in Anglesey the width is unusually narrow, rarely exceeding 15ft. (4.5m.).

Beyond the regular payment of the standard 1s. annual rental the tenure of a burgage also involved the performance of a number of other duties and obligations to the community as a whole. The terms of many borough charters, of course, usually exempted the burgesses from many of the more menial duties which were often carried out in return for land, as at Tenby where they were specifically exempted from guarding the lord's castle and mills,[37] while there may have been other tenants who were excluded from all services. Among this group were probably the 'burgesses of the wind' (de vento) who were only occasionally residents. They appear at Carmarthen and Cardigan in 1275 and 1280,[38] and again at Newcastle Emlyn in 1304 where they are entered in the accounts as 'men called burgesses de vento who hold neither burgages or lands, but pay in order that they may enjoy the same liberty'.[39] For the most part, however, the resident burgesses were obliged to play an active part in the welfare of the town as a whole and their most funda-mental duty centred on the defence of the borough. As Fox commented, the Anglo-Norman town, at least in its early years, was 'but the outer ward of the castle',[40] and accordingly each burgess had to be capable not only of defending his own plot, but taking an active part in the protection of the whole community. Often they were obliged to go on expedition beyond the borough in times of unrest, although this aspect of service had limitations imposed upon it; such sorties were only permissible if the town was left adequately defended while, as William de Beaumont's charter of 1153-84 to Swansea reveals, the burgesses were required to travel only such distances as enabled them to return home the same night.[41] Some interesting variations on this aspect are provided by the duties of the burgesses on the lands of the bishops of St David's; the men of St David's itself were bound to escort the bishop 'with the shrine of the Blessed David and with the relics on either side' provided they could return home that evening, while those of Llawhaden and New Moat performed the same service, but only as far as Carmarthen.[42]

While such mandatory duties were usually carried out they were not always welcomed by the burgesses, and it is not uncommon to read of disputes between them and the local lord. Such neglect of obligations came to the fore at Monmouth in 1308 when the men admitted neglecting their responsibility to keep watch 'and other trespasses' and agreed to pay 20 marks by way of recompense to the lord of the borough, Henry of Lancaster.[43] In principle, though, if not always in practice, burgage tenure continued to involve these duties throughout the medieval period; as late as 1563 the charter to the men of Holt shows that each plot there still bore the traditional military obligations.[44]

Market-Places, Market Halls and Town Halls

Among the principal and most coveted privileges of the medieval town was the regular holding of weekly markets and annual fairs. These rights were usually granted by the king, often on the supplication of the local seigneur, and were sufficiently prized by the inhabitants as to be the subject of frequent disputes between neighbouring communities highly sensitive to the threat of competition. It was, after all, the fear of the Montgomery burgesses for the success of their own market that persuaded Edward I to transfer, albeit temporarily, the Welshpool market to Trefnant, while similar disputes became common between the corporation of Tenby and the men of Narberth.[45] The market-place itself, as the commercial centre of the town, usually occupied a dominant position, and it is clear from the arrangement of the planned Anglo-Norman boroughs, in particular, that pride of place was given to its siting. Usually a large, triangular area was set aside for this purpose with the principal streets of the town laid out in such a way as to converge upon it. A market cross was erected in the centre—one of the few survivors can be seen at St David's—and on the specified market day this would be the focal point of considerable activity and revelry. Although many of these triangular market-places have been encroached upon in later years their basic outline remains a detectable feature of many present-day Welsh towns, including Caerphilly, Tregaron, Grosmont, Hay, Newcastle Emlyn, Painscastle, and Raglan. Occasionally, however, it was not always possible to allocate such a generous area within the central part of the town for this purpose. It was not uncommon, in fact, to find the early markets being held in the churchyard where the stocks might also be sited as a curious companion to the gravestones. At Llanelli, for example, the weekly Thursday market was held in the south-west corner of St Ellwy's churchyard right through to the 1820s, while the picture was the same in the case of St Mary's at Haverfordwest.[46] Elsewhere, where space was even more at a premium, it proved necessary to hold the market actually beyond the immediate confines of the town. In the case of Kidwelly the very small area of the walled borough necessitated the siting of the market-place outside the West Gate, while the market was likewise held beyond the walls at Caernarfon where the old Norman bailey, now the Castle Square area, was adopted as a suitable location.

In many towns the goods offered for sale on market days were displayed on temporary and easily-dismantled wooden stalls, but in others a permanent market house was built, usually in the middle of the market-place or the principal street. Often these halls had additional uses, doubling as a town hall with perhaps the undercroft, as at Neath, also serving as the borough prison. It is regrettable that the pressures of a later age have necessitated the destruction of many of these buildings whose very central positions had to be sacrificed to the pressures of increased town traffic. The finest examples, perhaps, survive at Llanidloes and Grosmont, though neither building is medieval, but elsewhere the majority were demolished in the 19th century, often with such scant notice that it is not always clear just how many towns contained public buildings of this type. What is evident, however, is that their frequency and distribution had surprisingly little to do with the varying size and prosperity of the early towns. While Cardiff had its own market house, mentioned in 1338 and mapped by Speed in 1610,[47] so also did Caerwys, New Radnor and Llangollen,[48] while at Newport (Dyfed) 'the old Sheere hall' had already fallen into disuse by 1594.[49] Like the distribution of town walls, basic need may have had much less to do with their building than considerations of prestige and civic pride.

The majority of market and town halls which survived right up to the last century stood on or very near the sites of previous halls, but the pedigree did not always extend back to the medieval period. The great age of town hall building was the 16th and 17 centuries, and in many Welsh towns the halls which are first recorded during these years do not appear to have had any predecessors. At Usk there are no indications of a market house before c. 1620;[50] the old town hall at Wrexham is not documented before 1562, although it was apparently then of some considerable age;[51] the market house at Swansea dates from 1652;[52] while Ruthin town hall was erected in 1663.[53] In other instances, however, there is clear evidence for a medieval predecessor and the overall frequency of earlier buildings may have been more common than the limited documentary evidence suggests. The 16th-century town hall at Newtown, demolished in 1852, is known to have had a medieval counterpart,[54] while another early example was that of Neath, recorded in 1397.[55] At Llantwit Major the first town hall dates from the late 13th century;[56] that at Llandovery from 1485;[57] the guild hall at Kenfig is recorded in 1330;[58] while Caernarfon's first town hall may have been erected as early as 1284.[59]

In some of the larger boroughs which functioned as administrative and judicial centres this range of civic and commercial buildings was much more sophisticated. While at declining Kidwelly the South Gate had to serve also as the town hall and the borough gaol,[60] regional capitals such as Brecon had their purpose-built gaols, in this case situated by the Water Gate above the Honddu. At Conwy excavations have suggested the presence of a whole range of judicial and administrative buildings in the area to the west of the castle,[61] while at Caernarfon the range was even more varied. As *caput* of the Principality of North Wales the borough had its Shire Hall, Town Hall, Justice's House, and, above the East Gate, the Exchequer Office.[62]

Fig. 4. The Town Hall, Llantwit Major
Dating originally from the late 13th century, this is one of the few surviving examples of its type
in Wales.

Town Mills

The mill was a common feature of the medieval landscape, and its presence was
as essential to the town dweller as to his rural counterpart. Indeed, the inhabitants
of most Welsh towns had their own mills which lay either within the immediate
urban area or not far removed and rarely more than half a mile away. While few
of these buildings or their successors have survived the test of time, enough
information can be gleaned from early maps and documentary sources to enable
the historian to draw some general conclusions regarding their sites and relationship
to the town. In the first instance, it is evident in the case of native towns like
Tregaron that the mills generally lay a greater distance from the communities they
served than was the case with the planned Anglo-Norman boroughs. With the
English towns, in fact, it is clear that the desire to create a self-contained and
defendable settlement also extended as far as the positioning of the mill which
was seen as an integral part of the borough. Inevitably there were exceptions, as
in the cases of Beaumaris, Denbigh, Cowbridge, and Llantrisant, where the chosen
town site was removed from a suitable water-course, but generally mills were sited
within the built-up area. At Ruthin, Newport (Gwent), New Radnor and possibly
Newcastle Emlyn the borough mills actually lay within the area enclosed by the

town defences, while elsewhere it stood as close to them as practical considerations allowed. At Kidwelly the successor to the medieval mill still stands by the Afon Gwendraeth Fach, immediately below the southern defences of the 'old town', while at Caernarfon the large mill-pool just beyond the East Gate was not filled in until the early 19th century. The many other examples of mills standing alongside the borough defences include Pembroke, Carmarthen, and Cardigan, while it was also common to find the mill sited in the shadow of the castle which provided much needed protection in the event of a Welsh attack, as at Cardiff, Harlech, Skenfrith, the two Newports, Laugharne, Monmouth, and Rhayader. Here much weight was evidently given to practical as well as defensive considerations since the mill was sometimes positioned along the same water-course which fed the castle moat.

Domestic Architecture

In attempting a review of the subject of medieval town houses in Wales it must be said at the onset that the historian is dealing with a subject which has yet to receive detailed study and any conclusions drawn can only be of a preliminary nature. Indeed, few detailed architectural surveys of Welsh towns have been made, while those available, including several published over sixty years ago, vary considerably in depth and coverage. In recent years, however, the work of the Royal Commission on Ancient Monuments together with a series of surveys made of the domestic buildings of Breconshire and Radnorshire (Powys) has yielded valuable information from which some general conclusions are forthcoming.[63] Most important of all in the present context is that very little domestic architecture older than the 16th century survives today beyond the occasional late 15th-century buildings such as 'The Old House' at Knighton.[64] While medieval roof-timbers and other structural details were subsequently incorporated into later buildings and remain in several towns the like of Bangor, Conwy and Caernarfon, the few complete remaining structures, such as the tower at Talgarth and the town hall at Llantwit Major, had an administrative rather than a domestic usage.

The explanation behind this negligible medieval survival is not hard to pinpoint. Throughout the 12th and 13th centuries many towns were consistently attacked and burnt by the Welsh, and suffered extensive damage again in the early 1400s at the hands of Owain Glyndŵr. In the event of such regular disturbance private dwellings seem unlikely to have amounted to more than basic, single-storey buildings which could be rebuilt with relative ease. The restrictions of space afforded by the burgage pattern would have determined a narrow, probably wooden frontage, with the house extending back to a depth which was probably as great, if not greater, than its width. It may well have been only with the increasing stability of the late medieval period that widespread development on this model took place with the addition of jettied or projecting upper storeys.[65] At the same time, however, the relative poverty of many Welsh towns in the 15th and 16th centuries might have meant that fewer more sophisticated dwellings were built, and that these would vary accordingly to the social class of the owner. The large *plasau* built for the gentry of Caernarfon and Conwy would undoubtedly have stood in marked contrast to the houses of the lesser burgesses. Eventually, through the natural processes of decay and replacement coupled with the advent of 'The Great Rebuilding' (the era of architectural advance which has been shown to have crossed Wales 'like a wave' from the 16th to the 19th century[66]) most of the old dwellings have been swept away so that very little remains which pre-dates this period of improvement.

Churches and Chapels

As well as making arrangments for the defence and commercial life of a community provision had also to be made for the spiritual needs of the inhabitants, and in an age of strong religious conviction the building of a church or chapel was often an early act in the process of town foundation. Indeed, such work in many cases appears to have been contemporary with the construction of the castle and walls, no better exemplified than at the Edwardian boroughs of Caernarfon, Beaumaris, and Rhuddlan, where in determining the plan of the new settlements the planners consistently chose to site the churches within the north-west chequer. Elsewhere, as we have seen, many existing churches, whether of Celtic or early Anglo-Norman foundation, often proved instrumental both in attracting native settlement and in the ultimate emergence of the Welsh towns, while others played a part in determining the sites of several English boroughs, which, like Llanelli, were founded alongside established centres of worship.[67]

By the early years of the 14th century it is clear that a church or chapel, or both, had become a central feature of the great majority of Welsh towns. The list of those without such provision is a short one and the absence can usually be accounted for in terms of the modest size of these towns, which include among them Dryslwyn, Caersws, Dinas Maddwy, and possibly Adpar.[68] Also, where a borough was sited within an existing parish and close to its church, as in the cases of Laugharne, Llandovery, Newborough, and Llawhaden, it was clearly unnecessary to provide additional places of worship. In contrast many boroughs housed a wide variety of religious buildings which as well as churches and guild chapels included priories, friaries and hospices for the sick and infirm. In general the number and range of such features within a given town was related to its size, prosperity and the benevolence of the local seigneur in the provision of land and endowments. This range also increased with the age of the community since those boroughs with a Norman background usually housed a greater number of ecclesiastical buildings which reflected stages in urban growth and the development of suburbs. Thus Cardiff boasted two churches: St John's and St Mary's, as well as the chapel of St Piran, which stood by the entrance of the castle.[69] Pembroke, likewise, had two churches within its walls, one a Norman foundation and the other a product of 13th-century expansion, while across the river stood on the one side the chapel of St Anne, and on the other the church of the Benedictine priory. Again there were three medieval churches at Haverfordwest which indicate stages in the development of the community first established by the Normans in the early 12th century. At Chepstow the priory church of St Mary also served the townsfolk, while within the walls of the borough, there were at least three early chapels, dedicated to SS Anne, Ewen, and Thomas.[70] Many of these chapels, it appears, were associated with particular crafts and professions carried out by the inhabitants; St Piran's at Cardiff was used by the Guild of Cordwainers, while St Julian's chapel at Tenby, conveniently sited on the borough quay, served the port's fishermen and mariners.[71]

Inevitably, however, there were occasional exceptions to this generalisation that the range of religious buildings was directly related to the size and wealth of the community. This was most apparent in the cases of those English boroughs planted within an established parish whose boundaries were not subsequently re-adjusted. In the case of Aberystwyth the 'clas' at Llanbadarn remained the parish church, and only a small chapel dedicated to St Michael was erected within the area of the walled borough.[72] Similarly small chapels had to suffice at Harlech, Denbigh, and Newcastle Emlyn, while no church was built at Bala until 1811, although a medieval chapel formerly occupied a central position in the High Street.[73] Even several of the lesser towns, however, had their chapels in addition to their churches; at Lampeter there are suggestions of a chapel dedicated to St Thomas;[74] while Llandeilo, in addition to the church of St Teilo, housed nearby a chapel which was dependent on Talley Abbey.[75]

From this account it is evident that most of the smaller town chapels fell into disuse and disrepair in the 16th and 17th centuries, and have not survived into the modern period. To the examples of vanished chapels already cited several additions can be made; Carmarthen housed the chapel of Prince Edward, located immediately below the castle;[76] alongside the town mill at Newport (Gwent) stood St Lawrence's chapel:[77] at Neath, St Giles' across the river;[78] St John's chapel at Hay occupied a site within the central market-place;[79] while a chapel dedicated to St Thomas lies buried beneath the sands which engulfed the old borough of Kenfig.[80]

Town churches, continually in use and frequently refurbished, have fared the test of time much better. Later modifications, and particularly the extensive programme of rebuilding which affected many of them in the 19th century, may have resulted in only the survival of the towers, and only partial structural remains from the medieval period, but the sites which their present successors occupy are essentially those of the original structures. Their dedications, also, survive as testimony to their antiquity and the circumstances of their foundation, with the Celtic dedications at Tregaron, Llantrisant, Cilgerran, and their like, standing in contrast to the 22 town church which retain the familiar dedication to the Virgin Mary, the most popular of saints among the Anglo-Norman conquerors.

Priories, Friaries and Hospices

For the Anglo-Norman conquerors of south and west Wales the granting of land to the various religious orders for the foundation of dependent houses was considered to be a normal aspect of the extension of their territorial possessions. Such action was regarded as a traditional act of piety and it proved to be a vital factor in the settlement of the country. The new monks, drawn in the main from their respective mother-houses in France and England, shared with the townsfolk all the isolation and vulnerability of frontier communities and, although technically free of secular interference, these foundations in practice had close cultural and economic links with the neighbouring boroughs in which they often held a considerable landholding interest.[81]

The Norman advance into Wales was contemporary with the rapid growth of monasticism in the west and in particular with the rise of the Benedictine Order. This was reflected in the boroughs of South Wales where, within 20 years of the building of the castles, the Order had established priories, in approximate chronological order, at Chepstow, Monmouth, Abergavenny, Cardiff, Carmarthen, Brecon, Llandovery, Kidwelly, and Cardigan, to which was later added a nunnery at Usk. This great burst of activity was followed by a relative lull in the later part of the 12th century which saw only the addition of St John's priory, a house of the Augustinians, at Carmarthen *ante* 1127, and the Cluniac priory at St Clear's, but in the following 100 years a new wave of foundation resulted in the additional appearance of friaries at Brecon, Cardiff, and Carmarthen, and the first cells at Bangor, Llanfaes, Haverfordwest, Rhuddlan, and perhaps also at Nefyn.[82] Finally, by the end of the 14th century the picture had been completed with the appearance of further establishments at Denbigh, Ruthin and Newport (Gwent) The distribution of these town priories and friaries was clearly related to that of the Anglo-Norman boroughs with only minor exceptions; Bangor was in all probability a mixed community, and the only thoroughly Welsh instance, apart from the dubious case of Nefyn, was Llanfaes in Anglesey where, in 1237–45, Llywelyn ab Iorwerth founded a Franciscan friary in memory of his deceased wife, Joan (*see* Table VI, p. 48).

As a demonstration of their detachment from secular controls and affairs most houses were founded on land which lay beyond the defences of the walled boroughs. In general, however, the distance between the two was often only nominal, although there were some noteworthy exceptions. The Dominican friary at Rhuddlan was built almost a mile from the borough, while Llywelyn's foundation at Llanfaes was also well removed from the site of the town. It seems probable, also, that the ill-fated priory at Llandovery, founded *c.* 1110, but dissolved in 1184, allegedly on account of the monks' misconduct, lay well to the north of the borough in the area of St Mary's church (Llanfair). Elsewhere, though, there was often no more than a short distance of perhaps a quarter of a mile between these houses and the limits of the civil settlements. This was particularly so with the earlier, and more vulnerable, foundations which were often sited so close to the Norman castles that subsequent extensions of the town defences sometimes resulted in their incorporation within the enlarged circuit. At Cardiff and Chepstow the extension of the initial defences took in the Benedictine priories there, while similar enlargement of the early defences at Abergavenny and Haverfordwest left the houses just a few metres beyond the new course of the walls.

Ultimately, however, the proximity of priories and friaries to the urban areas subsequently acted against the survival of their building complexes following the Dissolution of the Monasteries in the late 1530s. Many became private residences or were used as convenient supplies of building materials, but either way, with

TABLE VI

The Distribution of Town Priories and Friaries

Town	Foundation	Foundation Date	Order
Abergavenny	St Martin's priory	1087–1100	Benedictine
Bangor	friary	c. 1251	Dominican
Brecon	(1) St John's priory	c. 1110	Benedictine
	(2) friary	–1269	Dominican
Cardiff	(1) St Mary's priory	1106	Benedictine
	(2) Blackfriars	+1242	Dominican
	(3) Greyfriars	c. 1280	Franciscan
Cardigan	St Mary's priory	1110–15	Benedectine
Carmarthen	(1) St Peter's priory	c. 1110	Benedictine
	(2) St John's priory	–1127	Augustinian
	(3) friary	–1284	Franciscan
Chepstow	St Mary's priory	–1071	Benedictine
Denbigh	Henllan friary	1343–50	Carmelite
Haverfordwest	(1) St Thomas's priory	–1200	Augustinian
	(2) friary	–1246	Dominican
Kidwelly	St Mary's priory	1114	Benedictine
Llandovery	priory	c. 1110	Benedictine
		(dissolved 1184)	
Llanfaes	friary	1237–45	Franciscan
Monmouth	St Mary's priory	1074–86	Benedictine
Nefyn	priory	–1252	?
Newport (Gwent)	friary	–1377	Augustinian
Pembroke	Monckton priory	c. 1098	Benedictine
Rhuddlan	friary	–1260	Dominican
Ruthin	College of St Peter	1310	Bonhommes
St Clear's	St Mary's priory	1147–84	Cluniac
Templeton	preceptory?	–1185?	Knights Templar
Usk	St Mary's priory (for nuns)	–1236	Benedictine

Note.—This list includes only those foundations sited within the immediate area of the towns

the subsequent extension of the built-up areas together with all the pressures of urban renewal and redevelopment, few vestiges, save the priory churches and the notable exception of Usk, survive today. Rhuddlan friary, much of which was incorporated into a farm complex, is another exception, but even in the case of Llanfaes, which was also established in an area which has retained its rural character, only the church of St Catherine remains. Fortunately the efforts of the archaeologist have done much to elucidate the plans of such establishments and attention has been directed towards the houses at Chepstow, Cardiff (Blackfriars), and the Dominican friary at Haverfordwest, while details of the plan of the early priory buildings at Bangor were unearthed during building operations in 1898-9. Here the initial church, cloister garth and a number of other buildings were noted,[83] and excavations elsewhere have yielded similar findings. While the range of buildings at Chepstow, located to the south of St Mary's church, were found to have been unorthodox in plan,[84] the complexes at Haverfordwest Augustinian priory and

Blackfriars were compact and the buildings more sophisticated.[85] At both, the churches were revealed together with the chapter house, kitchen range and several additional domestic and agricultural buildings. Haverfordwest priory appears to have been a substantial house, and it was valued at £133 at the time of its dissolution in 1538. Sections of heavily overgrown walling are still visible.

In addition to their daily religious rituals and the more rudimentary agricultural work necessary to maintain themselves, the clergy were expected to provide food and accommodation in the houses for passing travellers and merchants, as were the hospices or hospitals which dotted the countryside. Some of these hospices, in fact, were dependencies of nearby priories, such as the hospice of the Holy Trinity at Monmouth, attached to St Mary's, and the hospice at Haverfordwest which was associated with the Dominican friary.[86] The majority of such foundations, however, appear to have been independent and purely secular establishments which depended on the generosity of local lords and the revenues forthcoming from their estates.[87] The work of these hospices, or 'spitals' as they were commonly known, appears to have varied; some concentrated on the needs of the poor and infirm, others on caring for the needs of poor travellers and pilgrims on their way to St David's, while a number catered primarily for the sick and sufferers from leprosy. Not surprisingly, in view of the latter aspect, such establishments tended to be sited well beyond the town boundaries and away from areas of concentrated settlement. An unusual exception to this rule was the hospital of St David at Swansea, founded in 1332, which was apparently within the defences of the borough,[88] but elsewhere these foundations were kept at a safe distance. The 14th-century spital at Cardiff was located at the end of Crockherbtown, well to the east of the borough,[89] while the hospice founded in 1287 at Llawhaden also stood beyond the western limit of the burgages.[90] Again, the leper house at Haverfordwest, recorded in 1246,[91] was removed from the built-up area and the evidence suggests that the *maladeria* recorded at Kenfig was also sited beyond the borough defences.[92]

The meagre level of documentation relating to these hospices together with the dearth of remains renders it extremely difficult to pronounce with any confidence on the overall number of such establishments associated with early towns. Additional examples are recorded from St David's, Tenby, Pembroke, and Usk, again all located beyond the boroughs, while Monmouth, by the late 15th century, had three hospitals.[93] A hospital of St John is also recorded at Rhuddlan in 1281, and it appears to have been sited to the north-east of the defences,[94] while the possibility of further foundations has been noted at Newcastle (Bridgend) and Wiston.[95] The evidence, clearly has a disproportionate bias towards South Wales and virtually nothing is known of similar establishments which may have been associated with the towns of the north. Overall, their actual frequency may have been greater than the surviving evidence suggests.

Suburbs

By the close of the Middle Ages the development of extra-mural settlements had become a feature of many of the larger Welsh boroughs. Yet this was far from a universal trend and there is evidence to suggest that the majority of towns remained unaffected by such manifestations of urban growth. Very few, in fact, of the lesser settlements, after experiencing a decline following the combined effects of the Black Death and the Glyndŵr revolt, breached their medieval limits, if at all, until the 19th century. Even several of the more substantial walled Anglo-Norman boroughs, as Speed's town maps of 1610 indicate, remained confined to their walled areas. Radnor and Flint had evidently contracted since their high point in the early 14th century, while Aberystwyth, apart from the growth of the vill of Trefechan across the Rheidol, experienced little extra-mural development until the early 1800s.[96] This was the case, also, at Tenby and Montgomery, while even Newport (Gwent) was unaffected by such expansion until the dawn of the Industrial Revolution.

Nevertheless, other towns were greatly modified by the appearance of suburbs and in many instances these first began to appear at a very early date and often within a decade of borough foundation. The reasons underlying such development varied from town to town, but the trend had much to do with the greater economic and administrative importance of the more favourably-sited English communities. Other common factors can also be detected and extra-mural growth, in particular, was frequently connected with the presence of religious and commercial establishments beyond the defences which focused attention away from the enclosed town at an early stage. Priories and similar religious foundations, often sited outside the town, proved particularly magnetic and were the focus of suburbs at Cardigan and Pembroke, while similar developments at Kidwelly were even more marked.[97] Here, by the early 15th century, the new town which had grown up on the south bank of the Afon Gwendraeth Fach around St Mary's priory had already outstripped the original walled borough. This example also reflects the importance of extra-mural commercial activities in such expansion since an additional suburb, known as 'Scholand', had earlier appeared beyond the West Gate where the weekly market was held.[98] At Caernarfon, likewise, restrictions of space within the town necessitated the holding of the market beyond the defences, which also proved a stimulus to further settlement, while outside the East Gate of the borough another suburb appeared in the area of the town mills.[99]

Clearly, the limit placed on later growth by the small areas enclosed within the walls proved to be an additional factor in these developments. In contrast to the 113 acres enclosed at Chepstow the great majority of walled boroughs in Wales had an area of less than 40 acres, most of which was already taken up by new burgesses within 20 years of the foundation date. Kidwelly had a defended area of only eight acres, while at Cowbridge only a portion, perhaps 25 per cent., of the 278 burgages recorded there in 1306 could have been accommodated within the walls.[100] In the case of Denbigh, founded in 1285 on the summit of a steep hill, the population of the extra-mural suburb had already quadrupled that of the defended town by 1305.[101]

Almost exclusively these early suburbs grew up beyond the main gates of the walled boroughs, flanking the principal roads which led to them. Bridgeheads and fording points also proved to be attractive locations, as at Bridgend, while at Conwy an extra-mural community had already appeared in the area of the ferry crossing to Degannwy by 1312.[102] From the evidence of Speed it is clear that many suburbs had assumed significant proportions by the early 17th century. To the list of these already mentioned can be added the names of Brecon, Monmouth and Beaumaris, while at Cardiff, Kidwelly and Cardigan these new areas of growth prospered while large areas within the walls lay empty and decayed. Already by the end of the Middle Ages townsfolk no longer required the security of stone walls which their predecessors had been at great pains to secure. The economic emphasis was gradually shifting from the old to the new, away from the confines of the medieval walled centres and out to the unrestricted expanse which lay beyond the old defences.

NOTES

Chapter One

1. For a full account of medieval town plantation *see* Beresford, M., *New Towns of the Middle Ages*, London, 1967.

2. 'Non urbe, non vico, non castris cohabitant', *Opera*, vi, 200. *See also* Lewis, *Medieval Boroughs of Snowdonia*, 1-12, and Carter, *Towns of Wales*, 7-13.

3. Lewis, *Medieval Boroughs of Snowdonia*, 3-4.

4. For the Roman background to these towns *see* the respective Gazetteer entries.

5. *Opera*, vi, 55.

6. Willis-Bund, J. W. (ed.), *The Black Book of St David's*, Cymm. Rec. Ser., v (London, 1902), 219-27, 277-81.

7. *Ibid.*, 17-35, 137-51.

8. *Cal. Ch. Rolls*, ii, 257.

9. Innes, J., *Old Llanelly* (Cardiff, 1902), 65, 81.

10. Speed, *Atlas of Wales*, 111. The market day at Wrexham was changed to Thursdays in 1331 (*Brut y Tywysogion*, 126).

11. *Mon. Angl.*, iv, 595; Kissack, M. E., *Medieval Monmouth*, The Monmouth Historical and Educational Trust (1974), 68.

12. Jack, R. I., 'Welsh and English in the medieval lordship of Ruthin', *T.D.H.S.*, xviii (1969), 38-9; *idem*, 'Records of Denbighshire Lordships: the Lordship of Dryffryn Clwd in 1324', *ibid.*, xvii (1968), 13-18.

13. Humphrey Bleaze's map of Welshpool, reproduced in Jones, M. C., 'Welshpool', *Mont. Coll.*, xiii (1880), *inter* 242-3.

14. *D.B.*, i, ff. 185b, 260b, 264b, 269; Tait, J., 'Flintshire in Domesday Book', *J.F.H.S.*, xi (1925), 4-5.

15. E 179/242/48, 57; Faraday, M. A., 'The Assessment for the 1/15th of 1293 on Radnor', *T.R.S.*, xliii (1973), 79-85, xliv (1974), 62-8.

16. Whitelock, D., et. al., *The Anglo-Saxon Chronicle; a revised translation* (London, 1961), 68; Taylor, A. J., *Rhuddlan Castle*: Official Guide (H.M.S.O., 1956), 3-4.

17. *Brut y Tywysogion*, 58; O'Brien, J., *Old Afan and Margam* (Port Talbot, 1926), 60-1; Clark, *Cartae*, iii, 922.

18. The fullest account remains Lloyd, *History of Wales*, Chaps. XI-XII.

19. *D.B.*, i, f. 162.

20. *Ibid.*, f. 269.

21. *Liber Landavensis*, 548; Nelson, L. H., *The Normans in South Wales* (Univ. of Texas, 1966), 30.

22. *D.B.*, i, f. 185b; Hogg and King, 'Early Castles', 107.

23. Ballard, A., *British Borough Charters, 1042-1216* (London, 1913), 18; Owen, *Cal. Pembs. Records*, iii, 208-10.

24. Ballard, A. and Tait, J., *British Borough Charters, 1216-1307* (London, 1923), p. 66.

25. Clark, *Cartae*, i, 136-8; Jones, W. H., *History of Swansea and Gower* (Carmarthen, 1920), 149-70.

26. The castle was attacked by a Welsh force in 1116 (*Brut y Tywysogion*, 40).

27. Richards, A. J., 'Kenfig Castle', *Arch. Camb.*, 7th ser., vii (1927), 163.

28. The motte at Caernarfon was built c. 1090, Jones, A. (ed.), *History of Gruffudd ap Cynan* (Manchester, 1910), 132; *R.C.A.M.W.M.*, *Caerns.*, ii, 125), that at Cardigan, although sited away from the later town, in 1093 (Hogg and King, 'Early Castles', 107).

29. Lewis, *Medieval Boroughs of Snowdonia*, 46; Beresford, *New Towns*, 545.

30. Clark, *Cartae*, i, 39.

31. Orderic Vitalis (ed. A. Le Prévost), *Historiae Ecclesiasticae Libri Tredecim*, Soc. de L'Hist. de France (5 vols., Paris, 1838-55), v. 110; Knowles and Hadcock, *Medieval Religious Houses*, 267.

32. *Cat. Pat. Rolls*, 1358-61, 7-8, contains an *inspeximus*—the original grant has not survived.

33. Round, J. H. (ed.), *Ancient Charters prior to A.D. 1200*, Pipe Roll Soc., x (1888), 8.

34. Galbraith, V. E. and Tait, J. (eds.), *The Herefordshire Domesday*, Pipe Roll Soc., xxv (1947-8), 79; Howse, W. H., 'Presteigne in Domesday', *T.R.S.*, xxi (1951), 48-9.

35. The castle's founder, Wizo the Fleming, who gave his name to the settlement, was dead by 1130 (*Pipe Roll, 31 Hen. I*, 136; Lloyd, *History of Wales*, ii, 425).

36. Round, *C.D.F.*, 367-8.

37. Radcliffe, F. and Knight, J., 'Excavations at Abergavenny, 1962-69, ii, Medieval and Later', *Mon. Antiq.*, ii (1968-9), 72.

38. Orderic Vitalis, *Hist. Eccles.*, viii, 3; Lloyd, *History of Wales*, ii, 382; *D.B.*, i, f. 269b.

39. Miles, H., 'Excavations at Rhuddlan, 1969-71; Interim Report', *J.F.H.S.*, xxv (1971-2), 2.

40. *Ann. Margam*, 4; *Mon. Angl.*, ii, 66.

41. *Atlas of Wales*, inter 105-6.

42. Rees, W., *Cardiff: A History of the City* (Cardiff, 1969), 19.

43. Nash-Williams, *Roman Frontier in Wales*, 73-4. The Roman and Welsh background has been summarised by Griffiths, R. A., 'Aberystwyth' in *idem* (ed.), *Boroughs of Medieval Wales* (Cardiff, 1978), 132-8.

44. Ballard and Tait, *British Borough Charters*, 66.

45. *Cal. Cl. Rolls*, ii, 199; *Cal. Pat. Rolls*, 1413-16, 308.

46. Lodwick, M. and E., *The Story of Carmarthen* (Carmarthen, 1953), 48.

47. Lloyd, *History of Wales*, ii, 424-5; Phillips, J. W., 'Haverfordwest Castle', *Arch. Camb.*, 6th ser., xiii (1913), 265-74; Owen, *Cal. Pembs. Records*, i, 158[n].

48. *Cal. Pat. Rolls*, 1258-66, 348; Owen, *Cal. Pembs. Records*, i, 86-7.

49. Mathias, A. G. O., 'Church of St Mary, Pembroke', *Arch. Camb.*, xciii (1938), 290-1.

50. Lloyd, *History of Wales*, ii, 496-500.

51. *Pipe Roll, 20 Hen. II*, 22.

52. *Brut y Tywysogion*, 58; O'Brien, *Old Afan and Margam*, 60-1; *Pipe Roll, 10 Hen. II*, 6.

53. Arber-Cooke, A. T., *Pages from the History of Llandovery*, i (Llandovery, 1975), 83; *Brut y Tywysogion*, 87, 95.

54. O'Neill, B. H. St J., 'The Castle and Borough of Llanidloes', *Mont. Coll.*, xliii (1934), 63.

55. *Brut y Tywysogion*, 58, 73, 90; Knowles and Hadcock, *Medieval Religious Houses*, 97, 102; Thomas, D. A., 'St Clear's in the Middle Ages, 1100-1500', *Carmarthen Historian*, vi (1969), 66-8.

56. Owen, G., *Baronia de Kemeys* (London, 1861), 49-51; Ballard and Tait, *British Borough Charters*, xxxi.

57. Owen, *Cal. Pembs. Records*, ii, 2, 10-11.

58. *Atlas of Wales*, inter 121-2, 123-4; *Annales Cambriae*, 108.

59. *Brut y Tywysogion*, 90.

60. *Cal. Ch. Rolls*, i, 10, ii, 479.

61. *Cal. Pat. Rolls*, 1247-47, 489.

62. *Cal. Pat. Rolls*, 1247-58, 609; *idem*, 1258-66, 67; Faraday, *op. cit.*, 83-4.

63. *Cal. Pat. Rolls*, 1225-32, 427.

64. S.C. 6/1201/1; *Glam. County Hist.*, iii, 340. Clark, *Cartae*, iii, 828.

65. *Ibid.*, ii, 532, iii, 845-60; Rees, W., *Caerphilly Castle: a history and descripion* (revd. edn., Caerphilly, 1971), 30.

66. Clark, *Cartae*, ii, 663.

67. *Cal. Ch. Rolls*, i, 328; Ballard and Tait, *British Borough Charters*, xliii; Banks, R. W., 'Early Charters to Towns in South Wales', *Arch. Camb.*, 4th ser., ix (1878), 99-100.

68. *Brut y Tywysogion*, 105; *Cal. Cl. Rolls*, 1247-51, 55; *Cal. Pat. Rolls*, 1257-58, 84.

69. *Cal. Pat. Rolls*, 1258-66, 348; Owen, *Cal. Pembs. Records*, i, 127.

70. *Cal. Pat Rolls*, 1232-47, 178; *Brut y Tywysogion*, 102.

71. Howse, W. H., 'Early Grant of a Weekly Market to Presteigne', *T.R.S.*, xxvi (1956), 43.

72. Craster, O. A., *Skenfrith Castle*: Official Guide (H.M.S.O., 1970), 7.

73. *Brut y Tywysogion*, 102.

74. Clark, *Cartae*, iii, 813-5; *Glam. County Hist.*, iii, 337-342; Rees, *Cardiff*, 30.

75. For the narrative of these events *see* Lloyd, *History of Wales*, ii, Ch. XX.

76. Edwards, J. G., 'Edward I's Castle Building in Wales', *Proc. Br. Acad.*, xxxii (1944), 15-81; *Cal. Welsh Rolls*, 165, 188; *Cal. Pat. Rolls*, 1272-81, 259; *Cal. Ch. Rolls*, ii, 206.

77. *Ibid.*, 276-7; Lewis, *Medieval Boroughs of Snowdonia*, 33, 171, 279-82.

78. Beresford, *New Towns*, 548. The original charter to the burgesses of Holt has not survived, but it is referred to in a confirmatory document of 1563 (Pratt, D., 'The 1563 Charter of Holt', *T.D.H.S.*, xxiii [1974], 104-25).

79. D.L. 42/1, ff. 30v, 31r, 31v. *See also* Owen, D. H., 'Denbigh', in Griffiths, *Boroughs of Medieval Wales*, 169.

80. *Cal. Ch. Rolls*, ii 372; E 101/351/15; 179/241/52; 179/242/52.

81. *Rec. Caern.*, 83-5, 178; Lewis, *Medieval Boroughs of Snowdonia*, 49-52, 282-3; *King's Works*, 395-7; Usher, G., 'The foundation of an Edwardian Borough: the Beaumaris Charter 1296', *T.A.A.S.* (1967), 1-16.

82. Harl. MS. 1240, ff. 67-8; *Cal. Ch. Rolls*, ii, 248; S.C. 6/1209/4.

83. S.C. 6/1218/9; Rhys, M. (ed.), *Minister's Accounts for West Wales, 1277-1305*, Cymm. Rec. Ser., xiii (London, 1936), 293, 307.

84. C 133/32/7; E 179/242/48; Owen, *Cal. Pembs. Records*, ii, 74-5, 148.

85. *Black Book*, 137-51.

86. *Ibid.*, 17-35, 127-36; *Cal. Ch. Rolls*, ii, 258.

87. *Black Book*, 263-9; *Brut y Tywysogion*, 87.

88. *Black Book*, 277, 291.

89. *Ibid.*, 241-9; Knowles and Hadcock, *Medieval Religious Houses*, 413, 419.

90. Beresford, *New Towns*, 538.

91. Faraday, *op. cit.*, 83-4; *C.I.M.P.*, iv, 161.

92. S.C. 6/1202/1; C 133/130.

93. T. Jones Pierce, 'The Old Borough of Nefyn, 1355-1882', *T.C.H.S.*, xviii (1957), 39-40; *idem*, 'Two Earl Caernarvonshire Accounts', *B.B.C.S.*, v (1931), 142-8.

94. Clark, *Cartae*, ii, 659; C 133/130; *Glam. County Hist.*, iii, 339.

95. Lewis, E. A., 'Chamberlains Accounts for West Wales', *B.B.C.S.*, ii (1925), 73; Rhys, *Minister's Accounts for West Wales*, 41, 71, 89, 195.

96. *See above*, Note 12.

97. *Cal. Ch. Rolls*, ii, 421.

98. Clark, *Cartae*, iii, 828; C 134/43.

99. *C.I.M.P.*, vi, No. 56; Evans, G., *The Ancient Churches of Llandovery* (London, 1913), 14, 118.

100. *Annales Cambriae*, 98; Owen, *Cal. Pembs. Records*, iii, 81, 221-2; C 134/4/1.

101. C 133/101/6; *C.I.P.M.*, iv, No. 41; C 133/114/8; *C.I.P.M.*, iv, No. 235.

102. S.C. 6/1247/21.

103. Beresford has calculated that 80 per cent. of England's planned boroughs had been laid out by 1300 (*New Towns*, 39).

104. Davies, J. C. (ed.), *The Welsh Assize Roll of 1277–84*, B.C.S., Hist. & Law Ser., vii (Cardiff, 1940), 148–54, 235–6; *Cal. Ch. Rolls*, ii, 263.

105. Williams, J., *The Records of Denbigh and its Lordship* (Wrexham, 1860), 107, 221–2; C 134/15/10; S.C. 11/970.

106. *Rec. Caern.*, 174; *Cal. Ch. Rolls*, iii, 467.

107. Williams-Jones, K., *The Merioneth Lay Subsidy Roll, 1292–3*, B.C.S., Hist. & Law Ser., xxix (Cardiff, 1976), 30.

108. Williams, J., *Records of Denbigh and its Lordship*, 230–1.

109. *Cal. Ch. Rolls*, ii, 276.

110. *Ibid.*, 325, 421; Rees, D. C., *Tregaron: Historical and Antiquarian* (Llandysul, 1936), 12–15; *Itinerary*, 121.

111. Ellis, T. P. (ed.), *The First Extent of Bromfield and Yale, A.D. 1315*, Cymm. Rec. Ser., xi (London, 1924), 47–57.

112. *Annales Cambriae*, S.A. 1245; *Brut y Tywysogion*, 116.

113. *Ibid.*, 103; Lewis, E. A., 'Chamberlains Accounts for West Wales', *op. cit.*, 75–6; Rhys, *Minister's Accounts for West Wales*, 71, 76, 89, 310–13, 377–80.

114. The text of the charter is in Lewis, *Medieval Boroughs of Snowdonia*, 287–91.

115. *See above*, Note 93.

116. T. Jones-Pierce, 'A Caernarvonshire Manorial Borough: Studies in the Medieval History of Pwllheli', in Smith, B. (ed.), *Medieval Welsh Society* (Cardiff, 1972), 132–9.

117. T. Jones-Pierce, 'The Growth of Commutation in Gwynedd during the Thirteenth Century', *ibid.*, 103–25.

118. *Brut y Tywysogion*, 117; *Cal. Pat. Rolls*, 1232–47, 460.

119. Seebohm, F., *The Welsh Tribal System* (London, 1904), Appendix A (a), 3–4; Lewis, *Medieval Boroughs of Snowdonia*, 49.

120. *See above*, Note 81.

121. *Cal. Ch. Rolls*, ii, 303; *Littere Wallie*, 164; Sanders, I. J., 'The Boroughs of Lampeter in the early fourteenth century', *Ceredigion*, iv (1960–3), 136–45.

122. Morgan, R., 'The foundation of the Borough of Welshpool', *Mont. Coll.*, lxv (1977), 9; E 179/242/54; S.C. 6/1146/52.

123. *Cal. Cl. Rolls*, 1272–9, 51; *Cal. Anct. Corresp.*, 86; *Brut y Tywysogion*, 118.

124. *Cal. Ch. Rolls*, ii, 236, 330.

125. Horsfall-Turner, E. R., *A Municipal History of Llanidloes* (Llanidloes, 1908), 256–7; Bridgeman, G. T. O., 'The Princes of Upper Powys', *Mont. Coll.*, i (1868), 152–62.

126. *Cal. Ch. Rolls*, ii, 408; Bridgeman, *op. cit.*, 141–2; E 179/242/54.

127. C 134/17/1.

128. The Welsh element in the English boroughs is discussed by Williams-Jones, *The Merioneth Lay Subsidy Roll*, lx–lxiv.

129. C 134/43.

130. Beresford, *New Towns*, 548.

131. S.C. 12/17/87; Griffiths, J., 'Documents relating to Conwy', *T.C.H.S.*, viii (1947), 6.

132. *Black Book*, 137–51.

133. *C.I.P.M.*, iv, 161.

134. Clark, *Cartae*, iii, 845; C 133/73/3; 133/120; Richards, H. P., *A Short History of Caerphilly* (Caerphilly, 1969), 42.

135. For the sources from which the following figures are derived *see* the relevant Gazetteer entries.

136. Russell, J. C., *British Medieval Population* (Albuquerque, 1948), 351; Williams-Jones, *The Merioneth Lay Subsidy Roll*, lix. For a fuller discussion of the evidence relating to population estimates *see ibid.*, xxxv–lix.

137. *See above* Note 111.

138. S.C. 11/771/4.

139. *See above* Note 93.

140. Williams, J., *The Records of Denbigh and its Lordship*, 107, 221–2. For the early surveys of Ruthin *see above*, Note 12.

141. As early as *c.* 1307 some 42 per cent. of the burgages were in Welsh hands. For a fuller discussion *see* Griffiths, R. A., 'Aberystwyth', in *idem, Boroughs of Medieval Wales*, 38–9.

142. Williams-Jones, *The Merioneth Lay Subsidy Roll*, lx.

143. *Ibid.,* cxliii, 51, 65–6.

144. *Cal. Welsh Rolls,* 287

145. E. 179/242/52; Evans, D. L. (ed.), *Flintshire Minister's Accounts, 1328–53*, 29, 50–1. For Knighton, *see above,* Note 15.

146. The effects of the Great Pestilence in Wales are considered by Rees, W., 'The Black Death in Wales', *T.R.H.S.*, 4th ser., iii (1920), 115–35, and *idem, South Wales and the March* (Oxford, 1924), 241–56.

147. *British Medieval Population,* 229–35, 367.

148. Rees, 'The Black Death in Wales', *op. cit.,* 120.

149. S.C. 6/783/1, 15; 1206/3; Rees, 'The Black Death in Wales', *op. cit.,* 119, 123.

150. S.C. 6/928/19; Rees, *South Wales and the March,* 247.

151. *Ibid.,* 242.

152. D.L. 29/1/2; S.C. 6/1183/9; Owen, D. H., 'Denbigh', in Griffiths, *Boroughs of Medieval Wales,* 170, 184.

153. C 134/83; Charles, B. G. (ed.), *Calendar of the Records of the Borough of Haverfordwest,* B.C.S., Hist. & Law Ser., xxiv (Cardiff, 1967), 1.

154. S.C. 6/1209/14.

155. The standard account of the rebellion remains Sir John Lloyd's *Owen Glendower,* Oxford, 1931.

156. Messham, J. E., 'The County of Flint and the Rebellion of Owen Glyndŵr in the Records of the Earldom of Chester', *J.F.H.S.,* xxiii (1967–8), 2.

157. Camden, *Britannia,* 669, a view echoed by Speed, *Atlas of Wales,* 123.

158. Lloyd, *Owen Glendower,* 103.

159. S.C. 6/775/1, Messham, J. E., *op. cit.,* 13.

160. Lewis, *Medieval Boroughs of Snowdonia,* 201.

161. Rees, W., *The Charters of the Borough of Newport in Gwynllwg* (Newport, 1951), xviii; Lloyd, *Owen Glendower,* 54.

162. S.C. 6/775/1; Messham, J. E., *loc. cit., Itinerary,* 67.

163. S.C. 6/1175/7–9, T. Jones-Pierce, *Medieval Welsh Society,* 156.

164. *Idem,* 'The Old Borough of Nefyn', *op. cit.,* 44.

165. Jones, D. D., *A History of Kidwelly* (Carmarthen, 1908), 126–30.

166. S.C. 6/1166/12; Evans, G., 'The Story of Newcastle Emlyn and Adpar', *Y Cymmrodor,* xxxii (1922), 127–8.

167. *Glam. County History,* iii, 353.

168. Mathews, J. H. (ed.), *Cardiff Records, Materials for a history of the County Borough,* i (Cardiff, 1898), 175.

169. Pratt, D., 'The Medieval Borough of Holt', *T.D.H.S.,* xiv (1965), 50.

170. *Itinerary,* 43.

171. Lewis, E. A., 'Records of Dynevor', *Trans. Hist. Soc. West Wales,* ii (1912), 106; Hingeston, F. C. (ed.), *Royal and Historical Letters of Henry IV* (R.S., 18), i, No. lx; *Itinerary,* 57.

172. Ellis, H. (ed.), *Original Letters illustrative of English History,* 2nd ser., i, 20.

173. For the full references *see* the List of Abbreviations under *Itinerary;* Owen, *Description of Pembrokeshire;* Camden, *Britannia;* and *Atlas of Wales,* (Speed).

174. 'The Population of Wales in the Sixteenth and Seventeenth Centuries', *Trans. Hon. Soc. Cymm.* (1959), 99–113.

175. *Ibid.,* 108; Camden, *Britannia,* 649.

176. Owen, L., *op. cit.,* 107, 109.

177. *Ibid.,* 108; *Itinerary,* 59.

178. Owen, L., *op. cit.,* 110.

179. *Ibid.,* 110.

180. Kissack, *Medieval Monmouth,* 57.

181. Camden, *Britannia*, 676.

182. *Itinerary*, 10, 32, 45, 53, 109.

183. Lewis, E. A. (ed.), *The Welsh Port Books, 1550-1603*, Cymm. Rec. Ser., xii (London, 1927), 310-11.

184. Rice Merrick, *Book of Glamorganshire Antiquities, 1578* (London, 1887), 106.

185. Owen, *Description of Pembrokeshire*, iii, 359; Owen, L., *op. cit.*, 112.

186. *Description of Pembrokeshire*, i, 142.

187. Bronwydd MS., 303; Charles, B. G., 'The Records of the Borough of Newport in Pembrokeshire', *N.L.W.J.*, vii (1951-2), 33-45, 120-37.

188. *Atlas of Wales, inter* 101-2.

189. E 179/242/54; Horsfall-Turner, *Municipal History of Llandidloes*, 257.

190. *Rec. Caern.*, 85-9; Carr, A. D., 'The Extent of Anglesey, 1352', *T.A.A.S.* (1971-2), 262-72; Owen, H., *Hanes Plwyf Niwbwrch ym Môn* (Caernarfon, 1952), 11-17.

191. Lewis, *Medieval Boroughs of Snowdonia*, 51; Owen, L., *op. cit.*, 107.

192. *Ibid.*, 111; Bridgeman, 'Princes of Upper Powys', *op. cit.*, 152-62.

193. *Atlas of Wales, inter* 111-2, 115-6, 117-7, 121-2.

194. *Itinerary*, 78.

195. *Ibid.*, 54, 80-1, 88, 113.

196. *Ibid.*, 14, 29, 45, 73, 88, 111, 134-5.

197. *Ibid.*, 56, 59-60, 62, 90.

198. Emmanuel Bowen, *Britannia Depicta or Ogilby Improved*, 4th Edn., London, 1753; Edward Lhuyd, *Parochialia*, Arch. Camb., Supplement, 1909-10; Gastineau, H., *Wales illustrated in a Series of Views*, 2nd edn., London, 1830.

199. *Itinerary*, 30; Bowen, *Britannia Depicta*, 38.

200. *Ibid.*, 127.

Chapter Two

1. *See above*, Nos. 3-15, and Margary, I. D., *Roman Roads in Britain*, revd. edn. (London, 1967), 315-8.

2. Davies, H. R. (ed.), *The Conwy and Menai Ferries*, B.C.S., Hist. & Law Ser., viii (Cardiff, 1942), *passim.*

3. D.L. 29/573/9063.

4. Jones, W. H., *History of Swansea and Gower* (Carmarthen, 1920), 310.

5. This was probably the *fossatum de Krenchey* mentioned in Richard III's charter to the burgesses of 1485 (*Cal. Ch. Rolls*, vi, 260-2).

6. Beresford, *New Towns*, 3-5.

7. S.C. 6/1158/10.

8. Gray, T., *The Buried City of Kenfig* (London, 1909), 58-9.

9. For a fuller discussion of medieval town planning *see* Beresford, *New Towns*, Chaps. 4-5, and Barley (ed.), *The Plans and Topography of Medieval Towns in England and Wales, passim.*

10. S.C. 6/1202/1; C 133/130.

11. This total includes Raglan and St David's, although in both cases the fortifications were slightly removed from the area of civil settlement.

12. T. Jones-Pierce, *Medieval Welsh Society*, 135, 184.

13. For further details of the history and architecture of the castles mentioned in the following account the reader is directed to the appropriate entry in the Gazetteer.

14. *Pipe Roll*, 1191-2, 77.

15. Murage grants were awarded in 1232 and 1237 (*Cal. Pat. Rolls*, 1225-32, 477; *idem*, 1232-47, 178).

16. For a fuller discussion of this subject *see* Turner, *Town Defences, passim*. The section devoted to Welsh towns, however, is only of limited value.

17. *Annales Cambriae*, 108.

18. *See* O'Neil, B. H. St J., 'The Castle and Borough of Llanidloes', *Mont. Coll.*, xliii (1933) 47–65.

19. Miles, H., 'Excavations at Rhuddlan, 1969–71', *op. cit.*, 8; *King's Works*, 323, 371.

20. O'Neill, B. H. St J. and Foster-Smith, A. H., 'Montgomery Town Wall', *Arch. Camb.*, xcv (1940), 217–28; Radcliffe, F. and Knight, J., 'Excavations at Abergavenny, 1962–69, ii, Medieval and Later', *Mon. Antiq.*, iii (1972–3), 72; *Archaeology in Wales*, xi (1971), n.43 (Flint); O'Neil, 'The Castle and Borough of Llanidloes', *loc. cit.*

21. *Rec. Caern.*, 174; *Cal. Ch. Rolls*, i, 378–9; iii, 467; iv, 214; *Cal. Pat. Rolls*, 1281–92, 2; *ibid.*, 1292–1301, 505.

22. *See above*, Nos. 12–15.

23. *Cal. Pat. Rolls*, 1413–6, 308.

24. *Archaeology in Wales*, xi (1971), No. 43.

25. Miles H., 'Excavations at Rhuddlan, 1969–71', *op. cit.*, 8.

26. As in the case of the walls at Beaumaris, Caernarfon, Conwy and Tenby.

27. Morgan, J., *A Short History of the Castle of Aberystwyth* (Aberyswyth, undated), 18.

28. *Cal. Pembs. Records.*, iii. 234–6;

29. Leland, *Itinerary*, 59.

30. James, W. E., *Guide Book to Cardigan and District* (Cardigan, 1899), 13.

31. Lewis, E. A., 'The Account Roll of the Chamberlain of the Principality of North Wales from Michaelmas 1304 to Michaelmas 1305', *B.B.C.S.*, i (1923), 262, 269; *Rec. Caern.*, 85–9; Griffiths, J., 'Documents relating to Conway', *T.C.H.S.*, viii (1947), 15–17;

32. At Old Dinefwr in 1298–1300, however, the tenants paid an annual rental of only 6d. (Rhys, *Minister's Accounts for West Wales*, 71, 89).

33 At Machynlleth and Fishguard, neither, of which were chartered boroughs, properties which changed hands in 1597 and 1653 were described as 'burgages' (Squires, H. L. and Morris, E. R., 'Early Montgomeryshire Wills at Somerset House', *Mont. Coll.*, xxi (1888), 220; *Report of the Royal Commission on Municipal Corporations*, Appendix I, 229).

34. S.C. 6/1170/4–5; Lewis, *Medieval Boroughs of Snowdonia*, 63.

35. Taylor, H., *Historic Notices of Flint* (London, 1883), 34.

36. Morgan, T., *History of Llantrisant* (Risca, 1975), 54.

37. *Cal. Pembs. Records*, iii, 209.

38. Cal. Inq. Misc., 33/31; Anct. Ext. Exch. K.R., No. 51.

39. Rhys, *Minister's Accounts for West Wales*, 293. Beresford has defined burgesses *de vento* as 'men . . . who thought it worth while having a stake in the new town but whose other interests— rural or urban—kept him on the move from place to place' (*New Towns*, 65, 225).

40. Fox, C., *Illustrated Regional Guide to Ancient Monuments, iv., South Wales* (London, 1938), 48.

41. Clark, *Cartae*, i, 136–8. For a valuable comparison *see* the Pembroke charter (*Cal. Pembs. Records*, iii, 209).

42. *Black Book*, 37, 133, 153.

43. Monmouth Borough Archives, D.L., f. 18, No. 8 (Great Cowcher); Kissack, *Medieval Monmouth*, 37.

44 Pratt, D., 'The 1563 Charter of Holt', *T.D.H.S.*, xxiii (1974), 109; *idem*, 'The Medieval Borough of Holt', *ibid*, xiv (1965), 15.

45. The full references appear below under the relevant Gazetteer entry.

46. Innes, J., *Old Llanelly* (Cardiff, 1902), 65, 81; Cobbe-Webbe, C., *Haverfordwest and its Story* (Haverfordwest, 1882), 168.

47. Rees, *Cardiff*, 37; Speed, *Atlas of Wales, inter*, 105–6.

48. Lewis, *Topographical Dictionary, sub* Caerwys; *Cal. Pat. Rolls*, 1560–6, 343–6; Simpson, W. T., *Some Account of Llangollen and its Vicinity*, 2nd edn. (London, 1845), 3.

49. Charles, B. G., 'The Records of the Borough of Newport in Pembrokeshire', *N.L.W.J.*, vii (1951–2), 128.

50. Bradney, *History of Monmouthshire*, iii, pt. i, 12, 23.

51. Palmer, A. N., *History of the Town of Wrexham* (Wrexham, 1893), 16, 39-44.

52. Thomas, N. L., *The Story of Swansea's Markets* (Neath, 1966), 12.

53. Tucker, N. (ed.), 'The Councell Booke of Ruthin, 1642-95', *T.D.H.S.*, x (1961), 39.

54. Williams R., 'Newtown: its ancient charter and Town Hall', *Mont. Coll.*, xii (1879), 92-3.

55. *Glam. County Hist.*, iii, 353.

56. Trevelyan, M., *Llantwit Major* (Newport, 1910), 38.

57. *Cal. Ch. Rolls*, vi, 260-2; Arber-Cooke, A. T., *Pages from the History of Llandovery*, i (Llandovery, 1975), 139; ii, 103-6, 172.

58. Clark, G. T., 'Kenfig Charters', *Arch. Camb.*, 4th ser., ii (1871), 248.

59. Provision for its building was made in Edward I's charter of that year (Lewis, *Medieval Boroughs of Snowdonia*, 33, 281).

60. Leland, *Itinerary*, 59.

61. Butler, L. A. S., 'Excavations at Conway, 1961-4', *T.C.H.S.*, xxvi (1965), 20-30.

62. *R.C.A.M.W.M.*, *Caerns.*, ii, 118; Jones, W. H., *Old Karnarvon* (Caernarfon, 1889), 77.

63. *R.C.A.M.W.M.*, County Inventories; Jones, S. R. and Smith, J. T., 'The Houses of Breconshire', *Brycheiniog*, ix-xiii (1963-9); Brooksby, H., 'The houses of Radnorshire: Part V, Town Houses', *T.R.S.*, xlii (1972), 39-54.

64. Jones, S. R and Smith, J. T., *op. cit.*, xi (1965), 43, 52-3.

65. *Ibid.*, 96.

66. Smith, P., *Houses of the Welsh Countryside* (H.M.S.O., 1975), 147.

67. *See above*, Nos. 4-6.

68. There may, however, have been a chapel at Adpar. *See* the Gazetteer entry, note 6.

69. Rees, *Cardiff*, 21, 47.

70. Bradney, *History of Monmouthshire*, iv, pt. i, 12, 23; Coxe, *Historical Tour through Monmouthshire, 1801*, 363-4.

71. Rees, Cardiff, *loc. cit.*, Owen, *Description of Pembrokeshire*, i, 22.

72. For the full references *see* the Gazetteer entry, notes 11-12.

73. Jenkins, R. T., 'The Borough of Bala, c. 1350', *B.B.C.S.*, ii (1941), 167; *R.C.A.M.W.M.*, *Mer.*, 1.

74. Lewis, *Topographical Dictionery*, *sub* Lampeter.

75. Davies, W., *Llandeilo Fawr and its Neighbourhood* (Llandeilo, 1858), 53.

76. *R.C.A.M.W.M.*, *Carms.*, 259.

77. Rees, *Newport Charters*, xvii, 6-7; Reeves, A. C., 'Newport', in Griffiths, *Boroughs of Medieval Wales*, 192.

78. The chapel is marked on a map of 1601, drawn as part of a survey of Cadoxton manor (Neath Corporation Muniments, reproduced in Birch, W. de Gray, *History of Neath Abbey* [Neath, 1902], 268.

79. Fairs, G. L., *A History of Hay* (Phillimore, 1972), 79-83; Jones, T., *History of Brecknock*, iii, 98.

80. A confirmatory charter of 1153-83 in favour of Tewkesbury Abbey refers to *ecclesiam St i. Jacobi de Kenefeg cum capella St i. Thomae in eadem villa* (*Cartae*, 134).

81. For a full discussion of this subject *see* Cowley, F. G., *The Monastic Order in South Wales, 1066-1349* (Cardiff, 1977), *passim*, and Knowles and Hadcock, *Medieval Religious Houses, passim*.

82. For the documentation relating to these foundations *see* the appropriate Gazetteer entries. Nothing is known of the priory of Nefyn beyond a reference to a prior in 1252 (*Rec. Caern.*, 252) and the element 'mynach' which appeared in former field names (*R.C.A.M.W.M.*, *Caerns.*, iii, 84).

83. *Ibid.*, ii, 12-13.

84. *Archaeology in Wales*, xiv (1974), 42.

85. Clapham, A. W., 'Haverfordwest Priory excavations, 1922', *Arch. Camb.*, 7th ser. ii (1922), 327-34; Rahbula, E. A. R., 'Further excavations at Haverfordwest Priory', *ibid.*, iv (1924), 334-9; Fowler, C. B., 'The Excavations carried out on the Site of the Blackfriars Monastery, Cardiff Castle', *Trans. Cardiff Nats. Soc.*, xxx (1897-8), 5-15.

86. *Cal. Lib. Rolls*, 1245-51, 91.

87. Knowles and Hadcock, *Medieval Religious Houses*, 311.

88. Clark, *Cartae*, iv, 1180-3.

89. *Cardiff Records*, v, 383, 418.

90. *Mon. Angl.*, v, 783.

91. *Ibid.*, vi, 445-6.

92. Birch, W. de Gray, *Penrice and Margam Manuscripts*, First Series, 28.

93. *Black Book*, 15 (St David's); *Cal. Papal Reg.*, i, 504; Walker, R. F., 'Tenby', in Griffiths, *Boroughs of Medieval Wales*, 303-4 (Tenby); *Mon. Angl.*, vi, 783 (Pembroke); *Cal. Ch. Rolls*, iii, 449 (Usk); Knowles and Hadcock, *Medieval Religious Houses*, 377 (Monmouth).

94. E 101/315/15; *Mon. Angl.*, vi, 782.

95. Rees, W., *The Order of St John of Jerusalem in Wales and on the Welsh Border* (London, 1947), 46 (Newcastle); *R.C.A.M.W.M., Pembs.*, 419 (Wiston).

96. *Atlas of Wales, inter* 111-2, 121-2; Lewis, W. J., 'Some aspects of the history of Aberystwyth', *Ceredigion*, iii (1959), 296.

97. *Atlas of Wales, inter* 101-2, 113-4.

98. Morris, W. H., 'A Kidwelly town rental of the early sixteenth century', *Carm. Antiq.*, 11 (1975), 64-5; Leland, *Itinerary*, 59.

99. Lewis, *Medieval Boroughs of Snowdonia*, 185; *Atlas of Wales, inter* 123-4.

100. C 134/43.

101. D.L. 29/1/2; Owen, 'Denbigh', in Griffiths, *Boroughs of Medieval Wales*, 170.

102. S.C.6/1170/4-9; Lewis, *Medieval Boroughs of Snowdonia*, 194.

GAZETTEER

ALPHABETICAL INDEX TO GAZETTEER

Town	County	Town	County
Aberafan - - -	- West Glamorgan	Harlech - - - -	- Gwynedd
Abergavenny - - -	- Gwent	Haverfordwest - - -	- Dyfed
Abergele - - -	- Clwd	Hay-on-Wye - - -	- Powys
Abergwili - - -	- Dyfed	Holt - - - -	- Clwyd
Aberystwyth - - -	- Dyfed	Holywell - - -	- Clwyd
Adpar - - -	- Dyfed	Hope - - - -	- Clwyd
Bala - - - -	- Gwynedd	Kenfig - - -	- West Glamorgan
Bangor - - -	- Gwynedd	Kidwelly - - -	- Dyfed
Beaumaris - - -	- Gwynedd	Knighton - - -	- Powys
Brecon - - -	- Powys	Knucklas - - -	- Powys
Bridgend - - -	- Mid Glamorgan		
Builth - - -	- Powys	Lampeter - - -	- Dyfed
		Laugharne - - -	- Dyfed
Caerleon - - -	- Gwent	Llandeilo - - -	- Dyfed
Caernarfon - - -	- Gwynedd	Llandovery - - -	- Dyfed
Caerphilly - - -	- Mid Glamorgan	Llanelli - - -	- Dyfed
Caersws - - -	- Powys	Llanfaes - - -	- Gwynedd
Caerwys - - -	- Clwyd	Llanfyllin - - -	- Powys
Cardiff - -	South Glamorgan	Llangadog - - -	- Dyfed
Cardigan - - -	- Dyfed	Llangollen - - -	- Clwyd
Carmarthen - - -	- Dyfed	Llanidloes - - -	- Powys
Castell y Bere - -	- Gwynedd	Llanrwst - - -	- Gwynedd
Cefnllys - - -	- Powys	Llantrisant - -	- Mid Glamorgan
Chepstow - - -	- Gwent	Llantwit Major -	- South Glamorgan
Cilgerran - - -	- Dyfed	Llawhaden - - -	- Dyfed
Conwy - - -	- Gwynedd	Loughor -	- West Glamorgan
Cowbridge - -	South Glamorgan		
Cricieth - - -	- Gwynedd	Machynlleth - - -	- Powys
Crickhowell - - -	- Powys	Monmouth - - -	- Gwent
		Montgomery - - -	- Powys
Degannwy - - -	- Gwynedd	Mostyn - - -	- Clwyd
Denbigh - - -	- Clwyd		
Dinas Mawddwy - -	- Gwynedd	Narbeth - - -	- Dyfed
Dinefwr - - -	- Dyfed	Neath - -	- West Glamorgan
Diserth - - -	- Clwyd	Nefyn - - -	- Gwynedd
Dolforwyn - - -	- Powys	Newborough - - -	- Gwynedd
Dolgellau - - -	- Gwynedd	Newcastle Emlyn - -	- Dyfed
Dryslwyn - - -	- Dyfed	Newmoat - - -	- Dyfed
		Newport - - -	- Dyfed
Fishguard - - -	- Dyfed	Newport - - -	- Gwent
Flint - - -	- Clwyd	New Radnor - - -	- Powys
		Newtown - - -	- Powys
Grosmont - - -	- Gwent	Overton - - -	- Clwyd

Painscastle	-	·	·	·	·	Powys	Swansea	-	·	·	- West Glamorgan

Painscastle	-	·	·	·	·	Powys		Swansea	-	·	·	- West Glamorgan
Pembroke	-	·	·	·	·	Dyfed						
Prestatyn	-	·	·	·	·	Clwyd		Talgarth	-	·	·	-	-	Powys
Presteigne	-	·	·	·	·	Powys		Templeton	-	·	·	-	-	Dyfed
Pwllheli	-	·	·	·	-	Gwynedd		Tenby	-	·	·	-	-	Dyfed
								Trefilan	-	·	·	-	-	Dyfed
Raglan	-	·	·	·	·	Gwent		Trefnant	-	·	·	-	-	Powys
Rhayader	-	·	·	·	·	Powys		Tregaron	-	·	·	-	-	Dyfed
Rhuddlan	-	·	·	·	·	Clwyd		Trelech	-	·	·	-	-	Gwent
Ruthin	-	·	·	·	·	Clwyd		Tywyn	-	·	·	-	-	Gwynedd
St Asaph	-	·	·	·	·	Clwyd		Usk	-	·	·	-	-	Gwent
St Clears	-	·	·	·	·	Dyfed		Welshpool	-	·	·	-	-	Powys
St David's	-	·	·	·	·	Dyfed		Wiston	-	·	·	-	-	Dyfed
Skenfrith	-	·	·	·	·	Gwent		Wrexham	-	·	·	-	-	Clwyd

With each entry the name of the town is followed by its Welsh form, where that differs from the English, then by the respective modern county, with the name of the old county in parenthesis, and finally by the Ordnance Survey National Grid Reference.

The Town Plans: Explanatory Note

All but 16 of the Gazetteer entries are accompanied by a plan which delineates the main areas of medieval settlement together with the principal topographical features, where it has been possible to identify and locate them, which made up the early townscape. The exceptions, omitted on grounds of insufficient evidence, are Aberafan, Abergele, Builth, Castell y Bere, Cefnllys, Degannwy, Dinefwr, Diserth, Dolforwyn, Holywell, Knucklas, Llanfaes, Mostyn, Prestatyn, Trefnant, and Wiston. It has not been possible to list the various sources on which these plans have been based in the case of each individual entry. References to the principal standing features are given in the notes, although a general statement of the evidence may be considered advantageous. Beyond the town maps of Speed, most of which were compiled in 1610, there are few plans of other urban communities earlier than the late 18th and early 19th centuries. Considerable use, therefore, has been made of documentary material, particularly early extents, which frequently refer to the presence of defences and other standing features while also naming the principal streets and thus the main areas of medieval occupation. Inevitably, however, considerable weight has had to be attached to later evidence, and in the main to topographical works and 19th-century maps and prints. Dominating this group are the writings of Leland, Camden, George Owen and Coxe, while the various maps employed range from the small, but nevertheless invaluable, ichnographs of Emmanuel Bowen to estate plans, the tithe maps of the 1840s, Municipal Corporations maps and surveys, to the earliest editions of the Ordnance Survey.

Scale.—To enable comparisons to be made between the overall size of towns and the various features within them all plans have been drawn to the standard scale of 1 : 7500 or 1in.: 600ft. (1 cm.: 75m. [approx.])

Key

::::	Built-up areas	——	Town defences, extant
*	Excavates sites	- - - -	", course of
(s)	Site of lost features	. . . .	", conjectural course
†	market-place		

ABERAFAN, West Glamorgan   SS 765902

The development of Port Talbot has virtually removed all traces of this small medieval borough which grew up at the mouth of the River Afan.[1] During the initial Norman advance into South Wales a motte-and-bailey castle was constructed here in a field adjoining the present churchyard, the remains of which were still visible in the 1830s,[2] but it is not known if any civil settlement was in being at this time. The castle was destroyed in 1153 by Rhys and Maredudd, sons of Gruffydd ap Rhys.[3] St Mary's church is first documented in the late 12th century,[4] and the borough was formerly incorporated by its local lord Leisian ap Morgan Fychan (1283-1314).[5]

Very little is known of the history of the medieval town which served as the *caput* of the lordship of 'Avene'. There is a tradition that the original settlement, like that of nearby Kenfig, has since been lost to the sea, and there are several references to the discovery of foundations at low water and during the construction of the modern docks.[6] These are more likely to have been individual farmsteads, however, and it would be reasonable to assume that the borough grew up in the shadow of the castle and church. It does not appear to have been fortified, and the only recorded defences were those thrown up against the encroaching sand.[7] When John Leland visited the area in the 1530s he observed only 'a poore village on the west ripe of Avon'[8] and his opinion was endorsed by successive commentators through to the growth of Port Talbot, which has engulfed the original settlement.[9] The process has been so thorough as to remove all vestiges of the early borough.

1. On the general history of Aberafan *see Glam. County Hist.*, iii, 341, 359; Davies, L., *Outlines of the History of the Aberavon District* (Aberafan, 1914); O'Brien, J., *Old Afan and Margam* (Port Talbot, 1926).
2. Lewis, *Topographical Dictionary, sub* Aberavon. The site was finally levelled in 1895 (O'Brien, *op. cit.*, 59).
3. *Brut y Tywysogion*, 58.
4. O'Brien, *op. cit.*, 60-1. The original medieval building was not demolished until 1857.
5. Clark, *Cartae*, iii, 922.
6. O'Brien, *op, cit.*, 47-54.
7. There are references to the 'King's Wall', 'Englishmens' Wall', 'Wall of the New Marsh', and 'Welsh Wall' (O'Brien, *op. cit.*, 49; Davies, *op. cit.*, 55-6).
8. *Itinerary*, 29.
9. The market had been discontinued by 1720 (Bowen, *Britannia Depicta*, 38), while it was described in 1789 as 'an inconsiderable place' (Hopkins, T. J. ed.), 'C.C.'s Tour in Glamorgan' *Glamorgan Historian*, ii (Cowbridge, 1965), 131.

ABERGAVENNY (Y Fenni), Gwent (Monmouthshire)   SO 300140

Abergavenny is traditionally known as 'the gateway to Wales' by virtue of its natural setting at the foot of three mountains, the Sugar Loaf, the Blorenge, and the Skirrid, at a point where the River Gavenny joins with the Usk. The value of the site was appreciated by the Romans who built here the fort of *Gobannium, c.* 50 A.D., and a series of recent excavations has revealed traces of the fort and its defences, the remains of several buildings, together with a cemetery to the northeast of the fort (SO 30251477).[1]

With the arrival of the Normans in South Wales the site came to assume new importance as both a military fortress and the local administrative capital of the Vale of Gwent. About 1090 Hamelin de Ballon constructed the first motte-and-bailey castle on the site of the later structure and set about the laying out of the town which was defended by an earthen bank, sections of which have been detected in Castle Street and on the Orchard site.[2] He also founded the Benedictine priory which stood beyond the East Gate together with its attendant church of St Mary's, also beyond the walls, and the church of St John.[3] The latter was originally the church of the walled town, but fell into decay once St Mary's ceased to cater only for the monastic community and opened its doors to the townspeople.

The early town had an eventful history and it was frequently the target of Welsh attacks, the most notable occurring in 1172, 1176 and 1262.[4] As a result of the ensuing destruction the burgesses decided to strengthen the original Norman defences and the town received its first murage grant in 1251, although a concentration of further grants in the period 1295–1301 and 1314–19 suggests that it was not walled in stone until the late 13th or early 14th centuries.[5] Recent archaeological

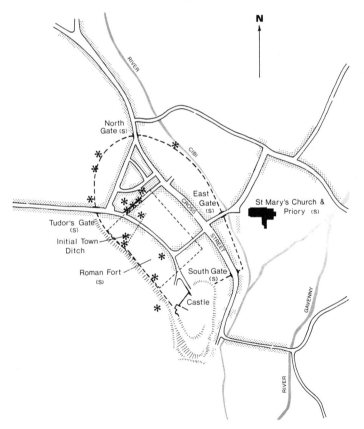

Fig. 5. Abergavenny

Fig. 6. Tudor's Gate, Abergavenny

A print of *c.* 1775. The gate, part of the medieval town defences, was
demolished in the mid–19th century.

investigation has suggested that the initial Norman town was smaller than the later
walled area and constituted a rectangle centring on Castle Street and extending
north-east to a point near the present Cross Street.[6] The later town was oval in
shape with the course of the walls known from the plan of the town by Coxe
(1800)[7] and through excavation. With the castle at the southern apex the wall ran
north-westwards for some 160m. to the Tudor Gate which was still standing in the
mid–19th century. Passing behind the houses on the left side of Nevill Street it

reached the North Gate at the junction of High Street, Nevill Street, and Frogmore Street, from which it followed a south-eastward course running behind the Town Hall and Cross Street, where portions could still be seen in the early 1960s. It continued along this course as far as the Monk or East Gate which led to St Mary's church and the priory. From this gate the wall veered to the south-east to rejoin the castle crossing Street near the *Sun* inn, where the South Gate was located. The medieval town thus enclosed was fashioned along two principal streets, Cross Street and Castle Street, which bisected it at right angles, with the old Market House standing in the middle of the former so as to leave only a narrow passage on either side.[8] Some of the original burgages can still be discerned—there were 230 in 1256-9[9]—but subsequent development has destroyed most of the pattern.

Probably contemporary with the construction of the town walls was the rebuilding of the castle in stone, of which only two towers, a gateway, and a length of curtain wall remain. Abergavenny was besieged by Owain Glyndŵr in 1404 and the attack appears to have inflicted considerable damage on both the castle and town. Indeed, the borough was all but destroyed, and it remained in a dilapidated state until Henry VIII issued a proclamation calling upon the burgesses to rebuild.[10] Much of the material for the resulting work came from the town walls which were quickly taken down, although in the 1530s there had still been sufficient remains for John Leland to call Abergavenny 'a faire waulled town'.[11] During the following century it regained much of its former status within the surrounding district and emerged as an important centre for local agriculture and industry. Owen saw it as 'a fine town and wealthie and thriving, the very best in the shire',[12] and it was noted for the manufacture of boots—there were large tanpits situated in Mill Street. The town was also noted for the production of a very fine white flannel which was widely distributed and even exported to India; the name of 'Flannel Street' is derived from this industry.[13]

1. Probert, L. A., *et al.*, 'Excavations at Abergavenny, 1962-69, i, Prehistoric and Roman', *Mon. Antiq.*, ii (1968-9), 163-99; Ashmore, P. J. and F. M., 'Excavations at Abergavenny Orchard Site 1972', *ibid.*, iii (1972-3), 104-10.

2. Radcliffe, F. and Knight, J., 'Excavations at Abergavenny, 1962-69, ii, Medieval and Later', *ibid.*, 72.

3. The evidence for the foundation of the town is contained in Hamelin's charter to the priory, printed in Round, *C.D.F.*, 367-8. The priory was a cell of the French Abbey of St-Vincent de Mans and was dissolved in 1536 when the buildings were converted into a private dwelling (Knowles and Hadcock, *Medieval Religious Houses*, 52, 54; Coxe, W., *A Historical Tour through Monmouthshire, 1801*, 2nd edn. (Brecon, 1904), 169-70.

4. Clark, J. H., *History of Monmouthshire* (Usk, 1869), 17-19.

5. Turner, *Town Defences*, 40-1, 208, 242-3.

6. Radcliffe and Knight, *op. cit.*, 72.

7. *Op cit.*, 166.

8. *Ibid.*, 167.

9. Roderick, A. J. and Rees, W., 'Ministers' Accounts for the Lordship of Abergavenny', *Trans. S. Wales and Mon. Record Soc.*, ii (1950), 73.

10. Bradney, J. A., *History of Monmouthshire*, part ii (London, 1906), 153.

11. *Itinerary*, 45. Also Camden, *Britannia*, 634.

12. *Description of Pembrokeshire*, iii, 302.

13. Coxe, *op. cit.*, 168-9.

ABERGELE, Clwyd (Denbighshire)   SH 945775

Abergele is situated on the North Wales coast along the course of the River Gele which formerly flowed into the sea at this point until the early 19th century when it was diverted eastwards into the Clwyd. The history of settlement here is confused because of the paucity of both documentary and archaeological evidence and recorded finds are few, the most notable being a hoard of some 800 Roman coins discovered in 1842 at Bron y Berllan farm near the town.[1] Little information is forthcoming for the medieval period, although in the 9th century Abergele church was regarded as the 'clas' or 'mother-church' of the surrounding district: the death of Ionathal, abbot of 'Abergelau' is recorded in 858.[2] Whether this religious house was situated on the same site as the present St Michael's church and had any associated civil settlement is not clear. The matter is complicated by an inscribed tombstone in the churchyard, apparently of medieval date, which records the death of one who lived three miles to the north, an area now well under the sea,[3] so it is possible that the church and also the town which appear in records from the 13th century were not in the area of the present St Michael's.[4]

Reliable evidence for a town at Abergele rests on the 24 burgages together with a mill, market and fair recorded in 1311.[5] There is little information for the remainder of the medieval period, however, and a supplication by the burgesses of Conwy to Henry VII regarding the encroachment of the Welsh into the towns of North Wales lists them, but makes no mention of Abergele.[6] In 1592 we find reference to 'lands and tenements in Abbergely',[7] and from this date the town grew, steadily encouraged by the development of the surrounding limestone industry. By 1831 the population had reached 2,506; there was a weekly market on Saturdays, and as many as seven annual fairs.[8]

1. O'Neill, B.H. St J., 'The Abergele Hoard of Roman Bronze Coins', *B.B.C.S.*, vii (1935), 64–72. A coin of Hadrian is also reported from the town (*ibid.*, ii [1925], 266), while prehistoric finds are limited to a Stone Age axe found in 1926 about 270m. N.N.E. of the church (Davies, E., *The Prehistoric and Roman Remains of Denbighshire* [Cardiff, 1929], 27–8).
2. *Brut y Tywysogion*, 4.
3. Lewis, *Topographical Dictionary*, sub Abergele; Edwards, G., 'Cantre 'r Gwaelod', *Arch. Camb.*, 1st ser., iv (1849), 159.
4. The church is mentioned in 1284 and 1389 (*Littere Wallie*, 128; *Cal. Anct. Petitions*, 412).
5. Williams, J., *The Records of Denbigh and its Lordship* (Wrexham, 1860), 107, 221–2.
6. The list is in Williams, R., *History of Aberconway* (Denbigh, 1835), 43–51.
7. Lewis, E. A. and Davies, J. C. (eds.), *Records of the Court of Augmentations Relating to Wales*, B.C.S., History and Law Ser., xiii (Cardiff, 1954), 371.
8. Lewis, *Topographical Dictionary, loc. cit.*

ABERGWILI, Dyfed (Carmarthenshire)   SN 439210

The small town of Abergwili is situated at the confluence of the Rivers Tywi and Gwili one mile to the east of Carmarthen. The medieval borough has very little recorded history and there is an absence of both archaeological investigation and stray finds. In 1022 this was the site of a battle between Llywelyn ap Seisyll of Gwynedd and an Irish leader named Rhain, but the degree of any settlement here

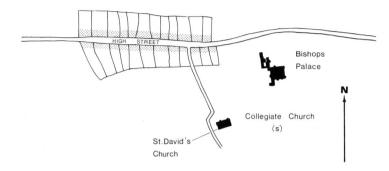

Fig. 7. Abergwili

at this time, if any existed, is not known.[1] It seems most likely that there was no organised township until Bishop Beck of St David's built the collegiate church in 1287 which functioned until 1541 when it was annexed to the new college at Brecon.[2] There are now no visible remains of this building which was located in the area between the parish church of St David and the later Bishop's Palace, now the County Museum.[3]

Medieval Abergwili was a small town and there were only 25 burgages here in 1326,[4] confined to the High Street. It boasted a weekly market on Fridays and at least one annual fair.[5] Some of the original burgage plots can still be detected, while the limits of the early borough are unlikely to have extended beyond the modern built-up area.

1. *Brut y Tywysogion*, 12.
2. Knowles and Hadcock, *Medieval Religious Houses*, 413, 419.
3. The church was originally dedicated to St Maurice, but this had been changed by 1395 (*R.C.A.M.W.M., Carms.*, 4). The Bishop's Palace dates from the episcopate of Bishop Barlow (1536–48), but the original building was destroyed by fire in 1903 when the present structure was built. It was noted in 1917 that 'foundations of buildings are traceable in the surrounding lawn, proving that the limits of the former residence extended beyond those of the present house' (*idem*). These can no longer be detected.
4. *Black Book*, 241–9.
5. *Ibid.*, 243.

ABERYSTWYTH, Dyfed (Cardiganshire)   SN 580815

Aberystwyth occupies an area of low-lying ground at a point where the Rivers Rheidol and Ystwyth join and flow on into Cardigan Bay. This was a planned town of the Edwardian conquest and the site chosen for the new borough was basically a peninsula with the inter-mural area lying below the 25ft. contour line.[1] The relatively late foundation date compared with Cardigan was due to the fact that the original Norman settlements in this immediate area were located further inland, the one at Tanycastell and its successor probably further north on the north bank of the Rheidol at Plas Crug.[2] In 1277 Edmund, Earl of Lancaster and brother of Edward I, elected to abandon the old sites and construct a new castle along with a

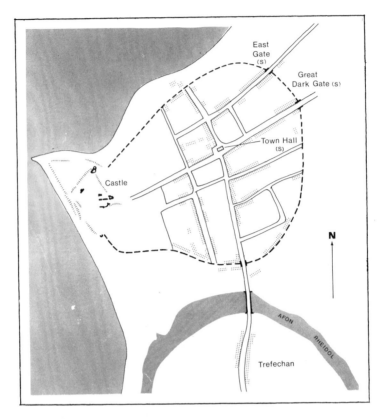

Fig. 8. Aberystwyth

fortified borough at the mouth of the river and the town received its charter in the same year.[3]

Of the castle which once dominated the English borough very little now survives, thanks mainly to the efforts of Cromwell's troops in 1647, who demolished the greater part of it.[4] The site was excavated in 1902 by Hughes, however, who concluded that the stronghold had consisted of two wards, an inner and outer, with both sets of containing walls forming a slightly irregular rectangle with the longest diameter lying north and south.[5] It was decided to further defend the town with a circuit of stone walls linked to the castle, and in 1280 alone nearly £200 was spent towards that end,[6] although the walls were destroyed during a Welsh attack two years later and had to be rebuilt.[7] Nothing now remains of these walls, and it would appear from early 19th-century maps and prints that the greater part had been removed by 1800.[8] The course of the defences has been well preserved, however, both in written sources and from the present street pattern which observes the original line. From a point slightly to the north-east of the Pier Pavilion the wall ran parallel to Crynfryn Row and continued along Baker Street and Chalybeate Street. From here it rounded to run along Mill Street and thence along South Road to link up with the castle. A map of Aberystwyth by Lewis Morris, c. 1748, shows sections standing in King Street indicating that the wall also continued along the seaward side of the town.[9] Morris also shows the survival of a large part of the southern wall in Mill Street, while excavations carried out in the early 1950s revealed further traces at the junction of South Road and Sea View Place.[10] Access to the defended town was provided by three gates, one at the junction of Eastgate Street (formerly Little Dark Gate Street) and Baker Street, the second slightly to the south where Great Dark Gate Street meets North Parade, and the third at the bridge which crosses the Rheidol.

The walled town exhibits many of the features typical of the Edwardian boroughs in Wales, especially in its lay-out whereby two principal streets cross at right angles in the centre of the town with the minor streets running parallel to them, the whole producing a rectilinear pattern similar to those achieved at Flint, Rhuddlan and Caernarfon. There was no medieval church within the walls, however, only a small chapel dedicated to St Michael, whose site has since been lost to the sea.[11] The mother-church was at Llanbadarn and it was not until 1784 that a full chapel-of-ease was built within the town.[12] To an extent the delayed appearance of a church can be seen as an indication that the new borough did not develop as rapidly as had been anticipated, and although there were 144 burgages by the early 14th century not all of them were taken up, and parts of the walled area appear to have remained unoccupied throughout the medieval period.[13] An excavation in 1971 at the rear of two partly-demolished houses in Princess Street produced no evidence of medieval settlement,[14] and despite close scrutiny of other development sites few finds from

Fig. 9. Aberystwyth

A print of 1799 showing the castle, Bridge Street and High Street. The view is from Trefechan looking north across the Rheidol.

this period have been noted, a pointer to the relative poverty of the early town.[15] Indeed, after the initial phase of development some contraction appears to have taken place as only 75 houses were noted in 1565,[16] while a succession of maps from the 1740s show unoccupied areas within the town, particularly in the western section near the castle.[17]

With the exception of the small settlement appropriately named Trefechan on the other side of the Rheidol there was little expansion beyond the borough walls until the beginning of the 19th century.[18] By 1832, however, Bath Street, Portland Street, North Parade, and Marine Terrace had all appeared,[19] growth which resulted mainly from the development of lead mining, slate quarrying, and the town's valuable herring fishery. Aberystwyth quickly rose to importance as a port, and in 1833 it boasted 133 registered vessels, thus displacing Cardigan as the principal trading centre on the west coast.[20] The population expanded accordingly and from an estimated figure of 1,000 in 1728 had risen to 4,128 by 1831, a total which nearly doubled again in the following half century as a result of the founding of the first University College of Wales in 1872 and as the town's attraction as a tourist resort—Wigstead called it the 'Cambrian Brighton'—became firmly established.[21]

1. For a discussion of the site *see* Carter, *Towns of Wales*, 208. The most recent account of the early history of the borough is Griffiths, R. A., 'Aberystwyth' in *idem, Boroughs of Medieval Wales*, 18–45.

2. *Idem*, 'The Three Castles of Aberystwyth', *Arch. Camb.*, cxxvi (1977), 74–87.

3. *Cal. Ch. Rolls*, ii, 206.

4. Morgan, T. O., *Guide to Aberystwyth* (Aberystwyth, 1824), 6.

5. Evans, G. E., *Aberystwyth and its Court Leet* (Aberystwyth, 1902), 198–201.

6. *King's Works*, 303–4.

7. *Brut y Tywysogion*, 120.

8. Prichard, T. J. L., *The New Aberystwyth Guide* (Aberystwyth, 1824), 6.

9. Reproduced in Carter, H., 'The Town in its Setting; the Geographical Approach', in Barley, M. W. (ed.), *The Plans and Topography of Medieval Towns in England and Wales*, C.B.A. Research Report, No. 14 (1975), 10.

10. *Ceredigion*, ii (1955), 276.

11. The chapel stood near the site of 'Castle House' which appears on Wood's map of 1834 (reproduced in Evans, G. E., *op. cit.*, 3, and Carter, H., 'The Town in its Setting', *op. cit.*, 12), and which later became part of the College buildings. The area eroded by the sea between the house and the chapel was known as Morfa Mawr, and human bones, presumably from the graveyard, were found here in the early 18th century. The loss of the chapel to the sea is mentioned in a presentment to the Court Leet in 1758 (Evans, G. E., *op. cit.*, 130–1).

12. Morgan, T. O., *op. cit.*, 15.

13. Sanders, I. J., 'The boroughs of Aberystwyth and Cardigan in the early fourteenth century', *B.B.C.S.*, xv (1954), 282; Griffiths, R. A., 'Aberystwyth', *op. cit.*, 42.

14. *Archaeology in Wales*, xi (1971), item 74.

15. Butler, L. A. S., 'Two medieval finds from Aberystwyth', *B.B.C.S.*, xx (1964), 74–5.

16. Lewis, E. A. (ed.), *The Welsh Port Books, 1550–1603*, Cymm. Rec. Ser., xii (London, 1927), 310–11.

17. Carter, H., 'The Town in its Setting', *op. cit.*, 10–12.

18. This is evident from a map of *c.* 1797 in *ibid.*, 12, and Lewis, W. J., 'Some aspects of the history of Aberystwyth', *Ceredigion*, iii (1959), 296.

19. *See* Wood's map in Evans, G. E., *op. cit.*, 3.

20. Carter, *Towns of Wales*, 209–12.

21. Wigstead, H., *Tour to North and South Wales* (1797), 49.

ADPAR, Dyfed (Cardiganshire) SN 309409

The village of Adpar lies on the north bank of the River Teifi immediately opposite Newcastle Emlyn, of which it is now virtually an extension. During the 14th century, however, Adpar was a flourishing borough in its own right, and under the control of the bishops of St David's it had developed into a community of 96 burgesses by 1326.[1] No date can be given for the actual foundation of the borough,[2] and very little is known of its subsequent history since the records of the corporation were destroyed by fire in 1752.[3] The names of the early burgesses, however, were predominantly Welsh and it would appear that the bishops simply reorganised an already existing settlement along English lines of burghal tenure.[4] The town was also occasionally known as 'Trehedyn', possibly the name of the original native 'tref'.[5]

A few vestiges of the medieval borough remain, the most obvious being the motte located on the eastern side of the present village, but this, unfortunately, has no recorded history. Associated with the early town was a weekly market, but there are no indications of the site of the market-place. The original burgage plots have, likewise, mostly disappeared, though the topography of the town would suggest that they were located on the western side of the bridge and that the present Lloyd Terrace was originally the main street. There was no medieval church within the borough as it lay within the parishes of, initially, Llandisiliogogo, and later, Llandyfriog.[6]

Although the respectable number of burgesses recorded in 1326 indicated a substantial community there were already indications of urban decay as 15½ plots lay empty for lack of tenants. In 1403 when neighbouring Newcastle Emlyn was attacked by Owain Glynŵr, half the houses were destroyed and there is no reason to suppose that Adpar escaped the spoliation of the Welsh rebels.[7] At all events, by the mid-16th century most of the original burgages had coalesced into a number of small estates, many of which were in the hands of the Lloyd family of Cilgwyn who came to control the corporation.[8] In 1741 the town was eventually deprived of its borough status and its identity has gradually been lost to the larger settlement across the river.[9]

1. *Black Book*, 291.

2. The name was recorded in 1297 (Evans, G. E., 'The story of Newcastle Emlyn and Atpar to 1531', *Y Cymmrodor*, xxxii (1922), 80-1.

3. *Ibid.*, 61; Lewis, *Topographical Dictionary*, sub Adpar.

4. *Black Book*, xxi

5. Evans, G. E., *op. cit.*, 85. Until the present century the place-name was traditionally spelt 'Atpar' but the etymology is uncertain (*ibid.*, 85–6).

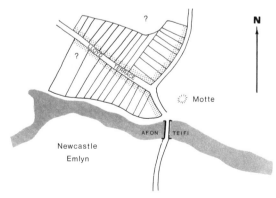

Fig. 10. Adpar

6. There may, however, have been a small chapel within the borough as the 1326 survey records the tenancies of both Gervase the Cleric and David the Chaplain (*Black Book*, 219–27; Evans, G. E., *op. cit.*, 103).

7. Lloyd, *Owen Glendower*, 67.

8. Evans, G. E., *op. cit.*, 148.

9. *Ibid.*, 153.

BALA, Gwynedd (Merionethshire)   SH 926360

Bala lies along the course of the main road to Dolgellau and the town is situated at the northern end of Bala Lake (Llyn Tegid) where the rivers Dee and Tryweryn meet. It represents the finest example of a planned English borough in Meirionnydd and the circumstances of its creation are recited in the foundation charter. During the later years of Edward II's reign the surrounding commote of Penllyn was in a state of disorder and virtually in the hands of marauding bands of thieves and robbers. In or about 1310, therefore, Roger Mortimer set about the foundation of the town in an attempt to bring stability to the area and so that the town could serve as as an administrative centre for the district. The borough was accordingly laid out with 53 burgages, and within a year all but nine had been taken up. The markets and fairs previously held at nearby Llanfor were transferred to the new settlements which received its formal grant of privileges in 1324.[1]

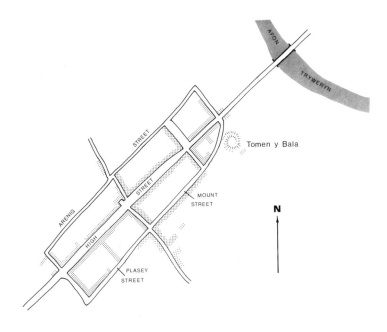

Fig. 11. Bala

Fig. 12. Bala

A gathering of Calvinistic Methodists in 1820. In the background the
dominance of the motte over the town is well illustrated.

The medieval town was small and its total area did not exceed one square mile.
Burgages were laid out along one principal street, the *Via Capitalis* mentioned in
1350, with two back lanes running parallel to it, now represented by Arenig and
Plasey/Mount Street. Subsequent development, however, has destroyed most of the
original plots. At the north-eastern end of the town stands a small motte, Tomen-y-
Bala, destroyed by Llywelyn ab Iorwerth in 1202,[2] and when Roger Mortimer
laid out the borough it was undoubtedly his intention to defend it with a wall and
ditch incorporating this existing fortification. Indeed, the 1324 charter makes
special provision for such work, but there is nothing to suggest that his instructions
were ever carried out.[3] An earthen bank may have been thrown up at the top of the
town, however, parallel to the Afon Tryweryn,[4] but the area has recently been
developed and no sections are visible. The other main feature of the medieval
topography was the small chapel which stood near the town cross of High Street.[5]
There was no church at Bala until the building of Christ Church in 1811, the town
being part of Llanycil parish, but the provision of the chapel appears to have been
contemporary with the foundation of the borough. It continued to serve the
community until the early 18th century when it was finally demolished and its
site together with that of the attached graveyard was built over.[6]

The later history of Bala is uneventful and in the absence of any maintained castle
the town does not figure in the Glyndŵr revolt, although a small garrison place
consisting of six timber houses was temporarily established. From the outset it was

a small settlement with the burgesses dependent solely on agriculture or trade, and within the following two centuries many of the original burgages fell into decay. John Leland (1532-4) described Bala as 'a little poore market' and a decade later only 13 taxpayers were recorded in the town,[8] a situation confirmed by Camden, who added that it was 'peopled with few inhabitants'.[9] During the 18th century, however, the beginnings of a hosiery industry appeared in the town which came to assume important proportions and led to much rebuilding. By the time of the 1842 Tithe Map the medieval area was again built-up and more recent development has enabled Bala to recapture its position as the market centre of Penllyn.[10]

1. *Rec. Caern*, 174; *Cal. Ch. Rolls*, iii, 467, iv, 214; Lewis, *Medieval Boroughs of Snowdonia*, 55, 283-7; Beresford, *New Towns*, 557.

2. *Brut y Tywysogion*, 82. This is the only documentary reference to the motte which does not appear to have been refortified. It was surrounded by a ditch, but this was later filled in when the present enclosing wall was built (*R.C.A.M.W.M., Mer.,* 1).

3. Lewis, *Medieval Boroughs of Snowdonia*, 61.

4. Owen, H. J., *Echoes of Old Merioneth* (Dolgellau, 1944), 4.

5. The Cross stood opposite the *White Lion* hotel (*R.C.A.M.W.M., Mer.,* 2).

6. Jenkins, R. T., 'The Borough of Bala *circa* 1350', *B.B.C.S.*, 99 (1941), 167; *R.C.M.W.M., Mer.,* 1).

7. The location of the houses, described in 1427 as 'long since burnt', is not known (S.C.6/ 1204/1; Lewis, *Medieval Boroughs of Snowdonia*, 118).

8. *Itinerary*, 78; Williams-Jones, *The Merioneth Lay Subsidy Roll*, xlvii.

9. Camden, *Britannia*, 666.

10. Nat. Lib. Wales, Map Collection.

BANGOR, Gwynedd (Caernarfonshire)   SH 575720

Bangor was not a planned town, and its development has been haphazard with an initial settlement clustered around the cathedral, followed by growth along the valley of the Afon Adda towards the sea. Its beginnings are to be associated with the founding in the 6th century of St Deiniol's monastery which became the principal ecclesiastical centre in North Wales,[1] functioning throughout the Dark Ages to emerge during the 11th century as the 'clas' or 'mother-church' of Arfon.[2] During the episcopacy of Bishop David (1120-39) a new cathedral church was constructed on the site of the present structure,[3] although some of the original buildings appear to have continued in use until at least the late 13th century before falling into decay.[4] No remains are now extant of the monastery complex and its actual site has been the subject of some debate. During the 1920s an early graveyard and stone chapel were discovered 100m. north of the Town Hall below the College, and these were thought to belong to the Celtic foundation.[5] Subsequent excavations, however, have failed to confirm this view, and the absence of other finds in the area has prompted the conclusion that the chapel was, in fact, medieval, probably that of Llanfair Garth Brenan mentioned in 1291, and that St Deiniol's monastery was on the right bank of the Adda and therefore beneath the present town.[6]

Nothing is known of any civilian settlement associated with either the monastery or the late 11th-century motte built a quarter of a mile north of the town.[7] It seems likely that there was little development until after the building of the new cathedral church when dwellings began to appear in its immediate area. A 'town' of Bangor is specifically mentioned in 1211 when it was burnt by King John's troops,[8] and Edward I is said to have erected some town defences in 1284, but their form and location is not known.[9] There is no mention of a medieval charter, although by the early 14th century Bangor had emerged as a town of some 53 householders,[10] which held its own weekly market, much to the annoyance of the Caernarfon burgesses who attempted to have it suppressed.[11] In 1402 Bangor was attacked by Owain Glyndŵr,[12]

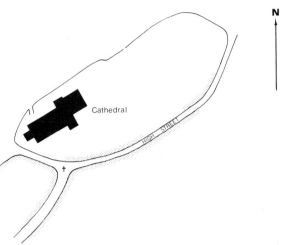

Fig. 13. Bangor

According to John Speed's map of 1610 the town consisted only of the High Street immediately south of the Cathedral and the extension of Glanyrafon which led down to the river.[14] The early cartographer also indicates the 16th-century Bishop's Palace, now the Town Hall, and the Free School, formerly the Dominican Friary.[15] The built-up areas, however, did not extend as far north as the old Friary until the late 18th century when the growth of the slate industry led to the development of the port of Hirael and the intermediate area along the modern Dean Street. From a total of 1,770 persons in 1801 Bangor's population rose to 4,571 in 1831, with this and subsequent development taking place nearer the sea and away from the site of the medieval town.[16]

1. Knowles and Hadcock, *Medieval Religious Houses*, 420.

2. *R.C.A.M.W.M., Caerns.*, ii (1960), 10; Johns, C. N., 'The Celtic Monasteries of North Wales', *T.C.H.S.*, xxi (1960), 14-18.

3. Ralegh-Radford, C. A., 'Bangor Cathedral in the twelfth and thirteenth centuries', *Arch. Camb.*, c (1949), 261.

4. *Littere Wallie*, Nos. 147, 245.

5. Hughes, H. H., 'An ancient Burial Ground at Bangor', *Arch. Camb.*, lxxix (1924), 395-6; *ibid.*, lxxx (1925), 432-6; *R.C.A.M.W.M., Caerns.*, 10-11.

6. *Archaeology in Wales*, xiv (1964), 16; White, R. B., 'Rescue Excavations at the New Theatre site, Bangor', *T.C.H.S.*, xxxii (1971), 246-7.

7. Hogg and King, 'Early Castles', 104-5. According to Samuel Lewis remains of the motte were still visible in the 1830s. (*Topographical Dictionary, sub* Bangor).

8. *Brut y Tywysogion*, 85.

9. *Annales Cambriae*, 108.

10. *Rec. Caern.*, 92-3.

11. *Cal. Anct. Petitions*, 459; Owen, H. and Jones, G. P., *Caernarvon Court Rolls*, Caer., Hist. Soc. Rec. Ser. i (1951), 137.

12. Camden, *Britannia*, 669; *R.C.A.M.W.M., Caerns.*, 1.

13. Leland, *Itinerary*, 81.

14. *Atlas of Wales, inter* 123-4.

15. The Friary was founded *c*. 1250 and was finally suppressed in 1538 when the buildings were converted into the Friars School. In or about 1800 the school was moved to its present site and the old buidings demolished (*R.C.A.M.W.M., Caerns.*, 12–13).

16. On the later growth of the town *see* Carter, *Towns of Wales*, 276–82, and Jones, P. E., 'The City of Bangor and its Environs at the time of the Tithe Survey 1840', *T.C.H.S.* xxxi (1970), 64–77.

BEAUMARIS (Biwmaris), Gwynedd (Anglesey)   SH 605761

Beaumaris represents the last of the Edwardian plantations in Wales and work was not begun on the new castle until April 1295.[1] It had been previously thought that Caernarfon was sufficient to control the Menai Straits, but the sacking of the town by Madog ap Llywelyn in September 1294 convinced Edward of the need for a second stronghold on the opposite shore. The site chosen was one of low-lying marshland which gave its name to the new castle-borough—'Beau Mareys' or 'Beautiful Marsh'. The small native settlement of Cerrig-y-gwyddyl which occupied the site was accordingly destroyed as the nearby Welsh township of Llanfaes (q.v.), and the inhabitants were moved to Newborough (q.v.) at the southern tip of the island.[2] By September 1296 work on the new castle was sufficiently advanced for a borough charter to be granted,[3] and the town grew rapidly with 132 burgages being

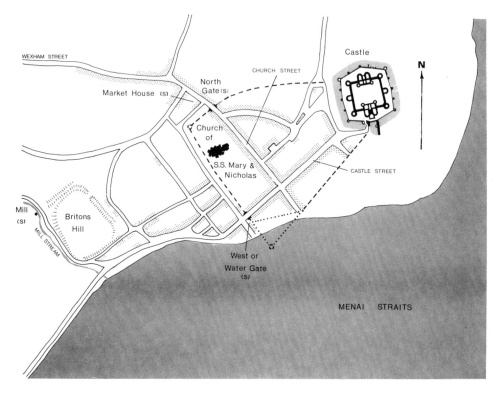

Fig. 14. Beaumaris

taken up during the first 10 years.[4] These were located immediately west of the castle with Church and Castle Streets as the principal lines of axis. The church of SS Mary and Nicholas was built in the north-west corner of the town, and was probably coeval with the castle although the present fabric dates from the 14th century.[5] Few other vestiges of the medieval town remain, although its overall plan and topography were recorded by John Speed in 1610.[6] By this date important suburbs had developed along Wexam Street and beyond the West Gate, while even the Market House was located outside the walled area on a site to the north-west of the church near Steeple Cottages. Speed also records the Free School founded by David Hughes in 1603 which stood on the site of the modern library together with the two town mills which stood together immediately west of Britons Hill.

Mention of the town walls raises the usual point that Beaumaris was not enclosed with stone defences at the outset, and there is no evidence that even earthen defences were constructed. The easing of the local political situation which allowed the castle to remain unfinished[7] may have rendered them unnecessary and no attempt was made to rectify the situation until the early 15th century. In 1403 Owain Glyndŵr attacked the town and burnt part of it, although he was unable to take the castle which did not fall to him until the following year.[8] It was retaken in 1405 and the episode was enough to convince the burgesses of the need to construct adequate town defences. In 1407 they received a royal donation of £10 'in aid of making a ditch around the aforesaid town',[9] and the wording implies that this was new work since it does not refer to the re-digging of an earlier ditch.

Later, in 1414, work was begun on building stone walls, which necessitated the destruction of 30 burgages,[10] and further additions were made in the years 1536-38.[11] From John Speed's plan of the town and from existing fragments the course of the wall can be traced with reasonable accuracy.[12] From the South Gate of the castle, where a section remains, the wall ran south-west as far as the landward end of the pier, its straight course indicated by the line of the former burgages off Castle Street. From the pier to the West Gate, which stood at the junction of Castle Street and Castle Row, the course is more problematical; Speed shows a direct line from the pier to the gate, but this is unlikely on topographical grounds. A more acceptable view is that the wall continued to follow a south-westerly course beyond the pier head to link up with the western section at a point some 35 metres below the present high-water mark. There are several references to the wall being breached by the sea, most notably in 1460,[13] and the additional work carried out in the 1530s may have resulted from this encroachment with perhaps the line being altered as depicted by Speed. From the West or Water Gate the course is clearer with the wall running north-west parallel to Steeple Lane which runs along the outer lip of the former ditch, partly excavated in 1975.[14] At the northern end of the land the wall turned and ran north-west across Church Street to connect with the surviving section behind Rating Row. It then continued to the castle moat and the line is indicated by the property boundaries behind Rating Row, but does not appear to have linked with the castle. There is no documentary reference to a North Gate along this stretch, but Speed's plan suggests that one was located at the top of Church Street.[15]

Although the walls were maintained throughout the 15th and 16th centuries no attack was made on Beaumaris which has an uneventful political history. The town prospered as a trading port,[16] and by the date of Speed's map it had emerged as a sizeable settlement with substantial extra-mural development. The only subsequent event of note occurred in 1646 when the castle was captured by a Parliamentarian force under the command of Major-General Mytton, although it escaped the attendant destruction which the Roundheads usually carried out.[17] Also associated with the Civil War was the earthwork constructed on Britons Hill a few years earlier, but much of this was destroyed in 1643.[18] In the early 17th century Beaumaris remained, as Camden observed, 'the principalle town'[19] of Anglesey with its trading activities and herring fishery, but both these concerns subsequently declined and the economic focal point has moved to the opposite end of the island.

1. *King's Works*, 396-7; *R.C.A.M.W.M., Anglesey*, 8-13.

2. Lewis, *Medieval Boroughs of Snowdonia*, 49-50.

3. *Ibid.*, 282, although incorrectly dated to 1295 (Usher, G., 'The foundation of an Edwardian Borough: the Beaumaris Charter 1296', *T.A.A.S.* [1967],1-16).

4. Lewis, *Medieval Boroughs of Snowdonia*, 51.

5. Hughes, H. H., 'Beaumaris Church', *T.A.A.S.* (1922), 72-3; *R.C.A.M.W.M., Anglesey*, 3.

6. *Atlas of Wales, inter* 125-6.

7. *King's Works*, 406.

8. Lloyd, *Owen Glendower*, 76, 99.

9. *King's Works*, 406.

10. S.C.6/1152-5;

11. Jones, G. P. and Knoop, D., 'The Repair of Beaumaris Town Walls 1536-8', *T.A.A.S.* (1935), 59-70.

12. The greater part of the walls had been removed by the mid–19th century (Pughe, D. W., *History of Beaumaris* [1852], 26).

13. *R.C.A.M.W.M., Anglesey*, cxlviii-ix.

14. *Archaeology in Wales*, xv (1975), 53.

15. *R.C.A.M.W.M., Anglesey*, cxlix.

16. Lewis, *Medieval Boroughs of Snowdonia*, 203-7.

17. *R.C.A.M.W.M., Anglesey*, 10.

18. Nat. Lib. Wales MS. 9081, f. 65; *R.C.A.M.W.M., Anglesey*, 16.

19. *Britannia*, 672.

BRECON (Aberhonddu), Powys (Breconshire)   SO 044287

The beginnings of settlement at Brecon are cloaked with the obscurity which surrounds many similar towns in Wales. It has been firmly established that during the Roman period the newcomers chose to establish their fort further up the valley of the Usk at Y Gaer[1] although there may have been some occupation of the area at the mouth of the Honddu; the site itself, an alluvial fan created by the confluence of the two rivers,[2] was ideal for settlement. The town derives its name from Brocan or Brychan, a semi-legendary leader whose Dark Age base may have been here. Whatever the details from this period, however, it is abundantly clear that the real origins of urban growth were associated with the coming of the Normans to the area in the late 11th and early 12th centuries. In 1093 Bernard de Neufmarché

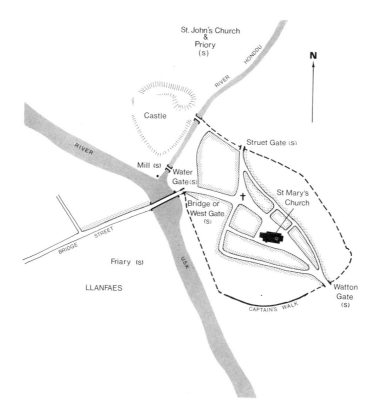

Fig. 15. Brecon

defeated the local ruler, Rhys ap Tewdwr, and followed this success with the erection of a motte-and-bailey castle on the site of the later structure.[3] At a comparatively early date this was reconstructed in stone, but little of it now remains, and much of the site is occupied by a hotel.[4] Alongside the motte a small town soon developed along the west bank of the Honddu and to promote further growth the inhabitants were assigned a three-mile stretch of land which extended from the Gludy to the Brynich brook.[5] At this stage there are no indications of settlement on the opposite side of the Honddu where the later borough was laid out, the Norman town being in the area of the Benedictine priory and its church, St John's, which had also been founded by Bernard before 1106.[6]

At some point in either the late 12th or early 13th century the original wooden castle was rebuilt in stone and a new town began to develop to the south on the east bank of the Usk. Despite being reduced to ashes by Llywelyn ab Iorwerth in 1231,[7] the settlement recovered and received its first charter from Humphrey de Bohun in 1277-82.[8] The borough was enclosed with an oval-shaped circuit of stone walls and from Speed's map of 1610 supplemented by that of Meredith Jones in 1744 it is possible to plot their course and identify the main features of the medieval town.[9] From the Honddu bridge which led from the castle the wall ran down the eastern side of Castle Street to the Struet Gate which stood at the junction with the High Street. From here it veered slightly to the south-east, running along the garden boundaries of Lion Street and across the old field, Clawdd y Gaer, where, in the early 19th century, the whole ditch and most of the walls were still visible.[10] Some remains can still be seen in the form of boundary walls. From here it rounded to the Watton or East Gate near the Shire Hall, and from there to the Usk along the course of Captain's Walk and then back to the Westgate which led to the bridge across the Usk. A section of the wall still remains along Captain's Walk, while traces of the ditch can still be seen along the river bank. The final course of the wall is the only part which raises some difficulty since it is not clear if it ran along the bank of the Honddu to link up with the castle bridge. It certainly did not end at the Westgate as there was another gate, the Watergate, facing the north bank of the Honddu, and the two were so close together that only one house separated them.[11] Speed then suggests that the wall continued along the river bank, but he is the only commentator to do so. Meredith Jones shows no defences here, and Theophilus Jones speaks of the bank as an 'impenetrable barrier' suggesting that the natural defences were sufficient. Along the course of the oval circuit were located a series of towers, 10 in all, while on the inner side was a raised walk, and on the outside a deep ditch which was probably flooded.

The subsequent history of the defences is shared by most of the walled boroughs in Wales. Owain Glyndŵr's attack on Brecon in 1404 ensured their upkeep after that date,[12] while Speed indicates that they were virtually intact in 1610. They were gradually robbed for building materials, however, and the destruction of the gates was ordered in 1775 on the grounds that they impeded the flow of traffic. By the later part of the following century large sections had been pulled down, but the course of the whole is still largely discernable from boundary plots.[13]

The medieval town thus enclosed, as depicted by John Speed, shows a close resemblance to the present street-pattern, while most of the original street-names have survived with the minimum of modification.[14] Essentially the main routes form a 'T'-shaped junction, with that from the south-east, the Watton, continuing along the Bulwark and High Street Inferior, joining those from the north, the Struet, and from the west, Bridge Street, at the junction of High Street Superior and Ship Street. The church of St Mary, built in the late 12th or early 13th century, occupies a central position within the walled area and the large triangular market-place was located immediately above it, although this had been built upon by Speed's time. The site of the original town hall is not known, the first recorded being that built in 1624 by John Abel.[15] Other features of the medieval town include the old gaol which adjoined the Struet Gate and near which was a chapel where the prisoners heard mass,[16] and the mill situated at the mouth of the Honddu under the castle wall, of which some remains are still visible.

It is clear from Speed's map of the town that by the early 17th century the walled area was no longer able to house all the townsfolk and important extra-mural suburbs had grown up. Brecon's geographical setting as the natural capital of the Middle Usk Lowlands together with the status conferred on the town by the Act of Union of 1536 which made it one of the four regional capitals of Wales were undoubtedly the essential factors in this urban growth. By 1610 much of Free Street, beyond the Watton Gate,[17] had been built up, while other important suburbs had appeared beyond the two other principal gates. To the north the Struet and Mount Street had been developed, while houses also lined the southern sides of Priory Hill. On the opposite side of the town, across the river, the suburb of Llanfaes had grown up around the Dominican friary, by now a secular college and grammar school.[18] By the end of the 17th century as many families were living beyond the walls as within them.[19] The town experienced further growth in the 18th century through some early industry and the construction of the Brecon and Monmouthshire canal.[20] Subsequent development has been more limited, however, and the area of the medieval town still represents the commercial core of modern Brecon.

1. Nash-Williams, *The Roman Frontier in Wales*, 48–51.

2. Carter, *Town of Wales*, 27.

3. Rees, W., *The Medieval Lordship of Brecon*, Brecknock Society (Brecon, 1968), 5.

4. Hogg and King, 'Early Castles', 106. In the 1530s the castle was still 'very large, strong, well mainteynid, and the keepe . . . very large and faire' (Leland, *Itinerary*, 105), but there was considerable robbing in the 17th and 18th centuries.

5. Rees, *Medieval Lordship of Brecon*, 42.

6. Banks, R. W. (ed.), 'Cartularium Prioratus, S. Johannis Evangeliste de Brecon', *Arch. Camb.*, 4th ser., xiv (1884), 142–3; Davies, R. R., 'Brecon', in Griffiths, *Boroughs of Medieval Wales*, 49.

7. *Brut y Tywysogion*, 102.

8. Rees, W., 'The Charters of the Boroughs of Brecon and Llandovery', *B.B.C.S.*, ii (1923–5), 244.

9. *Atlas of Wales*, inter 109–10. Meredith Jones's map is most accessible in Thomas, H., *Towards a seventeenth-century History of Brecknock* (Brecon, 1967), frontispiece; and Jones, T., *History of the County of Brecknock*, i (Brecon, 1909).

10. *Ibid.*, ii, 53–5.

11. Thomas, H., *op. cit.*, 13.

12. Lloyd, *Owen Glendower*, 63–4. In the same year the bailiff of Brecon was authorised to spend 100 marks on fortifying the gates, walls and ditches of the town (P.R.O., D.L., 42/15 f. 179v; *King's Works*, ii, 575).

13. Poole, E., *History of Brecon* (Brecon, 1876), 16.

14. Speed indicates that Castle Street was then 'Castle Lane', Michael Street was 'Lon y Popty', while Hugh Thomas writes 'Strowed' for Struet.

15. This occupied the site of the existing town hall at the junction of High Street Inferior and Tredegar Street. From a sketch by Dineley made during the 'Duke of Beaufort's Progress' in 1684 it is clear that Abel's building was constructed of timber (Thomas, H., *op. cit.*, 27; Jones, T., *op. cit.*, ii, 123).

16. In 1690 the old lock-up was replaced by a new gaol which was built near the Watergate. It was in turn pulled down in 1776.

17. Approximately a quarter of a mile beyond the Watton Gate stood another feature of the medieval town, the chapel and hospital of St Catherine. It was noted by Leland (*Itinerary*, 105), but by the late 17th century the building was being used as a barn, and there are now no remains (Thomas, H., *op. cit.*, 24).

18. Knowles and Hadcock, *Medieval Religious Houses*, 421; Clapham, A. W., 'The Architectural Remains of the Mendicant Orders in Wales', *Arch. Journ.*, lxxxiv (1927), 92–5.

19. Thomas, H., *op. cit.*, 23–6.

20. On the later history of the town *see* Gant, R. L., 'The Townscape and Economy of Brecon, 1800–60', *Brycheiniog*, xvi (1972), 103–4, and Minchenton, W. E., 'The place of Brecknock in the Industrialisation of South Wales', *ibid.*, vii (1961), 1–70.

BRIDGEND (Penybont ar Ogwr), Mid Glamorgan   SS 903799

The name Bridgend was not known during the medieval period, but the area covered by the present town incorporates the two early settlements of Newcastle, and, across the Ogwr, the smaller Nolton, known also as Oldcastle. The larger was Newcastle, which occupied a commanding position on rising ground on the west bank of the river. Its early history is obscure and although two stone crosses occur in St Illtyd's churchyard both are typologically late[1] and there is no definite evidence to suggest a settlement here before the arrival of the Normans under Robert fitz Hamon, c. 1106.[2] By that date he had constructed a castle at the top of the hill, later to be rebuilt in stone,[3] and founded the church of St Leonard (later re-dedicated to St Illtyd) alongside.[4] In the immediate area a small town grew up, initially around the castle, but later spreading down the hill which led to the Ogwr, halfway down which may have existed a hospice of the Order of St John.[5] A second street, now an overgrown path, also led from the hilltop following a

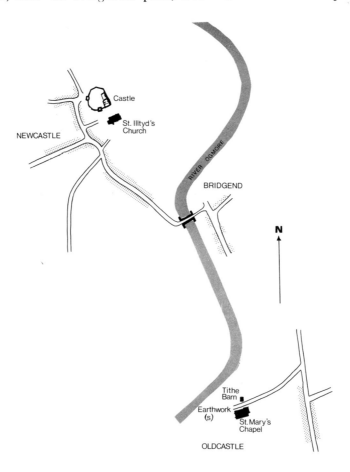

Fig. 16. Bridgend

semi-circular course across Park Fields, reaching the river at Pwll Clement near St Mary's church.[6] Although Newcastle emerged as an important market centre and hundredal town,[7] it did not enjoy borough status and accordingly there is a lack of information regarding the size of the medieval settlement.[8]

Across the river in the area of St Mary's was a second, albeit smaller medieval settlement which was known as both the Nolton and Oldcastle, noted by John Leland in the 1530s.[9] References to the vill date from the late 12th century,[10] and it had its own chapel which occupied the site of the present church.[11] Very little is known, however, of the 'Oldcastle' itself which may have been a Welsh earthwork. According to Samuel Lewis it was situated 'near the chapel . . . the tithe barn having subsequently been erected on part of its site'.[12] The latter is still standing on the north side of Merthyrmawr Road, while local government offices occupy the remainder of the site, but it is still possible to observe the northern slope of the mound.[13]

Throughout the medieval period Newcastle and the Nolton were the principal settlements along this stretch of the Ogwr. A bridge across the river was not built until the early 15th century,[14] and the development of a town on the east bank was slow. According to a manorial survey of 1631 the emerging Bridgend had only eight separate houses, while Nolton contained twenty-two,[15] and a century later their combined population was little more than three hundred. Again, in 1778, the Dunraven Estate Map marks Bridgend as a mere jumble of buildings near the river bend, still quite separate from Nolton, and inferior to both it and Newcastle.[16] It was not until the period after 1820 that this traditional settlement picture was transformed with the rapid industrialisation of Bridgend, which quickly engulfed the older communities.

1. They date from the late 11th or early 12th centuries, Nash-Williams, V. E., *The Early Christian Monuments of Wales* (Cardiff, 1950), 158–60.

2. Clark, *Cartae*, i, 39; Randall, H. J., *Bridgend, the Story of a Market Town* (Newport, 1955), 12.

3. O'Neil, H. B. St J. and Randall, H. J., *Newcastle Bridgend*, H.M.S.O. Guide; Hogg and King, 'Masonry Castles', 93; *Glamorgan County History*, iii, 432.

4. Clark, *Cartae*, i. 39. The present building dates essentially from the 19th century except for the mid 15th-century tower. Also mentioned in 1106 was the dependent chapelry of St Duotus, but its site is not known (Randall, *Bridgend*, 16).

5. Knowles and Hadcock, *Medieval Religious Houses*, 346. On the view that this did not belong to the Order, Randall, *Bridgend*, 23.

6. Randall, *Bridgend*, 75.

7. Corbett, J. A. (ed.), *Rice Merrick's Book of Glamorganshire Antiquities* (London, 1887), 90.

8. Randall, *Bridgend*, 13.

9. *Itinerary*, 29.

10. Clark, *Cartae*, ii, 235–6; Randall, *Bridgend*, 15.

11. The earliest mention of the 'chapel at Nolton' dates from 1631, but a drawing of it inserted on the Dunraven Estate Map of 1778 shows a building of medieval design. By the 1830s the chapel had fallen into disrepair and was demolished (Randall, *Bridgend*, 117–8).

12. Lewis, *Topographical Dictionary*, *sub* Bridgend.

13. The tithe barn, which appears to be late medieval in design, now houses the regional headquarters of the Red Cross Association (SS 905794).

14. Randall, *Bridgend*, 27.
15. The surveys are fully discussed by Randall, *ibid.*, 32.
16. The map is reprinted in Randall, *ibid., inter* 124-5.

BUILTH (Llanfair ym Muallt), Powys (Breconshire)   SO 040510

Builth is a small town situated in the valley of the River Wye which formerly enjoyed greater importance than it does today as the *caput* of the medieval lordship of Buellt.[1] No date is known for the actual foundation of the town, but this area was conquered by the Normans in the mid-1090s.[2] A civil settlement may have accompanied the building of the castle which is first mentioned in 1168.[3] Specific reference to the town is first made in 1217 when it was won by the Welsh from Reginald de Braose,[4] but there are no indications of its early size or of the medieval topography. The castle was destroyed by Llywelyn ap Gruffudd in 1260,[5] and not rebuilt until 1276, although there are indications that it had already been reconstructed in stone. In the following year the town received its first charter, but this appears to have been little more than a confirmation of already existing privileges.[7]

The street-pattern of modern Builth is irregular in form and there are no indications that this was a planned town. At the western end stands St Mary's church, but this was rebuilt in 1875 and only the 14th-century tower remains from the medieval period.[8] Adam of Usk (1377-1421) referred to Builth only as a 'village'[9] and there are no indications of any real urban character, although prior to the fire of 1690 the town is reputed to have extended from the east side of the castle westwards for a mile.[10] This is probably pure fancy, however, and in 1801 the population stood at only 677.

1. On the origin of the name *see* Williams, S. J., 'Some Breconshire Place-Names', *Brycheiniog*, vi (1965), 159.
2. Lloyd, *History of Wales*, ii, 402-3.
3. *Annales Cambriae*, 52.
4. *Brut y Tywysogion*, 95.
5. *Ibid.*, 112.
6. *Ibid.*, 118; King, D. J. C., 'Castles of Breconshire', *Brycheiniog*, vii (1961), 71-94.
7. *Cal. Ch. Rolls*, ii, 209.
8. Poole, E., *The Peoples' History of Brecon* (Brecon, 1876), 70.
9. Thompson, E. A. (ed.), *Chron. Adam de Usk* (London, 1904), 218.
10. Bowen, *Britannia Depicta*, 226; Jones, T., *History of Brecknock* (enlarged edn., Brecon, 1911), iii, 1-2.

CAERLEON (Caerllion), Gwent (Monmouthshire)   ST 340906

The town occupies an important site on the west bank of the Usk where the river takes a wide bend which affords considerable natural protection. This was appreciated by the Romans who constructed a legionary fortress here, naming it Isca after the river.[1] The remains of this fortress were still visible in the 12th century when Giraldus Cambrensis visited the site.[2] It has been extensively excavated,[3] and the medieval street-pattern of the town is seen to follow the regular Roman pattern whereby two principal streets meet almost at right-angles near the church.[4] At the end of the 3rd century the fortress was abandoned and the subsequent

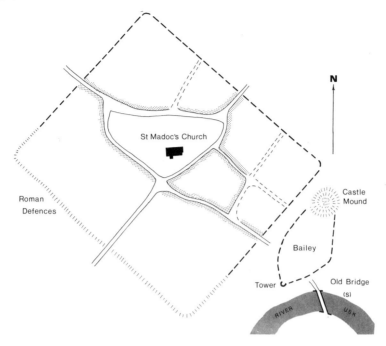

Fig. 17. Caerleon

history of the site is obscure since there is a dearth of finds from the Romano-British period. According to tradition St Dubricius (Dyfrig) is said to have founded a collegiate church here in the mid-6th century, but we know nothing of any associated civil settlement.[5]

The history of Caerleon recommences with the arrival of the Normans who had conquered this part of Gwent by the time of the Domesday Survey of 1086. There the small manor of 'Carlion' is entered in the Herefordshire *breve,* valued at 40s. and belonging to William de Scohies, one of the most important knights in that county.[6] A motte was constructed beyond the eastern corner of the old Roman fortress, either by the Normans or local lord Caradoc ap Gruffydd (d. 1069-70) or his son Owain. This was later topped by a stone keep and further defended by a walled bailey. The keep had disappeared by the late 18th century, but one of the bailey corner towers remained near the bridge, while the motte, known locally as the Mynd, is still visible.[7] Although Caerleon was within the area assigned to Robert fitz Hamon and his successors, the castle remained in Welsh hands throughout most of the 12th and early 13th centuries.[8] There can be little doubt that a town was also in existence by this time; it is specifically mentioned in 1171 when it was attacked by Iorwerth ab Owain while temporarily in the control of Henry II.[9] In the course of excavating the Roman site, moreover, a variety of medieval finds emerged dating from the 13th century onwards,[10] while St Cadoc's church probably also dates from this period.[11] It would appear that the town had to be rebuilt in the mid-13th century as Llywelyn ab Iorwerth is said to have 'reduced it to ashes' in

1231,[12] an event which may explain the absence of any borough charter until 1324 when a variety of previously existing privileges were confirmed.[13] An extent of the town taken in that year mentions the castle, two mills, a market, fair, fishery, and weir, and the whole borough yielded a rent of 102s.[14] There is no mention here or elsewhere of the Cistercian abbey which is supposed to have been located near the building known as 'The Priory' on the south side of the High Street,[15] the confusion arising from the occasional styling of nearby Llantarnam as 'Caerleon Abbey'.[16]

The later history of the town is largely uneventful except for Owain Glyndŵr's attack on it in August 1402.[17] Caerleon's long history of military importance, however, had gone and the castle was allowed to fall into disrepair and much of the masonry was removed for new building projects. By all accounts the borough was small, but not insignificant, being valued at £27 in 1532.[18] A survey carried out a century later gives the impression of a well-populated market town with a variety of trades and professions.[19] The picture does not appear to have changed markedly by the time of the first census in 1801, which recorded a population of 667, contained in 228 houses.[20]

1. Nash-Williams, *The Roman Frontier in Wales*, 29–33.

2. Dimock, J. F. (ed.), *Itin. Kamb.* (R.S.), I, vi (London, 1868), 55.

3. For a full summary *see* Boon, G. C., *Isca*, Nat. Museum of Wales, Cardiff, 1972.

4. This is considered to be the only instance of Roman influence on subsequent street-patterns in Wales, Carter, *Towns of Wales*, 6, 174.

5. Baring-Gould, S., *Lives of the Saints*, xvi (Edinburgh, 1914), 168; Bradney, J. A., *History of Monmouthshire*, iii, ii (London, 1923), 209–10.

6. *D.B.*, i, f. 185b; Nelson, L. H., *The Normans in South Wales* (University of Texas, 1966), 76.

7. Knight, J., 'The Keep of Caerleon Castle', *Mon. Antiq.*, i (1963), 71–2; Hogg and King, 'Masonry Castles', 94.

8. *Brut y Tywysogion*, 60, 70.

9. *Ibid.*, 66.

10. Lewis, J. M., 'Post-Roman Finds from the Caerleon Fortress Baths Excavation', *Mon. Antiq.*, ii (1967), 105–117.

11. The church, like many of the houses, is built of stone robbed from the Roman fortress (Boon, *Isca*, 13).

12. *Brut y Tywysogion*, 102.

13. *Cal. Ch. Rolls*, iii, 461. It was confirmed again in 1359 (*ibid.*, 164).

14. *C.I.P.M.*, iii, 244.

15. Marked on Bradney's map of the town, *op. cit.*, 188.

16. Williams, D. H., 'Llantarnam Abbey', *Mon. Antiq.*, ii (1967), 131–148.

17. Lloyd, *Owen Glendower*, 54.

18. Owen, E. (ed.), *Manuscripts Relating to Wales in the British Museum* (Cymm. Rec. Ser., iv, 1908), 606.

19. Bradney, *op. cit.*, 194.

20. *Ibid.*, 185. The total number of houses stated was 254 of which 26 were uninhabited.

CAERNARFON, Gwynedd (Caernarvonshire)   SH 478628

The castle and town of Caernarfon were founded by Edward I as part of his attempt to encircle the old kingdom of Gwynedd with a series of formidable defended towns. He was not the first to be attracted to the site, however, and organised settlement in the immediate area dates at least[1] from the Roman period with the construction of a fort, *Segontium,* on Llanbeblig Hill, half a mile to the south-east of the present town. This was maintained down to the late 4th century and may have been used for civil settlement after the Roman withdrawal, with St Peblig's church being built nearby. There is no direct evidence for continuity during the following centuries, and the area is not mentioned again until *c.* 1090 when Hugh of Avranches, Earl of Chester, built a motte on the north bank of the Afon Seiont.[3] This was later incorporated within the Edwardian castle, but the outline of the bailey beyond the east wall, the site of the medieval market-place, can still be detected.[4]

The Norman presence was short-lived and by 1115 the Welsh had regained the area and appear to have reoccupied the motte and established a small civil settlement.[5] Giraldus Cambrensis referred to 'Kairarvon' in 1188,[6] while Llywelyn ab Iorwerth issued a charter from here in 1221.[7] Later accounts of the castle-building refer to the displacement of the native community.[8] This work was begun

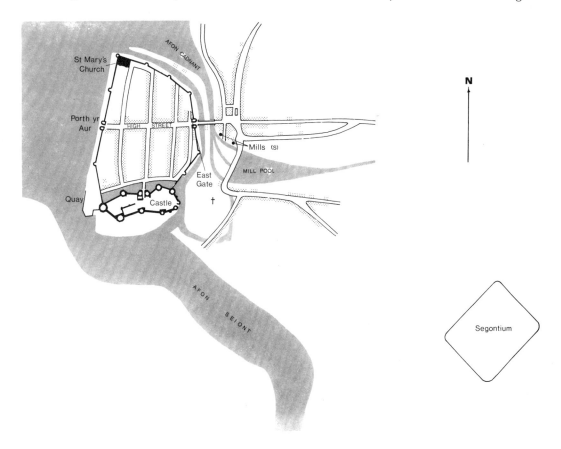

Fig. 18. Caernarfon

in June 1283, building materials partly coming from the old Roman fort at
Segontium,[9] and within a few years the castle, town walls, burgages, quay, bridge,
and mill-pool had all been laid out. By the Statute of Rhuddlan of 1284 Caernarfon
became the administrative and judicial capital of the Principality of North Wales
and the town received its charter in the same year.[10] Early growth was steady, the
walled area providing room for about 70 burgages which measured 60ft. by 80ft.[11]
and by the first rental of 1298, 59 had been taken up.[12] An attack on the town five
years previously by Madog ap Llywelyn, although resulting in the destruction of
much building, clearly had little effect on the development of the civil community.[13]

In comparison to the grandeur of the castle, medieval Caernarfon was a small
borough with more of an administrative than commercial importance. It was
enclosed with stone walls,[14] which replaced an earlier timber palisade originally
intended for Rhuddlan (q.v.),[15] and they remain substantially intact. At intervals
of 69m. they are flanked by a series of D-shaped towers and have two gatehouses
at the east and west ends of the High Street, namely the East Gate or Porth Mawr,
the principal entrance to the town, and the West Gate or Porth-yr-aur which led to
the quay. Other medieval entrances were a postern in the south-west corner, Water
Gate, and another in the south-east, the small Green Gate which gave access to
the market-place at Maes Glas.[16] When completed the walls thus enclosed a peninsula
bounded by the Seiont on the south and the Cadnant to the north, over which a
bridge was built leading out from the East Gate.[17] The influence of the rivers meant
that the town was not a regular rectangle as at Flint and this has modified the
street-pattern to the extent that none of the eight blocks or chequers is of the same
dimensions, although the difference is less marked on the south side of the principal
east-west axis, the High Street.[18]

Other features of the medieval town are well known from John Speed's plan of
1610,[19] supplemented by Jones's late-19th-century description.[20] The principal
non-military feature was St Mary's chapel, built in 1307 by Henry Ellerton on his
burgage in the north-west corner tower which became the vestry. The chapel was
substantially rebuilt in 1814, when remains of the early churchyard and several
skeletons were discovered.[22] With the importance of Caernarfon in the administration
of North Wales, moreover, the town housed a variety of buildings associated with
commerce and the judiciary. The Exchequer office was located above the East
Gate,[23] the Justice's house stood near the junction of Castle Ditch Street and Shire
Hall Street, while the Shire Hall itself, as shown by Speed, stood above it, but back
from the burgage frontages. Edward I's charter to the town also mentions *inter alia*
the right of the burgesses to build a town hall, and this was carried out on a site at
the junction of the High Street and Market Street. It eventually fell into ruin after
a new guildhall was built above the East Gate in 1767.[24] The importance of these
buildings was partly equalled in the domestic sphere with the walled area containing
a number of substantial properties or 'plasau', owned by the principal figures in the
commercial and administrative life of the town. None of them remain, but the
sites of at least six can be determined.[25]

Throughout the medieval period Caernarfon was largely confined to the walled
area, although by the early 15th century a small suburb had developed beyond

the East Gate which was destroyed during the Glyndŵr rebellion. By Speed's time this had largely recovered and he shows settlement in the area of modern Bangor Street and Penrallt and extending south along Mill Street. Speed also provides a valuable picture of the mill-pool which formerly existed along the Cadnant in the area of the present Pool Hill. Its construction appears to have been coeval with the castle and town when a mill was also built, although this was replaced in 1305.[27] The mill-pool was crossed by a bridge of five arches which Speed called 'Pount Prith' and it was not finally filled in until the early 19th century when the town was beginning a new phase of expansion.[28] This extra-mural area was again destroyed during the Civil War,[29] but it had re-established itself by 1776 when Griffith mapped the town,[30] and thereafter suburban growth increased as Caernarfon became the major outlet for the North Wales slate industry.[31]

1. A prehistoric hill-fort may have existed on nearby Twt Hill (Carter, H., 'Caernarvon', in Lobel, M. D. [ed.], *Historic Towns*, i [London, 1969], 1).

2. On *Segontium*, the 'gaer' which gave Caernarfon its name (caer yn arfon, 'the fort in the district of Arfon'), *see* Nash-Williams, *The Roman Frontier in Wales*, 59-64, and *R.C.A.M.W.M.*, *Caerns.*, ii, 158-64.

3. Jones, A. (ed.), *The History of Gruffydd ap Cynan* (Manchester, 1910), 310.

4. The motte has no recorded earlier history. Soundings concluded that it was both partly natural and partly artificial (*R.C.A.M.W.M.*, *op. cit.*, 127; *Archaeology in Wales*, ix (1969), 23.

5. Lewis, *Medieval Boroughs of Snowdonia*, 46.

6. *Opera*, vi, 124.

7. *Cal. Ch. Rolls*, ii, 459.

8. *R.C.A.M.W.M.*, *Caerns.*, ii, 115. Full structural and historical accounts of the castle can be found in *ibid.*, 124-50, and *King's Works*, 369-95.

9. This is suggested by the finding of silver pennies *temp.* Edward I on the site of the fort.

10. Lewis, *Medieval Boroughs of Snowdonia*, 33, 281; Jones, W. H., *Old Karnarvon* (Caernarfon, 1889), 43, 49.

11. S.C.6/1170/5; Lewis, *Medieval Boroughs of Snowdonia*, 63.

12. *Ibid.*, 66.

13. *R.C.A.M.W.M.*, *Caerns.*, ii, 150.

14. The walls are fully discussed in *ibid.*, 150-6, and Turner, *Town Defences*, 211.

15. *King's Works*, 323, 371.

16. This remained a very small entrance, hence the derivation of 'Hole-in-the-Wall Street', and was not enlarged until the early 19th century (Jones, *Old Karnarvon*, 77).

17. The river no longer flows along here, but the bridge was unearthed during demolition work in 1961 (*Archaeology in Wales*, ii [1962], 12).

18. Carter, *op. cit.*, 3.

19. *Atlas of Wales*, inter 123-4.

20. *Old Karnarvon*, passim.

21. *Rec. Caern.*, 224; *Cal. Pat. Rolls*, 1461-7, 310.

22. Jones, *Old Karnarvon*, 97.

23. *R.C.A.M.W.M.*, *Caerns.*, ii, 118.

24. Jones, *Old Karnarvon*, 77.

25. The Royal Commissioners located four: Plas Mawr, Plas Pulleston, Plas Spicer, and Plas Bowman (*R.A.M.W.M.*, *Caerns.*, ii, 117), while Jones adds a further two: Plas Isaf and Plas-y-Porth (*Old Karnarvon*, 100).

26. Lewis, *Medieval Boroughs of Snowdonia*, 185.

27. *Ibid.*, 185-6; *R.C.A.M.W.M.*, *Caerns.*, ii, 158; Jones, *Old Karnarvon*, 86.

28. 'Pount Prith' is probably derived from Pwnt Pridd or 'Earth Dam' (Carter, *op. cit.*, 4).

29. These events are best described by Jones, *Old Karnarvon*, 49–55.
30. Nat. Lib. Wales, MS., Langford James Collection.
31. On the later growth *see* Carter, *Towns of Wales*, 226–31.

CAERPHILLY (Caerffili), Mid Glamorgan   ST 157868

The town is impressively situated at the bottom of a steep-sided basin where the Nant Gledyr joins the Porset Brook. To the south it is bounded by Caerphilly Mountain, and in the north by Mynydd Eglwysilan. This was a planted borough but a late one as there is no evidence of medieval settlement before Gilbert de Clare began work on the first castle in 1268.[1] His chosen site lay along the course of a Roman road which led from Cardiff to Gelligaer and traces of a 1st-century auxiliary fort 90m. north-west of the castle were discovered in 1963.[2] In 1270 Llywelyn ap Gruffydd destroyed Gilbert's embryonic structure,[3] and a successor was not started until 1271, probably on the same site, when the beginnings of the town were also laid out. The initial settlement was modest with only 80 burgages, but by 1281 the number had risen to 116 burgages.[4] A further attack by the Welsh, however, succeeded in destroying the majority and by 1306 only 44 remained, of which another 26 were wasted during a siege on the castle 10 years later.[5] Thus what was intended as a substantial town to equal the splendour of the castle was reduced to a scattering of dwellings in its shadow. No borough charter has survived (there may never have been one), but the town boasted a weekly market until the mid-20th century.[6] Other burghal privileges, however, as Rice Merrick observed in 1578, had long since disappeared.[7]

The location of the small medieval town has been the subject of some discussion,[8] but it would be logical to place it behind the East Gate of the castle in the area of the present Castle and Market Streets, where natural protection is afforded by the Porset Brook and the Nant Gledyr.[9] The original market-place by the Twyn is preserved by the triangular shape of the modern car park, while there is evidence of 18th- and early-19th-century housing on the west side of Castle Street, since cleared, which may represent an earlier tradition of settlement. The modern town has grown up to the south of the castle, but this was still essentially agricultural land in the 1830s.[10] It is unfortunate that the lack of archaeological

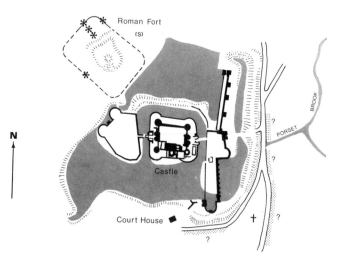

Fig. 19. Caerphilly

investigation and the absence of chance finds from other than the castle have prevented a satisfactory assessment of the area of medieval settlement.

Apart from the castle and the restored Court House which is situated immediately beyond the South Gate there are no further remains of the early town. No burgage pattern is apparent and there are no indications of defences, although the town may have been enclosed by a ditch and earthen bank.[11] Medieval Caerphilly had no early church, the inhabitants being served by nearby Eglwysilan, and the smallness of the borough is suggested by the absence of even a chapel-of-ease until St Martin's was built in 1552.[12] Total rents from the town amounted to £4 in 1631, less than one-third of the figure of Llantrisant. Caerphilly did not experience any marked growth until the early 19th century, and as late as 1795 the population amounted to a mere 200, occupying some 50 dwellings.[13]

1. There are several accounts of the history of the castle: Banks, R. W., 'Caerphilly Castle', *Arch Camb.*, 5th ser., iii (1886), 161-74; Clark, G. T., 'Contribution towards an account of Caerphilly Castle', *ibid.*, new ser., i (1850), 251-304; Rees, W., *Caerphilly Castle: a history and description*, revd. edn., Caerphilly, 1971.

2. Lewis, J. M., 'The Roman Fort and Civil War Earthwork at Caerphilly Castle', *Arch. Camb.*, xcv (1966), 67-87; Nash-Williams, *Roman Frontier in Wales*, 64-5.

3. *Brut y Tywysogion*, 115.

4. Rees, W., *op. cit.*, 30; Clark, *Cartae*, iii, 845.

5. C.133/73/3; 133/120; Richards, H. P., *A Short History of Caerphilly* (Caerphilly, 1969), 42.

6. Richards, *op. cit.*, 99-104.

7. *Book of Glamorganshire's Antiquities*, 106.

8. According to Rees (*op. cit.*, 31), the borough 'lay on both sides of the mountain road leading to the south gate of the Castle', viz., the present Cardiff Road.

9. Beresford, *New Towns*, 553.

10. Clark, G. T., *op. cit.*, 265.

11. Rees, W., *op. cit.*, 31.

12. Richards, *op. cit.*, 74.

13. On the growth of the town *see ibid.*, 109-128.

CAERSWS, Powys (Montgomeryshire)   SO 031920

Caersws is a small village situated some five miles due west of Newtown in the valley of the Severn. The site was strategically important with two lesser rivers, the Cerist and the Garno also meeting here, and the control which it offered over the three valleys was appreciated by the Romans, who constructed a large fort with an associated civil settlement immediately to the north-west of the present village.[1] Very little is known, however, of the medieval town; no date is recorded for the foundation of the borough, and there is no surviving charter. The rectangular street-pattern would suggest that it was planned,[2] while evidence from neighbouring boroughs points to a date in the late 12th or early 13th centuries.[3] There is some evidence to suggest that it was formerly more extensive than at present as the modern street-patterns appear to continue as field boundaries and surrounding lanes, but the decline must have been early as by Leland's time (1532-36) this was 'poor Caersws', where the weekly market had already been abandoned.[4]

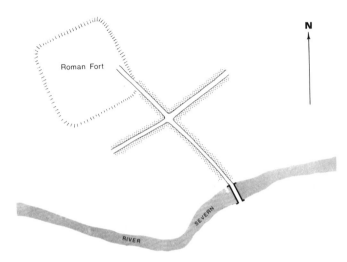

Fig. 20.   Caersws

Samuel Lewis (1832) mentions the former existence of a castle and 'at least one church', but this appears to be fiction.[5] 'Castle field', south of the fort, was presumably responsible for the growth of the first legend, but this evidently derives its name from the Roman stronghold, while the present church is Victorian and prior to its construction the inhabitants were served by the parish church of nearby Llanwnog.

Throughout the 16th century Caersws continued to be referred to as a borough and its inhabitants as burgesses,[6] but it ceased to retain an urban character and this has never been regained.

1. Nash-Williams, *The Roman Frontier in Wales*, 66–70. On recent excavations *see* Daniels, C. M., Jones, G. D. B., Putnam, W. G., 'Excavations at Caersws', *Mont. Coll.*, lix (1965-6), 112–115; *ibid.*, lxi (1969-70), 37–42.
2. Beresford, *New Towns*, 562-3.
3. O'Neill, B. H. St J., 'The Castle and Borough of Llanidloes', *Mont. Coll.*, xliii (1934), 63.
4. *Itinerary*, 54.
5. *Topographical Dictionary*, *sub* Caersws.
6. Hamer, H., 'Ancient Arwystli: Caersws', *Mont. Coll.*, ii (1869), 46-66.

CAERWYS, Clwyd (Flintshire)   SJ 128728

Caerwys is situated midway between two Edwardian foundations—Flint and Rhuddlan—and it belongs to the same chain of boroughs created to encircle the lands of the defeated Llywelyn. It received its first charter in 1290 and the regularity of the street-pattern suggests a planned borough, although it had evidently been laid out before that date as the document clearly refers to an already established community.[1] Indeed, the 'men of Kayroys' are mentioned in 1242,[2] and St Michael's church was also standing before the English arrival.[3] Unlike the other North Wales boroughs, moreover, Caerwys was a predominantly Welsh town throughout the medieval period,[4] and the absence of both castle and town defences suggests a commercial rather than a strategic role for the community.[5] Possibly we have here a small native vill which was reorganised and enlarged under Edwardian direction, and far from necessitating the removal of the existing community as happened at Llanfaes, other Welshmen from the surrounding areas were encouraged to take up burgages. Of the original parish church only the tower of late 13th- or early 14th-century date remains,[6] which suggests that the building may have been rebuilt at the time the borough was laid out.

Throughout the 14th century Caerwys was an important trading town with its own weekly market held in the central market-place, and its annual borough fairs. The hundred or commot court for Rhuddlan also met here occasionally.[7] Assizes were held in the town until 1672; the remains of the old gaol and town hall were still visible in the 1830s.[8] Caerwys was attacked by Glyndŵr, however,[9] and although the extent of the damage is not known the town thereafter fell increasingly under the influence of Rhuddlan and deteriorated in status. The markets, fairs and town mill continued to function, but with declining importance, and by the early 19th century they had lapsed altogether.[10]

St Michael's Church

Fig. 21. Caerwys

1. *Cal. Ch. Rolls,* iii, 372.

2. *Ibid.,* i, 275.

3. *Littere Wallie,* 86.

4. Of the 43 taxpayers named in 1292, 39 bore Welsh names (E 179/242/52).

5. A field near the town known as Erw'r Castell ('Castle Acre') had been variously regarded as the site of either a Roman fort or a medieval stronghold (Lewis, *Topographical Dictionary, sub* Caerwys), but the assertions are without foundation (Davies, E., *The Prehistoric and Roman Remains of Flintshire* [Cardiff, 1949], 63, 83–4).

6. *R.C.A.M.W.M., Flints.,* 8; Davies, E., 'Caerwys Church', *J.F.H.S.,* xviii (1960), 1–10.

7. Edwards, J. G., 'Flint Pleas, 1283–5', *J.F.H.S.,* viii (1922), liv–lv.

8. Lewis, *Topographical Dictionary, loc. cit.*

9. Messham, B. A., 'The County of Flint and the Rebellion of Owen Glyndŵr in the Records of the Earldom of Chester', *J.F.H.S.,* xxiii (1967–8), 11.

10. Lewis, *Topographical Dictionary, loc. cit.* The general history of Caerwys is discussed, although inadequately, by Owen, E., 'The Place of Caerwys in Welsh History', *Arch. Camb.,* 5th ser., viii (1891), 166–84.

CARDIFF (Caerdydd), South Glamorgan — ST 182763

Cardiff has traditionally held a senior position in the urban hierarchy of Wales ever since the Romans established a fort here at the end of the 1st century. The fort occupied the same site as the later Norman motte and 13th-century castle.[1] Beyond the fort, to the south, a civilian community also appears to have developed.[2] To what extent, if any, this continued to exist after the abandonment of the fort is unclear, however, since very little is known of Cardiff's history during the Dark Ages. There are suggestions of a Scandinavian presence,[3] even of a slave-trading post,[4] but archaeological excavation has so far failed to produce any real evidence of occupation from this period. While future excavations may modify this view at present the town is considered to be no older than the 1080s, when this area was secured by the Normans under the leadership of Robert fitz Hamon. The old Roman fort was reoccupied and an artificial motte thrown up near the North Gate, while the eastern area was cleared during the construction of the bailey.[5] A borough was laid out immediately to the south, incorporated in 1120–37, while fitz Hamon also appears to have been responsible for the foundation of St Mary's church which was initially a priory attached to Tewkesbury Abbey.[6] There are indications that this Norman borough was substantially smaller than its late medieval successor and parallels here can be drawn with Haverfordwest, Abergavenny, and Rhuddlan.

Professor Rees has drawn attention to the difference between the northern and southern sectors of the town as depicted on Speed's map of 1610.[7] The lower area, south of Wharton Street, was less congested, and was principally given over to gardens and enclosures. Occupation was concentrated in the upper part near the main town gates and where the streets followed a more regular pattern. The author of a recent study of medieval Cardiff has suggested that this northern sector may represent 'the garden . . . outside the town of Cardiff' referred to in a late-17th-

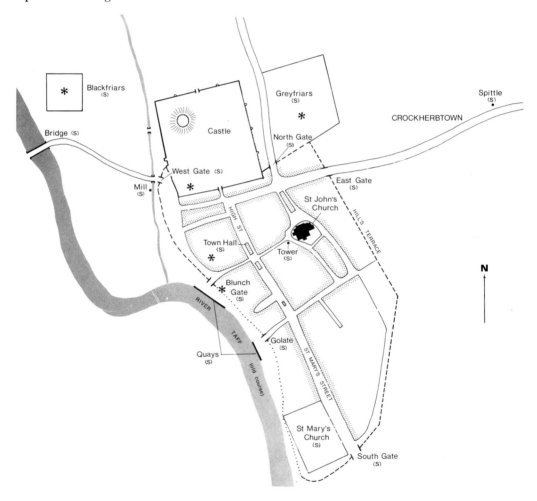

Fig. 22. Cardiff

century charter of William, Earl of Gloucester, the inference being that the initial borough lay beyond this area, in the vicinity of St Mary's.[8] In the absence of archaeological evidence no definite pronouncement can yet be made, but in the light of the evidence from other early Norman boroughs, where the civil settlements lay under the immediate shadow and protection of the castle, it seems unlikely that the first burgages at Cardiff would have been sited so far to the south. There are further indications which suggest that Norman Cardiff lay immediately beyond the south gate of the castle. Speed indicates a length of walling with a corner bastion running down the west side of Trinity Street, while another map of c. 1650 shows a further section running westwards from the tower along Church Street.[9] Here, in 1901, the remains of a thick wall running parallel with the south side of the castle were exposed during street alterations,[10] and this was presumably the wall of the Norman town which was made to run down Trinity Street in order to enclose St John's chapel.

Little is known of Cardiff's history during the 12th century, although it had become sufficiently important to be the victim of a Welsh attack in 1185 when both the town and castle were put to flames.[11] Its growth is confirmed by the appearance of the suburb of Crockherbtown which suggests that there were more prospective settlers than the walled enceinte could contain.[12] During the 13th century, when the borough and lordship had passed to the de Clares, more substantial growth took place, and Cardiff emerged as the largest town in Wales, with some 400 burgesses and perhaps a total population of 2,000 people.[13] In 1221 St Mary's priory was remodelled as a parish church to serve the southern sector of the town and beyond the borough two friaries appeared, the first being the Dominicans (Black Friars) on the left bank of the Taff,[14] followed in c. 1280 by the Franciscans (Grey Friars) whose house stood east of the castle beyond the North Gate.[15] Further additions were also made to the castle defences, while perhaps the most significant move was the walling of the town in stone which seems to have been completed by the early 14th century.[16] The wall has since disappeared, but its course can be reconstructed from Speed's map and the observations of later topographical writers. The northern wall was joined to the south-east bastion of the castle where a small portion is still visible. Here stood the North Gate (Leland's Senghenydd Gate) which led to the burgesses' holdings in Cathays, while nearby was the more important East Gate leading to Crockherbtown suburb along the modern Queen Street.[17] From here the wall followed a south-easterly course, which was later that of the Glamorganshire canal which followed the line of the town moat, running parallel with High Street and St Mary's Street as far as Cock's Tower. It then veered south down Mill Lane to the South Gate and then to the banks of the Taff, the river formerly flowing much closer to St Mary's Street than it does now, a 'new cut' being made in 1845–50.

It is not clear if the wall then continued northwards to link up with the West Gate or if the river itself was considered an adequate defensive barrier on this side. Speed's plan would suggest the latter, but it is quite clear by his day that this part of the town had been subject to extensive flooding and the corner of St Mary's churchyard had already disappeared. Subsequent excavations, moreover, have uncovered sections of the wall in this area, and in all likelihood it ran the full course on this western side, but had already been washed away by the 17th century. Two further gates stood here and provided access to the river. Blount's or Blunch Gate linked the High Street with the town quay and stood at the junction of Quay Street and Womanby Street,[19] while access to a lesser quay was through the Gully Gate or Golate located further to the south at the rear of the present *Queen's* hotel.

The increasing status of Cardiff suggested by the building of the walls was paralleled by other developments in town life during the course of the 14th century. In 1338 the burgesses were granted a plot of land in the High Street and the first town hall was constructed, its site shown by Speed as immediately to the north of the junction of Church Street and Quay Street with the High Street.[20] This housed both the Assizes and the Court of Common Council, while the lower half contained the corn market and a variety of traders' stalls. Immediately below it stood the town cross, while other features of the medieval topography marked by Speed include the poor house in Westgate Street, not demolished until 1851, and the leper hospital beyond the town which was located at the eastern extremity of Crockherbtown.[21] There had also been the chapel of St Piran serving the guild of Cordwainers in Shoemaker Street (now Duke Street), but this had been suppressed in 1548, although remains of the building were still visible near the castle entrance in the late 18th century.[22]

It is clear from Speed's map that the Cardiff of the early 17th century was smaller than it had been at its peak in the early 14th century. He indicates large areas of gardens and enclosures in the lower part of the walled area, while the suburbs of Crockherbtown beyond the East Gate and Soudrey beyond the South Gate appear smaller than is suggested by earlier records. Both the friaries had been suppressed, while St Mary's church was being undermined by the Taff and by the end of the century had almost disappeared. Borough revenues had also fallen sharply, and the number of burgages had sunk to about a hundred,[23] a situation which was undoubtedly linked, at least in part, with the outbreak of plague in 1348 and the attack on the town by Glyndŵr in 1404 when the greater part was put to flames.[24] While Cardiff nevertheless retained its dominant position in the Vale the borough remained below its medieval peak until the early 19th century; in 1810 the population stood at only 1,870, less than it had been 500 years earlier.[25]

1. On the Roman fort *see* Ward, J., 'Roman Cardiff', *Arch. Camb.*, lxiii (1908), 29–64, lxviii (1913), 159–64, lxix (1914), 407–10; Nash-Williams, *Roman Frontier in Wales*, 70–2; Webster, J. and P., *Morgannwg*, xx (1976), 71–4.

2. Storrie, J., 'Discovery of Ancient Remains at Cardiff', *Arch.Camb.*, xlviii (1893), 277–81; *Archaeology in Wales*, xii (1972), 29; Ward, *op. cit.* (1908), 63.

3. Paterson, D., 'Scandinavian influence in the place-name and early personal names of Glamorgan', *Arch. Camb.*, lxxv (1920), 35–6.

4. Bromberg, E. J., 'Wales and the Medieval Slave Trade', *Speculum*, xvii (1942), 263–9.

5. Rees, W., *Cardiff: A History of the City* (Cardiff, 1969), 10–13.

6. *Mon. Angl.*, ii, 66; *Rice Merrick's Book of Glamorganshire's Antiquities*, 93.

7. Rees, *Cardiff*, 10; Speed, *Atlas of Wales*, inter 105–6.

8. Walker, D. G., 'Cardiff', in Griffiths, *Borough of Medieval Wales*, 112–13.

9. Reproduced in *Arch. Camb.*, 6th ser., i (1901), inter 318–9 and Birch, W. de Gray, *History of Neath Abbey* (Neath, 1902), inter 216–7.

10. Rees, *Cardiff*, 19.

11. *Ann. Margam*, 17-18; *Pipe Roll*, 31 Hen. II, 5-6.

12. Clark, *Cartae*, i, 104.

13. Rees, *Cardiff*, 30. For the most recent account of medieval Cardiff *see* Walker, D. G., 'Cardiff', *op. cit.*, 103-28.

14. Rees, *Cardiff*, 23; Knowles and Hadcock, *Medieval Religious Houses*, 214.

15. Cronin, *op. cit.*, *passim*.

16. Repairs were carried out in 1315 following the revolt of Llywelyn Bren (*Borough Records*, i, 108; Rees, *Cardiff*, 16).

17. The gates were pulled down in the late 18th century (*ibid.*, 127-8).

18. *Ibid.*, 16[n].

19. Foundations of the quay were discovered during the demolition of the old fire station in Westgate Street (Webster, P., 'Excavations in Quay Street, Cardiff, 1973-74', *Arch. Camb.*, cxxvi [1977], 88-115).

20. Rees, *Cardiff*, 37; *Rice Merrick's Book of Glamorganshire's Antiquities*, 94. It was demolished in 1743 (Rees, *Cardiff*, 127).

21. Knowles and Hadcock, *Medieval Religious Houses*, 350; Rees, *Cardiff*, 18. This may have been the hospice at Cardiff granted to Neath Abbey in 1147-57 by William, Earl of Gloucester (Birch, *History of Neath Abbey*, 51).

22. Rees, *Cardiff*, 21, 47.

23. On the decline of late medieval Cardiff *see* Griffiths, *Glam. County Hist.*, iii, 348-50.

24. Lloyd, *Owen Glendower*, 89-90.

25. Rees, *Cardiff*, 152.

CARDIGAN (Aberteifi), Dyfed (Cardiganshire)   SN 178461

The medieval town grew up on a promontory site on the north bank of the Afon Teifi and near the estuary of the river, hence the origin of Cardigan's Welsh name. Urban origins date back to the Normans and the initial motte constructed by Roger de Montgomery in 1093 (then known as Din Geraint, but now as Hen Castell) was placed a mile to the west of the present town nearer the mouth of the river (SN 164465).[1] During the reign of Henry I this was deserted and the first castle was built at Cardigan under the direction of Gilbert de Clare.[2] It is likely that he also founded the Benedictine priory and St Mary's church a half-mile further east and the beginnings of the civil settlement probably date from these years.[3] In 1165 the Welsh under Rhys ap Gruffudd regained the castle and expelled the English monks from the priory,[4] granting it to Chertsey Abbey in Surrey, and a similar fate may have befallen de Clare's English townsfolk. In 1171 Rhys rebuilt the castle in stone,[5] but it changed hands frequently during the following 50 years until the 1240s when the English hold was firmly consolidated.[6] Five years later the castle was again rebuilt and work was begun on the construction of the town wall, although there are suggestions that the line of the defences had been previously laid out.[7] In 1249 Cardigan was granted the privilege of a guild merchant, and in 1284 received its first charter from Edward I,[8] although clearly this was more of a confirmation of existing privileges as a weekly market had been in operation for over a century[9] and there were already 128 burgages in 1274. The charter had the effect of increasing the growth rate, however, and from a burgage total of 130 in 1279 the figure rose to 172 in 1308.[10]

Of the stone walls that enclosed the medieval town there are no remains; in 1610 they were 'indifferent for re-paire',[11] while all traces had disap-peared by Samuel Lewis's day (1832).[12] Sections are shown on Speed's map, however, and the overall course is still discernible from the modern street-pat-tern. Starting at the eastern side of the castle the wall ran north following the

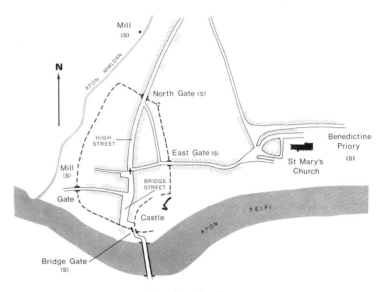

Fig. 23. Cardigan

slope below Chancery Lane, and there was a gate at the junction with St Mary's Street. From it here it continued northwards as far as College Row, and Speed shows a corner tower where the wall turned westwards. Here also was the North Gate which was still partly standing in 1843, when it was destroyed during the Rebecca Riots. At the corner of College Row and Queen's Terrace the wall turned south along the Mwldan and ran as far as the Teifi where it turned eastward until it joined the castle just above the bridge. A third gate was located at the juntion of Quay Street and Lower Mwldan, while Speed shows a fourth at the bottom of Bridge Street adjoining the western corner tower of the castle. The principal street within the walled area was the north-south axis, High Street, where stood the town cross, with the side streets—Quay Street, Market Street and St Mary's Street—constituting the medieval nucleus.

The significant growth rate which Cardigan exhibited during the 13th and early 14th centuries was not maintained and there is firm evidence that the town contracted during the later Middle Ages. By the mid–16th century the number of houses had fallen to about fifty-five, and in 1600 George Owen confirmed that the town was 'ruinous and decayed'.[14] Speed's map of 1610 indicates large areas of open space in the northern half of the walled town and the appearance of 'Souter's Street' (now Chancery Lane) which linked the East Gate with the upper part of the High Street by cutting across the rear of the burgages suggests the abandonment of organised tenure in this area. A decline is also suggested by the appearance of a single mill situated to the north-east of the town on the Mwldan Brook, whereas there had been two in the early 15th century, and three in the late 13th century.[15] On the credit side, however, extra-mural development had already begun beyond the North Gate, while there was a more substantial suburb to the east in the area of St Mary's church and the priory. Towards the end of the 17th century these areas began to expand as maritime trade revived, and there was much redevelopment within the walls, but this took the form of infilling.[16] The original street-pattern of the medieval town, with the exception of Chancery Lane, has survived intact.[17]

1. Hogg and King, Early Castles', 107.

2. *Idem*, 'Masonry Castles', 96.

3. On the history of the Priory *see* Pritchard, E. M., *Cardigan Priory*, London, 1904.

4. *Brut y Tywysogion*, 64.

5. *Ibid.*, 67.

6. *Ibid.*, 99, 105.

7. *Cal. Pat. Rolls*, 371; Turner, *Town Defences*, 212.

8. *Cal. Ch. Rolls*, ii, 280.

9. Sanders, I. J., 'Trade and Industry in some Cardiganshire towns in the Middle Ages', *Ceredigion*, iii (1959), 323,

10. Beresford, *New Towns*, 538.

11. Speed, *Atlas of Wales*, 113.

12. *Topographical Dictionary*, *sub* Cardigan.

13. James, W. E., *Guide Book to Cardigan and District* (Cardigan, 1899), 13.

14. *Description of Pembrokeshire*, iv, 479.

15. Sanders, *op. cit.*, 330.

16. On the later growth of Cardigan *see* Carter, *Towns of Wales*, 189–97.

17. The possibility of some change in the street-pattern has been tentatively suggested (Maynard, D., 'Excavations in Cardigan: Volk's Bakery, 1975', *Ceredigion*, vii [1974/5], 350–4) but is unlikely given the position of the town gates which determined a rib-like form.

CARMARTHEN (Caerfyrddin), Dyfed (Carmarthenshire)   SN 413200

The town occupies a river terrace on the north bank of the Afon Tywi, and in common with many similar Norman foundations in Wales this position was also the highest tidal point of the river which enabled relief by sea in the event of a Welsh siege.[1] The advantages of the site had been appreciated long before the arrival of the Normans, however, as a Roman auxiliary fort was established here *c.* A.D. 75–77, while immediately to its east a *vicus* developed to form the nucleus of *Moridunum,* the cantonal capital of the Demetae. Recent excavations have determined the position and outline of both features, while further east, beyond the site of St John's priory, an amphitheatre has also been located.[2] Little archaeological evidence of settlement has come to light in the period following the Roman withdrawal, but there is a strong tradition of an established native community. Documentary sources point to the presence of a Celtic church dedicated to St Teulyddog and this is considered to have stood in the area of the later priory. In all probability this was the centre of a Welsh community which was well established when William fitz Baldwin and his Norman followers arrived in 1094.[3]

Contrary to the procedure at Abergavenny and Cardiff the Normans decided against building their initial fortification within the area of the old Roman fort, although this was still visible, and a new site was chosen which overlooked the river. Known in its early years as Rhyd-y-Gors,[4] the castle was frequently the target of Welsh attack, and was several times rebuilt.[5] Immediately beyond its gates a

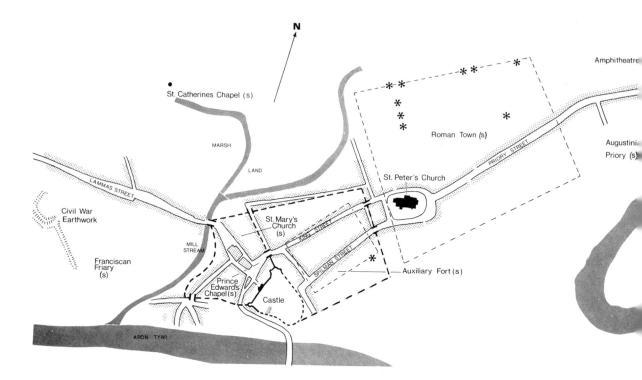

Fig. 24. Carmarthen

civilian community was established which received its first grant of privileges from Henry I in 1109.[6] At the same time the existing Welsh settlement to the east was allowed to remain and by a royal grant of Henry II it fell under the control of the prior of St John's which had been founded in 1127. Throughout the medieval period, therefore, there were two Carmarthens, the Anglo-Norman borough below the castle, and 'Old Carmarthen', the native township which had grown up around St Teulyddog's church.[7]

Throughout the 12th and 13th centuries Carmarthen was a relatively small town. In 1223 it received a grant of murage, the earliest known example in Wales, but only the area of the modern Guildhall Square, Quay Street, and Bridge Street, was enclosed.[8] On the east side of the guildhall St Mary's church, since demolished,[9] was built, while beyond the walls St Peter's was probably already in existence,[10] its position stimulating the growth of extra-mural settlement which soon outgrew the area of the walled borough. By the end of the 13th century Carmarthen housed in the region of 150–180 burgages, and it is very unlikely that little more than half of them could have been accommodated within the defences.[11]

Eventually, in 1415, it was decided to extend the walls,[12] a move prompted by Owain Glyndŵr's atacks in 1403 and 1405,[13] and Henry V granted £20 towards the cost of the operation. While few vestiges of these walls remain today they are clearly marked on John Speed's plan of 1610 and their course has been worked out in some detail.[14] It is important to note that it was dictated by the presence of two water-courses which flowed into the Tywi; the mill stream, now covered by Blue Street, ran from Glannant Road to St Catherine's mill, and then to John Street and Red Street, while a second stream flowed into the town from the present Springfield and Wellfield Road district. This ran to Francis Terrace and Little Water Street, where it turned to cross Orchard Street, eventually joining the other stream in Red Street. Together they formed a natural moat around the north and west walls of the medieval town, while also on the north side the presence of a large marsh in the John Street area, not drained until the late 17th century prevented any suburban development in that direction, Beginning, then, at the south-east tower of the castle the wall ran eastwards above Dan-y-banc and then turned north-west, crossing Spilman and King Street, where gates were located. From a point just past the East or White Gate in King Street the wall veered south-west down Wood's Row, passing through the lower end of Jackson's Lane as far as the Dark Gate in Lower Guildhall Square. From here it continued south following the curve of the former stream now covered by Blue Street and then turned eastwards to link up with the South Tower of the castle.

Apart from the gates already noted there were additional entrances to the town at the end of the Red Lion Yard leading into Chapel Street (SN 41232011) and two others at the bottom of Bridge and Quay Streets, where they join Little Bridge Street. Within the town was also the Prisoner's Gate, originally part of the smaller 13th-century defences, which separated King Street and Nott's Square.[15] It is shown by Speed and was not finally pulled down until 1792.

Although the circuit of town walls was not enlarged until the early 15th century it is clear that they then enclosed an area of existing settlement and that the borough had expanded significantly during the previous century. Burgage rents in 1301-2 totalled £9 4s. 0d., suggesting, at 1s. per plot, a figure of 184 burgages, while additional returns from the 'burgesses of the wind' amounted to a further £4 14s. 0d.[16] With these figures it would not be unreasonable to suggest a population of about a thousand, and there are indications that the figure increased still further as the century progressed. Carmarthen's developing trading activities were recognised in 1326 when it was made a staple port with licence to deal in wool, pelts, leather, lead and tin, while it was also the base for an important fishing industry. Since the death of the last Llywelyn, moreover, the borough had emerged as the *caput* of royal government in South Wales and the combined effects of economic and administrative importance produced a degree of urbanisation equalled only by Cardiff and in the north, Caernarfon. Much of the business was conducted from the castle, and there is no mention of a separate guildhall until 1576,[17] but other features of the medieval town are known from documentary sources and from Speed's map of 1610. Religious activities were especially well catered for, and apart from St John's priory and St Mary's church already mentioned, a Franciscan friary had been established off Lammas Street by 1284,[18] while also beyond the walled town stood St Catherine's chapel in the area of the present cattle market (SN 41002028).[19] A further chapel, St Edward's, also lay within the defences and its site appears to have been immediately below the castle in Nott Square.[20] The commercial life of the borough centred on the open market held in Guildhall Square where the town cross stood. Beyond the south wall lay the quay, shown by Speed, who also records the site of the mill as immediately beyond the Dark Gate. By the close of the 16th century Carmarthen had grown into a community of some 325 houses with a population estimated at 2,250, no longer confined to the walled area.[21] Speed indicates extra-mural settlement by the quay, along Lammas Street and along Priory Street beyond the eastern gates. From this period until the large-scale urbanisation of the early 19th century, Carmarthen remained the most populous town in Wales.

1. On the site of the town *see* Carter, *Towns of Wales*, 18-19, 27.

2. Nash-Williams, *Roman Frontier in Wales*, 73-4; Wacher, *Towns of Roman Britain*, 389-93. For a bibliography of Roman Carmarthen (to 1974) *see* Green A., *Carm. Antiq.*, x (1974), 47-9.

3. Baring-Gould, *Lives of the Saints*, iv, 251-2; Griffiths, R. A., 'The Making of Medieval Carmarthen', *Carm. Antiq.*, ix (1973), 86; *idem*, 'Carmarthen', in *Boroughs of Medieval Wales*, 137-8.

4. The traditional view that the original motte occupied a different site from its successor has been rejected (Lodwick, M. and E., *The Story of Carmarthen* (Carmarthen, 1953), 6, 17; Taylor, A. J., 'Carmarthen Castle', *Arch. Camb.*, c [1949], 123-4), although recently revived by Griffiths ('Carmarthen', *op. cit.*, 138-9).

5. *Brut y Tywysogion*, 54, 57, 100; Hogg and King, 'Early Castles', 107, 119; *idem*, 'Masonry Castles', 96.

6. Ballard and Tait, *British Borough Charters*, 66.

7. *Cal. Ch. Rolls*, i, 315; Phillipps, T. (ed.), *Cartularium S. Johannis Baptistae de Carmarthen* (Cheltenham, 1865), 28.

8. *Cal. Cl. Rolls*, ii, 199; Turner, *Town Defences*, 212; *R.C.A.M.W.M.*, *Carms.*, 251-2.

9. *Ibid.*, 258; *Cal. Pat. Rolls*, 1247-58, 123; Lodwick, *Carmarthen*, 48.

10. *Ibid.*, 39.

11. E 142/51; C 145/33/31.

12. *Cal. Pat. Rolls*, 1413-16, 308.

13. Lloyd, *Owen Glendower*, 67, 103; Griffiths, 'Carmarthen', *op. cit.*, 153.

14. *Atlas of Wales*, inter 103-4.

15. A recent excavation off Guildhall Street across the conjectured line of the 13th-century defences (SN 41242009) failed to locate the wall (*Archaeology in Wales*, xv [1975], 56), but it may have been robbed during the building of the larger circuit.

16. Lewis, E. A., 'Chamberlain's Account for West Wales', *B.B.C.S.*, ii (1925), 51, 53.

17. It was built within the area of the open market (Lodwick, *Carmarthen*, 99-100; *R.C.A.M.W.M.*, *Carms.*, 252).

18. The friary was dissolved in 1558 and all remains had been removed by the early 19th century (Knowles and Hadcock, *Medieval Religious Houses*, 224; *R.C.A.M.W.M.*, *Carms.*, 259).

19. *Ibid.*, 260; Lodwick, *Carmarthen*, 48.

20. It site is considered to have been at No 2 Nott Square (*R.C.A.M.W.M.*, *Carms.*, 259; Lodwick, *Carmarthen*, 48).

21. *Ibid.*, 135; Thomas, W. S. K., 'Tudor and Jacobean Swansea', *Morgannwg*, v (1961), 25-6.

CASTELL Y BERE, Gwynedd (Merionethshire)   SH 667085

The attempt by Edward I to establish this castle-borough in the inland parish of Llanfihangel-y-Pennant proved unsuccessful, and in little more than a decade both had been abandoned. This was not the result of bad siting, however, since the castle dominated the Dysynni River and formed an important link in the control of the whole area between the Dyfi and Mawddach, while also lying midway between Harlech and Aberystwyth. The value of the location, moreover, had been appreciated well before the king began to encircle Gwynedd since the castle was initially a Welsh foundation,[1] and the comparatively small sum which he spent on it suggests that it was repaired rather than rebuilt.[2] It was probably erected during the time of Llywelyn ab Iorwerth and may be identified as 'the castle of Meirionnydd', built in 1221, as its overall plan is consistent with those of other native fortifications in the north.[3] Edward I took it in April 1283[4] and set about repairs and the laying out of a small borough which received its charter in November of the following year.[5] The constable of the castle was made ex-officio mayor of the town, but the list of office-holders contains only three names[6] and the whole venture was abandoned after Madog's attack of 1294.[7] Excavation of the castle in the 1850s and again in 1949-66 produced only the occasional find later than the 13th century and large amounts of charcoal uncovered suggests that the castle was burnt down.[8] Of the borough very little is known. There were 16 taxpayers in 1292-3, of whom one-third were Welsh,[9] and in all probability this small community was destroyed along with the castle. Its exact site is not known; it may have been within the castle walls as at Dryslwyn or alternatively on the level plateau to the east, but this area has yet to be excavated since all efforts to date have been concentrated within the defences.[10]

1. On the castle, which was also known as 'Caerbellan', *see* Evans, E. D., 'Castell Y Bere', *J.M.H.R.S.*, iii (1957), 31-44; *R.C.A.M.W.M., Mer.*, 112-3; *King's Works*, 367-9.

2. Total expenditure to October 1290 amounted to only £262 (*ibid.,* 368).

3. *Brut y Tywysogion*, 98; *King's Works*, 367-8; Butler, L. A. S., 'Medieval Finds at Castell-y-Bere', *Arch. Camb.*, cxxiii (1974), 79.

4. *Littere Wallie*, 189; Morris, *Welsh Wars*, 193.

5. *Cal. Ch. Rolls*, ii, 280.

6. Lewis, *Medieval Borough of Snowdonia*, 36[n].

7. Morris, *Welsh Wars*, 252, Evans, *op. cit.*, 41-2; *King's Works*, 369.

8. Wynne, W., 'Castell y Bere', *Arch. Camb.*, 3rd ser., vii (1861), 106-7.

9. Williams-Jones, K. (ed.), *The Merioneth lay Subsidy Roll 1292-3*, cxliii, 51.

10. Beresford, *New Towns*, 558; Butler, *op. cit.*, 78.

CEFNLLYS, Powys (Radnorshire)   SO 089614

Both the castle and the borough were the creation of the Mortimer family who had been consolidating their hold over large areas of mid-Powys since the end of the 11th century. In or about 1100 Ralph Mortimer had built a motte-and-bailey at Alpine Bridge two miles further north (SO 09216304),[1] but this was abandoned during the period 1240-46 as part of Henry III's border campaign against the Welsh and a new stone castle was built at Cefnllys within an Iron Age fort on the hill since known as Castle Bank.[2] This was rebuilt in 1273-4[3] and a small borough was established although no firm date can be given for its foundation. It was in existence in 1297 when it appears in a general charter of Edmund Mortimer to the 'men of Malienydd'[4] and in 1304 there were 25 tenants together with a mill.[5] There is no evidence of further growth; in 1332 only 20 burgesses were recorded[6] and by 1383 10 burgages had fallen into decay.[7] It continued to be referred to as a borough, however, and this was the case down to the 19th century, although by then the term had come to refer to a much larger area encompassing one-fifth of Cefnllys parish.[8]

Since there are no remains of the medieval settlement its actual location has not been conclusively determined. The 14th-century evidence suggests that the population was small enough to be accommodated within the area of the castle or alternatively the burgages may have been concentrated around St Michael's church 300m. due east.[9] The second possibility seems the most likely as the mill must have been powered by the Afon Ieithon which flows behind the church and the burgesses were obliged to pay pontage on a bridge which was presumably the predecessor of the present Shaky Bridge nearby. A number of aerial photographs were taken of this area in 1946 which showed earthwork banks perhaps representing raised causeways across what is now wet and boggy land.[10] Two sunken roads are visible to the south of the church, one running down to the bridge, while on the east side ruins of a building are clearly visible. Immediately to the north of the ruins a scatter of stones and more earthworks would seem to indicate more buildings and these are near the farmhouse 'Neuadd' where the court leet was held after the abandonment of the castle.[11]

1. *Mon. Angl.*, vi, 349; *R.C.A.M.W.M., Rads.*, 29; Brown, A. E., 'The Castle, Borough and Park of Cefnllys', *T.R.S.*, xlii (1972), 12.

2. *Cal. Pat. Rolls*, 1237-47, 489; Hogg and King, 'Masonry Castles', 97; *R.C.A.M.W.M., Rads.*, 29-31; Brown, *op. cit.*, 12-15.

3. *Cal. Anct. Corresp.*, 94.

4. *Cal. Pat. Rolls*, 1292-1301, 290.

5. *C.I.P.M.*, iv, 162.

6. *Ibid.*, vii, 280; Beresford, *New Towns*, 570.

7. S.C. 6/1209/14.

8. *MSS. Relating to Wales*, 549; Lewis, *Topographical Dictionary*, *sub* Kevenlleece; Brown, *op. cit.*, 16.

9. The foundation date of the church is not known and the original structure was completely rebuilt in 1895 (*R.C.A.M.W.M., Rads.*, 31).

10. Brown, *op. cit.*, 16.

11. *Ibid.*, 15; Morris, T. E., 'The Parish Book of Cefnllys', *Arch., Camb.*, 6th ser., xix (1919), 35-95.

CHEPSTOW (Cas-gwent), Gwent (Monmouthshire)   ST 536940

Chepstow occupies a dominant position on the west bank of the River Wye where it is crossed by the main coast road from Gloucestershire into South Wales. This border situation allows for urban origins to be assigned to the early years of Norman power and there are good reasons for believing that the area was granted along with the earldom of Hereford to William fitz Osbern *c.* 1070.[1] The initial castle dates from this time,[2] as does St Mary's priory,[3] and a town had been laid out by 1075 when it was valued at £16 in total.[4]

Initially the town was known by the name of 'Stroguil' after the castle and surrounding lordship, but by the 14th century the present form had emerged to emphasise its commercial character—'cēapstow', indicating a 'market-place'.[5] By 1306 the burgage total had grown to an impressive 308, and Chepstow had established itself as a thriving borough and port.[6] The focal point was the castle situated in the north-west corner of the town which was improved by William Marshal in the late 12th century with further important additions carried out by Roger Bigod in the period 1270–1306. From its West Tower ran the town wall, known as the Port Wall, which enclosed an unusually large area of 113 acres, and

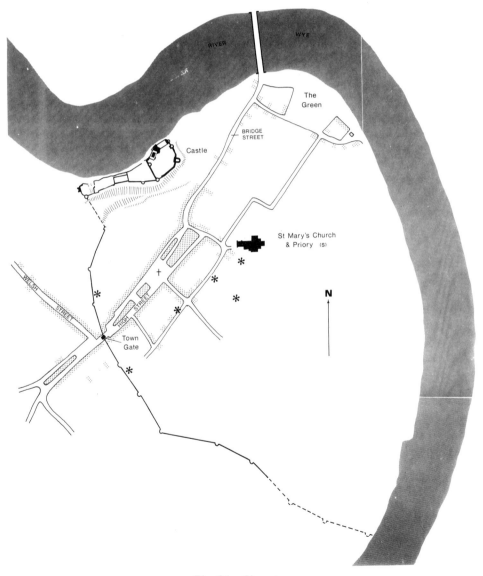

Fig. 25. Chepstow

there are substantial remains on this western side. As Leland noted,[7] it originally ran across the peninsula to the river bank, but the section east of the present railway line has since been lost. On the north and east sides there appear to have been no defences since the Wye was considered adequate to protect the town in this area.[8] There is some documentary evidence for the building of the wall, and the dating of 1272-78 by Perks has been supported by recent archaeological investigation which has produced evidence of 13th-century occupation prior to its construction. There was only one gate leading into the town, and this still stands at the junction of the High Street and Moor Street.

Despite the obvious size of medieval Chepstow the town enjoyed a quiet history and escaped the turmoil of the Welsh wars. Some features of its early topography are known, but the street-pattern must be in doubt. The High Street leading from the Town Gate and its continuation, Bridge Street, appear to be original—the bridge is mentioned in 1234.[10]—but the marked contraction of the borough in the late 15th and 16th centuries has left much of the remainder in doubt. Of the 11th-century priory there are now no remains except for the church of St Mary, but the site has been excavated and the ground plan elucidated.[11] Other religious houses which have since disappeared have also been noted: in Bridge Street stood St Anne's, described in 1695 as the 'old chapel', and which was still standing in the 19th century when it was used as a bark house.[12] Further down the street adjoining Powis's Almshouse was St Ewen's chapel, while in St Thomas's Street was a further chapel of that name, and a number of skeletons unearthed at the corner of Welsh Street and the High Street have indicated the site of its graveyard.[13]

By the early 16th century much of the southern section of the walled area had been deserted, and, as Leland observed, had been 'converted into little medowes and gardens'.[14] The earliest plan of the town, drawn by Millerd in 1686, shows settlement only in the High Street area, while evidence for medieval settlement further south has come from excavation of the former cattle market off Nelson Street (formerly Back Lane).[15] There was, however, some extra-mural development along Moor Street and Welsh Street, with the latter possibly indicating the area occupied by the Welsh after the English borough was founded. Morrice's map of 1800 shows that little change took place in the following century and the whole area east of the church and south of Back Lane was given over to agricultural use. It was only with 19th-century industrial and maritime activity coupled with the arrival of the railway that the whole of the walled area came back into urban use.

1. Wightman, W. E., 'The Palatine Earldom of William fitz Osbern in Gloucestershire and Worcestershire', *E.H.R.*, lxxvii (1962), 12. The suggestion of earlier settlement has been discarded by J. G. Wood (*The Lordship, Castle and Town of Chepstow* [Newport, 1910], 7; Beresford, *New Towns*, 559), although a significant volume of Roman material has emerged from recent excavations and further enquiry may yield more information on pre-Conquest settlement (*see Archaeology in Wales*, xi [1971], 33; xii [1972], 37; xiii [1973], 52; xiv [1974], 42).

2. Perks, J. C., *Chepstow Castle: Official Guide* (H.M.S.O.), 1967. Hogg and King, 'Early Castles', 109. The site is discussed by Morris, *Welsh Wars*, 311.

3. Knowles and Hadcock, *Medieval Religious Houses*, 53, 62.

4. *D.B.*, i, f. 162.

5. Bradney, *History of Monmouthshire*, iv, pt. i, 1.

6. *Ibid.*, 5; *Beresford, New Towns*, 559.

7. *Itinerary*, 43.

8. Perks, *op. cit.*; Coxe, *Historical Tour through Monmouthshire, 1801*, 294.

9. Excavations at ST 533939 (*Archaeology in Wales*, xii [1972], 37) and at ST 534927 (*Ibid.*, xi [1971], 33).

10. *Cal. Close Rolls, 1231-4*, 456.

11. *Archaeology in Wales*, xiv (1974), 42.

12. Bradney, *op. cit.*, 12; Coxe, *op. cit.*, 363-4; Clark,J . H., *History of Monmouthshire* (Usk, 1869), 74,

13. Bradney, *op. cit.*, 23.

14 *Itinerary*, 43; Camden noted both 'fields and orchards' within the town (*Britannia*, 663).

15. *Archaeology in Wales*, xii (1973), 52-3.

CILGERRAN, Dyfed (Pembrokeshire)   SN 195430

Cilgerran lies on the south bank of the Teifi four miles south-east of Cardigan. The town developed in the shadow of the castle which was built on a rising crag at a point where the Teifi is joined by the lesser Afon Plysgog and this was also the highest tidal limit which enabled supplies to be brought in by sea.

Although now little more than a village Cilgerran was previously a settlement of some note and was regarded as a borough, although by prescription only as no charter is known.[1] The regularity of the lay-out, with burgages on either side of the single street, suggests that it was planned, but no details are known and the town's early history is obscure.[2] The parish church of St Llawddog lies at the western end,[3] and this may have been the centre of an early Welsh settlement as

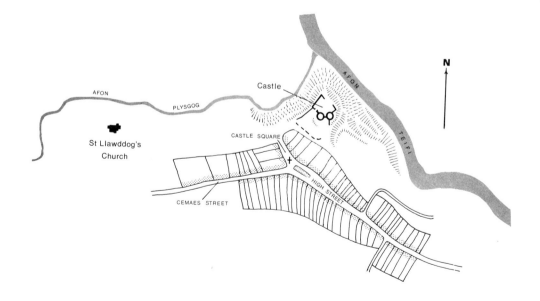

Fig. 26. Cilgerran

the dedication to a 6th-century saint together with the presence of an ogham-inscribed stone indicates a long-standing religious occupation of the site.[4] Documentary evidence, however, is not forthcoming until the mid 12th century; the castle is mentioned in 1166,[5] while the first specific reference to the town dates from 1204.[6] In the mid 13th century after a turbulent history the castle was rebuilt under the direction of William Marshall, and an outer ward added to the defences,[7] but there is no suggestion that further work was also carried out on the borough as only 22 taxpayers appear in 1292 and few of these bore English names.[8] Indeed, although Cilgerran functioned as the administrative centre of an independent lordship until 1536, it was never more than a small town and there is no truth in the fanciful suggestions of former glory advanced by some previous writers.[9] The surviving burgage pattern on the south side of the High Street and the settlement of Cemaes Street probably indicates the main area of medieval settlement with Castle Square representing the site of the weekly market which was held until the early 19th century.[10] Nearby, opposite the present Methodist chapel, stood the town gaol with the stocks and whipping-post outside.[11] Farming and fishing were the principal occupations of the townsfolk, and Cilgerran was particularly noted for the latter, with George Owen describing it as 'the chiefest weir of all Wales'.[12] The weir was located immediately below the castle as also was 'Ty'r goved', the building where the captured fish were taken to be weighed.[13] The coracles operated from the area at the bottom of Rhiw-Dôl-Badau where they can still be seen.

1. Phillips,J . R., *History of Cilgerran* (London, 1914), 37.

2. No archaeological material earlier than the mid 13th century has been forthcoming from the urban area (*R.C.A.M.W.M., Pembs.*, 70; *Arch. Camb.*, 3rd ser., v [1859] , 350).

3. On the history of the church, of which only the tower survives from the medieval period, *see* Phillips, *Cilgerran*, 49–73.

4. *Ibid.*, 50, 70–1; *R.C.A.M.W.M., Pembs.*, 69.

5. *Brut y Tywysogion*, 64; Craster, O. E., *Cilgerran Castle* (Official Guide, H.M.S.O., 1957), 6.

6. *Cal. Pembs. Records*, ii, 2.

7. *Brut y Tywysogion*, 100; Hogg and King, 'Early Castles', 109; *idem*, 'Masonry Castles', 98.

8. *Cal. Pembs. Records*, ii, 10–11.

9. Lewis, *Topographical Dictionary*, *sub* Kilgerren.

10. Speed lists Cilgerran among the principal market towns of Pembrokeshire (*Atlas of Wales, inter* 101–2), but the market had virtually ceased by the early 1900s (Phillips, *Cilgerran*, 46).

11. *Ibid.*, 34.

12. *Description of Pembs.*, i, 117. *See also* Camden, *Britannia*, 655.

13. Phillips, *Cilgerran*, 180.

CONWY, Gwynedd (Caernarfonshire)   SH 782775

Conwy, as an Edwardian borough whose circuit of medieval walls and gates remain virtually complete, has justifiably been termed 'the finest walled town in the country'.[1] The borough was founded in 1283 on the west bank of the River Conwy near its mouth, and almost opposite the earlier English foundation of Degannwy, whose castle had been destroyed in 1263, thus leaving this section of the main route into Gwynedd undefended.[2] The site chosen by Edward I was ideally

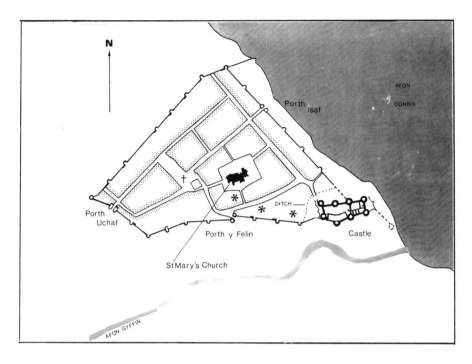

Fig. 27. Conwy

suited for town foundation, a rising spur of land flanked on the east by the Conwy River and on the south by its tributary, the Afon Gyffin, which gave additional defence as well as an outlet to the sea. There is no evidence to suggest any earlier settlement here, although part of the chosen area for the town was already occupied by a Cistercian abbey which had moved here from Rhedynog, near Caernarfon, c. 1192,[3] and was the burial place of several Welsh princes.[4] There was also a princely hall here, known later as 'Llywelyn's Hall', which Edward improved and used as his residence while work continued on the castle.[5] This site was accordingly acquired by the king who compensated the abbey and transferred it to Maenan further up the Conwy valley,[6] although the church was retained for the use of the burgesses and the borough was planned around it.[7]

By 1287 work on both the castle and town had virtually been completed.[8] Settlers had been encouraged to take up residence from the outset and the borough charter had been granted as early as 1284.[9] By 1295 112 burgages had been taken up by 99 burgesses,[10] and by 1312 the number of plots had risen to 124, the highest total recorded for Conwy, which made it about twice the size of Caernarfon, although slightly smaller than Beaumaris.[11] By this date, too, there was already a degree of extra-mural settlement with *placeae* mentioned on Twthill and in the area of the ferry.[12] The borough was enclosed with a wall 1,280m. in length, and along its course 21 half-round towers were built. Spurs at the northernmost and southernmost ends of the section facing the river gave added protection to the

To the Rt. Honble. FRANCIS SEYMOUR CONWAY Lord Conway Baron of Ragley. This Prospect is humbly Inscrib'd by his Lordships most Obedt. Servts. Saml. & Nathl. Buck.

Fig.28.   Conwy. The Edwardian borough as it appeared to the brothers Buck in 1742.

THIS Town is the Conovium of Antonius, seated on the River Conway; or rather the new Town of Conway or Aber-Conway, built about 1282. by K. Edw. I. at the Place where that River emptieth itself into the Sea in the most Northern part of this County, may be said to spring out of the Ruins of the Old Conovium; which stood something higher up the River, and it's memory is preserved by a small Village called Caer-hen or the Old City. In the Year 880. Anarawd Prince of North Wales gain'd a memorable Victory, near this Place, over Cadred ƴ Saxon Duke of Mercia.

AMORE

0. Road to Baumaris
1. Priestholme Isl.

Sam.ᵗ & Nath.ᵗ Buck delin et sculp. Publish'd according to Act of Parliament April 9ᵗ 1742.

Continued in Plate Nᵒ 79

quay. Initially there were three gates, all of which survive: Porth y Felin which provided access to the town mill on the Gyffin; Port Isaf or Lower Gate, leading to the quay; and Porth Uchaf, the principal entrance on the western stretch of wall and giving its name to Upper Gate Street.[13]

Inside the defences it was not possible to achieve a purely regular street-pattern because of the necessity to incorporate the existing church, and because of the course of the Gyffin which forced the southern wall to curve inwards. Rising ground to the west, also, provided an additional problem for the king's planners. The eventual decision was to make the principal streets run parallel to the north and east stretches of the wall with the addition of a third artery leading from Porth Uchaf through the market-place (now Lancaster Square), to Porth Isaf and the quay. A 17th-century view of Conwy suggests that the original pattern has largely survived, but with some later modifications off Chapel Street and High Street, and where the Bangor road later breached the wall.[14] Burgages fronted each of these streets, although the area immediately beyond the castle, the modern Rose Hill Street, does not appear to have been given over to domestic use. Recent excavations in this area have shown that a ditch 24m. wide and at least 9m. deep separated the castle from the borough, while no medieval house remains have been found fronting this street. On the contrary the discovery of substantial foundations between the street and the southern section of the wall suggest that this area was given over to a variety of administrative and judicial buildings.[15] It seems likely that they were destroyed in 1401 when Glyndŵr attacked the town and the area was not subsesequently redeveloped until the 19th century.[16]

After the early 14th century we know little about the size and development of the borough. The full extent of Glyndŵr's destruction is not recorded, although by the end of Henry IV's reign the town had almost fully recovered and only six burgages remained waste.[17] Despite the presence of the quay, however, Conwy did not emerge as an important port, and the absence of any noted industry suggests that it experienced a decline in the post-medieval period. In 1607 it was seriously hit by plague;[18] Camden noted that it was 'not replenished with inhabitants',[19] and by the 1830s large areas within the walls had been given over to gardens and the houses were 'comparatively few'.[20]

1. Hogg and King, Masonry Castles', 99.

2. On the foundation of the town and the building of the castle see R.C.A.M.W.M., Caerns., i, 38-9; King's Works, 337-54; Toy, S., 'The Town and Castle of Conway', Archaeologia, lxxxvi (1936), 163-93.

3. Hays, R., The History of the Abbey of Aberconway (Cardiff, 1963), 5.

4. For a list see Richards, G., 'The Church of St Mary and All Saints, Conway', Journ. Hist. Soc. Church in Wales, xvi (1966), 35.

5. R.C.M.W.M., Caerns., i, 57; Toy, op. cit., 174.

6. Hays, op. cit., 61-77; Ellis, H. (ed.), The Register of the Abbey of Aberconway, Camden Soc., xxxix (1847), 13; Lewis, Medieval Boroughs of Snowdonia, 44-6.

7. It seems likely that the abbey's domestic buildings stood to the north of the church in the area of the Castle hotel where masonry foundations have been noted (Hays, op. cit., 9; R.C.A.M.W.M., Caerns, i, 39; Williams, R., History of Aberconway (Denbigh, 1835), 75.

8. Taylor, A. J., Conway Castle, Official Guide (H.M.S.O., 1956), 3.

9. Lewis, Medieval Boroughs of Snowdonia, 171, 279-81.

10. S.C. 12/17/87; Griffiths, J., 'Documents relating to Conway', *T.C.H.S.*, viii (1947), 6.

11. Lewis, *Medieval Boroughs of Snowdonia*, 66.

12. S.C. 6/1170/4–9; Lewis, *Medieval Boroughs of Snowdonia*, 194.

13. On the walls *see R.C.A.M.W.M., Caerns.*, i, 55–7; Taylor, A. J., 'The Walls of Conway', *Arch. Camb.*, cxix (1970), 1–9; Turner, *Town Defences*, 212–3.

14. Published in Hemp, W. J., 'Conway Castle', *Arch. Camb.*, xcvi (1941), *inter* 168–9.

15. Butler, L. A. S., 'Excavations at Conway, 1961–4', *T.C.H.S.*, xxvi (1965), 20–30.

16. Lloyd, *Owen Glendower*, 37–8.

17. Lewis, *Medieval Boroughs of Snowdonia*, 191.

18. Williams, *History Aberconway*, 51.

19. *Britannia*, 669.

20. Lewis, *Topographical Dictionary, sub* Aberconway.

COWBRIDGE (Y Bontfaen), South Glamorgan   SS 994747

Cowbridge lies along the course of the former Roman road leading to Neath and West Wales. Throughout the medieval period much of the surrounding area was marshland and in a wet season this represented one of the few points at which the River Thaw could be crossed.[1] Not surprisingly, therefore, the antiquity of settlement pre-dates the founding of the 13th-century borough with some prehistoric finds,[2] while of even greater importance are the substantial Roman remains recently discovered which suggest the existence of a civil community within the area of a walled town. This appears to have disappeared by the end of the 4th century, and nothing further is known of settlement here until the creation of the medieval town.[3]

The foundation of medieval Cowbridge was a commercial rather than a military venture and no provision in the form of a castle was made for its defence, that at nearby Llanblethian being thought adequate in times of emergency. The inhabitants claimed their rights from a lost charter of 1254 granted by Richard de Clare,[4] and the borough quickly developed into an important trading centre with its weekly market and annual fairs. From a total of 58 burgages in 1262 the number had risen to 135 within 20 years,[5] and this had doubled to 278 by 1306, placing it among the foremost towns in 14th-century Wales.[6] Probably contemporary with the laying-out of the borough was the building of the church of the Holy Cross (St Mary's), initially a chapel-of-ease to Llanbleddian.[7] The town walls may also have been in existence by the end of the 13th century, though there is no documentary evidence for their construction.[8] In all they enclosed an area of some 30 acres with additional defence in the form of a outer ditch 8m. beyond, the last sections of which were not filled in until 1853. Sections of the wall still remain to the south and west, while other foundations have been periodically noted and the course of the remainder can be determined by the rear line of the former burgages. There were originally four gates, but only the South Gate, repaired in 1805 and 1853, survives. From here a section of the wall extends west and then turns north at the Butts as far as the main road, where stood the West Gate, which was removed in 1754.[9] It then continued northwards to the end of Eagle Lane, where it turned east along North Road. The North Gate was located midway along this stretch, but it was of little importance and John Leland failed even to note it.[10] It was smaller

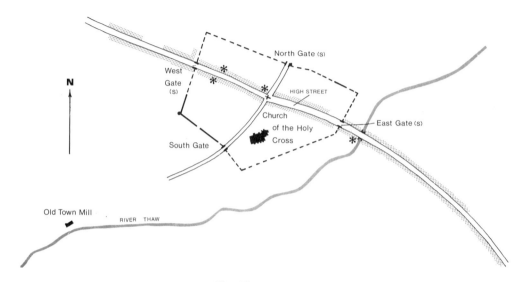

Fig. 29. Cowbridge

than the others and does not appear to have been a 'road gate', its probable function being to provide access to the northern meadows. From here the wall continued eastwards, where some remains are still visible,[11] until finally turning south behind the site of the present town hall to the East Gate which was demolished in 1775. At this point it veered south-west to the corner bastion at the bottom of the grammar school grounds and then west to link up with the South Gate, sometimes called Porth y Felin, since it led to the old town mill on the Thaw (SS 99007442).[12]

Within the walled area the town was laid out in a regular manner with two streets forming a simple cross with a gate at the end of each limb. At the junction stood the town hall which survived until 1830 with the market house adjoining and the market cross to the east.[13] Their eventual removal was necessitated by the increasing importance of the High Street as the principal route through South Wales. This importance also led to the decline of the north–south axis; the southern section of Church Street, formerly called Rood Street, has remained very narrow, while the northern extension leading to the North Gate has disappeared completely.

From the earliest records it is evident that the large number of recorded burgages could not be housed within this comparatively small area. While the size of the plots at Cowbridge is not given, they are well preserved on the north side of the High Street and on their example no more than 70 could have been accommodated, so that there must have been extensive suburban development. John Leland noted that 'the great suburbe' was *cispontem*,[14] referring to the area beyond the East Gate, and this long ribbon settlement was always more important than the west village, which consisted only of about thirty houses at the time the 1841 Tithe Map was drawn.[15] Although still an important town in Leland's time Cowbridge appears to have contracted significantly from its medieval peak with a 16th-century population of no more than about five hundred.[16] Nevertheless, according to Owen, it was still 'good for its bigness'[17] and it remained the main market, social and educational centre of the Vale of Glamorgan until Cardiff regained the ascendancy in the early 19th century.

1. Gunter, M., 'An Ancient Borough', *Vale of Glamorgan Series*, ii (1960), 38.

2. See *Archaeology in Wales*, ix (1960), 10; *B.B.C.S.*, iv (1927-9), 273.

3. *Archaeology in Wales*, xii (1972), 26; xiv (1974), 42; *Morgannwg*, xvii (1973), 59-60.

4. S.C. 6/1202/1; *Glam. County Hist.*, iii, 340; Beresford, *New Towns*, 554. A further charter of privileges was isued in 1324 (*Cal. Ch. Rolls*, iii, 461), which was confirmed in 1359 (*Idem*, v. 164).

5. Clark, *Cartae*, iii, 828.

6. C 134/43.

7. The original chapel was rebuilt in the early 14th century when the tower was added. There was a fishpond in the eastern part of the churchyard which was drained in the late 17th century. Although now known also as St Mary's, the name does not appear in church records until 1884 (Lewis, E., 'Two Vale Churches, Llanblethian and Cowbridge', *Vale of Glamorgan Series*, i [1959], 65-70).

8. Turner, *Town Defences*, 213.

9. Hopkin-James, L. J., *Old Cowbridge* (Cowbridge, 1922), 554.

10. *Itinerary*, 32; Richards, J., *The Cowbridge Story* (Cowbridge, 1956), 144.

11. A short section acts as the rear wall of No 23 High Street, but this is not shown on the Ordnance Survey 1:2500 plan.

12. This building survives in good condition and has been modernised as an outbuilding to 'Old Mill Cottage'.

13. The hall, market and cross are shown on the Dunraven Estate Plan of 1782 (Glam. Record Office, abstract in Moore, P., 'Glamorgan Town Plans', *Glam. Historian*, ix, *inter* 160-1).

14. *Itinerary*, 32.

15. Glam. Record Office.

16. On the late-medieval decline *see Glam. County Hist.*, iii, 355-9.

17. *Description of Pembrokeshire*, iii, 346.

CRICIETH, Gwynedd (Caernarfonshire)   SH 499377

This was an Edwardian castle-borough founded to control Tremadoc Bay and the main coast road into Llŷn and was one of the towns which encircled the old kingdom of Gwynedd. The importance of the site had itself been realised by the Welsh, and there was already a castle occupying an impressive promontory guarded by steep cliffs and the sea on three of its sides. Edward I added to it, but the structure dates essentially from the time of the two Llywelyns,[1] first mention of it being in 1239.[2] Whether there was also a native vill here prior to the creation of the borough is not known, although the church, St Catherine's, is thought to have had a Welsh predecessor.[3]

The castle fell into Edward's hands early in 1283 and the new borough received its first charter in November of the following year.[4] Development was slow, however, with only nine recorded burgesses in 1294,[5] and no attempt was made to wall the town, the castle presumably being thought adequate to protect the small civil community in times of emergency. By 1308 the burgage total had risen to 23, each plot measuring 80ft. by 60ft.,[6] but the highest number recorded was 25 and 5/6ths in 1319,[7] which made it the smallest of the Caernarfonshire boroughs. They were laid out only along Castle Street where some domestic buildings of late 16th-century date can still be discerned.[8] There was virtually no industrial activity in Cricieth and despite its coastal position there was little maritime trade, although it had most of the other borough perquisites, including a mill, a weekly market on Thursdays, two annual fairs,[9] and the right to hold its own courts.[10]

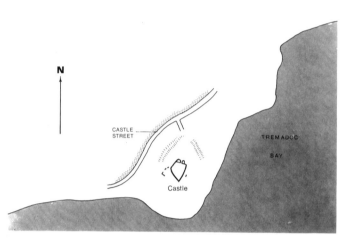

Fig. 30. Cricieth

The later history of the town is that of stagnation followed by decline. In 1404 it was attacked by Owain Glyndŵr and both the castle and the town were put to flames.[11] Although the town had largely recovered by the end of Henry V's reign,[12] the castle was not repaired and the withdrawal of the garrison had profound effects on the economic life of the borough. When John Leland visited Cricieth in the 1530s he noted only 'two or three poore houses' and added that it was 'clene decayed',[13] and almost a century later Speed failed to include it among his list of principal towns in the county.[14] Nevertheless, there had been some recovery in the intervening period, as 20 taxpayers appear in a late 16th-century rent roll, predominantly Welsh, in contrast to the original English inhabitants of the borough.[15] The church was also rebuilt at this time which is suggestive of an increasing population.[16] It seems likely that there was little later growth, however, as indicated by Fenton in the early 19th century when he described it as 'a village . . . and a most wretched place',[17] a view endorsed by Samuel Lewis, who added that the market had ceased to be held.[18]

1. *R.C.A.M.W.M., Caerns.,* ii, 59-62; O'Neil, B. H. St. J., 'Criccieth Castle', *Arch Camb.,* xcviii (1944), 1-51; *King's Works,* 365-7; Hogg and King, Masonry Castles', 99-100; Johns, C. N., *Criccieth Castle,* H.M.S.O. Guide, 1970. For the most recent view on the phases of building and the extent of the Welsh remains, *see* Gresham, C. A., 'The Development of Criccieth Castle', *T.C.H.S.,* xxxiv (1973), 14-22.

2. *Brut y Tywysogion,* 105.

3. Lloyd, J. E., 'The Dedication of Criccieth', *B.B.C.S.,* xii (1946), 26-7. The holy well of the original Celtic saint was at the rear of Holywell Terrace (SH 4992387), although it is now dry (*R.C.A.M.W.M., op. cit.,* 65).

4. *Cal. Ch. Rolls,* ii, 280. The text appears in full in *B.B.C.S.,* iv (1927-9), 229-30, and in part of Lewis, E. A., *Medieval Boroughs of Snowdonia,* 281.

5. *Ibid.,* 195.

6. S.C. 6/1170/6; Lewis, E. A., *op. cit.,* 49.

7. S.C. 6/1170/5; Lewis, E. A., *op. cit.,* 63. The Ministers' Accounts are most accessible in Jones, G., 'Ministers' Accounts for the Borough of Criccieth', *B.B.C.S.,* iii (1926), 62-71.

8. *R.C.A.M.W.M., op. cit.,* 62.

9. Lewis, E. A., *op. cit.*,195-7.

10. *See* Jones, W. G., 'Court Rolls of the Borough of Criccieth', *B.B.C.S.*, ii (1925), 149-60.

11. Lloyd, *Owen Glendower*, 78, 157. Evidence of the burning of the castle was uncovered during clearance of the northern tower (*Arch. Camb.*, xc [1935], 294).

12. Lewis, E. A., *op. cit.*, 134, 196.

13. *Itinerary*, 80, 84, 88.

14. *Atlas of Wales*, 123.

15. Pierce, T. Jones, 'A Criccieth Rent Roll', *T.C.H.S.*, xx (1959), 99-100.

16. Lloyd, J. E., *loc. cit.*

17. *Tours in Wales*, 224.

18. *Topographical Dictionary*, *sub* Cricieth. He described it as 'an inconsiderable village of mean appearance'.

CRICKHOWELL (Crucywel), Powys (Breconshire)   SO 217182

There was a small town here during the late 13th and 14th centuries, but very little is known of its origins and early history. During this period an older motte-and-bailey was replaced by a shell keep.[1] In 1281 the inhabitants received an award of murage, and it is clear from the wording of the grant that the town was already in existence.[2] There is no mention of any resulting defences, however, and there is nothing on the ground to suggest that they were every built. By the late 13th century Crickhowell had already acquired the status of a borough, although no charter is known[3] except for Edward I's confirmation, also in 1281, of existing markets and fairs.[4] Also contemporary with the rebuilding of the castle and the grant of murage was the construction of St Edmund's church which removed the necessity of travelling to St Mary's chapel 1½ miles beyond the town.[5] The building of the church is suggestive of an increasing population, but no lists of taxpayers have survived, while the relationship between the medieval town and the existing street-pattern is a matter for conjecture.

Crickhowell appears to have been a moderately-sized settlement throughout the 14th century which held its own weekly market on Mondays and enjoyed the benefits of several mills and a fishery.[6] In 1403, however, the castle was attacked, and there are no indications that it was rebuilt.[7] The borough accordingly experienced a decline, and by 1610 it was no longer listed as a market town.[8] Recovery was slow, and it is not until the early 19th century that we read of the market being revived,[9] although Fenton regarded it as 'the most cheerful looking town' he ever saw.[10]

1. On the castle *see* King, D. J. C., 'Castles of Breconshire', *Brycheiniog*, vii (1961), 76-7, and Clark, G. T., 'Tretower, Blaen Llynfi and Crickhowell Castles', *Arch. Camb.*, 4th ser., ii (1876), 276-84.

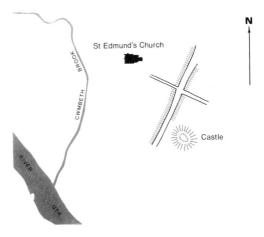

Fig. 31. Crickhowell

2. *Cal. Pat. Rolls*, 1281-92, 2.

3. Rees, W., *Medieval Lordship of Brecon*, 39.

4. *Cal. Ch. Rolls*, ii, 248.

5. The chapel was mentioned by Giraldus Cambrensis (*Opera*, iii, 308). It was later used as a farm building (Lewis, *Topographical Dictionary, sub* Crickhowell).

6. *C.I.P.M.*, iii, 317; Bowen, *Britannia Depicta*, 205.

7. *Cal. Cl. Rolls*, 1402-5, iii; King, *loc. cit.*

8. Speed, *Atlas of Wales, inter* 109-10.

9. Lewis, *loc. cit.*

10. *Tours in Wales*, 25.

DEGANNWY, Gwynedd (Caernarfonshire)   SH 782795

A town was planted at Degannwy by Henry III in the mid-13th century near a castle which had earlier been erected by the Welsh. The stronghold is twice mentioned in the 9th century, in 812 and 823,[1] while it was reputedly the seat of 6th-century ruler Maelgwyn Gwynedd. Recent excavations have shown that it was occupied during this period and even earlier, and some evidence dates from the late Roman period.[2] Late in the 11th century, however, a new castle on this site was built under the direction of Robert of Rhuddlan[3] and although it changed hands several times during the following century, nothing is known of any civil settlement during this period.[4] In 1241, in the face of Henry III's steady advance, Dafydd ap Llywelyn destroyed the stronghold and abandoned the site to the English.[5] Also in the same year, mention of 'tenements at Degannwy' suggests the emergence of a small vill of Welsh origin.[6] The castle was refortified in 1245,[7] and three years later Henry ordered free burgages to be assigned *apud Gannoc*,[8] while markets and fairs were granted in 1250.[9] The new borough received its royal charter in 1252 and this stipulated that 'the burgesses may enclose the said town with a dike and wall',[10] although there are no indications that such work was ever carried out. The whole venture, in fact, was short-lived since in 1263 Degannwy was attacked by Llywelyn ap Gruffudd when the castle, and presumably the nascent town, were destroyed.[11]

This was not completely the end, however, as subsequent references suggest the rebirth of a small commercial community dependent on Edward I's new foundation at Conwy on the opposite side of the river. By 1290 the market had reappeared,[12] and a list of Conwy burgesses drawn up before 1295 includes the names of six men who were *de Gannou*.[13] The monks of Aberconwy, by now moved to Maenan, held part of a weir here,[14] while a rental of 1305-6 lists *19 placeae in villa de Ganneu*, the majority in the hands of English tenants.[15] Just exactly where the settlement was located remains a matter for conjecture, although on topographical grounds it is more likely to have been near the river and the ferry crossing, thus facing a similar extra-mural vill beneath the walls of Conwy, than in the immediate area of the castle itself.

To what extent the township at Degannwy continued to exist throughout the later medieval period is far from clear, although the market was still being held in the late 15th century.[16] As Alcock has aptly obserbed, 'the end of Degannwy remains as enigmatic as its beginning'.[17]

1. *Brut y Tywysogion*, 3–4; *Annales Cambriae*, 12.

2. Alcock, L., 'Excavations at Degannwy Castle, 1961-6', *Arch. Journ.*, cxxiv (1967), 190-201; *Archaeology in Wales*, viii (1968), 20.

3. Orderic Vitalis, *Hist. Eccles.*, viii, 111.

4. *Brut y Tywysogion*, 84, 86, 88.

5. *Annales Cambriae*, 83.

6. *Littere Wallie*, 11.

7. *Brut y Tywysogion*, 107.

8. *Cal. Cl. Rolls*, 1247-51, 55; *Cal. Pat. Rolls*, 1247-58, 84.

9. *Cal. Cl. Rolls*, 1247-51, 314-5.

10. *Cal. Ch. Rolls*, i, 378-9.

11. *Brut y Tywysogion*, 113.

12. *Cal. Anct. Petitions*, 461.

13. Griffiths, J., 'Documents relating to Conway', *T.C.H.S.*, viii (1947), 7.

14. Hays, *History of the Abbey of Aberconway*, 75.

15. Griffiths, *op. cit.*, 15-17.

16. S.C. 6/1181/8; Lewis, *Medieval Boroughs of Snowdonia*, 194.

17. *Op. cit.*, 201.

DENBIGH (Dinbych), Clwyd (Denbighshire)   SJ 052658

Planned settlement at Denbigh dates from the reign of Edward I when a castle and walled borough were established by Henry de Lacy, Earl of Lincoln.[1] There are suggestions of earlier occupation, however, and the hilltop site on which the new town was built is traditionally regarded as the location of Dafydd ap Gruffudd's stronghold.[2]

Henry de Lacy granted the new borough's first charter of privileges in 1285 when 63 burgages are listed.[3] A second charter dating from the period 1295-1305 lists only 45 burgages,[4] the reduction stemming from the attack on the town by the Welsh rebels in 1294,[5] but it does mention the existence of the town walls which are absent from the earlier grant. The castle must also have been substantially completed by 1305 as the castle and walls were planned as a unity to enclose the hilltop area and command control of the Clwyd valley in association with Ruthin, which is of similar date. The walls of Denbigh remain substantially complete, as does the Burgess Gate, the principal entrance to the town, although the Exchequer Gate, the second entrance at the top of Bryn Secour, has since been removed.[6]

It is evident from the wording of the second charter that the new town had already expanded beyond the 9½ acres of the walled area with burgages spreading down the northern slopes of the hill. By 1305, in fact, the extra-mural area had come to outshadow the walled enceinte with some 183 burgages against only 52 within,[7] while by 1334 it had grown to cover an area of 57 acres.[8] Subsequent accounts record even further expansion in this area with 438 burgages recorded in 1373.[9] An early 16th-century survey noted that the suburbs extended for three quarters of a mile north of the castle.[10] The details of this development are fortunately recorded by John Speed in 1610, and his map indicates that the modern street-pattern was already firmly established with development along Love Lane, 'Chappel Lane' (the present Factory Ward area), High Street, 'Sandy Lane' (Beacon's Hill), 'Lower Street' (Vale Street), and 'Parke Lane' (Park Street).[11] The market

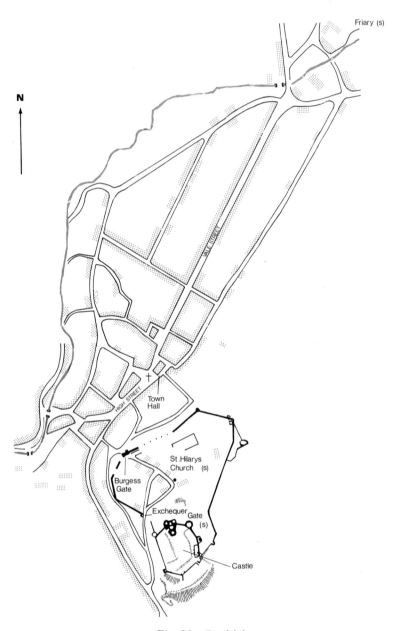

Fig. 32. Denbigh

house and the town cross[12] stood in Crown Square and the economic movement
away from the walled borough is shown by the virtual absence of dwellings within
the walls. St Hilary's chapel was, however, within the walls, although no church
was. The nearest church was at Llanfarchell (St Marcellus),[13] about a mile to the
east and beyond the Carmelite friary which had been founded in the mid-14th

century at the end of Vale Street (SJ 05956658).[14] St Hilary's is mentioned in the 1334 extent of the borough, and it was probably contemporary with the building of the castle and town walls.[15] It continued in use until 1904 when a faculty was obtained for its demolition, although the tower still stands. Near it Speed also shows the Earl of Leicester's church, begun, but never finished, in the 1580s.[17] Apart from a few tenements lining Tower Hill this was all the walled area housed and the decline continued throughout the following century. A drawing of Denbigh by Boydell in 1750, when its population was almost 2,000, shows relatively few buildings within the defences, although by the mid-19th century there had been some redevelopment as Williams (1856) listed as many as 46 cottages here, along Tower Lane, Exchequer Lane, and Castle Lane, the majority of which are no longer standing.[18]

The decline of the walled borough and the early development of substantial suburbs stemmed from the virtual inaccessibility of the chosen town site which was ideally suited to defensive, but not commercial, matters.[19] As early as 1334 records speak of 'a borough within the walls' and a 'market town without'[20] and the rapid growth of the latter in the 14th century testifies to the inadequacy of the Earl of Lincoln's initial scheme. With the market-place, the 16th-century town hall[21] and all the early industry concentrated without, only the chapel of St Hilary and, while it was maintained, the castle, drew the townsfolk up the steep hill to the old borough.

1. For a full account of early Denbigh *see* Owen, D. H., 'Denbigh', in Griffiths, *Boroughs of Medieval Wales*, 164-87. I am grateful to Dr Owen for providing me with a copy of this paper before it appeared in print.

2. Williams, J., *Ancient and Modern Denbigh* (Denbigh, 1856), 14; *R.C.A.M.W.M., Denbs.*, 39-40.

3. D.L. 42/1, ff. 30v, 31r, 31v; Owen, 'Denbigh', 169.

4. The charter is translated in Williams, J., *Ancient and Modern Denbigh*, 302-9.

5. Owen, 'Denbigh', 170.

6. Turner states that the Burgess Gate was the sole entrance to the borough (*Town Defences*, 213), but this is incorrect; the Exchequer Gate is mentioned by Leland (*Itinerary*, 96) and alluded to in a survey of the town drawn up late in the reign of Henry VIII as 'the Gate . . . north-west from the Gate of the Castle' (Williams, J., *Ancient and Modern Denbigh*, 89).

7. D.L. 29/1/2; Owen, 'Denbigh', 170.

8. *Ibid.*, 182; Beresford, *New Towns*, 548.

9. S.C. 6/1183/9; Owen, 'Denbigh', 184.

10. Williams, J., *Ancient and Modern Denbigh*, 90.

11. *Atlas of Wales*, inter 119-20.

12. The cross was *in situ* in the early 19th century (Fenton, *Tours of Wales*, 138), but was subsequently removed to the bowling green near the castle (*R.C.A.M.W.M., Denbs.*, 45).

13. On the church, recorded in 1271, *see* Williams, J., *Ancient and Modern Denbigh*, 342-56; *R.C.A.M.W.M., Denbs.*, 42-3.

14. Evans, W. A., 'The Carmelite Friary in Denbigh', *T.D.H.S.*, iv (1955), 20-5.

15. Williams, J., *The Records of Denbigh and its Lordship* (Wrexham, 1860), 58.

16. Lewis, *Topographical Dictionary*, sub Denbigh; *R.C.A.M.W.M., Denbs.*, 44.

17. For the story of Robert Dudley's abortive attempt to transfer the see of St Asaph to his new church at Denbigh, *see* Williams, J., *Ancient and Modern Denbigh*, 291-4, and Butler, L. A. S., 'Leicester's Church, Denbigh', *Journ. Br. Arch. Assoc.*, 3rd ser., xxvii (1974), 40-62.

To Sr ROBERT SALUSBURY COTTON, Bart
This Prospect is most gratefully Inscrib'd by
his much Oblig'd & very humble Servts
Saml & Nath Buck.

Fig. 33.   Denbigh
This view of 1742 shows the walled town to the south all but deserted. The first borough charter was granted by
Henry de Lacy in 1285 but within 20 years the extra-mural settlement was already four times greater than that
within the defences.

THIS *Abby of Black Monks of the Order of S.ᵗ Benedict was founded and endow'd by Adam Salusbury, in or about the time (as is suppos'd) of K. Hen: III. The Proprietor is S.ʳ Rob.ᵗ Salusbury Cotton Bar.ᵗ*

Sam.ˡ & Nath.ˡ Buck del. et sculp. Publish'd according to Act of Parliament April 9.ᵗʰ 1742.

1. Denbigh Town & Castle

18. This redevelopment is also indicated by Lewis, *Topographical Dictionary*, *sub* Denbigh.
19. This aspect is discussed by Carter, *Towns of Wales*, 201–5.
20. Williams, J., *Records of Denbigh*, 58.
21. Now the County Hall, the town hall was built on land granted for that purpose by Robert Dudley (Williams, J., *Ancient and Modern Denbigh*, 97–8).

DINAS MAWDDWY, Gwynedd (Merionethshire)   SJ 859149

Dinas Mawddwy occupies a river valley site in the south-eastern corner of Meirionnydd, near the confluence of the Rivers Cerist and Dyfi, the whole bounded on the west by the pass of Bwlch oer ddrws and on the north-east by that of Bwlch-y-Groes. Although no more than a village, the township was of greater importance during the medieval period when it served as the *caput* of the lordship of Mawddwy with its weekly market and several annual fairs.[1]

The origins of the town are obscure through the absence of both historical and archaeological evidence, and its exact legal status has been viewed with uncertainty. It enjoyed a variety of corporate privileges until the late 19th century, but there is no record of it being granted borough privileges. Since Mawddwy was not incorporated into Merioneth until 1536 nothing is forthcoming from documents such as the Subsidy Roll of 1292–3 which shed useful light on other boroughs in the county. There is, however, a 17th-century transcript made by Richard Vaughan of Hengwrt (1592–1667) of an *inspeximus* of 1423 by Hugh Burgh, Lord of Mawddwy, inspecting the charter of his father-in-law, John Mawddwy, granted in 1393. This specifically refers to Dinas Mawddwy as a borough and lists some 35 burgesses, overwhelmingly Welsh, as already residing there. There seems no reason to doubt the authenticity of the transcript, although the matter was investigated by the Municipal Corporations Commissioners in 1834 and again in 1880, but they were unable to confirm borough status and all corporate privileges were withdrawn in 1886.[2]

Although medieval Dinas Mawddwy was an important local centre with its commercial and administrative functions, it remained a small settlement, as indicated by the 35 burgesses recorded in 1393. This number could easily be accommodated within the area of the present village. Indeed, traces of the former plots are visible at its southern end. On the contrary, there may have been some contraction since only 14 burgesses were recorded as living within the liberty of the borough in 1592.[3] The settlement does not

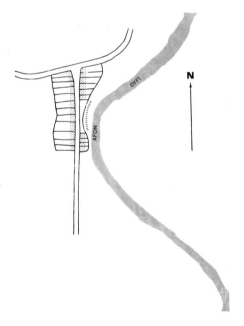

Fig. 34. Dinas Mawddwy

appear to have been defended, although there may have been a motte immediately to the south in a field known as Cae'r Bryn between the *Buckley Arms* hotel and the old Minllyn School-Room, now a youth hostel.[4]

The later history of the town is vague and unimpressive. While the corporation continued to exercise its various privileges they had little real significance,[5] and by the early 19th century even the market had virtually ceased to exist.[6] Fenton described the place as 'a miserable collection of mean houses making one street',[7] and it is unlikely to ever have been much more.

1. The general history of the town is related in Ashton, C., *A Guide to Dinas Mawddwy* (Aberystwyth), 1893.

2. Charles, B. G., 'Court Rolls of the borough of Dinas Mawddwy and the manor of Mawddwy', *J.M.H.R.S.*, i (1949), 44–68.

3. *Ibid.*, 48, citing *Llyfr John Brooke o Vawddwy* (Nat. Lib. Wales MS. 872), 394–6.

4. There are no documentary references to this supposed motte although inspection of the site revealed a definite mound and possible ditch which do not appear to be natural features.

5. On the surviving vestiges *see* Bridgeman, G. T. O., 'Relics of Dinas Mawddwy', *Mont. Coll.*, i (1868), 424; Owen, H. J., *Echoes of Old Merioneth* (Dolgellau, 1944), 15–23.

6. Lewis, *Topographical Dictionary*, sub Dinas Mowddwy.

7. *Tours in Wales*, 88.

DINEFWR, Dyfed (Carmarthenshire)   SN 611217

Nothing now remains of this medieval town which developed alongside the impressive Dinefwr Castle, some two miles west of Llandeilo. The stronghold,[1] occupying a hillside site which rises steeply above the Tywi, is mentioned in 1163 when it was seized by Rhys ap Gruffydd along with the rest of Cantref Mawr,[2] and it is generally recognised that the native princes of Deheubarth had resided here for at least the preceding two centuries.[3] There is no record of a dependent vill at this early date, however, and the first references to the town belong to the late 13th century with the appearance of burgages. In 1298–1300 the 'antiqua villa de Dynnevor' contained 26 plots, each rendering 6d. a year against the usual 1s., and there was also a mill and an annual fair together worth 31s. 8d.[4] Just how old the vill was is a matter of conjecture; it may have been a reorganised Welsh *tref* as at a number of similar sites like Llandeilo (q.v.) and Adpar (q.v.), or it may date from the late 12th or early 13th centuries when the castle was rebuilt. It certainly appears to have been of Welsh origin, however, and it is interesting that the tenants listed in a rental of 1302–3 were exclusively Welsh, while those of Dinefwr Newtown (Y Drenewydd), which had been founded in 1298 to the north of the original vill, were, with three or four exceptions, exclusively English.[5] By 1302 the latter had grown to some 60 holdings,[6] development which may partly have been at the expense of the Welsh town which had shrunk to only 11 burgages in 1301-2.[7] The new borough was badly burnt during the revolt of Llywelyn Bren in 1316,[8] but soon recovered, and the succeeding years also saw a revival of Old Dinefwr since in 1359 it was valued at £8 as against the £13 returned by the Newtown.[9]

Despite the satisfactory level of documentation concerning the two medieval settlements their eventual total disappearance coupled with the absence of archaeological activity in the area has left their exact locations open to doubt.[10] The site of the original Welsh Dinefwr presents the most difficulty although it was evidently in the area of the castle—perhaps within the bailey itself or immediately to the north where there is sufficient ground on the hilltop for burgages to be accommodated. The Newtown is known to have been planted further north and was separated from the castle by the lord's demesne lands. In the Exchequer Accounts of 1532 we learn that the newly-built mansion of Sir Rhys ap Thomas, 'Dynevor Castle', 'standith within the towne of Newtown'[11] and it is to be assumed that this building and its grounds occupy the area of the former borough which gradually declined after its sacking by Glyndŵr in 1403.[12] John Leland described it in the 1530s as consisting of 'one long street now ruinous,'[13] while Fenton (1804-13) added that the town lay on the west side of the mansion, although he does not add if any remains were still visible.[14] Traces of house platforms can still be detected on the east side also, however, flanking the track from Llandeilo,[15] and if Fenton can be relied upon, the mansion must occupy a central position along the course of the 'long strete'.

1. On the castle *see R.C.A.M.W.M., Carms.*, 107-9; *King's Works*, 633-4; Hogg and King, 'Early Castles', 110; *idem.*, 'Masonry Castles', 101.

2. *Brut y Tywysogion*, 62; *Annales Cambriae*, 69.

3. Giraldus, *Itin. Kamb.*, 80-1; Lloyd, J. E., *History of Carmarthenshire*, i, 147-8.

4. Rhys, *Minister's Accounts for West Wales*, 71, 89, 305.

5. Lewis, E. A., 'Records of Dynevor', *Trans. Hist. Soc. West Wales*, i (1911), 181-3. The foundation date is indicated by the entry which states that the new burgesses held their lands rent-free for the first seven years and 1304 is given as the sixth year (Rhys, *Minister's Accounts for West Wales*, 307).

6. S.C. 11/773; Beresford, *New Towns*, 544.

7. Rhys, *Minister's Accounts for West Wales*, 305, 373; Lewis, E. A., 'Chamberlain's Accounts for West Wales', *B.B.C.S.*, ii (1925), 73-4.

8. S.C 6/1219/5; Lewis, E. A., 'Records of Dynevor', *op. cit.*, i, 190; *Annales Cambriae*, 109; Griffiths, R. A., 'The Revolt of Rhys ap Maredudd, 1287-88', *W.H.R.*, iii (1966), 129. The destruction was sufficient for the townsfolk to be exempted from payment of a fifteenth tax in 1318 (*Cal. Pat. Rolls*, 1317-21, 266).

9. S.C. 6/1221/12; Lewis, E. A., 'Records of Dynevor', *op. cit.*, i, 209.

10. The only stray finds recorded from Dinefwr consist of a collection of Roman *denarii* from the Mansion House at SN 614224 (*R.C.A.M.W.M., Carms.*, 111).

11. Lewis, E. A., 'Records of Dynevor', ii (1912), 209.

12. *Ibid.*, 106; *Royal and Hist. Letters of Henry IV*, i, No. lx; Lloyd, *Owen Glendower*, 65.

13. *Itinerary*, 57.

14. *Tours in Wales*, 62. No traces of the borough are shown on the Tithe Map of 1841 (Llandyfeisant Parish, Carmarthen Record Office).

15. I am grateful to Mr Dilwyn Jones for bringing notice of these to my attention.

DISERTH, Clwyd (Flintshire)   SJ 060799

In 1241 Henry III began work on Diserth Castle,[1] known also as 'Dincolyn' or 'Caerfaelan', following the abandonment of an earlier scheme at a site further north.[2] The king chose for his site a steep hill 60m. above sea level which commanded extensive views over part of the Vale of Clwyd and the Irish Sea, and

Fig. 35. Diserth Castle

The castle, in the centre of this aerial view (58/RAF/2196), has been subjected to
intensive quarrying. The site of the lost borough planted here by Henry III in 1248-51
probably lay beyond the main entrance (marked).

which had been occupied intermittently since Neolithic times.[3] By 1248 work
had been virtually completed and in the same year prospective tenants were
invited to take up burgages 'near the castle', although the exact number of plots
is not stated.[4] Three years later the new borough was given the liberties of
Chester,[5] but its development was arrested in July 1263 when a Welsh force
under Gruffudd ap Madog completely destroyed the castle and probably most
of the town along with it.[6] The castle does not appear to have been refortified:
excavations have produced no finds later than the 13th century, while by 1292
the number of taxpayers in the borough had dwindled to twelve.[7]

It seems unlikely that the planned borough was laid out in the area of the
present village of Diserth, which lies half a mile to the south-west of the castle.
Admittedly, the church there is medieval, but its dedication to St Bridget
(Welsh Ffraid) together with the presence of two early crosses in the churchyard[8] and the appearance of vill of 'Dincolyn' in Domesday Book, points to
a pre-Conquest origin.[9] Moreover, the distance from the castle and the nature
of the intervening topography with the land rising very steeply is such that the
burgesses would not have been able to seek shelter there in times of unrest.
Since the burgages offered in 1248 were also 'near the castle' the likely spot
for the borough would appear to be the sheltered slopes immediately to the east
and south-east of the castle entrance, where the remains of a medieval building
known as Siambr Wen can still be seen.[10]

1. *Brut y Tywysogion*, 105. For an account of the castle, much of which has largely disappeared as a result of quarrying operations, *see* Edwards, T., *Arch. Camb.*, xii (1912), 263-94,
and Glenn, T. A., *et al.*, *ibid.*, xv (1915), 49-86, 249-52.
    2. *Cal. Pat. Rolls*, 1232-47, 258; *Cal. Lib. Rolls*, ii, 129.
    3. For the finds *see* Glenn, T. A., *loc. cit.*, and the summary in Davies, E., *The Prehistoric
and Roman Remains of Flintshire* (Cardiff, 1949), 108-17.
    4. *Cal. Cl. Rolls*, 1247-51, 55.
    5. *Cal. Pat. Rolls*, 1247-58, 84.
    6. *Annales Cambriae*, 101. During the excavations of 1914 evidence of the siege, including
quantities of molten lead, were discovered by T. A. Glenn.
    7. E 179/242/52.
    8. *R.C.A.M.W.M.*, *Flints.*, 22-4. The church is recorded in 1284 (*Littere Wallie*, 61).
    9. *D.B.*, i, f. 269a.
    10. The remains lie 200m. south of the castle near the course of the old Mineral Railway line.
For a description of them *see* *R.C.A.M.W.M.*, *Flints.*, 21-2.

DOLFORWYN, Powys (Montgomeryshire)   SO 153951

The site of the castle and attempted borough lies half a mile north of
Abermule on the opposite side of the Severn. Both were the work of Llywelyn
ap Gruffudd, who began operations on the castle in 1273, perhaps on the site
of an earlier structure,[1] and much to the annoyance of the English authorities
who issued an 'Inhibition . . . of his erecting a castle at Abrunol (Abermule) . . .
or a borough or town there, or a market . . . as the king learns that he proposes
to erect anew the said castle . . . and a borough or town and market',[2] Llywelyn
continued the work, however, and in 1277 the castle was besieged and taken by

Roger de Mortimer.[3] The 'vill of Dolforwyn' is specifically mentioned in the following year,[4] but nothing is known of its size or even its exact location. It must have been very small, perhaps, as Beresford suggests, located on the same hilltop as the castle,[5] and parallels may be drawn with Cefnllys and Bere. Just how long this 'town' continued to exist is a matter of conjecture, although an inventory of the castle contents taken in 1312-2 mentions an adjoining grange together with a variety of agricultural implements and land under cultivation which suggests the presence of a civil community.[6] It is usual to consider the castle as destroyed early, but it was still tenanted in 1383, and the borough may equally have lingered on until the end of the century.[7]

1. *R.C.A.M.W.M., Mont.*, 8–9; Hogg and King, 'Masonry Castles', 102; Spurgeon, C. J., 'The Castles of Montgomeryshire', *Mont. Coll.*, lix (1965-6), 39–42; On the documentation relating to the castle *see* Williams, R., 'Early Documents relating to Dolforwyn Castle', *ibid.*, xxviii (1894), 145-64.
2. *Cal. Cl. Rolls*, 1272-9, 51; For Llywelyn's reply, *see Cal. Anct. Corresp.*, 86.
3. *Brut y Tywysogion*, 118; Morris, *Welsh Wars*, 121. His tenure of the castle was confirmed in 1279, *Cal. Ch. Rolls*, ii, 211.
4. Davies, J. C. (ed.), *The Welsh Assize Roll of 1277-84*, B.C.S., Hist. and Law Ser., vii (Cardiff, 1940), 241, 255-6.
5. *New Towns*, 563; Spurgeon, *op. cit.*, 40.
6. Williams, R., *op. cit.*, 151-3.
7. *Cal. Pat. Rolls, 1381-5*, 318; By 1398, however, the castle was 'ruinous and worth nothing' (Chancery I.P.M., 5 Ric. II, No. 43, m. 32).

DOLGELLAU, Gwynedd (Merionethshire)   SH 729177

Dolgellau lies on the south bank of the River Maw and occupies a low-lying site in an area of predominantly high ground dominated by the formidable Cader Idris. Although the position is 12 miles inland from Cardigan Bay the Maw at this point is still navigable by small vessels, and it was by water that Dolgellau has been served for the greater part of its existence.

Unlike other medieval towns in Merionnydd, like Bala and Harlech, Dolgellau was not a planned borough, although its development owed much to the English conquest. Its early growth appears to have been organic with the appearance of a small native 'tref' at the bridgehead on the eastern side of St Mary's church. This was far from substantial, however, and at the time of Edward I's victory it was the smallest of vills with only three taxpayers recorded in 1292-3.[1] During the following century, though, Dolgellau experienced a period of pronounced growth when it was made the seat of the local hundred or commot court and with its weekly market it grew steadily to emerge as the principal town in the area.[2] This was a gradual process, however, and the ensuing street-pattern is haphazard and lacks the regularity of most medieval towns in Wales.

By the mid-16th century Dolgellau had come to overshadow Bala and the three taxpayers recorded in 1292-3 had grown to about twenty-three[3] by 1543. John Leland described it as 'the best village of this commote' and in the economic sphere it was known for the manufacture of coarse woollen cloth.

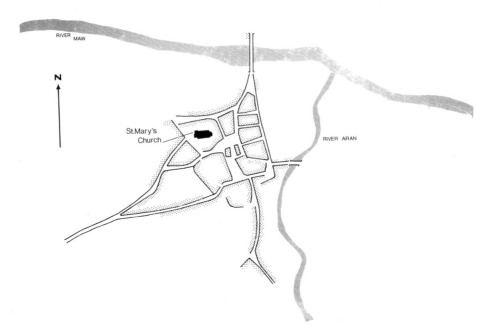

Fig. 36. Dolgellau

In 1552 the town was leased to one Lewis Owen for an annual farm of 38s. 4d., a respectable amount which indicates its growing importance.[5] The weekly market had developed considerably with stalls occupying large tracts of the surrounding waste ground, and there were now three annual fairs.[6] Other features of this steady urban development included the building of a gaol (at the rear of the *Clifton* hotel), and the almshouses, demolished in 1962 (to the west of the church off Marian Road). There was even a cock-fighting pit to the north-west of the town in the present Marian Mawr Recreation Ground.[7] Despite this growth, however, Dolgellau boasts no borough charter, although early-17th-century records invariably refer to the town as a borough and to the tenements as burgages.[8]

In the political sphere Dolgellau has little political history and even its association with Owain Glyndŵr and his so-called 'Parliament House'—'Cwrt Plas yn y Dre'—is now considered dubious.[9] The remoteness of the site has confined its importance to its immediate locality and restricted further growth; as late as 1832 Samuel Lewis observed that most goods and foodstuffs had still to be shipped from Liverpool to Barmouth and then conveyed up the Maw in smaller vessels.[10] The first satisfactory town plan drawn up a decade later shows that it did not then extend further south than Cader Road, except for Meyrick Street which was gradually being developed, and that there had been little growth on the east side of the River Aran.[11]

1. William-Jones, K. (ed.), *The Merioneth Lay Subsidy Roll of 1292/3*, xlvi, 49–50.
2. *Rec. of Carn.*, 136, 142.
3. William-Jones, *op. cit.*, xlvi–xlvii.

4. *Itinerary*, 77.

5. Lewis, E. A. and Davies, J. C. (eds.), *Records of the Court of Augmentations*, 430.

6. Jones, T. I. J. (ed.), *Exchequer Proceedings Concerning Wales tempore James I*, B.C.S., Hist and Law ser., xv (Cardiff, 1955), 224–5.

7. Known locally as 'Pant y Ceiliogod', the outlines of the pit were still visible in the early 1900s, but it can no longer be distinguished.

8. Jones, T. I. J., *op. cit.*, and 237.

9. On this building, which was later re-erected at Dolerw, Newtown, *see* Breese, E., *Arch. Camb.*, 4th ser., vii (1876), 135–41, and Owen, H. J., *J.M.H.R.S.*, ii (1954), 81–88.

10. *Topographical Dictionary*, *sub* Dolgelley.

11. Dolgellau Tithe Map of 1841, County Record Office, Dolgellau.

DRYSLWYN, Dyfed (Carmarthenshire)   SN 554204

The remains of Dryslwyn castle lie on the north bank of the Afon Tywi, 4½ miles west of Llandeilo.[1] During the 14th century there was also a small borough here, but this has all but disappeared, and the existing settlement consists only of a scattering of cottages to the north of the castle.

The origins of both are slightly obscure, but the castle at least was of Welsh foundation. It is mentioned in 1246, and in 1271, when control passed to Rhys ap Maredudd; the *Brut*, also refers to the 'town'.[3] After Rhys forfeited his lands to Edward I following the unsuccessful revolt of 1287,[4] it seems likely that the town was enlarged and reorganised along English lines with burgages laid out both within the castle defences and along the road down to the old ford. The Constable's Accounts for 1287–89 include expenditure on the ditch surrounding the castle and town,[5] while there are also references to the *villa subtus castrum de Drusselan*.[6]

By the end of the 13th century Dryslwyn had developed into a borough of 43 burgages with a mill and its own annual fair, and the burgesses were said to hold their lands *per cartam regis*.[7] This size was maintained throughout the following century with perhaps a little growth since in 1360 there were 34 burgages within the castle defences and a further 14 below in 'Briggestrete'.[8] The latter must correspond to the present road on the west side of the castle which formerly led to the ford 100m. east of the modern bridge.[9] In 1403, however, the castle was captured by Owain Glyndŵr and the absence of later references

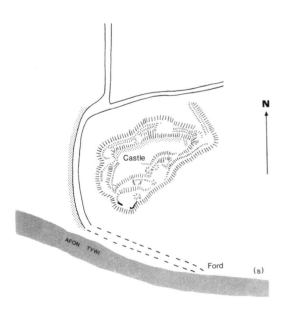

Fig. 37. Dryslwyn

to the community suggests that it was destroyed at that time and failed to recover.[10]

1. On the castle *see* Hogg and King, 'Masonry Castles', 102; *R.C.A.M.W.M., Carm.*, 155–6.

2. *Annales Cambriae*, 86.

3. *Brut Y Tywysogion*, 116.

4. Morris, *Welsh Wars*, 206–13; Griffiths, R. A., 'The Revolt of Rhys ap Maredudd', *op. cit.*, 122, 133.

5. Rhys, *Minister's Accounts for West Wales*, 41.

6. Lewis, E. A., 'Chamberlain's Accounts for West Wales', *op. cit.*, 73.

7. *Idem*; Rhys, *Minister's Accounts for West Wales*, 71, 89, 195; Griffiths, R. A., *op. cit.*, 141–2. Nothing is known of the charter alluded to in 1287–9, and the first detailed grant of privileges dates from 1324 (*Cal. Ch. Rolls*, iii, 461).

8. S.C. 6/1158/10.

9. The position of the ford is clearly shown on the 1841 Tithe Map, while the track to it is still detectable on the ground (Llangathen Parish, Nat. Lib. Wales).

10. Ellis, H., *Original Letters illustrative of English History*, 2nd ser., i, 20.

FISHGUARD (Abergwaun), Dyfed (Pembrokeshire)   SM 958370

A cloud of obscurity surrounds the early history of Fishguard, and very little is known beyond the circumstances of the town's foundation by the Normans in the late 11th century. Martin de Tours granted 'Abergwaun' to Jordan de Cantington along with the surrounding area which came to form the lordship of Cemaes.[1] There is no indication, however, of the town's early size or of any defences, although the most likely position for the settlement would have been in the area of St Mary's church. While the present building dates only from the mid-19th century the existence of the church is known from *c.* 1300,[2] while the outline of the adjoining market-place can be detected amid the street-pattern immediately to the south. The Tithe Map of 1844 shows that this was then the built-up area with the outline of the medieval field system of strip cultivation visible below the Square between the High Street and Wallis Street, land which has since been developed.[3]

Fig. 38. Fishguard

The virtual absence of early documentation suggests that medieval Fishguard was among the smallest of towns and even its status is uncertain. E. A. Lewis regarded it as a doubtful example of a borough[4] and it was not included by the author of a study of Pembrokeshire boroughs.[5] In 1835, however, the Municipal Corporations Commissioners referred to a tradition of borough status and cited a survey of 1653 which regarded the town as such and the holdings as burgages.[6]

1. Owen, G., *Baronia de Kemeys* (London, 1861), 52–3; *Cal. Pembs. Records*, iii, 6.

2. *Cal. Papal Registers*, 1305–42, 81.

3. Nat. Lib. Wales, *Map Coll.*, No. 94.

Fig. 39. Fishguard

A print of 1797 showing the early town confined to the rising ground above the bay.

4. *Medieval Boroughs of Snowdonia*, 16.
5. Sudbury, P. G., 'The Medieval Boroughs of Pembrokeshire', Univ. of Wales M.A. (1947), unpublished, 5.
6. *Report of the Royal Commission on Municipal Corporations*, Appendix I, 229.

FLINT (Y Fflint), Clwyd (Flintshire)   SJ 244730

Flint was the first of Edward I's Welsh bastides, and work began on both the castle and town defences in July 1277.[1] The chosen site was that of a rising outcrop of sandstone which was easily defensible, and, equally important, one that could be reached and supplied by sea.[2] The castle, designed with an inner and outer ward, was constructed at the northern apex,[3] and it could still be reached by sizeable vessels as late as the mid–19th century.[4] Immediately below it appears to have been a stretch of marshland rather than an outer ditch as once thought, with access to the town itself by means of a raised causeway.[5] The town was laid out in the fashion of a regular parallelogram as Speed indicates on his plan of 1610, although the original street-pattern had since been disturbed by the building of the Chester to Holyhead railway which bisected the medieval kernel and necessitated the construction of Corporation Street.[6]

Like its neighbour, Rhuddlan, Flint was enclosed with earthen rather than stone defences. This had been one of the initial tasks facing Edward I's workmen,[7] although their construction did not prevent the new borough—the charter was granted in September 1284[8]—from being burnt during the Welsh War of 1294-5 with a sizeable £300 worth of damages.[9] Nevertheless the defences were impressive, consisting of a double bank further protected by a flat-bottomed outer ditch which recent excavations have shown to have been 13.7m. wide and 2.7m. deep.[10] Some sections of the bank can still be traced at various points,[11] while its overall course is indicated by the lines of Swan Street and Duke Street on the east, Coleshill and Chapel Streets on the south, and on the west side by Earl Street.

Likewise with Rhuddlan, however, Flint's development did not live up to its original expectations. The population was probably at its height in the early 14th century,[12] and although the number of burgesses is not given they regularly rendered £36 for their lands in this period, which indicates a flourishing community.[13] But in 1400 the borough was ravaged by the Glyndŵr rebels and it was unable to achieve a speedy recovery.[14] John Speed, although indicating the full outline of the street-pattern and the course of the defences shows only about 60 buildings other than the castle and church and overall the town has a distinctly rural atmosphere.[15] The town hall is marked, but this was an Elizabethan structure and the apparent absence of a medieval predecessor is suggestive of this lack of urban character.[16] Two centuries later (1800) a drawing of the church by Parkes (although the building occupied a central position within the walled area), shows it surrounded by open space and gardens[17] and it was not until the late 18th and early 19th centuries with the development of the North Wales coalfield and its associated industries, that Flint reassumed the character and functions originally intended by its founder.

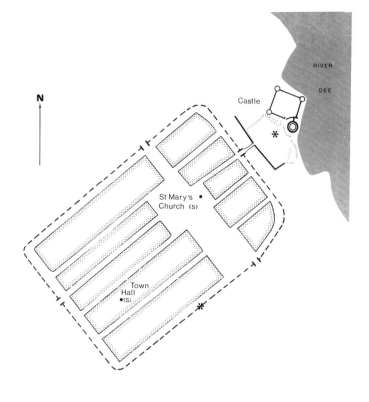

Fig. 40.   Flint

1. Edwards, J. G., 'The Building of Flint', *J.F.H.S.*, xii (1951), 5-20; *idem*, 'Edward I's Castle Building in Wales', *Proc. Br. Acad.*, xxxii (1944), 15-81; *King's Works*, 308-18.

2. Carter, *Towns of Wales*, 167-9.

3. On the castle *see* Hemp, W. J., *Flint Castle*, Official Guide (H.M.S.O., 1929), and Simpson, W. D., 'Flint Castle', *Arch. Camb.*, xcv (1940), 20-6.

4. This is clear from the drawing by J. Wrightson in Roscoe, T., *Wanderings in North Wales* (1836), facing p. 47.

5. Craster, O. E., 'The Supposed Outer Ditch of Flint Castle', *J. F. H. S.*, xxii (1965-6), 71-4.

6. Taylor, H., *Historic Notices of Flint* (London, 1883), 209.

7. *Brut y Tywysogion*, 118-9; *King's Works*, 310.

8. *Cal. Ch. Rolls*, ii, 277.

9. *Cal. Anct. Petitions*, 177.

10. *Archaeology in Wales*, xi (1971), No. 43.

11. *Idem*; *R.C.A.M.W.M., Flints.*, 29.

12. Beresford, *New Towns*, 550.

13. In 1301-2 the figure was £36 10s. 2d., while in 1347-8 it stood at £36 19s. 8d. (Jones, A. [ed.], *Flintshire Ministers' Accounts*, i, 1301-28, 5; ii, 1328-53, 15).

14. Lloyd, *Owen Glendower*, 32.

15. *Atlas of Wales*, inter 121-2.

16. Taylor, *Historic Notices of Flint*, 179. A new town hall was built on the same site in 1840.

17. The drawing is reproduced in Taylor, *op. cit.*, 119. The original medieval church was demolished in 1847 (*ibid.*, 207-8, 210; *R.C.A.M.W.M., Flints.*, 28).

GROSMONT (Y Grysmwnt), Gwent (Monmouthshire)   SO 406243

The village occupies an area of rising ground on the west bank of the Monnow where the river makes a sharp bend, and derives its name from the Graig, the nearby 'Gros Mont', or 'Great Hill'. Together with Skenfrith and Whitecastle, Grosmont castle was an important key to the control of Upper Gwent, and the creation of the town was a consequence of this defensive function. Unfortunately the foundation dates of both are unknown: the castle is mentioned in 1163,[1] but may have been in existence before 1137 when King Stephen acquired Grosmont, and there is no record of a borough charter. The borough was evidently later than the castle, however, and may date from 1219 when Reginald de Braose is recorded as clearing the wood,[2] perhaps to make room for the burgages. Certainly the town was well established by 1250 when borough rents amounted to £8 8s. 3d., suggesting as many as 160 plots.[3]

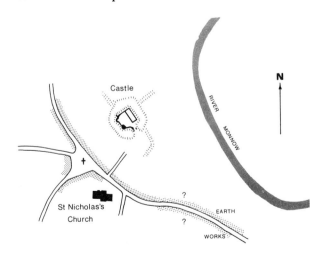

Fig. 41. Grosmont

It is clear from the modest nature of the present settlement that early medieval Grosmont must have been much more extensive than its modern successor. The size of St Nicholas's church, enlarged by Eleanor of Provence in the late 13th century, is a reflection of this former importance, as is also the value of the twice-weekly market held in the (since encroached upon) triangular market-place beyond. The Duchy of Lancaster Surveys (1609-13) record several cottages to the east of the castle,[4] but this area has since reverted to woodland. The borough also appears to have extended further along the principal street. William Coxe noted a number of deserted roads and causeways leading from the village,[5] and ribbon development along the road south to Lower Tresenny is suggested by the presence of earthworks still noticeable in the adjoining fields.

Very little is known of the later history of the borough and the reason for its decline must be linked with the eventual abandonment of the castle allied to the destruction caused by the Glyndŵr rebels in 1405, which appears to have been considerable.[6]

1. *Pipe Roll*, 10 Hen. II, 6.
2. *Cal. Anct. Corresp.*, 8.
3. *Cal. Inq. Misc.*, i, 1219-1307, 28; Beresford, *New Towns*, 559.
4. Rees, W. (ed.), *A Survey of the Duchy of Lancaster Lordships in Wales, 1609-13*, B.C.S., Hist. and Law Ser., xii (1953), 77.
5. *A Historical Tour through Monmouthshire*, 1801, 272.
6. Lloyd, *Owen Glendower*, 96.

HARLECH, Gwynedd (Merionethshire)   SH 582311

The castle and town of Harlech both occupy an impressive promontory site which overlooks Tremadoc Bay and across the Llŷn Peninsula. They were jointly conceived as part of the chain of castle-boroughs intended to encircle North Wales. Building operations began in 1283 and progress was sufficiently rapid for the new borough to receive its royal charter in the following year.[1] Despite the grandeur of the castle, which was largely complete by 1289,[2] the town proved to be the smallest of the Edwardian planned boroughs and only 12 taxpayers appear in the Subsidy Roll of 1292-3.[3] By 1305 the burgage total stood at 24½, and by 1312 it had risen to 29,[4] but neither figure suggests that the population of the community exceeded 150 persons.

Like nearby Cricieth the medieval settlement at Harlech was a poor companion to its splendid castle, although it had its commercial and administrative functions since both the hundred court and the county sessions met here, and there was also a weekly market on Saturdays together with four annual fairs.[5] No attempt was made to wall the borough, however, a decision which must have been regretted after Glyndŵr's attack when 46 houses, virtually the whole town, were destroyed.[6] Neither was a church built within the area of the early town, although there was a medieval chapel which Speed (1610) marks as standing in Stryd Fawr, immediately to the east of the castle in the area of the modern hotel.[7] He adds that the building was then 'decayed and without use',[8] and no traces of it remain, although its site appears to correspond with the area of the hotel car park since this land appears on the 1843 Tithe Map as 'Chapel Yard'.[9] Attached to the chapel was a small graveyard, and several burials were unearthed during building operations in 1808.[10] Few other vestiges of urban life are recorded. The borough had its mill, mentioned as early as 1305,[11] and Speed shows its position as beyond the north-eastern corner of the castle where the land falls sharply down to the caravan park. There was also an early town hall, but its site is not known; the building was ruinous at the beginning of the 19th century, and its site had been built on by 1813.[12]

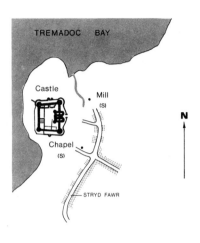

Fig. 42. Harlech

The later history of Harlech is poorly documented and appears to have been uneventful except for the role of the castle during the Wars of the Roses and the Civil War. Speed's plan suggests that the borough failed to recover from the ravages of Glyndŵr, who held the castle for nearly five years,[13] and he indicates a mere handful of tenements lining Stryd Fawr with the beginnings of a secondary street at right-angles to it, the present Pen Dref. A contemporary description of the borough referred to 'a verye poore towne . . . having no traphicke or trade',[14] and 200 years later Fenton was still able to observe that it was 'the most forlorn, beggarly place imaginable'.[15]

1. *Cal. Ch. Rolls*, ii, 280. The text appears in Lewis, *Medieval Boroughs of Snowdonia*, 282.
2. *King's Works*, 357-65.
3. Williams-Jones (ed.), *The Merioneth Lay Subsidy Roll of 1292/3*, 65-6.
4. Lewis, *Medieval Boroughs of Snowdonia*, 54; Beresford, *New Towns*, 46.
5. Lewis, *Medieval Boroughs of Snowdonia*, 171.
6. *Ibid.*, 201.
7. *Atlas of Wales, inter* 117-8.
8. *Ibid.*, 117.
9. Housed in the Meirionnydd Record Office, Dolgellau.
10. Fenton, *Tours in Wales*, 104-5.
11. Griffiths, J. (ed.), 'Early Accounts relating to North Wales *temp* Edward I', *B.B.C.S.*, xvi (1954-6), 114.
12. Fenton, *Tours in Wales*, 104, 129.
13. Lloyd, *Owen Glendower*, 81, 137.
14. Wynne, W. W. E. (ed.), 'Documents relating to the Town and Castle of Harlech', *Arch. Camb.*, i (1846), 255.
15. *Tours in Wales*, 104.

HAVERFORDWEST (Hwlffordd), Dyfed (Pembrokeshire)   SM 953157

The town is situated at the lowest bridging point of the Western Cleddau, and until recently the river was navigable this far inland, a vital factor in the defence, growth and development of the early borough. From a wider viewpoint

Haverfordwest occupies an almost central position within the county of Pembroke, which further enhanced its suitability as an administrative and market centre.

The foundation of both the castle and town date from the early Norman period as the work, *c.* 1110, of Gilbert de Clare, first Earl of Pembroke.[1] Under royal direction significant numbers of Flemish immigrants were encouraged to take up residence within the borough and its environs, and their arrival, which necessitated the expulsion of the native Welsh, earned for Haverfordwest recognition as capital of the 'Little England Beyond Wales'[2] The initial settlement was small and was confined to burgages west of the castle in the area of Queen's Square and St Martin's church, the whole defended by stone walls. There is no record of a borough charter earlier than that granted by William Marshal, Earl of Pembroke in 1189-1219,[3] and it was not until the 13th century that this insignificant community assumed any developed urban character. The Norman castle was rebuilt in stone at this time and with it came the enlargement of the early borough and its protection by surrounding walls.[4] This work probably began after a murage grant was obtained in 1264,[5] but since there are little or no extant remains their course must remain partly conjectural, in spite of a number of 19th-century observations and prints valuable in an attempted reconstruction.[6]

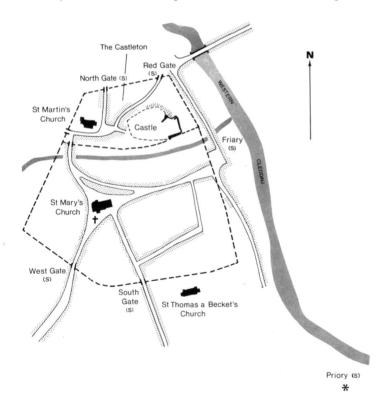

Fig. 43. Haverfordwest

In the first instance it is clear that the Castleton, the initial Norman settlement, was perhaps as much as four times smaller than the later medieval borough.[7] Its defences ran from Bridge Street behind Gloucester Terrace across North Street to Perrott's Road, where they turned and continued south behind St Martin's church and then east along Castle Street and Castle Back. The later extension of the town was achieved simply by continuing the eastern and western walls southwards with the latter extending along Barn Street as far as the vicarage. At this point it turned east, although the continued course across to Quay Street is difficult to determine; it may have crossed over to Dew Street by the top of Market Street and then down Goat Street, although on topographical grounds it is more likely to have traversed Dew Street in the region of its junction with Horns Lane, where the West Gate would have stood. From this point it would have run parallel to Horns Lane to the South Gate in Upper Market Street, and then on to the edge of the ridge above Quay Street, then turning north, running behind the houses on the west side of the street before linking up with the Castleton defences in Bridge Street. Reeve accounts of 1404-5 mention six gates along the course of the defences:[8] the West and South Gates already mentioned; the North Gate and Red Gate above the castle, the latter leading to the bridge across the Cleddau; another in the Castleton defences at the junction of Church Street and Barn Street; and another gate nearby in Perrot Avenue, which led from the old Castleton into the extended borough. Also separating the two parts of the town was a stream, 'Schitrikislake', which flowed from the river between the southern wall of the Castleton and the High Street.[9]

Medieval Haverfordwest was consequently a town of significant proportions— it was larger than any of the Edwardian boroughs on North Wales—and there may have been 360 burgages here in 1324,[10] and 422 by 1376.[11] The walled area also housed two churches, St Martin's in the Castleton and St Mary's at the end of the High Street, while beyond the walls stood St Thomas's, the Augustinian priory. This was founded in the 12th century, probably by Robert fitz Tancred, and was situated in Quay Street, where some remains are still visible.[12] It was an important foundation, valued at £133 at the time of its dissolution in 1536, and its ground plan is known from excavations conducted in 1922-4.[13] A second religious house also stood beyond the walls, a Dominican friary founded in the mid 13th century and situated in Bridge Street between the two lanes known as the Friars and the Hole in the Wall.[14] The early town also had its own leper hospital, recorded in 1246,[15] which stood at the bottom of Merlin's Hill where remains of the chapel could still be seen in the early 19th century.

Economically the borough's importance was primarily associated with the Cleddau which was navigable for barges as far as the old bridge, and to a point just below the town, for vessels of 250 tons. An important trade developed with Ireland and the Continent, while incoming goods were sold at the weekly market which was held every Sunday in St Mary's churchyard.[16] When the town was besieged by Llywelyn ab Iorwerth in 1221 it was the river that enabled the inhabitants to receive supplies.[17] Owain Glyndŵr's determination to reduce the town in 1405, although he failed to take the castle,[18] bears witness to Haverfordwest's importance as an economic and administrative focal point.

Later, in the 16th century, a valuable coastal trade developed with Bristol in brass and pewter, and this appears to have been a particularly prosperous period in the history of the borough, one of Queen Elizabeth's surveyors describing it as 'the best buylt, the most civill and quickest occupied . . . in South Wales'.[19] A century later, however, it was badly hit by plague and there were over 400 deaths, representing a fifth of the total population.[20] Further expansion was thus checked, while the silting of the Cleddau, together with the expansion of nearby Milford Haven as a port confirmed this trend, although Haverfordwest has been able to retain much of its status as a local market and social centre.

1. Lloyd, *History of Wales*, ii, 424.

2. Sudbury, P. G., 'The Medieval Boroughs of Pembrokeshire', University of Wales M.A. (1947), 163-7.

3. Owen, *Cal. Pembs. Records*, i, 131; Ballard, *British Borough Charters*, xxix.

4. On the castle *see* Phillips, J. W., 'Harverfordwest Castle', *Arch. Camb.*, 6th ser. xiii (1913), 265-74.

5. *Cal. Pat. Rolls*, 1258-66, 348; Owen, *Cal. Pembs. Records*, i, 127.

6. *See, for example*, that by Nesta Williams, published in Brown, J., *The History of Haverford-west* (Haverfordwest, 1914), *inter* 116-70.

7. Phillips, J. W., *op. cit.*, 274.

8. Owen, *Cal. Pembs. Records*, i, 86-7.

9. *Ibid.*, 158[n].

10. C 134/83.

11. Charles, B. G. (ed.), *Calendar of the Records of the Boroughs of Haverfordwest, 1539-1660*, B.C.S., Hist. and Law Ser., xxiv (Cardiff, 1967), 1.

12. Knowles and Hadcock, *Medieval Religious Houses*, 140, 159.

13. James, D., *The Town and County of Haverfordwest* (Haverfordwest, 1957), 28-9.

14. Knowles and Hadcock, *Medieval Religious Houses*, 214, 216.

15. *Cal. Lib. Rolls*, iii, 91.

16. Owen, *Cal. Pembs. Records*, i, 126-7.

17. *Brut y Tywysogion*, 98.

18. Lloyd, *Owen Glendower*, 103.

19. Charles, *Records of Haverfordwest*, 2; Owen, H., 'A Survey of the Lordship of Haverford-west in 1577', *Arch. Camb.*, 6th ser., iii (1903), 39, 46.

20. In 1651-2 the mayor estimated the population of the borough to be some '2,000 souls' (Charles, *Records of Haverfordwest*, n. 580, p. 100).

HAY-ON-WYE (Y Gelli), Powys (Breconshire)   SO 230425

The small town of Hay lies on the south bank of the River Wye at the meeting point of three counties—Breconshire, Radnorshire, and Herefordshire. The river runs along the western side, while flowing into it from the south-east is the Dulas Brook which gives the town its triangular form as well as affording additional protection.

During the Norman period this border region fell under the control of Bernard de Neufmarché, who granted Hay and its environs to William Revel, the probable builder of the motte which lies beyond the West Gate of the later walled town (SO 226422). This 'castello de haia' is mentioned in 1121.[1] Also recorded early in the 12th century was the nearby church of St Mary, which had been granted to the Benedictine priory at Brecon.[2]

As for the early town, the circumstances of its foundation are not known and there is no record of any borough charter, Hay being a borough by prescription only.[3] It was certainly in existence by the early 13th century, since both the castle and town were burnt by King John in 1216,[4] and again by Llywelyn ab Iorwerth in 1231.[5] In the following year, not surprisingly, the inhabitants secured their first grant of murage,[6] which was followed by a second in 1237.[7] Associated with the building of the wall was the construction of a new stone castle to the north-east

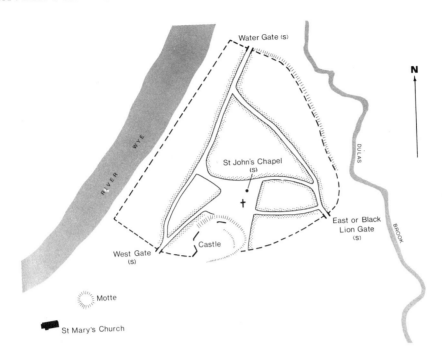

Fig. 44. Hay-on-Wye

·of the Norman motte, but little of this now remains, and much of the site is
occupied by a private dwelling.[8]

Of the surrounding defences little also survives, although their overall course is
well-preserved by street and boundary lines. Beginning at the south-west corner of
the castle, the wall crossed westwards to the West Gate in Castle Street, from where
it continued to the river bank and then turned north-east to run parallel with Broad
Street as far as Wye Ford Road and the Water Gate. At this point it swerved
south-east—its line is indicated by the property boundaries off Heol y Dŵr—and
continued as far as the East Gate which stood near the junction of Lion Street
and Bear Street, finally running east to link with the castle at Bell Bank. The
disappearance of the walls has been relatively recent, for in 1804 Fenton noted
that the eastern section was 'pretty entire' and that the gates had been removed
within living memory.[9] Sections of the west wall also survived into the 19th
century, and were not finally demolished until the building of the now-dismantled
railway in 1864.[10]

Within the walled area burgages were principally laid out along three main streets:
Belmont Road and its extension, Broad Street, running north; Heol y Dŵr, running
south-east; and Lion Street, which traversed the town from east to west. Immediately north of the castle in the area of the present Bull Ring and High Town
was the large medieval market-place,[11] the market being held on Thursdays,[12]
while also located in this area was a guild chapel dedicated to St John.[13] This ceased

to be used for divine service in the 17th century, and most of the building fell down in 1700, but a drawing of it has fortunately been preserved in Dineley's account of the Duke of Beaufort's Progress.[14] This is also of interest since it shows the area immediately north of the castle—the triangle bounded by Broad Street, Heol y Dŵr and Lion Street—to be largely open space, whereas this must have been built-up in 1298 in order to accommodate the 183¾ burgages then recorded in the borough.[15] This apparent late-medieval decline was also noted by Leland, who observed that 'within the waulles is wonderfully decaied'[16] and this may partly have resulted from the destruction caused by Glyndŵr's attack on the town in 1400.[17]

1. Round, J. H. (ed.), *Ancient Charters Prior to A.D. 1200*, Pipe Roll, Soc., x (London, (1888), 8.
2. Banks, R. W., 'Cartularium Prioratus S. Johannis Evang. de Brecon', *Arch. Camb.*, 4th ser., xiv (1883), 40-1, Jones, T., *History of Brecknock*, iii, 99.
3. Rees, W., *Medieval Lordship of Brecon*, 40; Lewis, *Topographical Dictionary*, sub Hay; Jones, T., *History of Brecknock*, iii, 100.
4. *Brut y Tywysogion*, 93.
5. *Ibid.*,102.
6. *Cal. Pat. Rolls*, 1225-32, 477; Turner, *Town Defences*, 205.
7. *Cal. Pat. Rolls*, 1232-47, 178.
8. King, D. J. C., 'Castles of Breconshire', *Brycheiniog*, vii (1961), 78-9; Hogg and King, 'Masonry Castles', 106.
9. *Tours in Wales*, 22.
10. Fairs, G. L., *A History of The Hay* (Phillimore, 1972), 230.
11. *Ibid.*, 49.
12. Lewis, *Topographical Dictionary*, loc. cit.
13. Fairs, *op. cit.*, 79-83; Jones, T., *History of Brecknock*, iii, 98.
14. *The Account of the Official Progress of His Grace, Henry I, Duke of Beaufort, through Wales in 1684* (London, 1888), 142.
15. C 133/92/7; Beresford, *New Towns*, 537; Rees, W., *Medieval Lordship of Brecon*, 39.
16. *Itinerary*, 111.
17. Jones, T., *History of Brecknock*, iii, 97; Rees, W., *Medieval Lordship of Brecon*, 39; John Speed wrote of the finding of several Roman coins during rebuilding after the attack, but nothing is known of any Roman settlement at Hay (*Atlas of Wales*, 109).

HOLT, Clwyd (Denbighshire)   SJ 410540

Holt is situated on the west bank of the Dee, where the river makes a pronounced bend to the south-west, and with Cheshire on the opposite side it is the most easterly of the medieval boroughs in North Wales. A half-mile to the north-west of the town an extensive Roman tile and pottery works has been discovered and partly excavated,[1] but there is no evidence of any settlement at Holt itself before the reign of Edward I. In 1282 the lands of Bromfield and Yale were granted to John de Warenne, Earl of Surrey, as a reward for war service against the Welsh and the planting of an English castle-borough soon followed.[2] No original charter has survived, but a confirmatory document by Elizabeth I in 1563 refers to an earlier version issued in 1285,[3] and the first indication of the castle's existence dates from 1304.[4]

Medieval Holt was a town of some importance; in 1315 the borough was surveyed and 159 burgesses were recorded, together with about two hundred other tenants.[5]

The burgage plots were laid out along a regular street-pattern and they can still be traced in places. North-west of the castle lay the triangular market-place from which all the main roads of the town radiated. Two parallel streets, Cross Street and Church Street, ran north to the bridge, while there was also a track, now disappeared, which ran from the bridge immediately in front of St Chad's church to the castle.[6] To the south ran Castle Street, and to the west Frog Lane, the latter being the most important according to Norden's Survey of the town in 1620,[7] though it appears to have contracted since. On the east side of the market-place stood two halls, the so-called Welsh court house in the castle precinct, and the town hall on Cross Green, which stood until 1897.[8] Apart from the castle—which for defensive considerations was badly sited and fell into decay at an early date[9]—and a tower defending the bridge,[10] Holt had no further protection, although provision for an enclosing stone wall had been made from the onset, but never carried out.[11]

From the sizeable number of tenants recorded in the early 14th century Holt's population probably exceeded 1,000 at that time, making it one of the largest of the Welsh boroughs. Agriculture was the principal occupation of the inhabitants, although there was also some early mining and in 1412 the burgesses received the right to take coal from the nearby wastes of Coedpoeth and Brymbo.[12] The Dee was also navigable as far as Holt, and some trading activities were carried on with the town quay situated just below the bridge.[13] From this early peak, however, the population declined drastically after the Black Death, and

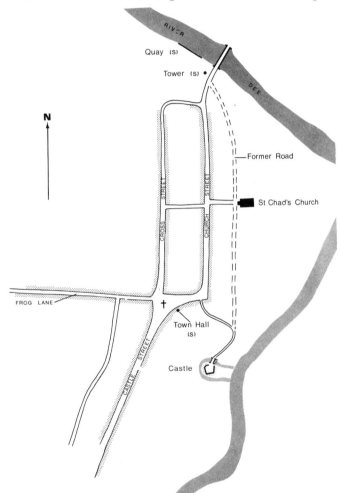

Fig. 45. Holt

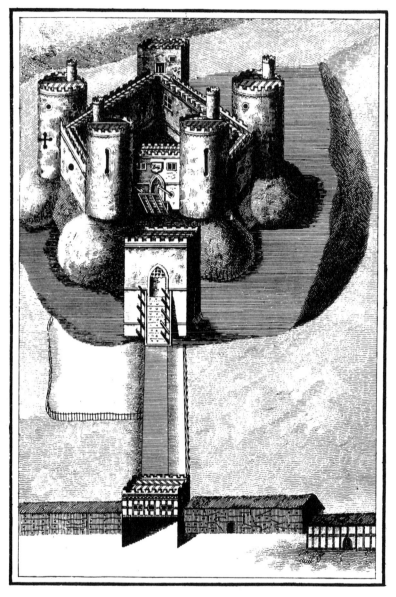

Fig. 46. Holt Castle
This imaginative reconstruction contrasts sharply with the scant remains
of today. Much of the stone was removed in 1675–83 to provide building material for Sir Thomas Grosvenor's Eaton Hall.

by the mid 15th century it has been estimated at less than three hundred.[14] The
fall may also be partly ascribed to Glyndŵr's attack on the town which resulted
in many decayed burgages and also in hostility against the Welsh inhabitants, who
had gradually been increasing in number.[15] By the end of the 16th century, however,

Holt appears to have recovered and Leland was able to regard it as 'a praty, riche Walsch toune'.[16] Norden's Survey of 1620, although it lists only 65 freeholders and burgesses, indicates a substantial community spread over the full medieval areas of settlement.[17]

1. On the Roman site *see* Grimes, W. F., 'Holt, Denbighshire; the works depot of the 20th legion at Castle Lyons', *Y Cymmrodor*, xli (1930), *passim*.

2. *Cal. Chanc. Rolls Var.*, 1277-1326, 240; Morris, *Welsh Wars*, 178; Palmer, A. N., *History of Holt and Isycoed* (London, 1910), 32-3. The latter work originally appeared in *Arch. Camb.* between 1906-10, but reference is here given to the collected volume.

3. Pratt, D., 'The 1563 Charter of Holt', *T.D.H.S.*, xxiii (1974), 104-25; Palmer, *op. cit.*, 37-9, 50-5.

4. Pratt, D., 'The Medieval Borough of Holt', *T.D.H.S.*, xiv (1965), 13. This is a reference to castle service, whereas the first notice of the structure dates from 1311, *Cal. Pat. Rolls*, 1307-13, 405.

5. Beresford, *New Towns*, 548.

6. On the church, which appears to have been contemporary with the castle, *see R.C.A.M.W.M., Denbighshire*, 75-6; Palmer, *op. cit.*, 169-99.

7. *Ibid.*, 83-128.

8. *Ibid.*, 59[n], 93, 98, 138.

9. Little of the castle survives, but its plan is known from the so-called 'Tidderley's Survey' of Holt (Palmer, *op. cit.*, 60-2), and from Norden's drawing of 1620 (*ibid.*, 91). It was surrounded by a moat, 10m. deep, which connected with the Dee at two points (*ibid.*, 61).

10. *Ibid.*, 129.

11. *Ibid.*, 39.

12. Edwards, I., 'The burgesses of Holt and Pentre Saeson', *T.D.H.S.*, xix (1970), 222-3.

13. Pratt, D., 'The Medieval Borough of Holt', *op. cit.*, 43, 56.

14. *Ibid.*, 50.

15. On this aspect *see idem*, 'The 1563 Charter of Holt', *op. cit.*, 110, and 'A Holt Petition *c.* 1429', *ibid.*, xxvi (1977), 153-5.

16. *Itinerary*, 69.

17. Palmer, *op. cit.*, 101.

HOLYWELL (Treffynnon), Clwyd (Flintshire)   SJ 185759

The early history of Holywell is poorly documented, but there is some evidence to suggest the existence of a small town during the medieval period. Its origins are to be associated with the neighbouring holy wells of St Winefride and St Beuno which lie at the head of the Greenfield stream a half-mile inland from the Dee estuary.[1] Also important in encouraging early settlement was the founding of nearby Basingwerk Abbey and the securing of a market by the monks,[2] coupled with the building in 1210 by Ranulf, Earl of Chester, of a motte to the north-east of St Winefride's Well.[3] Since St James's church, situated immediately west of the well, also dates from the 13th century,[4] this would appear to have been the period of town foundation, and though there is little housing in this area now, as the modern town developed further south off the High Street, it seems likely that the medieval settlement was concentrated in this area.

Holywell was not granted borough status, and there are no indications of its extent or population. Apart from the trade associated with the weekly market it was essentially a mining community and lead was exploited on the common above as early as 1302. By that date the miners were already an established community enjoying a collection of privileges, including the right to appoint their own steward and mayor.[5] While this mining activity continued throughout the following centuries, however, Holywell failed to develop and perhaps even declined since its market ceased to be held.[6] In 1703, however, it was revived by royal charter granted to Sir John Egerton[7] and towards the end of the century the town began to grow rapidly with the development of the North Wales textile and metallurgical industries.[8] Before that time, however, it was 'very inconsiderable and the houses few',[9] and it seems that the later growth has largely ignored the earlier areas of settlement.

1. On the site see Carter, Towns of Wales, 282–3.

2. Pennant, T., The History of the Parishes of Holywell and Whiteford (London, 1796), 246.

3. Brut y Tywysogion, 84. There are no subsequent references to this 'castell Trefynnawn'.

4. The church is mentioned in 1284 (Littere Wallie, 76, 81), and, although it was rebuilt in 1769 (Pennant, op. cit., 237), the original tower survives (R.C.A.M.W.M., Flints., 43–4). It appears to have originally been dedicated to St Winefride (Poole, J., History of Holywell, Flint, St Asaph and Rhuddlan [Holywell, 1831], 39–50).

5. Rees, W., Industry Before the Industrial Revolution (Cardiff, 1968), 42, 52; Evans, D. L. (ed.), Flintshire Ministers Accounts, 1328–53, lxx.

6. Pennant, op. cit., 245.

7. For a translation of the charter see Arch. Camb., i (1846), 409–10.

8. Dodd, A. H., 'The North Wales coal industry during the Industrial Revolution', ibid., lxxxiv (1929), 209–10.

9. Pennant, op. cit., 245–6. Camden called it a 'Little towne' (Brittania, 680).

HOPE (Yr Hôb), Clwyd (Flintshire)   SJ 309583

Hope is a small town built on rising ground which slopes down to the River Alyn, lying only six miles south-east of Chester, of which earldom it and the surrounding Hopedale formed part. It appears in the Flintshire Domesday Book when it was held by Gilbert de Venables,[1] but there are no real indications of urban life at this early period and it is to the 13th century that the town's real development must be ascribed. No charter is known from this period, but 35 taxpayers appear in 1292.[2] There may have been some corporate life earlier in the century associated with the caput of the lordship, Caergwrle Castle, a mile to the west, and which may have been standing long before it is first recorded in 1277.[3] The church, St Cynfarch's, is first documented in 1254, but the dedication suggests a much earlier foundation, and since there is no evidence of town plantation this must have been another likely stimulus to civil settlement.[4] The churchyard is very much the centre of the town with the streets radiating from it, and the pattern is similar to Dolgellau and Llantwit Major where urban development also had a strong native element.

Hope did not receive its first borough charter until 1351 when the townsfolk successfully petitioned the Black Prince and secured a series of privileges based on those already granted to Rhuddlan.[5] The town had already been regarded as a borough, however, and it was so described in 1347 and again in 1349–50, when the 'borough rents' amounted to 101s. 6d.[6] It was very much a racially-mixed community, with Welsh and English both holding burgages, although this situation

changed after the charter,
which specifically excluded
the Welsh whose burgages
were confiscated and redis-
tributed. The animosity
which this created soon had
an opportunity to vent itself
and it is hardly surprising
that Hope was an early
target for Owain Glyndŵr
and his supporters. The
town was attacked in Feb-
ruary 1403 when it was
'burnt and completely destroyed' and there is record
of many English burgesses
moving out through fear.[7]
The limited number of subsequent references to the
borough suggest that recov-

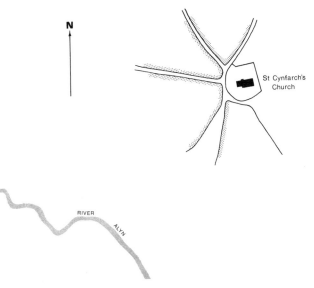

Fig. 47. Hope

ery was a long and slow process and even by 1610 it was not sufficiently important
for Speed to list it among the principal Flintshire towns.[8] Two hundred years later
Samuel Lewis observed that it was still 'an insignificant village'.[9]

1. Tait, J., 'Flintshire in Domesday Book', *J.F.H.S.*, xi (1925), 4–5.

2. E 179/242/52,

3. The date when Edward I granted it to Dafydd up Gruffudd (*Cal. Pat. Rolls*, 1277–81, 227).
On the possibility of an earlier foundation *see* Taylor, A. J., 'The Earliest Reference to works at
Hope Castle', *J.F.H.S.*, xxii (1965–6), 76–7.

4. Lloyd, G., 'Hope Church', *ibid.*, xix (1961), 21–31. The church originally appears to have
been dedicated to St Cyngar (*ibid.*, 21; *R.C.A.M.W.M., Flints.*, 48[n]).

5. Evans, D. L. (ed.), *Flintshire Ministers Accounts, 1328–53*, xl, xliv, 50–1. The charter was
confirmed by Richard II in 1278 (*Cal. Pat. Rolls*, 1377–81, 233).

6. Evans, D. L., *op. cit.*, 29.

7. S.C. 6/774/15; Messham, J. E., 'The County of Flint and the Rebellion of Owain Glyndŵr'
op. cit., 7, 13.

8. *Atlas of Wales, inter* 121–2.

9. *Topographical Dictionary, sub* Hope.

KENFIG (Cynffig), West Glamorgan   SS 800824

Kenfig is potentially one of the most interesting medieval archaeological sites in
Wales since under the sand dunes a town of considerable extent lies virtually intact.
The area lies to the west of the modern village which did not develop until the
16th century following the substantial sand encroachments over the initial site, but
all that is now visible are a few sections of the castle walling rising above the dunes.[1]

Although Kenfig was a Norman foundation a variety of archaeological finds from
the area of the borough indicate that it was favoured for settlement from an early

date. Beginning with a number of Neolithic implements, there is evidence of further occupation through and after the Roman period,[2] while from the late 9th century Kenfig begins to appear in written sources. In 893 the *Brut* records a Danish attack on the Glamorgan coast when the area was sacked, together with Llantwit Major and Llancarfan, and the same document again mentions Kenfig in 1080 when Iestyn ap Gwrgan, the last native ruler of Morgannwg, strengthened his castle there.[3] Just where this structure was situated is not known as no traces of it, or of the Norman motte which succeeded it, were discovered when the surviving late 12th-century castle was excavated in 1924.[4]

No date has been recorded for the foundation of the borough, although it was probably contemporary with nearby Newcastle (Bridgend), where the motte had been built by 1106. Both Kenfig Castle and the church of St James are first mentioned in the period 1135-54,[5] and it is clear that a town had been established by that date and had already been surrounded by an earth and timber palisade.[6] These defences were obviously needed, as Kenfig had a violent history right through to its capitulation to the encroaching sands. In 1167 the borough was completely destroyed by the Welsh and had to be rebuilt, only to be further damaged by a second attack in 1183, when parts of the town were again burnt and the mill destroyed.[7] Further damage was inflicted by the Welsh in 1232, 1242 and 1294-5, but Kenfig survived and housed 142 burgages in 1307.[8] Some 42 of these were later destoyed by Llywelyn Bren when he attacked the town and castle in 1316, but by 1349 the figure had again recovered to reach 144 burgages.[9]

As Kenfig in the mid 14th century was still a substantial borough of perhaps 700-800 persons there can have been little sand encroachment by that time.[10] During the following century, however, the situation changed markedly, and by 1470 the town had been virtually abandoned. In the following year the burgesses were instructed to leave their church and move to that at Pyle[11] and a whole new settlement was developing along the route from Ewenny to Mawdlam.[12] Leland, in the 1530s, noted only 'a village on the Est side of Kenfik, and a Castel, both in ruines and almost shokid and devoured with the Sandes that the Severne Se there castith up'.[13] By 1572 only three burgages remained,[14] while a borough survey of 1665 recorded only a single family, living 'on the site of the ould Castle'.[15]

The town that appears so vividly in 14th-century records now lies completely buried and the volume of overlying sand is so great that much of it is unlikely ever to be excavated. From the records, however, something of the

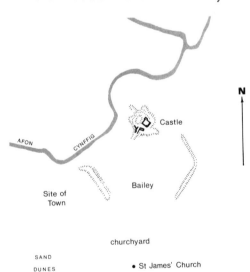

Fig. 48. Kenfig

borough's lay-out and topography can be reconstructed. Immediately south of the
castle was the bailey which was surrounded by an earth wall and moat which
linked up with the Afon Cynffig, and traces of this ditch can still be seen. The
bailey was unusually large, encompassing eight acres (3.24h.),[16] and part of the town
lay within it since several deeds mention houses inside.[17] The position of the
borough church, St James's, is indicated on the Ordnance Survey as lying immediately south of the bailey, while the churchyard appears to have been between the
two as a late-12th-century deed mentions a messuage 'within the bailey near the
wall of the cemetery.[18] Early in the present century a worked stone was found
on the site of the church, while outlines of graves and human remains have also been
periodically noted. Most of the burgages lay west of the church towards the coast,
no doubt along the 'High Street', which appears in the 1330 Ordinances. Other
streets mentioned are East Street and West Street, suggesting that the town had a
rectilinear street-pattern, and Monekin and Monk's Streets where the Margam monks
held land. There was also a chapel dedicated to St Thomas, but its location is not
known as is the case with the guildhall, which also appears in the Ordinances. Kenfig
also had its *maladeria*—hospital or leper-house—which is mentioned in a land grant
by Richard de Dunster to Margam Abbey *ante* 1186. With the probable exception
of the latter, the borough was enclosed with walls which are mentioned in 1147,
but we know nothing of their course. They were initially of earth and timber and
were rebuilt with the same materials after the Welsh attack of 1183 when one Hywel
of Caerleon was charged with despatching stakes from Chepstow 'in order to enclose
the town and castle'. The 'Town Walls and Gates' are further mentioned in the 1330
Ordinances, but there is nothing to suggest that they were ever reconstructed in
stone.[19]

1. The history of Kenfig has been investigated by Gray, T., *The Buried City of Kenfig* (London,
1909); Llewellyn, R. W., 'The Borough of Kenfig', *Arch. Camb.*, xv, 5th ser. (1898), 132-53;
Evans, A. L., *The Story of Kenfig* (Port Talbot, 1960); and Lewis, J. H., 'The History of the
Borough of Kenfig to 1485', Univ. of Wales M.A., 1922 (unpublished). For a valuable summary
see Griffiths, R. A., in *Glam. County Hist.*, iii, 338, 344, 351-2, 354.

2. For the finds *see* Gray, T., *op. cit.*, Chap. I; David, H. E. and Lethbridge, T. C., 'A brooch
of the Dark Ages from Kenfig', *Arch. Camb.*, lxxxiii (1928), 200-2; Grimes, W. F., 'A Stone
Axe from Kenfig', *ibid.*, lxxxiv (1929), 149.

3. Richards, A. J., 'Kenfig Castle', *ibid.*, 7th ser., vii (1927), 162-3.

4. Evans, *op. cit.*, 21-2.

5. Clark, *Cartae*, i, 111; *idem.*, Kenfig Charters', *Arch. Camb.*, 4th ser., ii (1871), 174; Richards,
op. cit., 163.

6. *Ibid.*, 163.

7. On the attacks *see* Richards, *loc. cit.*; Griffiths, *op. cit.*, 338, 340.

8. C 133/130; Beresford, *New Towns*, 555; Richards, *op. cit.*, 162-3.

9. Clark, *Cartae*, iii, 837-8; Beresford, *op. cit.*, 555; Griffiths, *op. cit.*, 344.

10. On this aspect *see* Higgins, W. F., 'An investigation into the problem of the sand dune areas
on the South Wales coast', *Arch. Camb.*, lxviii (1933), 26-27.

11. Richards, *op. cit.*, 191; Evans, *op. cit.*, 35.

12. *Ibid.*, 21-2; Richards, *op. cit.*, 181.

13. *Itinerary*, 124-5.

14. Clark, 'Kenfig Charters', *op. cit.*, 245.

15. Evans, *op. cit.*, 39-40. For a discussion of what may have been the remains of this dwelling

see Jones, D. and Soulsby, I. N., 'A Late-Medieval building at Old Kenfig, Glamorgan', *Arch. Camb.*, cxxxvi (1977), 145-7.

16. Richards, *op. cit.*, 164.
17. Gray, *op. cit.*, 58-9.
18. Llewellyn, *op. cit.*, 135.
19. Clark, 'Kenfig Charters', *op. cit.*, 244.

KIDWELLY (Cydweli [Cedweli]), Dyfed (Carmarthenshire)   SN 409070

Kidwelly lies some nine miles south of Carmarthen at a point where the Afon Gwendraeth Fach flows into Carmarthen Bay. As at Pembroke, the place-name was originally applied to the larger area of a Welsh commot, although we know nothing of any native settlement here prior to the arrival of the Normans.[1] The town was essentially a military foundation and was planned as part of a chain of castle-boroughs along the South Wales coast. The Normans first reached the area in 1093 when the new lord of Ogwr, William de Londres, is said to have wrested Kidwelly from the Welsh, but if he built a stronghold there it was not maintained as he lost control of the territory in the following year. The Norman hold was not re-established for another decade until Roger, Bishop of Salisbury, built the castle and laid out the town on the north bank of the Gwendraeth, c. 1110.[2] During the following century the Welsh proved reluctant to accept this foreign domination, and several attempts were made to secure control, most successfully in 1190 when the Lord Rhys rebuilt the castle.[3] By 1201, however, the English had regained Kidwelly, and further Welsh control was sporadic, although attacks continued when Llywelyn ab Iorwerth burned much of the town and church in 1223.[4] By the reign of Edward I the English hold had strengthened considerably, and it was during this period that the castle was again rebuilt and the borough defended by stone walls and an outer ditch.[5]

The medieval town was initially centred on the Norman motte with burgages laid out within the castle bailey to the south-west, which was defended by a bank and ditch. A similar area to the north of the castle was also allocated for settlement, but this was abandoned at an early date, although the defences here are still visible. The early town was thus confined to an area of only eight acres, and consequently there is evidence of the growth of suburbs at an early date. A number of 14th-century deeds record extra-mural development beyond the West Gate in the area then called 'Scholand', now the lower parts of Ferry Road and Water Street, where the market cross also stood. They also indicate the beginnings of settlement south of the river which was eventually to outstrip the original 'little town'. Burgages were lining 'Le Cawsay' (Bridge Street) and its continuation along Lady Street and south to the beginnings of Monksford Street. Branching off Bridge Street was 'Frogmerstrete', now the town end of Station Road and originally the pathway to the burgesses' holdings on West Hill.[6] This 'new town' on the south bank of the Gwendraeth Fach had its origins in the settlement of the tenants of the Benedictine priory, of which the present St Mary's church was originally a part. This was founded by Roger, Bishop of Salisbury, in 1114 and was a dependency of Sherborne Abbey.[7] There are now no remains of the domestic buildings, although some vestiges

were still visible in the
1830s[8] and pieces of carved
freestone are still evident
in the area. It is likely that
the priory stood imme-
diately north of the church
leading down to the river.[9]
A cemetery associated with
the priory, known as Myn-
went Domos, was located
on the far side of the town
'about 300 yards from the
castle adjoining the Llan-
saint Road'.[10]

By the 14th century the
development across the river
was clearly well-advanced,
but it had not yet out-
stripped the area of the
original town. When Patrick
de Chaworth secured a
murage grant in 1280,[11]
no attempt was made to

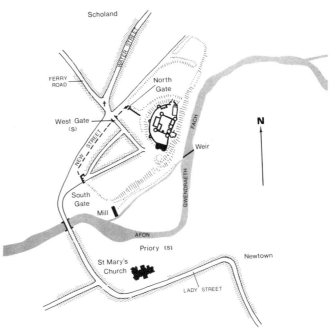

Fig. 49. Kidwelly

incorporate the suburbs by extending the line of the early defences as occurred at
Haverfordwest. Instead only the southern part of the original area was walled, and
of these defences only a short section by the North Gate remains, although the
whole course is known since it followed that of the Norman bank. From a point
almost midway along the western ditch of the castle the wall ran north-west to
the surviving North Gate and then turned south-west to the West Gate, which stood
at the junction of Castle Road and Ferry Road. From here it continued south-
westwards along New Street, formerly known as Ditch Street,[12] to the surviving
South Gate. At this point it veered south-eastwards to link up with the natural scarp
which protected the town on the river side. All three gates were mentioned by
John Leland as extant in the 1530s, and he added that the medieval town hall
was located above the South Gate, while its basement was used as the borough
'lock-up'.[13]

The growth of Kidwelly can largely be attributed to the development of the
cloth industry established here by Flemish settlers in the 12th century. By the
early 13th century the town had also emerged as an important trading port, with
links with Ireland, Gascony, and Aquitaine. It was a reflection of this improvement
that the borough attracted the attention of the Glyndŵr rebels in 1403, when a
force under Henry Donne succeeded in breaching the walls and destroying the
old town, although they were unable to take the castle.[14] Although this was
subsequently repaired and the ditch surrounding the wall town re-dug,[15] the
attack proved to be almost the death-blow for the old town, and the subsequent

history of Kidwelly belongs largely to the developing suburbs. When Henry VI granted a new charter in 1444 it was described as being 'waste and desolate',[16] while a century later Leland noted that 'the old Toun is near desolate' and that the new was 'three times as bigge as the Old'.[17] According to a borough survey of 1609-13 most of the bailey had been given over to gardens with a number of holdings down to a mere 18 as against a total of 171 for the town as a whole. Beyond the West Gate 'Scholand' was flourishing with 42½ burgages lining Water Street and another 32 along Ferry Road. Across the bridge the survey also confirms the importance of the 'new town' by recording tenements along Bridge Street, 'Longestrete' (Lady Street?) and the upper part of Station Road.[18] By this time a new town hall had also been built here[19] and that above the South Gate abandoned, sure testimony to the desertion of the old walled area.

1. Morris, W. H., 'A Kidwelly town rental of the early sixteenth century', *Carm. Antiq.*, 11 (1975), 57.

2. *Ibid.*, 57-62.

3. *Brut y Tywysogion*, 74.

4. *Ibid.*, 100.

5. On the castle *see* Ralegh-Radford, C. A., *Kidwelly Castle*; Official Guide (H.M.S.O., 1952); *R.C.A.M.W.M.*, *Carms.*, 45-9; Fox, C. and Ralegh-Radford, C. A., 'Kidwelly Castle', *Archaeologia*, lxxxiii (1933), 93-107.

6. Morris, *op. cit.*, 64-5. The burgesses were granted two weekly markets in 1268 (*Cal. Ch. Rolls*, 1257-1300, 113), but this was more a confirmation of existing privileges since 'the men of Cadweli' had been granted freedom from tolls as early as 1106-14 (Morris, *op. cit.*, 62).

7. Jones, D. D., *A History of Kidwelly* (Carmarthen, 1908), 47-55; Knowles and Hadcock, *Medieval Religious Houses*, 55, 68.

8. Lewis, *Topographical Dictionary*, *sub* Kidwelly.

9. Jones, D. D., *op. cit.*, 50.

10. *Ibid.*, 56-7. This area has since been developed, but nothing was discovered in the process to enable the exact position of the cemetery to be determined.

11. *Cal. Pat. Rolls*, 1272-81, 418, 427.

12. The course of the ditch can still be seen by the marked slope of the gravestones on the western side of the Siloam Baptist Chapel graveyard.

13. *Itinerary*, 59.

14. Mathews, T. (ed.), *Welsh Records in Paris* (Carmarthen, 1910), xxv; Lloyd, *Owen Glendower*, 76; Morris, W. H., 'Cydweli and the Glyndŵr Revolt', *Carm. Antiq.*, iii (1959), 4-16.

15. D.L. 29/584/9242; Morris, 'Kidwelly town rental of the early sixteenth century', *op. cit.*, 58.

16. A translation is in Jones, D. D., *op. cit.*, 126-30. The earliest known charter to the Kidwelly burgesses dates from *ante* 1309 (Weinbaum, M., *British Borough Charters, 1307-1660* (London, 1943), 141; Beresford, *New Towns*, 541).

17. *Itinerary*, 59.

18. Rees, W. (ed.), *A Survey of the Duchy of Lancaster Lordships in Wales, 1609-13*, B.C.S., Hist. and Law Ser., xii (Cardiff, 1953), 179-96.

19. This is thought to have stood on or very near the site of the present hall at the junction of Lady Street and Causeway Street.

KNIGHTON (Trefyclawdd), Powys (Radnorshire)   SO 284722

Knighton is a small town situated at the head of a deep and narrow vale on the southern bank of the River Teme, which here acts as the border between England and Wales. Like most of the Radnorshire towns it was conquered early and was in Norman hands at the time of Domesday Survey, where it appears as a waste manor in the Shropshire *breve*.[1] At its eastern end lies Bryn y Castell, the remains of a probable Norman motte which is not documented.[2] There is no suggestion of any town existing here until at least the end of the 12th century.

In 1191–2 William de Braose appears in the *Pipe Rolls* as a castle-builder at Knighton,[3] and this is probably a reference to initial work on the new castle, whose remains are still visible in the centre of the town, 460m. east of the old motte.[4] Some encouragement may have been given at this point to potential settlers, but although Knighton was a borough there is no record of any charter, and no date can be reliably given for the foundation of the town. Certainly it had emerged by 1292–3, when there were 71 taxpayers,[5] but the fact that as many as 60 per cent. of them were Welsh points against plantation alone for its creation. It is more reasonable to regard Knighton as a vill enlarged by plantation' as by 1304 it had grown to accommodate 126 burgesses holding 162 and a third burgages.[6] The borough church, St Edward's, had also been built by this date[7] and its English dedication, together with its situation at the eastern end of the town may indicate the direction of this secondary growth. Most of the plots, however, could easily have been accommodated below the castle, and Market Street, High Street, Plough

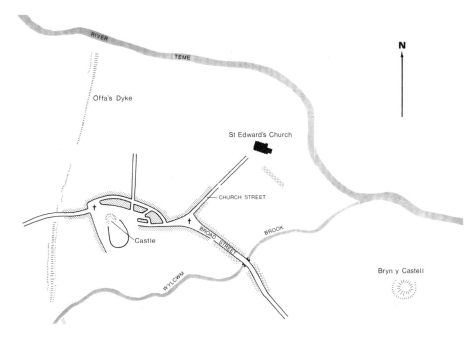

Fig. 50. Knighton

Road and Broad Street constituted the core of the medieval town. The original market-place was here, immediately north of the castle,[8] but this area was later built-up and the site was moved to the junction of the High Street and Broad Street.

In 1260 Knighton secured a grant of murage for the construction of town walls, but if they were built nothing is known of their course. It is more reasonable to imagine earth and timber defences than a stone wall, since later observers would not have failed to note traces of the latter. Moreover, the town would have been relatively easy to defend as it was virtually enclosed by existing lines: to the north and east it is bounded by the River Teme, on the west by Offa's Dyke;[10] and on the south by the Wylcwm Brook, the western end of which flows through a steep-sided valley. It is possible that any man-made defences were partly destroyed by Owain Glyndŵr who took over the town in 1402.

The subsequent history of Knighton was uneventful and there was no further expansion beyond the medieval confines until the 19th century. Its chief asset, described by Speed, was the weekly Thursday market,[11] while John Leland noted that it was 'praty . . . aftar the Walsche buildings'.[12]

1. *D.B.*, f. 260b; *V.C.H., Shrops.*, i, 348.
2. All traces of the bailey have been removed by farming, although a 6m.-high mound survives (*R.C.A.M.W.M., Rads.*, 55-6).
3. *Pipe Roll*, 1191-2, 77.
4. *R.C.A.M.W.M., op. cit.*, 55; Hogg and King, 'Early Castles', 113.
5. Faraday, M. A., 'The Assessment for the 1/15th of 1293 on Radnor', *T.R.S.*, xliii (1973), 83-4; Beresford, *New Towns*, 571.
6. *C.I.P.M.*, iv, 161. The inquisition also indicates the existence of a mill by this date.
7. It is mentioned in 1284 (*Cal. Pat. Rolls*, 1281-91, 135). On the building *see R.C.A.M.W.M., Rads.*, 56-7; Williams, J., *History of Radnorshire*, 224-5.
8. *See also* Woodfield, P., 'The Houses of Radnorshire: Knighton', *T.R.S.*, xliii (1973), 51.
9. *Cal. Pat. Rolls*, 1258-66, 67; Turner, *Town Defences*, 207.
10. Hence the Welsh name for Knighton which signifies 'the town on the ditch'.
11. *Atlas of Wales*, 111. *Cf.* Bowen, *Britannia Depicta*, 187.
12. *Itinerary*, 10.

KNUCKLAS (Cnwclas), Powys (Radnorshire)   SO 250745

The inclusion of Knucklas here rests on very slender grounds, and the 'town' which appears in documentary sources in reality has been little more than a scattering of dwellings completely lacking in urban characteristics. Nevertheless there was an important castle here, the remains of which can still be seen occupying a commanding hill near the right bank of the River Teme 2½ miles north-west of Knighton.[1] This was a creation of the Mortimers in the 1240s, and although no charter has survived it was probably they who founded the small borough similar to the one they attached to Cefnllys Castle.[2] Little of its history is known, and it may have all but disappeared along with the castle which was not maintained after being captured in 1262.[3] However, the few inhabitants succeeded in retaining many of their privileges, and burgages were still being recorded in 1649.[4] Knucklas's rights as a contributory borough remained until the early 19th century. At that time

Samuel Lewis described it as a mere 'village of about a dozen cottages situated not very close to each other'.[5]

1. The castle is described in *R.C.A.M.W.M., Rads.*, 24-5. It may have been built on the site of a former hill-fort (Hogg and King, 'Masonry Castles', 108).

2. It is mentioned in 1246 (*Cal. Pat. Rolls*, 1232-47, 489).

3. *Ann. Camb.*, s.a. The castle is not included in the list of Mortimer castles seized in 1322, and by 1406 the lordship was regarded as having no castle (*Cal. Pat. Rolls*, 1405-8, 145).

4. Lloyd, J., 'Surveys of the Manors of Radnorshire; the town and borough of Knucklas', *Arch. Camb.*, 5th ser., xvii (1900), 17.

5. *Topographical Dictionary, sub* Cnwclas. A similar description is given by Williams, J., *History of Radnorshire*, 212-3.

LAMPETER (Llanbedr Pont Steffan), Dyfed (Cardiganshire)   SN 578481

The town lies on the north bank of the River Teifi and its site is flanked on both sides by two parallel-flowing tributaries, the Creuddyn and the Dulas. During the Norman period a motte was erected here, the remains of which can still be seen in the grounds of St David's College,[1] but the borough itself was a Welsh foundation and dates from 1285 when Rhys ap Maredudd was granted the right to hold a weekly market together with an annual fair on the feast of St Denus.[2] The church was also standing by this time—it is mentioned in 1284[3]— and its dedication to St Peter coupled with the name of Stephen, perhaps a Norman bridge-builder, has given us the town's Welsh name from which 'Lampeter' itself is also derived.

Initially the borough was small and in 1298-1300 the 'villa de Lampadar' rendered only 6s. 7½d. in rents, although it already had the benefit of its own mill on the Dulas.[4] During the period 1300-1 the number of burgages increased from 13 to 19½,[5] and by 1317 there were 26, virtually all in Welsh hands.[6] There are no reliable figures for the later history of Lampeter, but every indication is that it remained a small borough with little in the way of industry to stimulate further growth. The annual fair was important, although the weekly market was insignificant[7] and in extent the town was confined solely to the High Street, where the former burgage pattern can still be detected. As late as 1758 the inhabitants were ordered to clear muck from 'the Street',[8] while a plan of 1845 indicates little change with no development as yet along Market Street, College Street, or Bridge Street.[9] The medieval topography was accordingly sparse and there was not even a town hall until 1741 since the members of the court-leet were easily accommodated in one of the public houses.[10] There may, however, have been another chapel dedicated to St Thomas which has given its name to one of the streets, at the bottom of which, according to Samuel Lewis, was 'Mynwent Twmas' (St Thomas's graveyard). The site has since been developed, although Lewis mentions the frequent finding of coffins, and adds that masonry remains were still visible in the 17th century.[11]

Since the mid 19th century Lampeter has experienced steady growth, which has stemmed in part from the foundation of St David's College in 1827.

1. The castle was destroyed by Owain Gwynedd in 1137 (*Brut y Tywysogion*, 52).

2. *Cal. Ch. Rolls*, ii, 303; *Littere Wallie*, 164; Davey, W. H., 'Charters connected with Lampeter

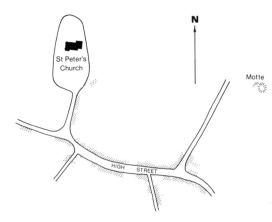

Fig. 51. Lampeter

and Llanbadarn Fawr', *Arch. Camb.*, 5th ser., ix (1892), 308.

3. When the advowson was granted to St David's (*Cal. Ch. Rolls*, ii, 303; *Littere Wallie*, 80).

4. Rhys, M. (ed.), *Minister's Accounts for West Wales*, 85; Lewis, E. A., 'Chamberlains' Accounts for West Wales', *op. cit.*, 69. The position of the mill is indicated on the 1843 Tithe Map (Nat. Lib. Wales).

5. Lewis, E. A., *op. cit.*, 75; Rhys, *op. cit.*, 205.

6. Sanders, I. J., 'The Borough of Lampeter in the early fourteenth century', *Ceredigion*, iv (1960–3), 136–45. On the racial composition of the burgesses *see ibid.*, 139.

7. In 1304 the market rendered only 1s., while the fair yielded 30s. (Rhys, *op. cit.*, 309; Sanders, I. J., 'Trade and Industry in some Cardiganshire towns in the Middle Ages', *Ceredigion*, iii (1959), 321.

8. Evans, G. E., *Lampeter* (Aberystwyth, 1905), 33.

9. Printed in Lewis, W. J., *Cardiganshire Historical Atlas* (1969), 87.

10. Evans, G. E., *op. cit.*, 29, 48.

11. *Topographical Dictionary, sub* Lampeter.

LAUGHARNE (Talacharn), Dyfed (Carmarthenshire)   SN 301108

The town, which appears as 'Talacharn' or 'Abercoran' in early sources,[1] is situated on the southern Dyfed coast where the small River Coran flows into Carmarthen Bay. The impressive castle, rebuilt as a mansion in the 1580s by Sir John Perrot, lies at the lower end and dates from the 1170s, although it seems to have pre-dated any organised burghal settlement by almost a century.[2] Llywelyn ab Iorwerth reduced it in 1215[3] and the subsequent rebuilding provided a suitable opportunity for the laying-out of the borough. In 1247 Guy de Brionne was granted an annual fair here, together with a weekly market to be held on Thursdays,[4] but 10 years later the town was burnt by a force under Rhys Fychan.[5] The indications are that recovery was slow and the new borough was not granted its charter until 1278–82.[6] The church of St Martin also dates from the 13th century but its position well to the north of the castle and early town suggests that it may have replaced an earlier, perhaps Welsh, structure.[7]

Laugharne was laid out immediately above the castle and the former burgage plots are easily discernible along the course of the principal thoroughfare, King Street. At its southern end, by the town hall,[8] several lesser streets radiate from it, principally Victoria Street, Market Lane, and Wogan Street; and a similar burgage pattern is noticeable off them also. The Frogmore Street area across the Coran was also built-up at an early date and there are associations nearby with 'The Grist'. This is traditionally regarded as the site of a religious house (Welsh: *Crist* = Christ), and although documentary evidence is lacking, human remains, perhaps from a graveyard, have been periodically noted from the immediate area.[9] The town mill was also here, off the north side of Wogan Street, although the stream which formerly powered it has since been re-channelled to flow past the east rather than the west side of nearby Island House.[10]

The principal problem relating to the history of medieval Laugharne concerns the matter of the town's defences. The borough's historian has asserted that it was, indeed, walled,[11] although in 1835 the Municipal Commissioners stated a contrary opinion.[12] There is no record of any murage grant, although authority to enclose the town was given in 1465. Curtis states that one of the gates was located above the bridge in Wogan Street, near Island House; a second at the eastern end of Victoria Street; and another, removed c. 1780, stood by the Mariners' Corner.[13] Although these were presumably built of stone, the walls are unlikely to have been more than an

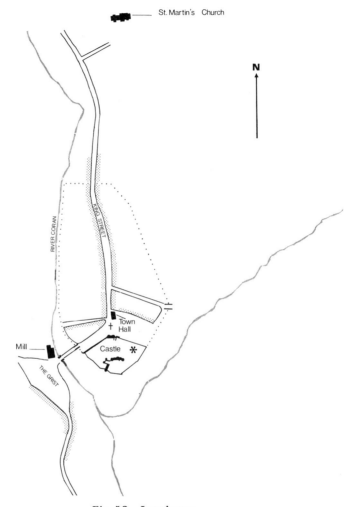

Fig. 52. Laugharne

earthen bank and ditch since no masonry remains were noticed by later observers. Assuming the existence of these defences, then, it is possible to postulate their course, although in the absence of both documentation and excavation this can be no more than speculative. On the west the River Coran forms a natural line of defence, while on the east a track runs along the boundaries of the former burgage plots which suggests a course on this side. The burgage pattern itself does not extend northwards beyond the house known as 'The Limes', and this may have been the point where the wall veered across King Street to link up with the western section.

Laugharne has not changed significantly in size and area since the Middle Ages; in 1566 it was described as 'a vyllage of ninety houses'[14] with the inhabitants principally involved in agriculture and some coastal trade with Bristol and Ireland.

During the reign of Elizabeth I the town was noted as a centre for piracy, but all this maritime activity was short-lived and by the early 19th century Laugharne had reverted to being a purely farming community.[15]

1. *Brut y Tywysogion*, 41, 73.

2. Lloyd, *History of Wales*, ii, 543; *R.C.A.M.W.M., Carms.*, 62-6; Curtis, M., *The Antiquities of Laugharne and Pendine* (London, 1871), 27. The castle was excavated in 1976 (Avent, R. and Read, M., 'Laugharne Castle, 1976', *Carm. Antiq.*, xiii (1977), 17-41; and xiv (1978), 21-35.

3. *Brut y Tywysogion*, 91.

4. Nat. Lib. Wales MS., 460 D; *Cal. Ch. Rolls*, i, 328.

5. *Brut y Tywysogion*, 111.

6. Ballard and Tait, *British Borough Charters*, xlii; Banks, R. W., 'Early Charters to Towns in South Wales', *op. cit.*, 99-100.

7. *R.C.A.M.W.M., Carms.*, 64-6; Curtis, *Antiquities of Laugharne*, 30, 43.

8. The present town hall dates from 1746, but it stands on or very near the site of the medieval guildhall (*ibid.*, 5; *R.C.A.M.W.M., Carms.*, 64).

9. *Ibid.*, 66; Curtis, *Antiquities of Laugharne*, 66.

10. *Ibid.*, 58.

11. *Ibid.*, 36.

12. *Municipal Corporations Report* (1835), 288; *R.C.A.M.W.M., Carms.*, 64.

13. Curtis, *Antiquities of Laugharne*, 36. The town is also stated to have been walled by Lloyd, J. E., *History of Carmarthenshire*, i, 317.

14. *Ibid.*, ii, 14.

15. The economic history of Laugharne has been investigated by Sudbury, P. G., 'The Medieval Boroughs of Pembrokeshire', University of Wales, M.A. (1947, unpublished), 182-4.

LLANDEILO, Dyfed (Carmarthenshire)   SN 629222

The town lies in the Vale of Tywi and is situated on the north bank of the river where it is joined by the smaller Afon Cennen. Its early growth resulted from the patronage of the bishops of St David's who came to control the area in the late 13th century when the town was laid out and potential settlers encouraged. Llandeilo, however, was not a planted town *per se* since a small Welsh community had long been established here around the church of St Teilo, supposedly founded in the 6th century.[1] There are no real indications of the size of this initial settlement although it appears to have been confined to the area immediately south of the church along Church and Bridge Streets. The town is mentioned in 1213 when it was attacked and destroyed by Rhys Grug,[2] but it recovered and the 'villa de Lanteilo' appears again in 1304.[3] By 1326 the bishop of St David's had 30 burgesses there, plus 11 other tenants, who paid 4d. a year for the lord's protection. Mention is also made of a mill, while the town was granted a weekly market plus three annual fairs.[4]

The medieval town originated by the bridge, which is mentioned in 1289,[5] and gradually extended northwards to surround the church with the development of King Street, Church Street, and Abbey Terrace. The upper part of the town could only be reached by either King Street, which was formerly much narrower than at present, or by the lesser Church Street, since the main road which now bisects the churchyard was not constructed until the early 19th century. The site of the old market-place is remembered in the present Market Street, where a

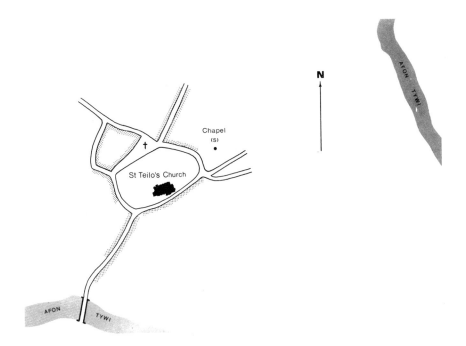

Fig. 53. Llandeilo

triangular block of houses was built after it had ceased to function.[6] Later growth of the town was immediately to the north and west with the appearance of Carmarthen and Rhosmaen Streets. Only the lower part of the latter was built-up in 1800, except for some 'straw-thatched houses of the poorest description', while much of Carmarthen Street was given over to stables and stores.[7] Another feature of the early topography was a chapel which stood east of Abbey Terrace behind the present Baptist church. It was a dependency of the abbey of Talley, but almost nothing is known of the building's design, and the site is now too heavily wooded for any remains to be discerned.[8]

The later history of Llandeilo was uneventful except for Owain Glyndŵr's attack in 1403 when much of the town was put to flames.[9] John Leland was here in the 1530s, but he had nothing to say of Landeilo's size or condition.[10] However, the decline of nearby Dinefwr at this time may have proved beneficial for the market. From the late 18th century there was renewed growth to the north and west, and this is indicated on the Tithe Map of 1841.[11] The town was regarded as important enough then for the county Midsummer Quarter Sessions to be held there.[12]

1. Samuel, W., *Guide to Llandeilo and its Neighbourhood* (Carmarthen, 1869), 74. Knowles and Hadcock, *Medieval Religious Houses*, 476.

2. *Brut y Tywysogion*, 87.

3. Rhys, M. (ed.), *Minister's Accounts for West Wales*, 307, 373.

4. *Black Book*, 263–9;

5. Rhys, *op. cit.*, 53.

6. Davies, W., *Llandeilo Fawr and its Neighbourhood* (Llandeilo, 1858), 8.

7. Samuel, *op. cit.*, 66.

8. Davies, *op. cit.*, 53. There must have been a Tithe Barn here also as the track to the east is known as Ysgubor Abad ('The Abbot's Barn'), while the chapel stood in Cae Ysgubor Abad ('the field of the Abbot's Barn').

9. Lloyd, J. E., *History of Carmarthenshire*, i, 253.

10. Leland's solitary remark was that the town continued to be held by St David's (*Itinerary*, 58).

11. Llandyfeisant Parish, Nat. Lib. Wales.

12. Lewis, *Topographical Dictionary*, sub Llandeilo.

LLANDOVERY (Llanymddyfri), Dyfed (Carmarthenshire)   SN 767343

Llandovery is a small market town lying in the Tywi valley at a point where two of its tributaries, the Bran and the Gwydderig, meet, and it has traditionally been important since its position lay along the course of the main route from Brecon to St David's. While nearby St Dingat's church would appear to have been a Celtic foundation,[1] however, the recorded history of the town does not begin until the arrival of the Normans in the early 12th century. Richard fitz Pons erected a motte-and-bailey on the north bank of the Afon Gwydderig, about a mile to the south of a Roman fort at Llanfair. This castle is first mentioned in 1116, when it was attacked by Gruffydd ap Rhys,[2] but there is no record of a town at this early date, although the founding of a Benedictine priory may also have been accompanied by some civil settlement.[3] By the end of the century it was certainly in being, and English burgesses are recorded in 1185.[4] Both the town and castle are frequently mentioned in the fighting of the following century, when control regularly alternated between English and Welsh.[5] The vill had little chance to develop until stability was restored during the reign of Edward I, and the growth of the borough can be dated to *post* 1276, when Llandovery was granted to John Giffard, a Gloucestershire knight, who encouraged expansion, and strengthened the castle, perhaps rebuilding it in stone.[6] From a burgage total of 37 in 1299 the figure had risen to 81 in 1317.[7]

The medieval town consisted essentially of one main street and the market square above the castle, following the line of the Gwydderig. The area of settlement extended from Broad Street eastwards to Market Square and King's Road and then continued down the line of the High Street almost to the ford across the Afon Bran. For the most part burgages lined either side of this main thoroughfare except for the area of the castle bailey which is now the site of the livestock market.[8] On the west side Garden Street perfectly preserves the back land of the old plots. There were no town walls, and for the most part the borough was well defended by natural features. To the south flowed the Gwydderig, and joining it at the eastern end of the High Street was the Bran which flowed southwards from the Roman fort. On the west the (now vanished) eastern channel of the Tywi ran parallel to the present college road and was forded at the junction of Broad Street with Church Bank.[9] Within the town was another stream, the Bawddwr, originally known as the Dyfi, which flowed down through the market-place and into Broad Street, while a small section which joined the Gwydderig was incorporated into the castle moat. For the most part the Bawddwr is now culverted. It was only on the north side that the town lay unguarded, and it is possible that the 'fossatum de Krenchey', the ditch mentioned in Richard III's 1485 charter to the burgesses,[10] ran east-west, parallel to Garden Street.[11] There was no church within

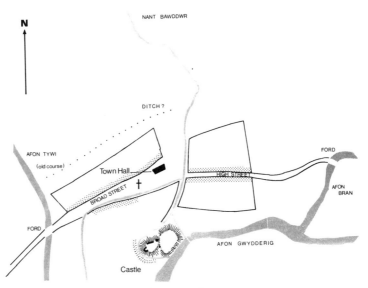

Fig. 54. Llandovery

the borough since St Dingat's, off Lower Road, was probably already standing when the Normans first arrived; while a second, St Mary's, was built within the area of the old Roman fort.[12] Other than the castle which, along with the town, was taken by Owain Glyndŵr in 1403,[13] the remaining noteworthy feature of the medieval topography was the town hall, situated in Market Square. Provision for its building was made by Richard III in his charter of 1485 and it seems to have occupied the same site as the present structure, which dates from 1858.[14]

The later history of Llandovery is largely uneventful and the borough declined after Glyndŵr's attack, which caused considerable damage.[15] John Leland, writing a century later, observed that it had 'a poore market . . . but one strete, and that poorely builded of thatchid houses'.[16] In 1659 the town was surveyed, and it was then found that there had been sufficient recovery for the early-14th-century burgage total to be reached again. In all 76 burgages are recorded, and the survey is particularly valuable in that it assigns them to their respective streets. The Broad Street/Market Square area housed 23, and there was constant distribution elsewhere with 14 in Queen Street, 11 in Castle Street, 15 in the High Street, and 13 in Lower Street.[17] Thus there had been little development beyond the medieval areas of settlement with Stone Street, now one of the principal areas of the town, still a mere trackway leading north to Llanfair.

1. Evans, G., *The Ancient Churches of Llandovery* (London, 1913), 59–65. The church is mentioned in 1250 (*Cal. Anct. Corresp.*, 52).

2. *Brut y Tywysogion*, 40.

3. The Priory was short-lived, being dissolved in 1185, supposedly because of the scandalous misconduct of the monks (Lloyd, *Hist. Carms.*, i, 331; Knowles and Hadcock, *Medieval Religious Houses*, 69). Its site is not definitely known, but it probably corresponds to that of St Mary's church at Llanfair to the north of the town, which was very likely the priory church (Evans, *Ancient Churches of Llandovery*, 122; Fenton, *Tours in Wales*, 16).

4. Arber-Cooke, A. T., *Pages from the History of Llandovery*, i (Llandovery, 1975), 83.

5. For an account of this period *see ibid.*, 77–103, and Evans, *Ancient Churches of Llandovery*, 92–105.

6. *Cal. Pat. Rolls*, 1272–81, 212. For a description of the castle *see R.C.A.M.W.M., Carms.*, 94–5, and Arber-Cooke, *op. cit.*, ii, 86–95.

7. *C.I.P.M.*, vi, No. 56; Evans, *Ancient Churches of Llandovery*, 14, 118; Arber-Cooke, *op. cit.*, i, 112.

8. Evans, *Ancient Churches of Llandovery*, 40–1.

9. Arber-Cooke, *op. cit.*, i, 413, 415.

10. *Cal. Ch. Rolls*, vi, 260–2. A translation also in Arber-Cooke, *op. cit.*, i 135–40.

11. *Ibid.*, 153–4.

12. The building of St Mary's has traditionally been ascribed to the 15th century, but for a much earlier dating *see* Evans, *Ancient Churches of Llandovery*, 65–8.

13. Hingeston, F. C. (ed.), *Royal and Historical Letters during the Reign of Henry IV* (R.S. 18), i, 139.

14. Arber-Cooke, *op. cit.*, i, 139, ii, 103–6. The original hall was rebuilt in 1592 (*ibid.*, 172).

15. *Ibid.*, 130.

16. *Itinerary*, 113.

17. Arber-Cooke, *op. cit.*, i, 188.

LLANELLI, Dyfed (Carmarthenshire)   SN 505004

The rapid industrialisation of south-east Carmarthenshire since the late 19th century and the emergence of Llanelli as the largest town in the area has tended to obscure the antiquity of settlement here, which is firmly rooted in the medieval period. Like nearby Kidwelly, this was an Anglo-Norman borough attached to a small castle functioning as the *caput* of the lordship of Carnwyllion, later part of the extensive West Wales holdings of the Duchy of Lancaster. The church, dedicated to St Ellwy, was an even older foundation and there is a late 11th-century reference to it in the *Book of Llandaf*.[1] We know nothing, however, of any associated vill existing at this time, and indeed Llanelli's history throughout the Middle Ages is sparsely documented. There is no record of a borough charter,[2] and no date is available for the foundation of the town itself. The castle is first mentioned in 1190 when it was destroyed, but it appears again in 1215 when the stronghold was under the control of Rhys Ieuanc.[3] It subsequently disappears from the records and its apparent abandonment must have had its effect on the nascent borough which is lost for the remainder of the medieval period.[4]

The antiquary, John Leland, writing in the 1530s, observed that Llanelli was only 'a village where the inhabitants digge Coles'[5] and we can envisage nothing more than a cluster of dwellings in the area of the old church. In 1609 a survey of Llanelli was carried out by the Duchy of Lancaster and only 59 freeholders were listed;[6] this modest size is confirmed by the earliest town plan, the Stepney Estate map of 1761.[7] This shows tenements surrounding the church and along Wind Street, which had not as yet been bisected by Hall Street. Other built-up areas of the town were the present Union Terrace; parts of the modern car park north of the Town Hall Square; and houses were to be found across the Afon Lliedi, along Water Street and Swanfield Place. This basic street-pattern has survived with only a few modifications. There has been some change in the immediate area of the church

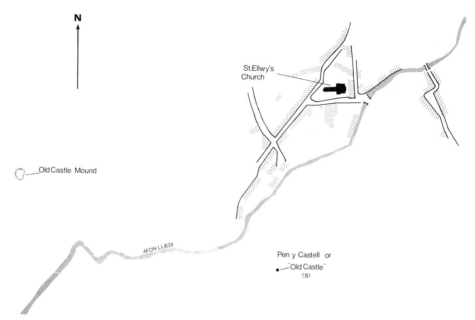

Fig. 55. Llanelli

since the graveyard was originally larger than at present—during the 1840s Bridge Street was widened at its expense. The original extent of the graveyard is suggested by the discovery of human bones close to the nearby Falcon Bridge,[8] although these areas had already been encroached upon by 1761. Until the 1820s Llanelli's weekly market was held in the south-west corner of the graveyard, where the town stocks were also located.[9]

Throughout the greater part of the 19th century Llanelli remained a town of little importance. A painting of 1821 indicates only a small village clustered around the church[10] and Fenton noted that there were only 51 houses.[11] A local authority map of 1851 refers to it as a 'borough hamlet',[12] while another, based on the Tithe Map, but dated as late as 1891, continues to show a town of modest proportions.[13] This indicates, however, new development across the Lliedi where, as at Kidwelly, a new market hall had been built, thus encouraging further growth away from the old town which has since been steadily decaying.[14]

1. *Liber Landavensis*, 279.

2. Beresford, (*New Towns*, 543. Llanelli was a borough by prescription only (Lewis, *Topographical Dictionary*, sub Llanelly).

3. *Brut y Tywysogion*, 90.

4. The site of 'Castell Carnwyllion', or 'Carnwallon' is not entirely clear. The Ordnance Survey map (SN 5000) places it to the west of the medieval borough in People's Park (50040037), and this siting is also given by Hogg and King ('Early Castles', 114). There is still a mound here, but the issue is complicated by a second site, 'Pen y Castell', some 500m. east of this 'Old Castle', now the rear of John Street (50570081). Until the development of this area in the late 19th century a square mound was here, and it is indicated on the Stepney Map of 1761. Innes observed

its removal, but saw nothing that might have shed light on its origin (*Old Llanelly* [Cardiff, 1902], 7; also Mee, A. [ed.], *Carmarthenshire Notes* [Llanelli, 1889], 143). Given the position of Llanelli, however, as midway between the Roman fort at Loughor and the *civitas* at Carmarthen, the John Street mound may have been a Roman marching camp which would leave the 'Old Castle Mound' as the site of Castell Carnwallon.

5. *Itinerary*, 60–1. On the early coal industry of Llanelli *see* Rees, W., *Industry Before the Industrial Revolution*, 82, 99–100.

6. *Idem* (ed.), *A Survey of the Duchy of Lancaster Lordships in Wales*, 1609–13, 253–63.

7. Reproduced in Innes, *Old Llanelly*, 5.

8. *Ibid.*, 76–81.

9. *Ibid.*, 65, 81.

10. *Ibid.*, 11.

11. *Tours in Wales*, 338.

12. Llanelli Water Works Plan, Carmarthen Record Office.

13. Nat. Lib. Wales, Map Coll.

14. This modern growth has been summarised by Carter, *Towns of Wales*, 286–7.

LLANFAES, Gwynedd (Anglesey)   SH 604778

Llanfaes, situated immediately to the north of Beaumaris, near the northern end of the Menai Straits, is today a hamlet of a dozen cottages clustered around the church of St Catherine. During the 13th century, however, this ranked among the principal communities of Gwynedd, a prosperous borough fostered and developed by the Welsh princes. No date is known for its foundation, and there is no record of the charters by which the burgesses held their lands but organised settlement dates from the later years of the first half of the 13th century. Between 1237–45 Llywelyn ab Iorwerth founded a Franciscan friary here near the coast,[1] while under Llywelyn ap Gruffudd the town achieved considerable importance with about one hundred and twenty tenements.[2] Its proximity to the sea encouraged its development, and a ferry across the Straits was operated. Fishing and trading both in local traffic and the Gascon wine trade were also important for the prosperity of Llanfaes.[3]

As a borough and a commercial enterprise, however, Llanfaes was short-lived. It was burnt by Madoc ap Llywelyn during his revolt of 1294[4] which in turn convinced Edward I of the need to re-occupy North Wales and secure the region's peace. A Welsh town, a product of the native princes, could not be allowed to remain, and more practically the decision to build a castle-borough at nearby Beaumaris rendered Llanfaes superfluous. Accordingly, Edward ordered its destruction, and the site was used as a base for the new building operations. By 1303 nearly all the inhabitants had been moved, some to Beaumaris itself, but the majority to the new foundation of Newborough at the other end of the island. By 1318 it was reported that the town stood unrepaired and uninhabited,[5] although the church survived[6] encouraging the later building of the few dwellings which now constitute the village.

Nothing remains of Llanfaes except for the church and the site of the friary, and the much of the intervening area is now given over to industrial use. The exact location of what was undoubtedly a substantial town, therefore, cannot be stated with certainty. Its maritime connections would suggest a site adjoining the coast, but the friary which is likely to have been *beyond* the town was situated there. To the north there is a small stream, presumably the borough's water supply as well as the power for its mill, and the town may have been sited here, immediately to the east of the church, but until the area is excavated this must all be speculation.[7]

1. Llywelyn is said to have built the friary around the grave of his wife, Joan, who died in 1237 (*Brut y Tywysogion*, 117). In 1245 the friars were granted the royal protection (*Cal. Pat. Rolls*, 1232-47, 460). The site is now occupied by a modern dwelling, 'Fryars', and its grounds, although human remains and a variety of gravestones have periodically been noted (*see* Bloxam, M. H., 'Some account of the friary of Llanvaes, near Beaumaris', *Arch. Camb.*, 4th ser., iv [1875], 137-44; Wright, E. G., 'Llanfaes Priory', *T.A.A.S.* [1953], 48-9).

2. *See* the 1294 extent reproduced in Seebohm, F., *The Welsh Tribal System* (London, 1904), Appendix A (a), 3-4; Lewis, *Medieval Boroughs of Snowdonia*, 49.

3. *King's Works*, 395.

4. *Cal. Cl. Rolls*, 1318-23, 71.

5. C 145/79/12.

6. The original structure was rebuilt in the years following 1811 (*R.C.A.M.W.M.*, *Anglesey*, 65).

7. During the laying of an oil pipeline in 1973 what was alleged to have been the town ditch was noted, but no exact location given, and the identification remains to be definitely confirmed (*Archaeology in Wales*, xiii [1973], 12).

LLANFYLLIN, Powys (Montgomeryshire)   SJ 142195

Llanfyllin is a small market town lying in the valley of the Afon Cain along the road from Shrewsbury to Bala.[1] The river is joined at this point by the Nant Abel, which formerly flowed through the main street until being culverted in the late 19th century.[2]

The borough was a Welsh foundation by the princes of Upper Powys and is ascribed to the 1290s, although a more accurate dating is possible; in December 1293 Llywelyn ap Gruffud de La Pole, Lord of Mechain Uwch Coed and Mochnant Uwch Rhaeadr, granted a weekly market and annual fair 'at his manor of Llanveclin'—there is no mention of the borough[3]—while the actual foundation charter cannot have been later than his death in June 1295.[4] The town, however, was not a substantial creation, and there were only 30 burgages in 1310,[5] laid out along the single street which led down to

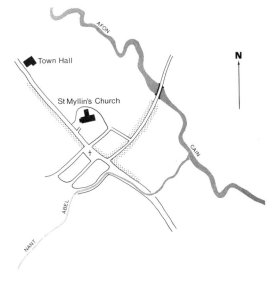

Fig. 56. Llanfyllin

the river. There was a medieval town hall—a wooden building on the site of the present structure which replaced it in 1791.[6] The early topography also included the church of St Myllin occupying the north-west corner of the borough, but this was already standing; it was listed in Pope Nicholas's *Taxatio* of 1291,[7] and its Celtic dedication coupled with the presence of the Saint's well, Ffynnon Myllin, 330m. to the west, suggests that it had been there for a considerable time. As Beresford has observed, however, nothing is known of any associated native *tref*.[8]

Throughout the Middle Ages Llanfyllin remained a small town confined to the one street. There was no castle and there is nothing to suggest the presence of any defences. It appears to have existed solely as a commercial centre with its Saturday market, and it was important enough for Speed to list as one of the principal market towns of Montgomeryshire,[9] although Camden added that the town itself was only 'little'.[10]

1. The history of the borough is told by Williams, R., 'A History of the Parish of Llanfyllin', *Mont. Coll.*, iii (1870), 51-112, and the later period by Dugdale, J. M., 'A History of the Parish of Llanfyllin, 1862-1915', *ibid.*, xxxviii (1918), 1-128.

2. Lewis, *Topographical Dictionary*, *sub* Llanvyllin; Fenton, *Tours in Wales*, 38.

3. *Cal. Ch. Rolls*, ii, 433.

4. Bridgeman, G. T. O., 'The Princes of Upper Powys', *Mont. Coll.*, i (1868), 63; Richards, R., 'The Medieval Castles of North Montgomeryshire', *ibid.*, il (1946), 173. The original charter has not survived, but is recited in an *inspeximus* of Elizabeth, translated in full by Williams, *op. cit.*, 91-4.

5. C 134/17/1.

6. Williams, R., *op. cit.*, 62.

7. *Ibid.*, 69. The church was rebuilt in 1706 on the same site (*ibid.*, 69-79; *R.C.A.M.W.M.*, *Mont.*, 96).

8. Beresford, *New Towns*, 563.

9. *Atlas of Wales, inter* 115-6.

10. *Britannia*, 662.

LLANGADOG, Dyfed (Carmarthenshire)   SN 706284

Llangadog is a small town and parish straddling the road from Llandovery to Llandeilo occupying an area of low ground on the south bank of the Afon Brân near its confluence with the larger Afon Tywi. Although by modern standards it may appear to be little more than a village, the settlement is an old one which was of greater status during the medieval period. It developed two miles north of an earlier Roman settlement[1] as a borough under the patronage of the bishops of St David's, who were originally responsible for its development.[2] There was a weekly market on Thursdays, and at its height there were as many as seven annual fairs.[3]

No date can be given for the foundation of the town as settlement had probably begun before the bishops of St David's came to control it. The place-name is derived from St Cadog's church which appears in the *Book of Llandaf*,[4] and there may have been a *tref* associated either with this or with Castell Meurig, mentioned in 1203,[5] which lies a mile to the south. The names of the burgesses recorded in the 14th century were all Welsh which suggests a reorgansation along burghal lines rather than a foundation *de novo*.[6]

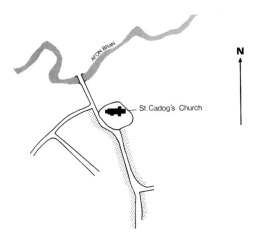

Fig. 57. Llangadog

In 1281 the right to hold a market and annual fairs was granted[7] and two years later Bishop Bek founded a college here, albeit short-lived.[8] By 1326 Llangadog was a vill of 33 burgesses, together with eight other tenants who paid for their lord's protection.[9] The burgage plots were laid out south of the Brân along either side of Church Street, and although they are no longer detectable the pattern can be seen on the 1841 Tithe Map.[10] On the west side Back Way clearly represents the rear boundary line.

Virtually nothing has been recorded of the later history of Llangadog which functioned as a small local centre, not growing beyond its medieval confines, and largely dependent on its market and fairs which continued to be held until the present century.

1. At SN 705255. See Jarrett, M. G., 'Excavations at Llys Brychan, Llangadog', *Carm. Antiq.*, iv (1962), 2-8.
2. *Black Book*, 277-81.
3. Lewis, *Topographical Dictionary, sub* Llangattock.
4. *Liber Landavensis*, 551.
5. *Brut y Tywysogion*, 82.
6. *Black Book, loc. cit.*
7. *Cal. Ch. Rolls*, ii, 257.
8. The college was transferred to Abergwili in 1287 (Thompson, A. H., 'Notes on Colleges of Secular Canons in England', *Arch. Journ.*, lxxiv (1917), 83-5.
9. *Black Book*, 277.
10. Llangadog Parish, Nat. Lib. Wales Map Coll.

LLANGOLLEN, Clwyd (Denbighshire)   SJ 216419

Llangollen is situated in a deep and narrow valley on the south side of the Dee at one of the river's principal bridging points. The town's recorded history dates from July 1284 when Edward I granted the manor to Roger Mortimer and gave his consent to the holding of a weekly market and two annual fairs.[1] This was not the language of plantation, however, rather the conferring of privileges on an existing community which had grown up around St Collen's church, mentioned in the same year.[2] This was probably a *tref* associated with the nearby Welsh castle of Dinas Brân which appears to have been founded by Gruffudd ap Madoc *c.* 1270.[3]

There are no indications of the population of medieval Llangollen, and no burgage pattern has survived to indicate the areas of early settlement. Also in 1284, however, Roger Mortimer had been granted pontage for three years to construct the bridge,[4] and we can envisage the appearance of tenements aligning Bridge Street

which leads to the church. The market
house also lay along this road near the
present *Hand* hotel.[5] There is nothing
to suggest that this small town was
defended, although the Dee provided
a natural barrier to the north, while
a small brook afforded additional protection on the east side.

Little is known of the later history
of Llangollen, and Leland's reference
to it as a 'village'[6] suggests that it remained
a small settlement right through to the
19th century when it expanded as a
result of its position along the main
coach road from London through
Shrewsbury to Holyhead. Several local
industries also developed, principally
limestone, slate quarrying and the
manufacture of woollens and fabrics.

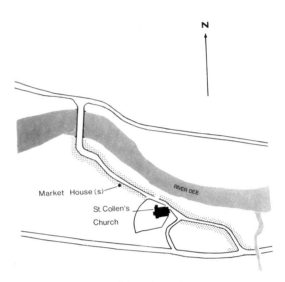

Fig. 58. Llangollen

With the arrival of the railway in 1862 came tourism which is now the mainstay
of the local economy.[7]

1. *Cal. Ch. Rolls*, ii, 276.
2. *Littere Wallie*, 62.
3. *R.C.A.M.W.M.*, Denbs., 120-1.
4. *Cal. Pat. Rolls*, 1281-92, 125; *Cal. Anct. Corresp.*, 141. The bridge is said to have been
rebuilt in 1345 by John Trevor, Bishop of St Asaph (Simpson, W. T., *Some Account of Llangollen
and its Vicinity*, 2nd edn. [London, 1845], 75; *R.C.A.M.W.M.*, Denbs., 124).
5. Simpson, *op. cit.*, 3.
6. *Itinerary*, 90.
7. Edwards, I, *et al.*, 'Industry at Llangollen', *T.D.H.S.*, xviii (1969), 136-53.

LLANIDLOES, Powys (Montgomeryshire)   SN 955845

Llanidloes occupies a good natural site with the old town laid out on a bluff on
the east bank of the Severn near the river's junction with the Afon Clywedog.
Several lesser streams, now for the most part culverted, also flanked the town on
the south and east sides, so that it was well defended by natural features.

The borough's original charter has not survived although the date of its
foundation can be confidently ascribed to the reign of Edward I. The vill is first
mentioned in 1263,[1] while in 1280 Owain de la Pole was granted a weekly market
and two annual fairs *apud villam suum de Thlanydleys*,[2] later confirmed in 1286.[3]
A lay subsidy roll of 1292 records the names of 13 taxpayers, a mixture of English
and Welsh,[4] while in the following year the borough courts are first recorded.[5]
Growth then appears to have been substantial and by 1309 the number of
burgesses had risen to 66, each paying the standard 1s. a year rent.[6]

Llanidloes, being a planted borough, was laid out in a regular manner and consisted essentially of two principal streets running east-west and north-south, meeting at the market cross, which was replaced *c.* 1600 by the Old Market Hall.[7] The church lies in the north-west corner, but its Celtic dedication suggests that it was already standing and had to be incorporated into the design. Nothing now remains of the motte-and-bailey castle which stood at the bottom of China Street, and which gave its name to Mount Street,[8] or of the borough defences, although their course can be reconstructed.[9] Beginning on the west side at the end of Short Bridge Street where High Gate led to the medieval bridge across the Severn; there the river itself provided adequate protection, and artificial defences did not begin before the rear of the churchyard was reached. At the churchyard a scarp was topped with timber stakes and this continued right across the

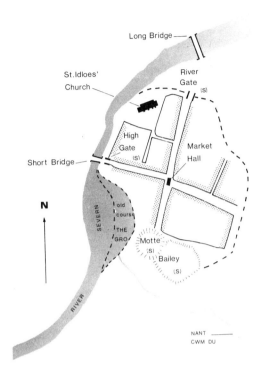

Fig. 59. Llanidloes

north of the town and beyond the River Gate or Severn Porte, which stood at the end of Long Bridge Street. Just east of the gate the defences turned south-east and ran parallel to Brook Street, which represented the course of a dingle of the Lletty Coch Nant, now culverted, providing additional cover on this side. At the bottom of Brook Street the natural scarp ended, so it was necessary to complete the circuit and link up with the motte by digging a ditch on the eastern side of the High Street. The castle defences were then utilised with further protection provided by the Nant Cwm Du which flowed along Smithfield Street, while to the west between the motte and High Gate the Severn originally flowed over the area known as The Gro and afforded natural cover on this side.[10]

Little has come down of the town's later history, and burgage totals are unknown after the 66 recorded in 1309. The fairs and weekly market, held on Saturdays,[11] were important and together returned £4 in 1401, although 20 years later the figure had fallen to 23s. 4d.,[12] probably as a result of the ravages of the Glyndŵr rebels, although there is no record of the town itself being attacked. In 1545 some 59 taxpayers were recorded, overwhelmingly Welsh,[13] and the indications are that Llanidloes remained confined to its medieval limits until the growth of the textile industry in the late 18th and 19th centuries.[14] The town has since resumed its original function as a modest commercial centre.

1. O'Neil, B. H. St J., 'The Castle and Borough of Llanidloes', *Mont. Coll.*, xliii (1933), 56.

2. *Cal. Ch. Rolls*, ii, 236. The grant can be seen in full in Hamer, E., 'Parochial Account of Llanidloes', *Mont. Coll.*, viii (1875), 224-5; Horsfall-Turner, E. R., *A Municipal History of Llanidloes* (Llanidloes, 1908), 38-9; and O'Neil, *op. cit.*, 47.

3. *Cal. Ch. Rolls*, ii, 330. Transcribed in full in Hamer, *op. cit.*, 225-6; Horsfall-Turner, *op. cit.*, 40-1; and Bridgeman, G. T. O., 'The Princes of Upper Powys', *op. cit.*, 132.

4. Horsfall-Turner, *op. cit.*, 256-7.

5. *Ibid.*, 232.

6. The figure is given in an inquisition on the death of Griffin de la Pole, in Bridgeman, *op. cit.*, 152-62.

7. *See* Owen, C. E. V., 'Llanidloes Market Hall', *Mont. Coll.*, lxi (1969-70), 58-64.

8. On the motte *see* O'Neill, *op. cit.*, 49-54, and Spurgeon, C. J., 'The Castles of Montgomeryshire', *Mont. Coll.*, lix (1965-6), 26-7.

9. The following account rests heavily on that prepared by O'Neill, *op. cit.*, 59-62.

10. The Gro remained under the river until it was drained in 1830 (Horsfall-Turner, *op. cit.*, 206).

11. The market was still being held on Saturdays in Samuel Lewis's time (*Topographical Dictionary*, *sub* Llanidloes).

12. Horsfall-Turner, *op. cit.*, 24.

13. *Ibid.*, 257-8.

14. On the later expansion of the town *see* Carter, *Towns of Wales*, 197-201. An interesting near-contemporary account of the physical growth can be read in Davies, D., 'An Essay on Llanidloes', *Mont. Coll.*, lxi (1969-70), 105-6.

LLANRWST, Gwynedd (Denbighshire)   SH 799618

Apart from the record of a Welsh battle fought at or near Llanrwst in 954 very little is known of the town's early history.[1] By the 14th century there was a borough on the site, but there is no record of its foundation, and as the majority of the burgesses were Welsh—there were 21 burgages in 1334[2]—the pointers are to a reorganisation of a native vill rather than a foundation *de novo*.[3] Indeed, the town developed on the eastern side of the Conwy where the river was still navigable by sizeable ships and this was traditionally one of the chief fording points, all of which would have encouraged early settlement just as they had led to the foundation of St Grwst's church by the river bank.[4] Some of the recorded burgesses, moreover, were already holding several plots, and this aggregation of property is suggestive of a developed town by the date of the 1334 survey.[5] A few years later we find the burgesses petitioning the Black Prince, and paying 40 marks to have their town enfranchised.[6] There was to be no further growth for the remainder of the medieval period, however, largely as a result of Glyndŵr's attack on the town which, it was recorded, 'brought such a desolacion, that greene grasse grewe one the market place in llanroose called Brin y Botten. And the deare fed in the churchyard'.[7]

By the early 17th century Llanrwst was beginning to recover its position in the locality, and although, as Camden observed, it was still 'small and ill-built' the weekly market was flourishing.[8] Through the efforts of the Wynn family of nearby Gwydir the old ford across the Conwy was replaced with Pont Fawr, an impressive bridge traditionally associated with Inigo Jones,[9] and a chapel was built in 1633 on the south side of the church.[10] Also near the church Sir John Wynn had earlier in the century (1612-14) established almshouses for 'twelve poore men' and a school, which together went under the comprehensive title of 'Jesus College'.[11] The town was further improved in 1661 when a town hall, recently demolished, was erected in the centre of the spacious market-place.[12]

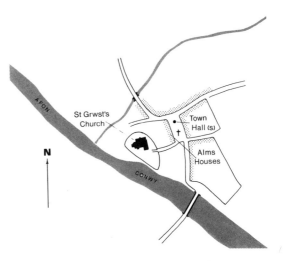

Fig. 60. Llanrwst

1. *Brut y Tywysogion*, 7; Lloyd, J. E., *History of Wales*, i, 344–5;

2. Williams, J., *Records of Denbigh and its Lordship*, 230–1.

3. For a full discussion of this evidence *see* Owen, D. H., 'The Medieval Lordship of Denbigh', Univ. of Wales Ph.D., 233–4.

4. There is a description in *R.C.A.M.W.M., Denbs.*, 147–8;

5. Owen, D. H., *op. cit.*, 235.

6. Jones, A. (ed.), *Flintshire Ministers' Accounts, 1328–53*, xlii.

7. Ballinger, J. (ed.), *History of the Gwydir Family* (Cardiff, 1927), 52–3. I am grateful to Dr J. Gwynfor Jones for this reference.

8. *Britannia*, 676.

9. *R.C.A.M.W.M., Denbs.*, 148; *idem, Caerns.*, i, 191. On the association with Inigo Jones *see* O'Neil, B. H. St J., 'Llanrwst Bridge', *Arch. Camb.*, lxxxviii (1933), 348–9.

10. Described in *R.C.A.M.W.M., Denbs.*, 147–8.

11. Williams, A. H., 'The Origins of the old Endowed Grammar Schools of Denbighshire', *T.D.H.S.*, ii (1953), 52–4. The almshouses have since been converted into private dwellings.

12. Lewis, *Topographical Dictionary, sub* Llanrwst.

LLANTRISANT, Mid Glamorgan   ST 047834

Although Llantrisant has grown significantly since the end of the Second World War both the residential and commercial focal points have moved away from the old town to Talbot Green and the surrounding lowland with the result that the original borough has been by-passed and is steadily decaying. During the 14th and early 15th centuries, however, this was a thriving settlement with its own weekly market and annual fairs and served as the chief town of one of the 10 hundreds of Glamorgan.

The precise origins of both the town and castle are unknown, but the pointers are to the middle years of the 13th century. Mention of the castle is first recorded in 1246,[1] and it was impressively sited on the summit of a hill immediately to the north of the juncture of the Clun and Ely rivers which commanded extensive views over the Vale of Glamorgan. The first burgesses are recorded in 1262, but the settlement was obviously in its infancy at this time, for their rents amounted only to 13s. 4d.[2] and they were all Welsh, a fact which may suggest that the nascent borough at this stage was no more than a reorganised *tref* surrounding the old church of Saints Illtyd, Tyfodwg and Gwyno which pre-dated the castle.[3] In the

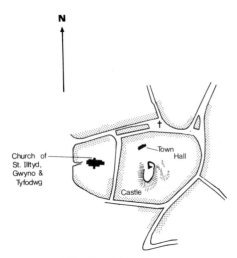

Fig. 61. Llantrisant

later part of the 13th century this picture changed markedly, however, and Llantrisant experienced a period of rapid growth. By 1306-7 the burgage total had reached 145½, and despite a series of attacks by Llywelyn Bren, when many plots were wasted, the figure had grown to 198 by 1316.[5] No charter has survived from this period, but there must have been one since the earliest recorded document, a grant of 1346, evidently refers to existing privileges, and from the wording it is clear that Llantrisant was already a borough.[6]

The medieval borough was confined to its hilltop location, and this dictated both its size and limits. With the castle already occupying a central position and the church to the west the burgages had to be laid out in a circular fashion along either side of the High Street, Church Street, and Swan Street, and they are best preserved on the latter's northern side. A presentment to the corporation in 1631 revealed that a burgage at Llantrisant was traditionally 24ft. long and 20ft. wide, with a garden plot at the rear.[7] The commercial centre of the old town lay immediately north of the castle, with the market-place (known locally as the Bull Ring) situated at the junction of the High Street and Swan Street and the town hall, built within the area of the castle bailey, standing nearby. The present building dates from 1773, but it replaces an earlier structure on the same site, which also housed the corn market.[8]

Llantrisant, like many of the Welsh boroughs, appears to have reached its peak in the middle years of the 14th century and suffered a decline in the late-medieval period. The castle was attacked in 1321, and was probably abandoned soon after and allowed to fall into decay.[9] The loss of military importance would have had its effects on the civil community. By the end of the 15th century 60 burgages stood unoccupied, and early in the 16th century even the courts and markets were temporarily abandoned.[10] The early development of the mining industry in Glamorgan prevented further decline, however, and with the building of a smelting works at Llantrisant in 1531 and the exploitation of the surrounding coal reserves,[11] the town was saved from the fate that befell similarly sited hilltop towns such as Denbigh.

1. Clark, *Cartae*, ii, 532. Rice Merrick suggested that it was founded by Robert Curthose, son of William the Conqueror, but this appears as pure fancy (*Book of Glamorganshire Antiquities*, 53).

2. The extent is in Clark, *Cartae*, ii, 659, and a translation in Morgan, T., *History of Llantrisant* (Cardiff, 1898), 36-7.

3. The church underwent an extensive restoration in 1873, but there remain indications of Norman work by the South Door and the lower part of the western arch of the nave (Morgan, T., *op. cit.*, 74-7; Lewis, D., *The History of Llantrisant* (Risca, 1975), 20-2.

4. C 133/130; Beresford, *New Towns*, 555; *Glam. County History*, iii, 339.

5. In 1314 47 burgages lay empty, while in Michaelmas 1316 a further attack had destroyed 90 (Beresford, *New Towns, loc. cit., Glam. County History*, iii, 339, 344).

6. The charter is recited in a later grant of privileges by Richard Despenser in 1424 (Clark G. T., 'Llantrisant Charter', *Arch. Journ.*, xxix (1872), 351-9; Morgan, T., *op. cit.*, 40-44).

7. *Ibid.*, 54.

8. Glamorgan County Records Committee, *Two Ancient Boroughs: Cowbridge and Llantrisant* (Cardiff, 1951), 16.

9. *Cal. Cl. Rolls*, 1318-23, 542; John Leland described the castle as being 'in ruine' (*Itinerary*, 20-1).

10. *Glam. County History*, iii, 353.

11. Rees, W., *Industry Before the Industrial Revolution*, 142-5.

LLANTWIT MAJOR (Llanilltud Fawr), South Glamorgan   SS 966687

Llantwit Major is situated at the southern tip of the Vale of Glamorgan with the town occupying the crest of a gentle slope which leads down to the Bristol Channel less than a mile away.[1] The position has encouraged settlement from very early times, and a number of Bronze Age artefacts were unearthed off Colhugh Street in 1887.[2] Just to the east of the town lie the remains of 'Castle Ditches', an Iron Age Fort,[3] and on the higher ground to the north a number of Bronze Age barrows.[4] The Romans, in turn, were also attracted to the locality, and between the barrows and the town, on Morfa farm, a villa has been extensively excavated.[5] Whether there was any settlement in the area of the later town at this time is unknown, but within two centuries of the Roman withdrawal a prominent religious community had been established and with it the nucleus of urban development.

Lantwit Major takes its name from the 6th-century St Illtud, and according to tradition he established a religious centre of such importance, that, along with Amesbury and Glastonbury, it was regarded as one of the three great monasteries of Dark Age Britain.[6] Archaeological investigation has as yet been unable to locate its site, but there is no reason to doubt its existence, which is documented in later centuries. In 988, for example, it was sacked by Danish raiders,[7] and its importance in the pre-Norman period is indicated by the presence of a group of inscribed funerary stones which suggest that it was the burial-place of local kings.[8] The Normans themselves did nothing to hinder this level of religious activity, and during the reign of Henry I Robert fitz Hamon granted the monastery to Tewkesbury Abbey and the association resulted in some rebuilding.[9] The grange was located immediately west of the church in the three fields known as 'The Bishop's Palace Field', 'The Monastery Field', and 'the Dovecot Field', and excavations carried out in 1912-13 and 1937 revealed a complex of monastic buildings, and finds dating from the 13th to the 16th centuries, while the enclosing wall can still be traced on the outskirts of the fields.[10] Other buildings from this period of improvement are still partly extant and include the chantry house in the southern part of the church-yard, the gatehouse on the northern side of Church Lane, the dovecot, and the nearby remains of the tithe barn.[11]

The town itself developed immediately to the east of the monastery across the small Ogney Brook. We can only speculate as to its beginnings and on the size of

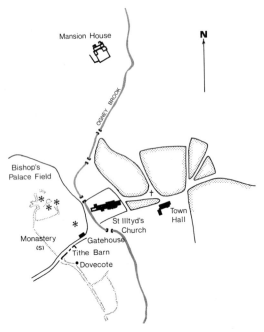

Fig. 62.   Llantwit Major

any community developing in the shadow of the church, although there is unlikely to have been any urban character until the period of the Tewkesbury influence, and the 13th-century rebuilding. This was no planted town, however, a fact evident from the haphazard character of the street-pattern which makes it difficult to identify positively the areas of medieval occupation. The evidence suggests, however, that the original town lay in the area of Church Street, Wine Street and Commercial Street. The 13th-century town hall is situated here,[12] as is the market cross, and there are records of markets being held at Llantwit Major from this period.[13] This was a commercial rather than a military settlement, and there is nothing to suggest that the town was ever defended. Apart from the weekly market the inhabitants were principally involved in agriculture, although there was also a steady trade carried out from the nearby port of Colhugh with the south-west and other ports of South Wales.[14]

Very little is known of the municipal and later history of the town. It was never a borough and any privileges which it may have enjoyed had disappeared by the reign of Henry VII, apparently revoked because of the inhabitants support for Glyndŵr.[15] Both Lewis and Trevelyan point to considerable contraction in the 17th and 18th centuries,[16] while the 1840 Tithe Map shows that the area between the High Street and West Street as far as 'The Mansion', which now contains Wesley Street, Ashgrove and Castle Court was entirely farmland.[17]

1. On the general history of the town *see* Davies, W. H., *The Story of Llantwit Major* (Llantwit Major, 1938), and 'Llantwit Major: History and Legend', *Vale of Glamorgan Series*, ii (1960), 11–25; Trevelyan, M., *Llantwit Major* (Newport, 1910); and Fryer, A. C., *Llantwit Major: A Fifth Century University* (London, 1893).

2. This was the so-called 'Founder's Hoard' discovered on the site of Hayes Cottage, 80m. due south from the Town Hall (Davies, W. H., 'Llantwit Major: History and Legend', *op. cit.*, 12).

3. Fox, C., 'Llantwit Major', *Arch. Camb.*, 7th ser., viii (1928), 408.

4. Nash-Williams, V. E., 'The Medieval Settlement at Llantwit Major, Glam.', *B.B.C.S.*, xiv (1952), 315.

5. *Idem*, 'The Roman Villa at Llantwit Major, Glam.', *ibid.*, ix (1939), 290–1, x (1941), 191–3, xiii (1950), 163–6.

6. *Liber Landavensis*, 313; Knowles and Hadcock, *Medieval Religious Houses*, 477; Lloyd, J. E., *History of Wales*, i, 143–5, 205–6, 222.

7. *Brut y Tywysogion*, 10.

8. Nash-Williams, *Early Christian Monuments of Wales*, 140.

9. Rees, W., 'The Possessions of the Abbey of Tewkesbury in Glamorgan', *Trans. S. Wales and Mon. Rec. Soc.*, ii (1950), 140; Clark, *Cartae*, i, 39.

10. Rodger, J. W., 'Excavations at Llantwit Major', *Arch. Camb.*, 6th ser., xiii (1913), 151-2, xv (1915), 141-56; Nash-Williams, V. E., 'The Medieval Settlement at Llantwit Major', *op. cit.*, 319-33.

11. *Ibid.*, 315-6.

12. Its building is generally attributed to Gilbert de Clare (d. 1297). The ground floor housed trading stalls, while cells were located beneath the western section (Trevelyan, M., *op. cit.*, 38, 113; Davies, W. H., 'Llantwit Major: History and Legend', *op. cit.*, 20).

13. Clark, *Cartae*, ii, 663.

14. Trevelyan, M., *op. cit.*, 10. The port appears to have functioned well into the post-medieval period and in 1833 Samuel Lewis noted that 'the remains of the ancient harbour may still be traced, and not withstanding the great encroachment made by the sea, the foundations of the pier and the piles of wood by which it was defended on the western side, are still visible at low water' (*Topographical Dictionary*, *sub* Lantwit Major). These piles, known locally as 'The Black Men', could be seen until 1940 when they were flattened by a wrecked ship (Davies, W. H., 'Llantwit Major: History and Legend', *op. cit.*, 15).

15. Trevelyan, M., *op. cit.*, 40, 113.

16. *Ibid.*, 21-2; *Topographical Dictionary*, *loc. cit.*

17. Glam. Rec. Office.

LLAWHADEN (Llanhuadain), Dyfed (Pembrokeshire)   SN 072174

Today Llawhaden is little more than a pleasant village lying on the west bank of the Eastern Cleddau River, but during the 13th and 14th centuries it functioned as an imporant and sizeable borough under the control of the bishops of St David's. Earlier a ring motte had been built here, which was mentioned by Giraldus Cambrensis,[1] but destroyed by Rhys ap Gruffudd in 1193.[2] The church of St Aidan by the river, together with the early mill, were also standing at this time, but no details are known of any associated settlement.[3]

The creation of the borough is associated with the building of the Bishop's Palace, on the site of the earlier motte, by Bishop Bek in the period 1280-93.[4] A weekly market on Mondays, and two annual fairs were granted in 1281,[5] and a start was made on laying out the town on the level ground which runs westwards from the castle. It seems likely that the old church was also rebuilt at this time,[6] while in 1287, just beyond the western limits of the borough, the bishop founded a hospital for the poor and aged.[7] Some remains of the building, now badly overgrown, can still be seen in Chapel Field.[8] The first burgesses at Llawhaden appear in 1292,[9] the number grew rapidly, and by 1326 the town housed 174½ burgages held by 126, predominantly English, burgesses.[10] It was easily the most important of the bishopric's boroughs, even surpassing St David's, and the palace was the principal episcopal residence, where courts were also held and felons imprisoned.

While Llawhaden is now completely lacking in any urban character and the former burgage plots difficult to discern, it seems reasonable to assume that the medieval borough lay along the road leading from the castle with its westernmost limit represented by the hospital which, since it also served as a leper house, must

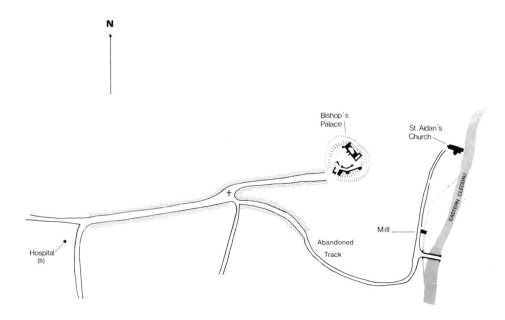

Fig. 63. Llawhaden

have been on the outskirts. In view of the large number of burgages recorded in 1326, however, which could not all have been accommodated along this stretch, other areas must have been built up, and it is probable that plots also lined the now overgrown roadway which leads from the decayed market square down to the bridge, where the remains of several dwellings are still detectable amidst the overgrowth. The settlement does not appear to have been defended, and although the *Black Book* records the rents for buildings *infra muros*,[11] these are likely to have been on the episcopal demesne lands to the south of the castle which were enclosed with formidable stone walls, sections of which are still standing.

Almost nothing is known of the later history of Llawhaden beyond references to the castle. During the revolt of Owain Glyndŵr Henry IV ordered it to be re-fortified in case of attack,[12] but it was eventually dismantled during the episcopacy of Bishop Barlow, 1536–47.[13] The 16th century also witnessed the dissolution of the hospital,[14] and the borough decayed considerably with the weekly market falling into disuse.[15]

1. *Opera*, i, 26, vi, 82.

2. *Brut y Tywysogion*, 75.

3. Giraldus Cambrensis, *Opera*, i, 56, iii, 73, 227; *MSS. Relating to Wales*, ii, 236.

4. For a description and plan of the castle *see R.C.A.M.W.M., Pembs.*, 139–41; Ralegh-Radford, C. A., *Llawhaden Castle* (H.M.S.O. Guide, 1947); Craster, O. E., 'Llawhaden Castle', *Arch. Journ.*, cxix (1962), 327-8.

5. *Cal. Ch. Rolls*, ii, 257, 259.

6. *R.C.A.M.W.M., Pembs.*, 141-3.

7. *Mon. Angl.*, vi, 783; *MSS. Relating to Wales*, iii, 226; Knowles and Hadcock, *Medieval Religious Houses*, 371.

8. These consist of a stone-vaulted chamber, 8m. by 5½m., later used as a stable, which may represent the chapel to the hospital (*R.C.A.M.W.M., Pembs.*, 143).

9. E 179/242/48.

10. *Black Book*, 137–51.

11. *Ibid.*, 137.

12. *Cal. Anct. Corresp.*, 199; *Cal. Cl. Rolls*, 1402–5, 111.

13. Craster, O. E., *loc. cit.*

14. Knowles and Hadcock, *Medieval Religious Houses*, 325.

15. Owen, *Description of Pembrokeshire*, i, 142. The authority to hold a new market was re-granted in 1652 (Charles, B. G. [ed.], *Records of Haverfordwest*, 125, 127).

LOUGHOR (Casllwchwr), West Glamorgan   SS 564979

Modern development has largely ignored the area of the old borough which developed to the west of the present town immediately overlooking the Loughor Estuary. The site has traditionally been an important one since it commanded the river at its narrowest crossing point and offered unrestricted views over much of Gower and the Carmarthen hills, considerations which prompted the Romans to build the recently-discovered fort within which the medieval borough was founded.

The existence of a Roman fort at Loughor—possibly the *Leucarum* of the Antonine Itinerary—has long been suspected, and excavations in 1969–73 located it beneath the later borough whose streets probably followed the rectangular lay-out of the fort and utilised its gates.[1] This appears to have been abandoned *c.* A.D. 300.[2] but no information was forthcoming on any Dark-Age occupation of the site. Its strategic importance, however, was again recognised *c.* 1100 when a Norman ringwork was constructed above the south-east corner of the fort, its highest point, and a square stone tower, still partly standing, was built into the slope on the west side. Later, probably early in the 13th century, further protection was provided by the addition of an outer curtain wall.[3]

In 1151 the castle was destroyed by the Welsh[4] and in 1215 captured again by Rhys Ieuanc,[5] but there is no mention of the town at this time, although St Michael's chapel, the predecessor to the present church, which lies just to the west of the castle, is recorded in 1208,[6] and we may envisage a cluster of dwellings around it protected by the old Roman defences. Loughor, in fact, has no charter, and there is no foundation date for the borough, although the pointers are to the later 13th century following Guy de Brion's securement of an annual fair in 1247.[7] In 1319 mention is made of the 'villam de Logher',[8] and there was definitely a town here in 1322 when the castle was granted to Hugh le Despenser.[9] It was most certainly a small settlement, however, confined largely to the area of the old fort, and its roughly rectangular plan with the east-west axis, Castle Street, crossed at right-angles by Ferry Road and its southern continuation, Station Road, apparently following the Roman pattern.[10] Other than the medieval ferry across the estuary to Llanelli [11] the place was of little importance once the military situation had stabilised and the castle abandoned and its recorded history is meagre. An inquisition in 1469–70 on the death of William Herbert, Earl of

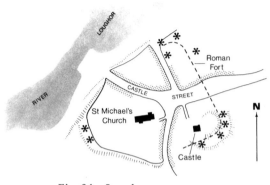

Fig. 64. Loughor

Pembroke, referred to the *castrum et manerium de Llonghour*,[12] not even accrediting it with the status of a town, while half a century later John Leland noted the remains of the castle, but was sufficiently unimpressed with the town as to ignore it.[13] During the 16th and 17th century the advent of coal mining within the boundary of the borough stimulated a small recovery,[14] although in 1833 it was still 'of very small extent and mostly of rather mean appearance',[15]

1. Ling, R. and L. A., 'Excavations at Loughor, Glamorgan: The North-East and South-East Angles of the Roman Fort', *Arch. Camb.*, cxxii (1973), 99–125.
2. *Ibid.*, 116.
3. Lewis, J. M., 'Loughor Castle', *Morgannwg* xvii (1973), 60–2.
4. *Brut y Tywysogion*, 57.
5. *Ibid.*, 203.
6. Clark, *Cartae*, ii, 316.
7. *Cal. Ch. Rolls*, i, 328.
8. Clark, *Cartae*, iii, 1066.
9. *C.I.P.M.*, vi, 216; *Cal. Ch. Rolls*, iii, 448.
10. Ling, *op. cit.*, 113.
11. D.L. 29/573/9063, Beresford, *New Towns*, 556.
12. Clark, *Cartae*, v, 1692.
13. *Itinerary*, 127.
14. Rees, W., *Industry Before the Industrial Revolution*, 96.
15. Lewis, *Topographical Dictionary*, *sub* Loughor.

MACHYNLLETH, Powys (Montgomeryshire)   SH 745009

Machynlleth is situated in the westernmost part of the old county of Montgomery on the south bank of the Afon Dyfi, the river being navigable to within 1½ miles of the town.[1] This was a Welsh foundation of the late 13th century and dates from December 1291, when Owain de la Pole was granted a weekly market to be held on Wednesdays, together with two annual fairs.[2] By the end of the century it had developed sufficiently to house 61 taxpayers[3] and its town status is clear from the inquisition on the death of Griffin de la Pole in 1310, which referred to the 'villa mercatoria de Maghentleyt'.[4]

The early growth took the form of a 'T'-shaped layout with one street running north-south and another east-west which met at the market-place, although the market house which now occupies the site was not built until 1783.[5] A will of 1597 refers to 'Stryte gwir deheubarth' and again to 'a street called y maen gwynn', the latter the town's principal thoroughfare. The will interestingly refers to the tenements as burgages, although Machynlleth was not a properly constituted borough.[6] The place has little recorded history and is best known for its association with Owain Glyndŵr, who held a 'parliament' here in 1404,[7] although the so-called 'Parliament House' in which it was allegedly held is considered a later building.[8] In 1545 there were 51 taxpayers[9] and the town was essentially a commercial concern with the now twice-weekly markets, and a considerable amount of trade carried

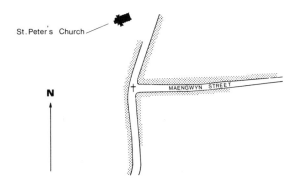

St. Peter's Church

N

MAENGWYN STREET

Fig. 65. Machynlleth

out along the Dyfi.[10] Samuel Lewis was sufficiently impressed to observe that 'the streets are wide and spacious, the houses are in general neat and well built, and the whole town . . . has a regular and prepossessing appearance'.[11]

1. Fenton, *Tours in Wales*, 83.
2. *Cal. Ch. Rolls*, ii, 408. The charter is printed in full in Bridgeman, G. T. O., 'The Princes of Upper Powys', *op. cit.*, 141-2.
3. E 179/242/54.
4. *C.I.P.M.*, v, 114; Bridgeman, *op. cit.*, 57, 162.
5. Jones, E., *Darlundraeth o Fachynlleth a'i Hamgylchoedd* (Machynlleth, 1855), 21.
6. Squires, H. L. and Morris, E. R., 'Early Montgomeryshire Wills at Somerset House', *Mont. Coll.*, xxi (1888), 220.
7. *Chron. Adam de Usk*, 86; Lloyd, *Owen Glendower*, 12.
8. *R.C.A.M.W.M., Mont.*, 145.
9. Horsfall-Turner, E. R., *A Municipal History of Llanidloes* (Llanidloes, 1908), 257.
10. Bowen, *Britannia Depicta*, 174; Fenton, *Tours in Wales*, 84.
11. *Topographical Dictionary*, *sub* Machynlleth.

MONMOUTH (Trefynwy), Gwent (Monmouthshire)   SO 508129

Monmouth represents one of the earliest Welsh foundations and the beginnings of the borough can be linked with William fitz Osbern's construction (*c.* 1070) of the initial motte on the site of the later masonry castle.[1] There appears, however, to have been an existing, well-established settlement on the site long before the Norman arrival, although we can only speculate as to its extent. The Roman station of *Blestium* is generally considered to be at or near Monmouth,[2] and Roman material from the area of the town has come to light through excavation.[3] Other recent finds have hinted at some Dark Age settlement,[4] while property at 'Aber Myngui' during the 8th century is referred to in the *Book of Llandaf*.[5] On the Norman arrival, moreover, the Celtic church of St Cadoc was already standing,[6] probably on the slopes of the hill chosen as the site of the motte,[7] while it may have been that the native Welsh displaced by the creation of the borough settled across the Monnow in the area of St Thomas's church where the detached suburb of Overmonnow existed throughout the Middle Ages.

As a defensible site Monmouth was ideally suited for town foundation. To the south flows the River Wye, and on the north side the Monnow which curves eastwards to join with it and create a peninsula with water on three sides. At the highest point by the Monnow, fitz Osbern built his motte, while in the period 1075-82 his successor, the Breton Wihenoc, established nearby a Benedictine priory together with St Mary's church, originally the priory church,[8] which was dedicated in 1101-2.[9] Immediately below the castle a market-place was cleared, and the foundations thus laid for burghal development. While no borough had come into being by the date of the Domesday Survey in 1086,[10] there appears to

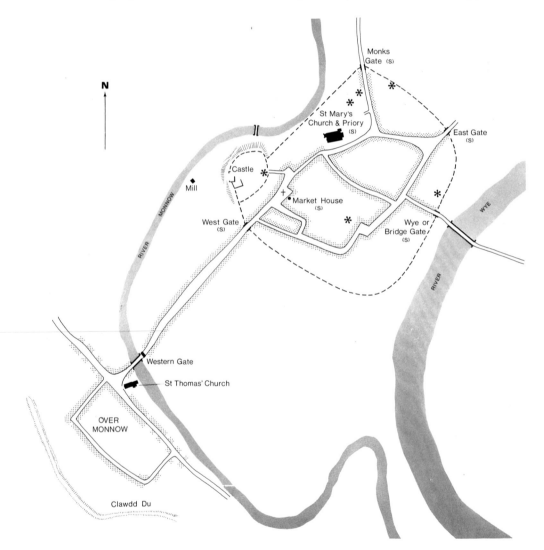

Fig. 66. Monmouth

Fig.67. Monmouth: The Monnow or Western Gate

The gate, which still remains, guarded the western approach to the borough
and the bridge over the river Monnow

have been substantial growth in the following century. By 1186 St Thomas's church
across the Monnow had come into existence,[11] while the early town was also
supporting some industry, for in 1166-77 Baderon of Monmouth granted three
forges to the prior 'on the banks of the Wye'.[12] It also seems likely that by this time
the town had been enclosed with a bank and ditch,[13] although no date can be
speculated for the digging of Clawdd Du, the defences of Overmonnow.

No early charter has survived from Monmouth except for a grant of privileges
in 1256[14] and it was not until 1447 that Henry VI formerly incorporated the
borough.[15] By that time there were 201 burgesses, and the town as Speed
depicted it in 1610—much as it stands today—had been laid out.[16] The early
defences had been replaced with stone walls following murage grants in 1297 and
1315.[17] Access was provided by four gates, no traces of which remain except for
fragments of the flanking tower of the East Gate incorporated into the 'Nag's
Head' on the south side of Old Dixton Road. According to Leland[18] and
Camden[19] the town was only walled on the north side where it was not defended
by water, an opinion endorsed by Speed, who shows no wall between the West
Gate in Monnow Street and the East or Dixton Gate which stood on the south
side of Old Dixton Road.[20] A fortified gatehouse guarded the bridge over the Wye,

while another, although apparently not part of the defences, provided access to the grazing land at Chippenham.[21] It is inconceivable that these gatehouses stood alone. Perhaps this southern section was not reconstructed in stone, but there certainly must have been defences here, and their course is indicated by property boundaries on the south side of Glendower Street. The town's fourth entry point, the Monk's Gate, was located immediately above the junction of Monk Street and Priory Street.[22] To the west stood the surviving Western Gate commanding the Monnow and affording protection to the sizeable suburb which had developed along the line of Monnow Street. The enclosed street-pattern bore considerable resemblance to that of present-day Monmouth, with the notable exception of Priory Street, which is not indicated by Speed or by Coxe in 1801.[23] Speed's plan is also valuable because it gives the position of the old Market House as south-east of the castle on a site which corresponds to that now occupied by the town hall.

As a substantial borough commanding one of the principal entry points into South Wales and the *caput* of an independent marcher lordship, medieval Monmouth was a settlement of considerable importance. The castle, which was gradually rebuilt during the 13th and 14th centuries,[24] served as the local administrative centre, while the town was also prominent in commercial matters with its market, the growth of the iron industry, and the manufacture of caps for which it was noted. Camden called it 'the chief town of the shire', adding that it 'hath flourished and bin of name'.[25] There were 266 burgesses in 1610,[26] an increase on the number recorded at the time of the 1447 charter. The later growth of Abergavenny, however, together with the industrialisation of the western parts of the county arrested this development and prevented Monmouth from establishing itself as the dominant town of the shire.

1. *Liber Landavensis*, 548; Nelson, *The Normans in South Wales*, 30.

2. Coxe, *Historical Tour through Monmouthshire, 1801*, 248.

3. Some Roman pottery was discovered during excavations in 1968 near the corner of Priory Street and Monk Street (*Archaeology in Wales*, viii [1968], 24-5), and during the clearing of the car park off Glendower Street in 1969 (*ibid.*, ix [1969], 28).

4. *Ibid.*, xiii (1973), 52.

5. *Liber Landavensis*, 175, 186.

6. The church is mentioned in the foundation charter of Monmouth Priory (*Mon. Angl.*, iv, 595).

7. For a discussion of the possible site *see* Kissack, K. E., *Medieval Monmouth*, The Monmouth Historical and Educational Trust (1974), 68.

8. *Mon. Angl.*, iv, 595; Knowles and Hadcock, *Medieval Religious Houses*, 71.

9. Round, *C.D.F.*, 406; Kissack, *Medieval Monmouth*, 16, 70.

10. The castle and manor are entered in the Herefordshire *breve* (*D.B.*, i, f. 180b).

11. Round, *C.D.F.*, 404.

12. *Mon. Angl.*, iv, 596; Kissack, *Medieval Monmouth*, 71. The remains of what were tentatively suggested as Roman iron-workings were partically unearthed off Wyebridge Street by the river during excavations in 1973 (*Archaeology in Wales*, xiii [1973], 52), but in the light of this document they may equally have been those belonging to the priory.

13. A bank 40m. south of Dixton Road and assumed to be part of the early defences was partially excavated in 1973. It was found to have been of one-phase construction and yielded some 14th-century pottery (*Archaeology in Wales*, xiii [1973], 52).

14. C 146/9843; Kissack, *Medieval Monmouth*, 72.

15. D.L. 37/15/27; Kissack, *Medieval Monmouth*, 56.

16. *Ibid.*, 57.

17. *Cal. Pat. Rolls*, 1292–1301, 307; *ibid.*, 1313–17, 297.

18. *Itinerary*, 45–6.

19. *Britannia*, 632.

20. *Atlas of Wales, inter* 107–8; also endorsed by Coxe, *Historical Tour through Monmouth-shire*, 1801, 248.

21. Kissack, *Medieval Monmouth*, 33, 36.

22. The gate was removed in 1710 (*ibid.*, 36).

23. *Atlas of Wales, loc. cit.*; Coxe, *Historical Tour through Monmouthshire*, 238.

24. For an account of the castle *see* Taylor, *Monmouth Castle*, H.M.S.O. Guide, 1951.

25. *Britannia*, 632.

26. Rees, *A Survey of the Duchy of Lancaster Lordships in Wales*, 11–26.

MONTGOMERY (Trefaldwyn), Powys (Montgomeryshire)   SO 223965

Montgomery was a planted town, and, as its border position suggests, one of the earliest in the county. The site lay 1½ miles south-east of an existing motte at Hen Domen, but this was not rebuilt,[1] and work began on a new castle in 1223.[2] It seems likely that a town was also envisaged from the outset since Henry III was already encouraging potential settlers to take up residence by offering them the liberties and customs already enjoyed by the burgesses of Shrewsbury.[3] The new borough received its charter in 1227,[4] and two years later the burgesses took the town at farm for £40.[5] By 1364–5 the rents alone had reached an impressive figure of almost £22.[6]

Montgomery was conceived primarily as a military base and the main reason for building it here was the presence of a large, steep-sided outcrop of igneous rock which was ideally suited, as Mathew Paris observed, 'for the erection of an impregnable castle'.[7] From here control could be exercised both over the south-eastern entry to the Severn Valley and the river's important crossing-point at Rhyd Whiman. The location was less suited to town foundation, however, and it proved impossible for the planners to achieve a regular lay-out, although something of a grid pattern can be seen in the southern section where St Nicholas's church and the market hall were sited. It proved possible, nevertheless, to enclose the town with walls and an outer ditch and substantial remains of these defences can still be seen.

The walls of Montgomery have been studied in detail by O'Neill and Foster-Smith who also conducted a series of small excavations along their course.[8] They concluded that they were built of stone, which had been subjected to extensive robbing in later centuries, and not of earth and timber as had traditionally been thought. This view is supported by the testimony of John Speed, whose plan of the town indicates that stretches of the north-east wall were still standing in 1610.[9] John Leland had earlier observed that 'in the waulls yet remayne broken towrets, of the wiche the whit toure is now the most notable'.[10] No evidence was found, in fact, to suggest any earlier defences and the writers concluded that the walls were built shortly after the completion of the castle, *c.* 1230. The opinion has been questioned by Taylor, who has argued in favour of an early wooden palisade replaced in stone in 1279–80.[11] The situation is further complicated by the existence of a murage grant in 1267 which suggests that the town had not by then been walled in stone.[12] This apparently contradictory evidence will no doubt remain puzzling until the walls have been subjected to a programme of extensive excavation. The 1930 study, however, remains invaluable for its reconstruction of the line of defences which is detectable for all but a few short sections. There are substantial remains on the west side below the castle and from the bottom of the cliff here a narrow bank runs south to the site of the Cedewain Gate which straddled the Newtown road. Below it the mound of the wall is also well preserved, running uphill to the south-west corner where a tower formerly stood. From this point the wall turned a right-angle to the Ceri Gate, and then continued straight down the hillside, although

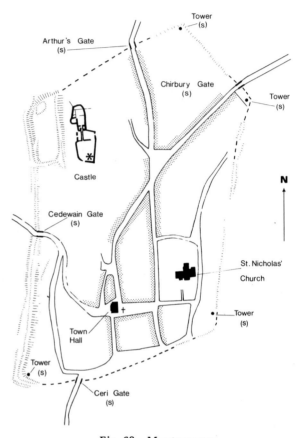

Fig. 68. Montgomery

traces of this southern stretch are only visible at the rear of the rectory. A second tower guarded the south-east corner, and from here the defences can be seen running due north in a straight line for 300m. with the outer ditch also still detectable for the most part. The north-east corner also had its tower, and the Chirbury Gate stood nearby, and from here the wall ran north-west for 180m. as far as another corner tower which was still standing in Speed's day. At this point it turned south-west with Arthur's Gate located at the junction of Forden Street and Station Road. This was also standing in 1610, but like the other three gates has long since been removed. The final section of the defences continued beneath the slopes of the hill to link with the western section immediately north-west of the castle.

From the surviving 13th- and 14th-century financial records viewed in the light of the substantial area of the walled town, medieval Montgomery appears to have been a sizeable borough. There was a weekly market held in Broad Street—the Market House is indicated by Speed[13]—and as many as four annual fairs.[14] By the early 17th century, however, it had experienced a decline, and although still important, large areas of the walled town lay empty and undeveloped. Speed shows that most of the burgages in the northern area had been abandoned with little settlement off Pool Road and Chirbury Road. No doubt this resulted partly from Glyndŵr's attack[15] and also from the lessening significance of the castle which fell into decay during the 14th century, and the town's military role consequently disappeared, although the castle itself was later restored as a private residence by the Herberts.[16]

1. Spurgeon, C. J., 'The Castles of Montgomeryshire', *Mont. Coll.*, lix (1965–6), 20–5.

2. *Cal. Pat Rolls*, 1216–25, 386. For an account of the castle, which was destroyed by Cromwell in 1649, *see* Sandford, G., 'Montgomery Castle', *Mont. Coll.*, x (1877), 61–124; Clark, G. T., *ibid.*, 313–8, *King's Works*, 739–42.

3. *Cal. Pat Rolls*, 1216–25, 414.

4. *Cal. Ch. Rolls*, i, 10. The borough charters are most accessible in *Mont. Coll.*, xxi (1887), 1–34, and xxii (1888), 1–8.

5. *Cal. Ch. Rolls*, i, 100–1.

6. S.C. 6/1306/3; Beresford, *New Towns*, 564–5.

7. *Ad inexpugnabile castrum construendum*, *Hist. Angl.* (R.S.), ii, 247.

8. O'Neil, B. H. St J. and Foster-Smith, A. H., 'Montgomery Town Wall', *Arch. Camb.*, xcv (1940), 217–28.

9. *Atlas of Wales*, inter 115–6.

10. *Itinerary*, 11.

11. Taylor, A. J., 'Montgomery Town Wall', *Arch. Camb.*, xcix (1947), 281–3.

12. *Cal. Pat Rolls*, 1166–72, 106; Turner, *Town Defences*, 217.

13. From Speed's map it would appear that the hall stood in the centre of Broad Street, a little to the east of the present building (Lloyd, J. D. K., 'Montgomery Town Hall and its architect', *Mont. Coll.*, lv [1957–8], 128–32).

14. Bowen, *Britannia Depicta*, 187.

15. Clark, G. T., *op. cit.*, 104. Leland noted that the town had been 'defloriched by Owen Glindour' (*Itinerary*, 41).

16. Lloyd, J. D. K., 'Montgomery Castle and the Herberts', *Arch. Camb.*, civ (1955–6), 52–64; Lewis, J. M., 'The excavation of the "new building" at Montgomery Castle', *ibid.*, cxvii (1968), 127–56.

MOSTYN, Clwyd (Flintshire)   SJ 157802

As Professor Beresford has pointed out, the evidence for an early town at Mostyn is slender and rests mainly on the 20 English taxpayers recorded at the 'nova villa de Moston' in 1292, which has the wording of plantion about it.[1] Three years later the manor was granted to Edward I's castle-builder, Master James of St George,[2] an extent made,[3] but there is little suggestion of real urban status. Almost nothing is known of the settlement for the remainder of the medieval period, and by the 16th century it was regarded only as a vill.[4] Coal and lead were being mined within the township by this time,[5] but Mostyn remained sufficiently insignificant to be omitted by Speed from his map of the county drawn up in 1610.[6]

The present village occupies a ridge running inland from the Dee and is similar in plan to Llawhaden, but there is no castle, and it is impossible to say if the house plots represent a medieval burgage pattern.

1. *New Towns*, 550-1, citing E 179/241/52.

2. *Cal. Cl. Rolls*, 1288-96, 423.

3. *Cal. Inq. Misc.*, i, No. 1692.

4. *Records of the Court of Augmentations*, 396, 403-5, 407.

5. Rees, *Industry Before the Industrial Revolution*, 74, 125, 478.

6. *Atlas of Wales, inter* 121-2.

NARBERTH (Arberth), Dyfed (Pembrokeshire)   SN 110145

The town of Narberth is built on rising ground just to the north of a small tributary of the Eastern Cleddau, and takes it name, as does Pembroke, from that of the surrounding district, being 'yn arberth'.

There is no direct evidence on the origins of settlement and the town may have been of either Welsh or English foundation. Following the conquest of Pembrokeshire by the Normans under Arnulf de Montgomery, Narberth is said to have been granted to Stephen Perrott.[1] It is unlikely, however, that he constructed any fortifications here, and the castle 'that was near Arberth' recorded in 1116[2] was probably Sentence Castle at Templeton. Midway between Narberth and Templeton stand the remains of another stronghold on Camp Hill which has also been attributed to Perrott, and it may well be that there was no castle at Narberth itself until after 1257, when Llywelyn ap Gruffudd destroyed the 'old fort'—either Camp Hill or Sentence Castle.[4] Certainly the visible masonry remains of Narberth Castle are no earlier than the late 13th or early 14th century.

Very little is known of Narberth during the medieval period beyond a few references to the castle. The borough seems to have come into being along with the castle, and by 1282 it had its own mill, and there was a yearly fair on the feast of St Andrew.[5] The church, dedicated to the same saint, also dates from the 13th century—it appears in the *taxatio* of 1291[6]—and it gave its name to Church Street, one of the principal areas of the early town. In 1532 there were only 30 burgages here[7] and John Leland, four years later, noted it only as 'a poore village'.[8] The principal development, in fact, was post-medieval, associated with the granting of a Thursday market in 1652, which was fostered by a certain Richard Castle.[9] The market expanded rapidly, mainly at the expense of that at Tenby, and as a result the Tenby burgesses applied to the king in 1671 for its suppression. This was granted in 1676, but by 1688 it had been re-established.[10] The town continued to grow steadily with the development of some local industry, principally the manufacture of hats and limestone quarrying.[11]

This developing 17th-century town centred on the Market Square which lies immediately north of the castle gates. The population at this time has been estimated at about seven hundred,[12] but in view of the small number of burgages recorded a century earlier before the granting of the market it seems unlikely that there was much settlement along the High Street and St James's Street during the medieval period. Indeed, the early town may not have been little more than a cluster of dwellings along Church Street, Castle Street, and Picton Place, with what was later to be the Market Square representing the northern limits of development.

1. Lewis, *Topographical Dictionary*, *sub* Narberth.

2. *Brut y Tywysogion*, 40.

3. Hogg and King, 'Early Castles', 117.

4. *Brut y Tywysogion*, 111; Hogg and King, 'Masonry Castles', 114.

5. Owen, *Cal. Pembs. Records*, ii, 74-5, 148. Owen, *Description of Pembrokeshire*, i, 143. The mill lay to the south of the town by the bridge, as indicated   by the names of Mill Farm, Mill Lane and Mill Pond Road.

6. *Record Commissioners edn.*, 274. Hugh de Mortimer appears as parson of *Nerberd* church in 1297 (Owen, *Cal. Pembs. Records*, ii, 75). The building, with the exception of the tower, was completely rebuilt in 1879.

7. *Ibid.*, 95-7. By 1547 the figure had risen by just two (*ibid.*, 119-20).

8. *Itinerary*, 62.

9. Charles, B. G. (ed.), *Records of Haverfordwest*, 125, 127; Howells, B. E. and K. A., *Pembrokeshire Life: 1572-1843*, Pembrokeshire Record Society (1972), 32. Bowen states that the market was on Wednesdays (*Britannia Depicta*, 40), but Lewis gives Thursdays (*Topographical Dictionary*, *loc. cit.*) as in the original grant.

10. Howells, *Pembrokeshire Life*, 48-52.

11. Lewis, *Topographical Dictionary*, *loc. cit.*

12. Archer, *The Welsh Post Towns Before 1840*, 88.

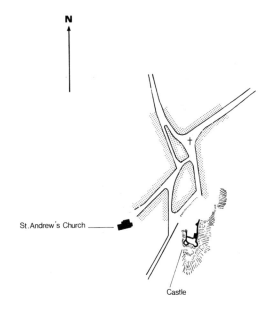

N

St.Andrew's Church

Castle

Fig. 69. Narberth

NEATH (Castell Nedd), West Glamorgan   SS 751978

The Neath district fell into Norman control during the second decade of the 12th century, and their hold was consolidated in 1129-30 when Richard de Granville, brother of Robert fitz Hamon, founded Neath Abbey on the east bank of the river.[1] There was also by this date an unlocated motte nearby, and a small, apparently defended, settlement appears to have been established in the shadow of the abbey since the foundation charter refers 'ad fossatum nove ville'.[2] The castle had ceased to stand by 1207, however,[3] and nothing further is heard of the township, which probably disappeared in the absence of adequate protection.

In the second half of the 12th century another attempt at town foundation was made with the building of a new castle, but this time on the opposite side of the river facing the old Roman fort of *Nidum*.[4] The site chosen was a terrace edge at what was traditionally the river's lowest crossing point prior to the construction of the modern bridge at Briton Ferry. The castle is first mentioned in 1185, when it was attacked by the Welsh,[5] who destroyed it again in 1231.[6] In the more detailed account of this second episode in the *Margam Annals* we find the first reference to the town which was also razed to the ground, and the inhabitants slain.[7] The 13th century was, in fact, a turbulent period for Neath, and the borough was again attacked in 1258,[8] the full extent of the damage revealed four years later in an inquisition on the death of Richard de Clare, when 150 houses lay destroyed. Burgess rents still amounted to 112s., however, so there must have been a flourishing town here before the attack.[9]

During the following years attempts were made to restore the community to its former extent, and recent excavation of the castle has indicated that its rebuilding dates from this period when the great gatehouse was added and an existing ring-wall capped with circular towers.[10] A fair was granted in 1280, but an account compiled in the following year reveals that 80 burgages and the town mill had again been destroyed by the Welsh, although 70 still paid rent, and that the tolls for the market and fair were only 6s., but 'not more because of the war'.[11] The situation had recovered again by 1294 when 104 burgages paid rent and the figure had risen further to 128 in 1314.[12] With the end of the Welsh risings the borough was able to enjoy a period of prosperity in the 14th century, receiving further grants of privileges in 1324 and 1340[13] and a major charter in 1359 when Edward le Despenser restricted all trade within the lordship to the borough.[14]

Despite the severity of the Welsh attacks it is clear from the burgage totals that early Neath was a substantial borough with a sound economy protected and fostered by charter. Curiously, however, its only defence appears to have been the castle, and there is no evidence to support the view that the town was walled or even protected with a bank and ditch,[15] although the possibility of at least the latter must remain until the question has been investigated archaeologically. In its

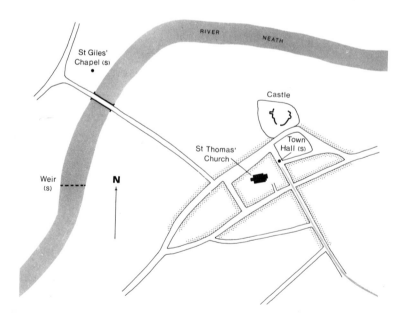

Fig. 70. Neath

lay-out the medieval town was compact and developed along the edge of the river terrace immediately east of the castle with the church of St Thomas as the natural core. The church appears to have been roughly contemporary with the castle, perhaps originally the garrison chapel,[16] for we find a certain 'Ralph persona [parson] de Neath' attesting an early 13th-century charter.[17]

Two plans of early Neath are known, included in a survey of Cadoxton Manor in 1601[18] and the Mackworth Estate map of 1720.[19] Both show virtually the same picture with the streets forming a square around the church with extensions to the north and south, and tenements also lining the road running south-east towards Briton Ferry. The earlier map is additionally valuable as it shows the position of the decayed weir below the bridge, which, as Leland noted, was timber-built,[20] and the site of St Giles's chapel on the west bank of the river. Neither plan, however, indicates the old town hall which stood in the middle of Old Market Street where it is joined by the High Street.[21] This building appears under the guise of 'le Court-house' in the 1397 charter and again as 'le Bottehalle' in 1491-2 when it was in ruins.[22] It was subsequently repaired and is mentioned again in the borough ordinances of 1542[23] and in an indenture dated 1612.[24] It was still standing in 1811 when it appears on the Gnoll Estate map[25] and was not finally demolished until the new town hall was built in 1821.[26] A final aspect of the early topography which has also disappeared was the stream which ran through the town and gave Water Street its name. In 1686 Anne Morgan was presented to the court-leet 'for throwing of rubbish into the common brook running through the said town', and it was misuse of this kind which eventually led to it being culverted.[27]

In common with the majority of Welsh towns Neath failed to experience any post-medieval growth, and the town may even have suffered a decline symptomised by the decay of the town hall. During the early 16th century the tolls from the market and fair ceased to be collected[28] and John Leland noted only a 'litle town',[29] with a population estimated at 600,[30] far fewer than must have lived there before the Welsh attack of 1258 when there were more than 250 houses. The surrounding coal industry and the borough's port functions which were responsible for the development of the modern town were already well established,[31] but the growth was comparatively late and the extent of settlement indicated on the 1811 map shows little change from the earlier plans, and is unlikely to have differed noticeably from the area occupied by medieval Neath.[32]

1. The foundation charter is in Clark, *Cartae*, i, 74-5; Francis, G. G., *Original charters and materials for the history of Neath and its Abbey* (Swansea, 1845), unpaginated, and Birch, W. de Gray, *History of Neath Abbey* (Neath, 1902), 30-1, 309-10.

2. Clark, *Cartae*, i, 75, 'The old Castle of Neth, in the Westerside of the River' is mentioned by Rice Merrick (*Book of Glamorganshire Antiquities*, 69).

3. Birch, *op. cit.*, 21-2.

4. On the fort *see* Nash-Williams, *Roman Frontier in Wales*, 98-101.

5. *Ann. Margam*, 18.

6. *Brut y Tywysogion*, 102.

7. *Ann. Margam*, 39.

8. *Annales de Theokesberia* in *Ann. Monastici*, i, 167.

9. Clark, *Cartae*, ii, 661-2; Birch, *op. cit.*, 230, 233-4.

10. *Med. Arch.*, x (1966), 194-5; Brooksby, H., 'Neath Castle', *Morgannwg*, xvii (1973), 62-4.

11. *Et non plus causa guerre*, Clark, *Cartae*, iii, 837; Birch, *op. cit.*, 235.

12. C 133/120, 134/43; Beresford, *New Towns*, 556; *Glam. County Hist.*, iii, 343.

13. *Ibid.*, 352; *Cal. Ch. Rolls*, iii, 461.

14. *Ibid.*, v, 164; Clark, *Cartae*, iv, 1419-22; Francis, *op. cit.* The borough was granted a further charter in 1397 (*ibid.*; Clark, *Cartae*, iv, 1422-26).

15. Neath is stated to have been walled by Lewis (*Topographical Dictionary sub* Neath) and by Clark (*Cartae*, i, 76; *The Land of Morgan* [London, 1883], 133). There are several references to ditches in the area of the town, such as the *veteri fossato*, mentioned in a late 13th- or early 14th-century deed (*Cal. Anct. Deeds*, ii, No. B 2737), but nothing to indicate a connection with defence.

16. Birch, *op. cit.*, 228.

17. Clark, *Cartae*, iii, 926.

18. Neath Corporation Muniments, reproduced in Francis, *op. cit.*, and Birch, *op. cit.*, 268.

19. In the possession of the Neath Antiquarian Society, reproduced in Birch, *op. cit.*, *inter* 226-7.

20. 'Ponte Castelle Nethe of timber' (*Itinerary*, 38).

21. Sanders, H. G., 'Neath, 1678-88', *Trans. Neath Antiq. Soc.*, 2nd ser., vi (1936-7), 66. The old borough prison was located underneath the hall.

22. *Glam. County Hist.*, iii, 353.

23. Francis, *op. cit.*

24. Birch, *op. cit.*, 273.

25. Glam. Record Office.

26. Taylor, G. A., 'Neath Town Hall', *Trans Neath Antiq. Soc., op. cit.*, 76-7.

27. Francis, *op. cit.*, extracts from the Presentments to the Courts Leet. *See also* Thomas, G. S., 'Some Neath Street Names', *Trans. Neath Antiq. Soc., op. cit.*, 97-100.

28. *Glam. County Hist.*, iii, 353.

29. *Itinerary*, 30.

30. Thomas, W. S. K., 'Tudor and Jacobean Swansea', *Morgannwg*, v (1961), 25.

31. Trott, C. D. J., 'Coal Mining in the borough of Neath in the Seventeenth and early Eighteenth Century', *ibid.*, xiii (1969), 47-74. Bowen noted 'a town trading much in coales' (*Britannia Depicta*, 38).

32. There is a valuable discussion of the later growth of the town in Carter, *Towns of Wales*, 234-44.

NEFYN, Gwynedd (Caernarvonshire)   SH 308407

Nefyn occupies an area of fairly level ground on the north coast of the Llŷn peninsula, the old town being only a quarter of a mile from the sea, and it was the rich herring stocks of Caernarfon Bay which underlay the growth of this Welsh vill.[1] It was also, as T. Jones Pierce has emphasised, situated at an important point on the pilgrim road to Bardsey and supplying the needs of the travellers was a second major factor behind its development.[2] Although there is a motte nearby,[3] nucleated settlement does not appear to have been earlier than the late 12th century when the church is first mentioned as being in the possession of the Augustinian canons of Haughmond Abbey.[4] Two burgesses of Nefyn also appear attesting an early 13th-century charter,[5] but it was under the two Llywelyns that the settlement developed into the administrative centre of the commot of Dinllaen and came to rank among the principal towns of Gwynedd. The Welsh princes, indeed, had a residence there, repaired in 1284[6] and again in 1306-7 for probable use by royal officers,[7] and the name of Palace Street provides an indication

of its former position. Nefyn also had its priory
—a prior is mentioned in 1252[8]—and although
the religious house has little documentary history its probable site has been suggested as
south-east of the church by the children's
modern playground, where former field-names
incorporated the word 'mynach'.[9]

Following Edward I's defeat of Llywelyn
ap Gruffudd Nefyn fell into English hands,
and it was here in the summer of 1284 that
the king chose to celebrate his victory by
holding a grand tournament.[10] The town was
surveyed in the same year and was immediately recognised by the officials as a *burgus,*
containing 50 households, holding its own
markets and carrying out some seaborne
trade.[11] This developing community was
immediately encouraged to expand further,
though few Englishmen ventured this far into
Wales to take up burgages, and by the time
of a second extent made in 1293 the popu-

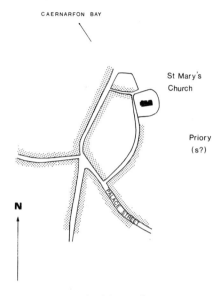

Fig. 71. Nefyn

lation had almost doubled to 93 taxpayers.[12] Their number included several
tradesmen, a goldsmith and an innkeeper, and Madoc the priest, and it is significant
that half of the total possessed fishing nets, indicating the mainstay of the economy.
No further surveys are known, and the town was subsequently let out at farm.[13]
In 1355 the burgesses, like those of Pwllheli on the south coast, petitioned Edward
the Black Prince and secured a charter of privileges. This confirmed the existing
Saturday market, gave the addition of two annual fairs, and further consolidated
the town's dominant position within Dinllaen by ordering that all the commot's
trade was to be conducted within the borough.[14]

The physical framework of the early town is not well documented, but in all
probability the burgages were centred around the church and along Palace Street
where some small 18th-century houses remain.[15] The borough itself was not
defended, and the absence of walls must have been regretted in 1400 when
Glyndŵr devastated the town.[16] The attack caused considerable damage and led
to the virtual abandonment of the borough, it being recorded in 1413 that no one
wished to live there. A community was established a few years later, however,
though on a much reduced scale, and the extent of the damage is indicated by the
population's exemption from rent throughout Henry IV's reign.[17] Nefyn, in fact,
was unable to regain its medieval extent, and even the weekly market had
temporarily lapsed by the 1530s,[18] although it had been revived by Camden's
time. The place was then no more than 'a village',[19] however, and even by the
early 19th century there had been no improvement and Fenton noted only 'a poor
straggling miserable place . . . neither dignified with Town Hall or handsome
Church'.[20]

1. For an account of the town's history *see* T. Jones Pierce, 'The Old Borough of Nefyn, 1355-1882', *T.C.H.S.*, xviii (1957), 36-53.

2. *Ibid.*, 39, and *idem*, 'Two Early Caernarvonshire Accounts', *B.B.C.S.*, v (1931), 142.

3. The motte has no documentary history (T. Jones Pierce, 'Old Borough of Nefyn', *op. cit.*, 38). It is crowned with the remains of a tower but this appears to be no older than the early 19th century (*R.C.A.M.W.M.*, *Caerns.*, iii, 85) and was probably used in connection with the fishing industry as a watch-tower, similar to the Cornish 'Huer's huts'.

4. Cartulary of Haughmond Abbey, Shrewsbury Public Library MS., i, ff. 149-50; *R.C.A.M.W.M.*, *Caerns.*, iii, 83.

5. Cartulary of Haughmond Abbey, f. 149; *R.C.A.M.W.M.*, *Caerns.*, iii, 83.

6. *Cal. Welsh Rolls*, 293.

7. T. Jones Pierce, 'Two Early Caernarvonshire Accounts', *op. cit.*, 150-1. The itemised expenditure indicates that it was a thatched building, constructed of timber and wattle, and apparently with an upper storey.

8. *Rec. Caern.*, 252.

9. *R.C.A.M.W.M.*, *Caerns.*, iii, 84, citing the Tithe Award Schedule, Nat. Lib. Wales.

10. *Brut y Tywysogion*, 121; *Annales Monastici*, ii, 402; iii, 313; iv, 491.

11. T. Jones Pierce, 'The Old Borough of Nefyn', *op. cit.*, 39-40.

12. *Idem*, 'Two Early Caernarvonshire Accounts', *op. cit.*, 142-8.

13. In 1316 it was farmed to a Welshman, Gruffydd ap Hywel (*Cal. Fine Rolls, 1307-19*, 271).

14. The text is in Lewis, *Medieval Boroughs of Snowdonia*, 287-9.

15. There were only a few dwellings in the area of the motte to the west of the town (T. Jones Pierce, 'The Old Borough of Nefyn', *op. cit.*, 39).

16. *Ibid.*, 44.

17. S.C. 6/1175/7-9; Lewis, *Medieval Boroughs of Snowdonia*, 198; T. Jones Pierce, 'The Old Borough of Nefyn', *op. cit.*, 44.

18. Leland, *Itinerary*, 87.

19. *Britannia*, 668.

20. *Tours in Wales*, 47. His contemporary Samuel Lewis was equally uncomplimentary (*Topographical Dictionary*, *sub* Nevin).

NEWBOROUGH (Niwbwrch), Gwynedd (Anglesey)   SH 424656

Newborough was a planted borough of English instigation, but whose inhabitants were almost exclusively Welsh. Its foundation stemmed from the need to re-accommodate the displaced inhabitants of Llanfaes, whose town had been destroyed with the building of Beaumaris. Accordingly Edward I's surveyors appropriated 90½ acres of land in the south-west corner of the island and established the borough around the existing village of Rhosyn (Rhosfair), itself a sizeable settlement and the *caput* of the commot of Menai.[1] The date of the transfer from Llanfaes has been assigned to 1303,[2] and by Michaelmas Newborough was well-established, the inhabitants receiving their charter, and by it the privileges of Rhuddlan in the same year.[3] The accounts for 1304-5 record the construction of a new mill and indicate that the borough rents already amounted to £8 8s. 6d. a year.[4] In 1349 the burgesses secured the right to elect their own mayor[5] and a survey carried out three years later shows that Newborough continued to prosper, recording the names of 58 taxpayers, seven of whom—the beginnings of an urban aristocrary—held six or more plots.[6]

In its plan Newborough exhibits the essential characteristics of a planted borough. It was rapidly established, perhaps more so than any other Welsh town, with the plots (termed *placeae* rather than burgages) set out along two streets which cross at right-angles. For the most part they are still easily detectable and apart from development to the north of Pendref Street the present town does not appear to be much larger than its medieval counterpart. No early buildings have survived, however, the majority being two-storeyed 19th-century dwellings and strikingly small since there has been little coalescing of the original

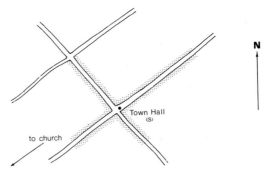

Fig. 72. Newborough

plots. At the junction of the two thoroughfares stood the site of the weekly Thursday market, while just to the east at the beginning of Pendref Street stood the old town hall. The building has since been removed, but it is indicated as 'the Shire Hall' on a crude plan of 1738-9 when it was 'in ruins'.[7] Notably absent from the early topography was the presence of a castle and there is nothing to suggest that the town was defended either with walls or a bank and ditch. Neither was there a borough church since the town was laid out only 300m. north-east of the existing parish church of St Peter which originally served the inhabitants of Rhosyr.[8]

As a corporation Newborough was at its height during the 14th century, but for the remainder of the medieval period it remained an important settlement despite its experiences at the hands of Glyndŵr's supporters which left several burgages unoccupied throughout Henry V's reign.[9] In 1507 Henry VII enhanced its status by transferring the county courts from Beaumaris,[10] but this had to be reversed in 1549 when it was said that the town had become impoverished and was no longer capable of supporting its pre-eminence in the shire.[11] Nevertheless, a survey carried out at this time (*c.* 1547) continued to indicate a sizeable town of 93 houses, 12 crofts, 13 gardens, and an orchard.[12] The decline in the borough's financial position was attributed to extensive sand drifts which had gradually been covering large areas of surrounding land. As early as 1331 the drifts had destroyed several farms and some 186 acres of pasture.[13] In 1561, to prevent further destruction, Elizabeth I granted an order forbidding the pulling up of 'mor-hesg' (marram grass), which alone could stave off further encroachment.[14] This protection of the grass proved beneficial to Newborough in another way, providing the inhabitants with the raw material to carry out mat and basket weaving, for which the town became noted.[15] However, by the end of the 17th century it had lost much of its urban character and functions. Fenton regarded it as 'a wretched place'[16] and even the weekly market had been abandoned by the early 19th century.[17]

1. *Rec. Caern.*, 83–5; Lewis, *Medieval Boroughs of Snowdonia*, 52; Beresford, *New Towns*, 535.

2. Davies, H. R., *The Conway and Menai Ferries*, B.C.S., Hist and Law Ser., viii (Cardiff, 1942), 24–7, correcting Lewis, who assigned the move *ante* 1302 (*Medieval Boroughs of Snowdonia*, 52).

3. The text is in *Rec. Caern.*, 178, and Lewis, *Medieval Boroughs of Snowdonia*, 283.

   4. Lewis, E. A., 'The Account Roll of the Chamberlain of the Principality of North Wales from Michaelmas 1304 to Michaelmas 1305', *B.B.C.S.*, i (1923), 262, 269.
   5. *Register of Edward, the Black Prince*, 1, 155. The grant, however, stipulated that the mayor had to be an Englishman, which severely limited the choice.
   6. *Rec. Caern.*, 85–9; Carr, A. D., 'The Extent of Anglesey, 1352', *T.A.A.S.* (1971–2), 262–72; Owen, H., *Hanes Plwyf Niwbwrch ym Môn* (Caernarfon, 1952), 11–16.
   7. Appended to Owen, *Hanes Niwbwrch*.
   8. *R.C.A.M.W.M.*, *Anglesey*, 118. This is likely to have been 'the church of Peter in Anglesey' ravaged by Henry II's troops in 1157 (*Brut y Tywysogion*, 59).
   9. Lewis, *Medieval Boroughs of Snowdonia*, 208, 250.
   10. *Ibid.*, 209; Owen, *Hanes Niwbwrch*, 25.
   11. Bowen, *Statutes of Wales*, lxxviii; Hughes, *Hanes Niwbwrch*, 26–8.
   12. Lloyd, A., *History of Mona* (Ruthin, 1833), 317; Hughes, *Hanes Niwbwrch*, 17.
   13. S.C. 6/1152/4; Owen, *Hanes Niwbwrch*, 9. *Cf.* Camden, *Britannia*, 672.
   14. *Rec. Caern.*, 298.
   15. Hughes, M., 'The Marram Grass Industry of Newborough, Anglesey', *T.A.A.S.* (1956), 22–8; Owen, H., 'The Mat-Weaving Industry in Newborough', *ibid.* (1923), 62–4.
   16. *Tours in Wales*, 270.
   17. Lewis, *Topographical Dictionary*, *sub* Newborough.

NEWCASTLE EMLYN (Castellnewydd Emlyn), Dyfed (Carmarthenshire)

SN 310407

Newcastle Emlyn is situated on the southern bank of the Afon Teifi with both the castle and medieval town occupying a striking peninsula formed by a deep incised meander of the river.[1] The site was obviously chosen for reasons of defence and the castle appears first, preceding the town by more than half a century. In 1240 the cantref of Emlyn was partitioned by Henry III between Walter Marshall and Maredudd ap Rhys and the Welshman is considered to have been the builder of the castle.[2] It quickly emerged as the administrative centre of the lordship of Emlyn uwch Cuch and became known as the 'new castle of Emlyn' to distinguish it from the 'old castle' at Cilgerran.[3] In 1287 the stronghold was attacked by Rhys ap Maredudd and changed hands three times in the same year, but none of the sources indicate the existence of an associated town.[4] Indeed, the evidence for its foundation is quite specific and the pointers are firmly to 1303 with 26 burgages recorded in the following year, each paying the statutory 12d. a year rent,[5] together with an unspecified number of burgesses *de vento* who collectively rendered 5s. 6d.[6] The vill expanded quickly and in the following year the burgess total had risen to fifty-four.[7] The borough had its bailiff and held its own courts, and tolls from two annual fairs are first recorded in 1307–8.[8] This growth continued, and by 1316 there were 62 burgages together with a further 24 other tenants.[9] The castle was also partly rebuilt and strengthened during these years[10] and the borough's first century of existence was generally a period of considerable prosperity.

The location and form of the early town was determined by the position of the castle. This was sited within an inverted 'S' bend of the river which almost made a complete natural moat. The town developed beyond the castle gate with the main street running parallel to the meander. The bridge across the Teifi to Adpar was

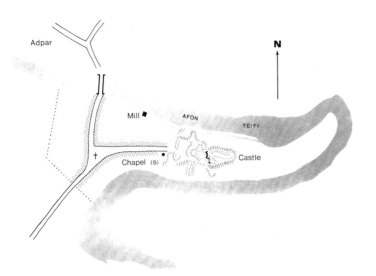

Fig. 73. Newcastle Emlyn

already in being before the foundation of the borough, and its position led to the appearance of a secondary street which connected with Castle Street at a right angle.[11] Here also was located the site of the weekly Friday market, although the area has been much encroached upon since the 18th century.[12]

The tenants recorded in 1316 could easily be accommodated along the 'T'-shape formed by Bridge Street and Castle Street and several of the former burgage plots can still be seen, notably on the south side of Castle Street, where they run down to the river. There is no archaeological or documentary evidence to suggest that the medieval borough was defended, but the possibility of at least a bank and ditch cannot be overruled. The selection of this site for the castle and town was obviously determined by considerations of defence, and it would have taken comparatively little effort to defend the town by throwing up a bank across the narrow neck of the peninsula. A possible line is suggested by the regular course of property boundaries on the west side of Bridge Street. There was no church within the confines of the early town since it was planted within the existing parish of Cenarth, and the church of the Holy Trinity dates only from 1842. There was a medieval chapel, however, with the same dedication, and its position lay close to the outer earthworks of the castle.[13] Remains were still visible in 1838 when it was shown on the Tithe Plan, but all traces have since disappeared.[14]

From its height in the 14th century Newcastle Emlyn experiences a marked decline in the 15th century. In 1403 the borough was attacked by Glyndŵr, and there appears to have been considerable resistance but with disastrous results.[15] Twenty years later the townsfolk were still £36 in arrears, and from this time the borough virtually disappears from the records for the remainder of the medieval period.[16] Something is known of the castle—it was rebuilt by Sir Rhys ap Thomas in the 1480s[17] and eventually demolished by Cromwell's troops in 1644[18]—but the town drifted into obscurity and its borough status was almost forgotten.

1. On the general history of the town and castle *see* Evans, G., 'The Story of Newcastle Emlyn and Adpar' *Y Cymmrodor*, xxxii (1922), 58–170.

2. Cole, H. (ed.), *Documents Illustrative of English History in the Thirteenth and Fourteenth Centuries* (London, 1844), 47–8; Lloyd, *History of Wales*, ii, 726.

3. *Ibid.*, 726; Evans, G., *op. cit.*, 72. D. J. C. King, however, thought that the 'old castle' of Emlyn was the motte at Cenarth (*Arch. Camb.*, cxxii [1973], 210).

4. *Annales Cambriae*, 110; *Cal. Anct. Corresp.*, 158; Griffiths, R., 'The Revolt of Rhys ap Maredudd', *op. cit.*, 135.

5. The foundation date is discussed by Beresford, *New Towns*, 543, and Evans, G., *op. cit.*, 89.

6. S.C. 6/1218/9; Rhys, *Ministers' Accounts for West Wales*, 293.

7. *Ibid.*, 361.

8. S.C. 6/1218/6.

9. S.C. 6/1217/6-7.

10. *King's Works*, 646-7; Hogg and King, 'Masonry Castles', 115.

11. The bridge is mentioned in 1257 (*Littere Wallie*, 171; *Cal. Pat. Rolls*, 1247-58, 582).

12. Lewis, *Topographical Dictionary*, *sub* Newcastle Emlyn.

13. Evans, G., *op. cit.*, 91, 157.

14. Carmarthenshire Record Office.

15. Ellis, H. (ed.), *Original Letters illustrative of English History*, 2nd ser., i, 15, 19; Evans, G., *op. cit.*, 122-6.

16. S.C. 6/1166/12; Evans, G., *op. cit.*, 127-8.

17. Leland, *Itinerary*, 57; *King's Works*, 647.

18. Phillips, *Memoirs of the Civil War in Wales and the Marches* (London, 1874), i, 234, 337-9; ii, 190, 192, 358.

NEW MOAT (Y Mot), Dyfed (Pembrokeshire)   SN 064254

New Moat lies eight miles north-east of Haverfordwest and is now little more than a village with a scattering of houses around St Nicholas's church and the site of an old motte. During the 14th century, however, this was a manor of the bishops of St David's, who were responsible for erecting the stronghold and fostering the development of a not insignificant borough.

The remains of the motte, now no more than 10.5m. in height, can be seen off the east side of the main road facing the newly-built Beech Court. There are no signs of any masonry, and it is unlikely that the castle was ever built in stone. The bailey can be detected to the west and north and was formerly mistaken for the remains of a Roman camp, being so marked on the 1907 edition of the Ordnance Survey map.[1] The name of 'New Moat', however, does imply the existence of an earlier structure which has been variously identified as nearby Henry's Moat or the camp of Rhyd y Brwyn.[2] Equally this may be an allusion to 'The Mote' which the 1907 map records south-west of the church beyond Awel y Coed Farm. This is still partly visible and traces of the outer bailey in the form of a shallow ditch and low outer bank cutting diagonally across the field can be seen running in a north-easterly direction towards the church. These defences appear to have been earlier and distinct from those associated with the episcopal borough of the 14th century, but, unfortunately, neither fortification has any recorded history.

It seems likely that the old motte gave protection to a small burgess community which was later expanded by the bishops of St David's. Adam de Rupe's foundation charter to Pill Priory *c.* 1200 indicates that the church was already standing, while he also granted *inter alia* 'in the township of New Moat a burgage by the East Gate and one burgage on the north side.[3] The reference to the 'East Gate' is particularly interesting since it suggests that this early vill was

defended, perhaps lying within the bailey walls
as at Dryslwyn. During the late 13th and early
14th centuries, associated with the buildings
of the bisop's motte, new tenants were encouraged to take up burgages and the borough came
into being. In 1291 a twice yearly fair was
granted at Michaelmas and on the feast of
St Nicholas[4] and by 1326 the burgess total
had risen to 42 holding 89 plots.[5] They were
overwhelmingly English, and they held their
lands by deed which suggests that the settlement
was still comparatively recent.

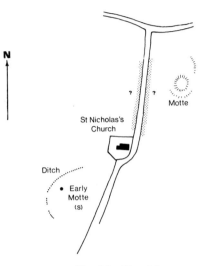

Fig. 74. New Moat

There is little in the appearance of modern
New Moat to indicate the site of this borough,
but it is unlikely to have corresponded with
the vill of *c.* 1200 and the old motte south of
the church. Indeed, the construction of a new
stronghold only 500m. further north suggests
a new location, and the indications are to the
area of what is now pasture immediately across the road. There are several earthworks in this area together with what appear to be house platforms, while the field
boundaries run parallel to the road, but set back, which suggests the perimeter
of the settlement.

Nothing is known of the later history of New Moat or of the circumstances which
led to its decline and virtual disappearance.

1. *See also* Lewis, *Topographical Dictionary, sub* New Moat; *R.C.A.M.W.M., Pembs.*, 268.
2. *Ibid.*, 268.
3. *In villa de Nova Mota quoddam burgagium proximum portae orientali* (*Mon. Angl.*, iv,
503; Pritchard, E. M., *History of St Dogmael's Abbey* [London, 1907], 124–6). On the revised
dating of the charter *see* Knowles and Hadcock, *Medieval Religious Houses*, 107.
4. *Cal. Ch. Rolls*, ii, 405.
5. *Black Book*, 127–36.

NEWPORT (Trefdraeth), Dyfed (Pembrokeshire)   SN 057391

Newport lies along the road from Fishguard to Cardigan at a point where the
River Nevern flows into Cardigan Bay. The town dates from the late 12th century
and the regularity of its street-pattern confirms the documentary evidence that this
was a planted borough created within the lordship of Cemaes. The Normans had
originally chosen nearby Nevern as this district's *caput*, but the castle there was
destroyed by the Welsh in 1195.[1] William de Tours elected to build its successor
on a new site half a mile inland, and within two years it was completed.[2] Probably
contemporary with it was St Mary's church,[3] and a charter of incorporation issued
to the newly-settled inhabitants of the *novum burgum* which included the right to
hold a weekly market on Thursdays and an annual fair on 16 June.[4]

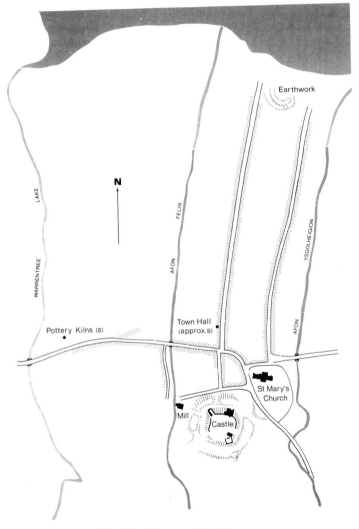

Fig. 75. Newport, Dyfed

It is not known if this new borough displaced an existing Welsh vill as was sometimes the case. The traditional Welsh name for Newport is 'Trefdraeth', which denotes a 'settlement on the sand', and it has been suggested than an earlier settlement existed by the shore at Parrog which has since been lost through sand encroachment.[5] The theory is plausible enough— sand overran Kenfig and perhaps also Prestatyn—but in this case the view appears to have developed because late-medieval contraction of the borough left 19th-century commentators unaware of the fact that it had originally extended right down to the Nevern Estuary when it had occupied almost twice its present area. Newport, in fact, ranked among the largest of the medieval Welsh towns functioning as the head of the independent lordships of Cemaes. The lords exercised *jura regalia* rights within their own territory and their own gaol and gallows were located just beyond the town near Cnwcau Farm on the Penfeidr road (SN 049390).[6] A borough rental of 1324 realised 46s., which, if the burgages were let at the standard 1s. each, meant only 46 plots, but there are reasons for assuming that this was a serious undervaluation[7] and we derive a more satisfactory impression of the town from a full extent compiled in 1434.[8] This included a detailed list of the burgesses and their holdings and assigns each plot to its respective street. There were 223 plots in all, with 20 on the south side of West Street

'beginning near the stream called Warentrelak' and running east towards the
castle; 20 off Bridge Street; 24½ along Goat Street; and 11½ along an unidentified
Vicus Mabudrud. Also, and particularly important are the totals for Long Street
and St Mary's Street which run north from the castle to the sea. Along the former
there were 88 burgages which began with that held by 'Thomas Jordan . . . next
the sea near the old castle', a reference to the earthwork situated only 70m. from
the shoreline; and another 59 along St Mary's Street, again 'beginning along the sea
(*per mare*) towards the church'. Clearly the early town was considerably more
substantial than its modern counterpart and extended northwards right to the
estuary with important extensions also east and west of the castle. Within the
present built-up area the burgage plots are for the most part still visible with those
off Long Street and St Mary's Street, bounded respectively by the Afon Felin and
Afon Ysgolheigion which flow past the castle on either side following a parallel
course down to the sea. Beyond modern Newport, north of Maes Morga, the
burgages have been coalesced into small fields and the recreation ground, and the
original pattern can no longer be discerned.

From the 1434 survey analysed with the evidence from another detailed extent
of 1594,[9] it is possible to reconstruct a little more of the early town's topography.
The lord's mill, mentioned in 1275,[10] still stands along the Afon Felin
immediately below the castle, while on the east side St. Mary's churchyard was
originally much smaller and burgages lined its northern edge.[11] Adjoining was the
old vicarage, known locally as 'The Court', which remained until 1800[12] although
some vestiges were still visible 30 years later when Lewis visited the town.[13] There
is no documentary proof for the suggestion that the borough also housed an
Augustinian priory and that St Mary's was originally the priory church,[14] and
writers appear to have been misled by the same order's house founded in 1377
at Newport, Gwent.[15] Seventy metres north-west of the church at the junction of
Church Street and Bridge Street stood the small market-place, while immediately
north on the west side of Long Street was the town hall, although the building had
ceased to be used for administrative purposes by the late 16th century.[16] Finally,
at the end of West Street, near Warrentree Lake (conveniently sited on the outskirts
of the borough where the fire risk could be minimised), was an area set aside for
use by the town's potters. Two kilns dating from the late 14th and early 15th
centuries were discovered here in 1921 by workmen laying the foundations of the
Memorial Hall.[17]

From its height in the early 15th century when Newport must have housed a
population in the region of 1,000 the borough declined drastically and,
according to a rental of 1594, all but 50 of the 233 burgages recorded in 1434 had
fallen into decay and stood untenanted.[18] Many of the plots had been completely
abandoned, and the boundaries ploughed, and even the town's weekly market
had ceased to be held. Other plots had also been sacrificed with the building of
Bridge Street which transferred the Cardigan to Fishguard traffic away from the
congested area of The Square and St Mary's church.[19] The reasons behind this
sudden decline are unclear, and the evidence conflicts with the traditional view
of 16th-century Newport as the centre of an important woollen industry with

its port.[20] The development of Fishguard during this period is said to have resulted from the migration of many Newport inhabitants fleeing from plague,[21] and although the story has been described as a myth there may well be much truth in it,[22] particularly since another outbreak recorded in 1665 was sufficiently severe to necessitate the removal of the revived market to a village four miles away, where it was still being held in 1714.[23]

1. *Annales Cambriae*, 60.

2. For a description of the castle, which was attacked by the Welsh in 1215 and 1257 (*ibid.*, 71; *Brut y Tywysogion*, 91, 111) see *R.C.A.M.W.M., Pembs.*, 274–6 and *Arch. Journ.*, cxix (1962), 340.

3. Jones, E., *A Historical Sketch of Newport* (Solva, 1890), 14–15.

4. Owen, G., *Baronia de Kemeys* (London, 1861), 49–51; Ballard and Tait, *British Borough Charters*, xxxi.

5. Jones, E., *op. cit.*, 7; *Arch. Camb.*, 3rd ser., x (1964), 313.

6. Owen, *Baronia de Kemeys*, 22–3; Jones, E., *op. cit.*, 33.

7. C 134/88/18; Beresford, *New Towns*, 568.

8. Bronwydd MS., 303; Charles, B. G., 'The Records of the Borough of Newport in Pembroke-shire', *Nat. Lib. Wales Journ.*, vii (1951–2), 120–7.

9. Bronwydd MS., 303; Charles, B. G., *op. cit.*, 127–34.

10. Owen, *Cal. Pembs. Records*, iii, 7–8.

11. The churchyard was enlarged in 1886 (Jones, E., *op. cit.*, 17).

12. *Ibid.*, 22.

13. Lewis, misled by the building's name, assumed it to have been the town's record office (*Topographical Dictionary*, sub Newport).

14. *Mon. Angl.*, vi, 1603, echoed by Jones, E., *op. cit.*, 18–19.

15. Knowles and Hadcock, *Medieval Religious Houses*, 246.

16. An entry in the town rental of 1594 refers to 'a burgage on the west side of Long Street called "the old Sheere hall"' (Charles, B. G., *op. cit.*, 128). Since the Long Street entry begins 'on the west side . . . near the castle and thus descending towards the river', and this was the seventh burgage listed, the hall must have been off the present Market Street.

17. *R.C.A.M.W.M., Pembs.*, 277; Talbot, E. J., 'Welsh Ceramics: A Documentary and Archaeo-logical Survey', *Post-Med. Arch.*, ii (1968), 122–7.

18. Above, Note 9.

19. This 'highway through the middle of the town towards Fishguard' is listed separately from (Upper) Bridge Street and West Street, the old road through Newport, but it does not appear in the 1434 rental.

20. Lewis, *Topographical Dictionary*, *loc cit.*; Evans, E., *op. cit.*, 38.

21. Lewis, *Topographical Dictionary*, sub Fishguard.

22. Beresford, *New Towns*, 569.

23. Bronwydd MS., 1009; Charles, B. G., *op. cit.*, 136.

NEWPORT (Casnewydd), Gwent (Monmouthshire)   ST 311882

Modern Newport ranks among the largest of Welsh towns, and is a leading distribution centre for the importers and exporters of South Wales and the Midlands. Despite the town's misleading name this is one of the oldest nucleated settlements in Gwent, and its history is firmly rooted in the medieval period when the borough was founded by the Normans. Indeed, town origins, or at least settlement history, appear to be even older, and there are suggestions of a community here during the post-Roman era. The Dark Age leader, Gwynllyw, is said to have established his court here, probably at Allt Gwynllwg, later to be known as Stow Hill. The nearby church of St Woolos is named after him, and its existence later encouraged the Normans to erect their first castle nearby, possibly on the site of Gwynllyw's old *maerdref*.[1]

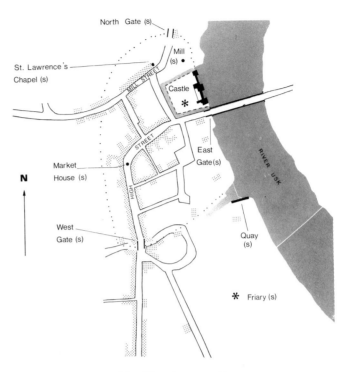

Fig. 76. Newport, Gwent

The Norman motte was thrown up *c.* 1090 by Robert fitz Hamon as part of a comprehensive thrust into South Wales, and it was still visible in 1801 when Coxe's map was drawn up, although it was later removed during construction of the railway.[2] The patronage of St Woolos's church and its tithes were granted to the Benedictine Abbey of Gloucester, and it is likely that a small English community came into being encouraged by the presence of a military garrison. During the early part of the 12th century it was decided to abandon the motte and construct a new castle on lower ground by the river, the predecessor of the structure whose remains can be seen by the modern bridge. Initially built of wood, the castle was well established by 1185–6 when it was repaired following a Welsh attack[3] and must have been standing in 1172 when Henry II passed through 'the new town on Usk'.[4] Early in the following century it was rebuilt in stone and surrounded by a moat,[5] of which the western part was later incorporated into the Monmouthshire canal, and the borough quickly came to dominate the lordship with its commercial life fostered by exclusive trading privileges and the right to levy tolls on those who passed through the town.[6] By 1263 the burgage total stood at 242[7] and by 1314 the figure had risen to 275,[8] which points to a total population in the region of about a thousand. No early charter is known, although confirmation of borough status was given in 1385 by Hugh, Earl of Stafford, and endorsed by his successor, Humphrey, in 1427.[9] The second document sets out the bounds of the medieval borough, although it is clear that the town itself covered a much smaller area by the castle. A plan of 1752 shows that it was confined to the High Street, and the lower part of Stow Hill, and there were only 192 tenants with 'an even fewer number of habitable houses'.[10]

Although confined to a small area, medieval Newport nevertheless boasted an interesting and varied urban topography. Inevitably the site was dominated by the castle which continued to be maintained long after the damage inflicted by Owain Glyndŵr in 1402, and in 1521 it was still 'a proper castle'.[11] It was surrounded by a moat fed by the River Usk which in turn provided the power for the town mill, mentioned in the charter of 1385, which was situated immediately to the north. The building was still standing when the 1844 Ordnance Survey map was compiled, but was finally removed later in the century. The chapel of St Lawrence also stood in Mill Street, and it continued to hold services until the early 16th century, but its site had been developed by the early 1800s. Both features lay within the town walls, although we know very little about the history of Newport's defences.

John Leland enumerated three gates in the 1530s; the East Gate by the bridge; the North Gate above the castle; and the West Gate which stood at the junction of Commercial Street and Stow Hill, but he curiously added that he 'marked not whyther ye were waulled or no'.[12] Obviously all traces had already disappeared and the total absence of remains at this relatively early date suggest that the town was not walled in stone and was defended only by an earthen bank with perhaps an outer ditch, only the gates being masonry structures. The early plans add nothing to our knowledge of the subject, although Coxe states that the borough was walled.[13] The position of the town gates studied in conjunction with the street-pattern preserved by the earliest Ordnance Survey map suggests a likely course. As natural barriers the river on the east and the town pill to the south are likely to have been incorporated and the position of the latter, which corresponds to the inlet beyond Skinner Street, suggests that the southern defences ran from the river past the north side of the pill as far as the West Gate. From here they appear to have turned north following a course parallel to High Street, where the burgage pattern is well preserved and the present Cambrian Road originally represented their rear boundary line with the defensive ditch beyond. With the mill and St Lawrence's chapel both within the enclosed area the ditch must have continued northwards across the railway line and Mill Street as far as the North Gate, which stood by the river.

Other features of early Newport's physical framework include the Market House which stood in the middle of the High Street, opposite the post office. It is marked on the 1752 town map, but was eventually demolished in 1793. Beyond the defences stood the borough quay mentioned by Leland and marked on the map of 1752 which also shows a lime kiln situated nearby. Further south was the Augustinian friary founded *ante* 1377 by Hugh, Earl of Stafford,[14] and mentioned by Leland as the 'house of religion by the key beneth the bridg'. It was dissolved in 1538, but there were still considerable remains north of Llanarth Street in 1801, although the site has recently been completely developed. The nearby friary cemetery was discovered and excavated in 1933 when several skeletons were unearthed, probably all of former brothers.

From being one of the largest Welsh boroughs in the early 14th century Newport declined significantly during the late medieval period. The town was put to flames

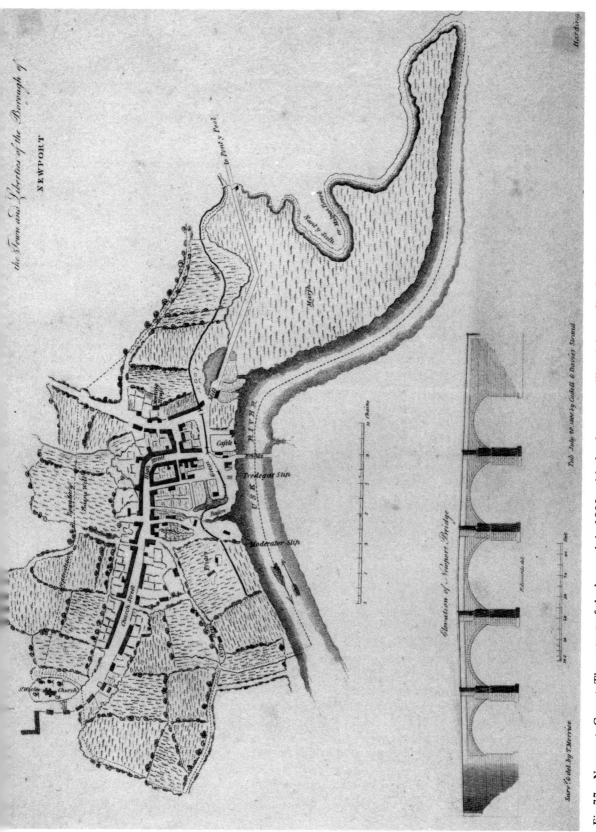

Fig. 77. Newport, Gwent. The extent of the borough in 1800, with development still mainly confined to the one principal street. The map also indicates the position of the town mill and the Augustinian friary.

by Glyndŵr in 1402 and the bridge destroyed, and the attack was so severe as to render the value of the whole lordship as 'nil' in a survey carried out in the following year.[15] John Leland, while describing the place as a 'bigge towne', added that it was concentrated 'all yn one streate' and was 'yn ruine',[16] a view later endorsed by Owen, who added that it was 'poor and decayed'.[17] In 1648 Newport became involved in the Civil War when Cromwell's forces took the castle and caused considerable damage to the town, and the effects can be seen on the 1752 map which shows tenements confined to Mill Street and the High Street. It was not until the early 19th century with the construction of the Monmouth and Brecon canals that the old town began on a phase of rapid expansion which was to place it firmly near the top of the Welsh urban hierarchy.

1. Rees, W., *The Charters of the Borough of Newport in Gwynllwg* (Newport, 1951), xi–xii.
2. *Historical Tour through Monmouthshire*, 64.
3. *Pipe Roll*, 31 Hen. II, 5–10, 127, 144, 155; *idem*, 32, Hen. II, 29; *King's Works*, 67, 651.
4. *Brut y Tywysogion*, 68.
5. *King's Works*, loc. cit.
6. The town of *Novus Burgus* is mentioned by Giraldus Cambrensis in 1188 (*Opera*, iii, 215). In 1147–83 William, Earl of Gloucester exempted members of the Abbey of Gloucester from the customary payment of tolls collected on passing through the borough (Mathews, J. H., *Cardiff Records*, i, 2).
7. S.C. 6/1201/1; Beresford, *New Towns* 560.
8. C 134/43; Beresford, *New Towns*, loc. cit.
9. Rees, *Newport Charters*, 3–15.
10. *A Survey of the lands of the Earl of Powis in Monmouthshire*, by Thomas Thorpe, 1752, County Record Office.
11. Rees, *Newport Charters*, xix.
12. *Itinerary*,, 45. The West Gate was still standing when the 1752 map was drawn up.
13. *Historical Tour through Monmouthshire*, 66. The view is endorsed by Rees, *Newport Charters*, xiv.
14. Knowles and Hadcock, *Medieval Religious Houses*, 242.
15. Lloyd, *Owen Glendower*, 54; Rees, *Newport Charters*, xviii.
16. *Itinerary*, 14.
17. *Description of Pembrokeshire*, iii, 302.

NEW RADNOR (Maesyfed), Powys (Radnorshire)   SO 212609

New Radnor was founded as the successor to the small village of Old Radnor some two miles to the south-east, where a motte had earlier been erected. The move to the new settlement is generally ascribed to the mid–13th century, but there is some evidence to suggest that it may have taken place earlier[1] and that the 'castle of Radenoure' reduced by Llywelyn ab Iorwerth in 1231 was, in fact, the new structure.[2] The borough created in its shadow was, as the circumstances suggest, a planted town, and Speed's plan of 1610 indicates the defences with streets laid out in a regular pattern running east-west and north-south with the town cross and market-place at the junction of the High Street and Broad Street.[3]

The early development of New Radnor appears to have been slow, but followed by a period of rapid expansion early in the 14th century. The town is specifically mentioned in 1257 when Roger Mortimer obtained a grant of murage,[4] and in 1301

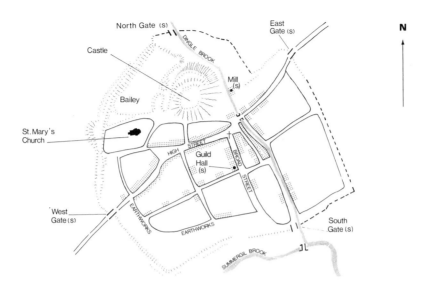

Fig. 78. New Radnor

there were 97 burgesses here.[5] By 1304, however, the number had doubled to 189, holding 262½ plots. There was already a weekly market held on Tuesdays,[6] while in 1306 the town obtained a charter for a yearly fair to be held on 18 October.[7] No details of any borough charter have survived the medieval period, however, and the town records are said to have been destroyed during Owain Glyndŵr's attack in 1401.[8] The earliest known charter dates from 1562, but it makes no mention in its preamble to any earlier grant of privileges.[9]

The castle was the dominant feature of the early town, and it was built on the highest point to command the only route into the district of Elfael. The present remains consist only of a number of earthworks, although Speed indicated an impressive stone structure with the main entrance from the High Street.[10] Immediately adjoining the bailey stands St Mary's church, and although a church at Radnor is mentioned in 1291 the reference appears to have been to another building.[11] John Leland wrote of 'the olde church stondynge now as a chapell by the castle', but added that 'not very farre is the new paroche churche buildyd by one William Bachefeld and Flory his wyfe'.[12] By the early 19th century this building had fallen into ruin and it was rebuilt in 1843-5. Immediately south of the castle and church lies the town itself, stretching as far down as the Summergil Brook, and sections of the defences which enclosed it are still visible. Work on these probably began shortly after 1257 when Roger Mortimer secured his murage grant, although further grants were made in 1280, 1283 and 1290 following the Welsh rising under Llywelyn ap Gruffudd.[14] In all an area of 26 acres was enclosed by a bank and ditch which may also have been topped with a wooden palisade. The western section is shown by Speed running north of the church to link up with the moat surrounding the castle mound. Remains are easily detectable here as well as on the southern side of the town where the brook was considered to be insufficient natural protection. On the east the defences ran parallel to Water Street, also to connect with the castle moat, but here they have experienced greater decay and are now barely discernable.

Leland noted four town gates,[15] whose positions at the four cardinal points were indicated by Williams on his map of 1800.[16] The West Gate was at the end of Church Street, which leads to Rhayader; the South Gate at the bottom of Water Street, just before the Grove Bridge; and the East Gate stood near the Baptist chapel on the Presteigne Road. The North Gate, which seems to have been a minor access point leading only to Radnor Forest and the burgesses's holdings beyond the town, lay beyond the castle hill where the outward entrenchment was bisected by the mill stream. The stream itself, known as the Dingle Brook, originally flowed down through the town to join the Summergil Brook, hence the name of Water Street whose line it followed. The mill, called 'Heynesmyll' in the 1562 charter,[17] is shown by Speed to have stood along the Dingle where it skirts the eastern side of the castle mound. A final aspect of New Radnor's early topography and itself a reflection of the town's fomer importance was the town hall which stood at the junction of Hall Lane and Broad Street. It also appears in the charter of Elizabeth I under the guise of 'The Buthall'[18] and was partly demolished by rioters in 1697.[19] By 1800 it had 'the semblance of a barn' and it was eventually removed later in the century.[20]

From Speed's plan of 1610 which indicates large areas of empty spaces within the walled town, it is clear that the thriving borough of the early 14th century had suffered a serious decline in the intervening centuries. Glyndŵr appears to have been partly responsible, and the castle ceased to be maintained after the revolt and New Radnor lost its military significance. By the end of the 17th century the courts of Great Sessions had been transferred to Presteigne and even the weekly market had ceased to be held.[21] The gradual reduction of the built-up area can be appreciated by comparing the maps of Speed and Williams with that of the present town. Clearly the medieval town was more densely developed than its modern counterpart, and Speed indicates a number of streets which either no longer exist or have been reduced to footpaths. Hall Lane is shown as continuing to the west, as also is the lower half of Rectory Lane, while west of Brookside Farm was another street running diagonally from the High Street to Water Street which was heavily built-up. In the western part of the town indications of its former extent can be detected in the form of earthworks lining Church Street, and the former extended course of Hall Lane. Williams adds another street which ran parallel and immediately inside the eastern defences, but only its northern section now remains.

1. Beresford, *New Towns*, 572.
2. *Brut y Tywysogion*, 102; *Annales Cambriae*, 78; *Annales de Wigornia*, in *Annales Monastici*, iv, 422.
3. *Atlas of Wales*, inter 111-2.
4. *Cal. Pat. Rolls*, 1247-58, 609.
5. C 133/101/6; *C.I.P.M.*, iv, No. 41.

6. C 133/114/8; *C.I.P.M.*, iv, No. 235.

7. *Cal. Ch. Rolls*, iii, 68.

8. Williams, J., *History of Radnorshire*, 180.

9. *Cal. Pat. Rolls*, 1560-6, 343-6; Cole, E. J. L., 'New Radnor Town Charters', *T.R.S.*, xxiii (1953), 30-9.

10. For a description of the castle *see R.C.A.M.W.M., Rads.,* 129-30.

11. *Taxatio Ecclesiastica* (Rec. Comm.), 159.

12. *Itinerary*, 10.

13. Lewis, *Topographical Dictionary, sub* Radnor (New); Howse, W. E., 'The Church of New Radnor', *T.R.S.*, xv (1945), 8-14.

14. *Cal. Pat. Rolls*, 1247-58, 609; *ibid.*, 1281-92, 277; Cole, E. J. L., 'New Radnor Murage Grant, 1283', *T.R.S.*, xxvii (1957), 25-6.

15. *Itinerary*, 10.

16. Williams, J., *History of Radnorshire, inter* 188-9.

17. Above, Note 9.

18. *Idem.*

19. Jones, E. D., 'Gleanings from Radnorshire Files of Great Sessions Papers, 1691-99', *T.R.S.*, xiii (1943), 22.

20. Williams, J., *History of Radnorshire*, 180.

21. *Ibid.*, 181. The market appears to have been revived by the mid-18th century (Bowen, *Britannia Depicta*, 225).

NEWTOWN (Y Drenewydd), Powys (Montgomeryshire)   SO 108918

Newtown lies on the south bank of the River Severn and the early settlement was planted in an ideal position for town development, lying on a tract of nearly level ground within a marked bend of the river and bounded on the north-west by a small stream flowing south. These natural defences were supplemented on the east side by an existing, although undocumented motte, now in the grounds of Newtown Hall, whose bailey appears to have extended right down to the river.[1]

The earliest sources refer to the surrounding district as Llanfair Cedewain, a name which was current throughout the medieval period surviving in occasional usage through to the 16th century. The chapel of Llanfair (St Mary's) is mentioned in 1253, and it proved to be the focal point of the new borough.[2] In January 1279 Cedewain was granted to Roger Mortimer,[3] and in the following year he secured from Edward I the right to hold a weekly market and annual fair within the manor.[4] By 1291 Llanfair had emerged as a rectory independent of the mother-church of Llanllwchaiarn, and it seems likely that the town had already taken shape, although there are no references to Newtown before the mid-1300s.[5] Iolo Goch referred in one of his works to 'Y Drenewydd';[6] a document dated 1331 mentions the 'Nova Villa de Kedenwywg';[7] and it is clear from this and other 14th-century records that the place was already considered to be a borough—but there is no known charter.[8]

There are no satisfactory indications of the size of the medieval town, although in the 16th century Leland observed that it was 'meately welle buildyd after the Walche fascion'[9] and there were 55 taxpayers recorded here in 1545.[10] A map of 1798,[11] compiled before Newtown's marked period of expansion in the 19th century as a result of the development of the flannel industry, indicates that the

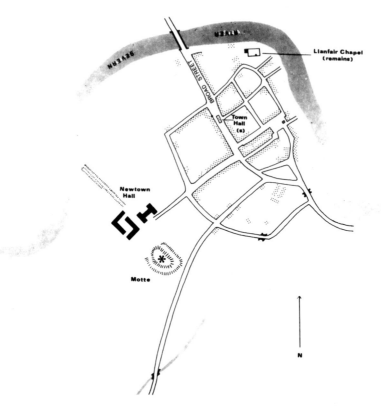

Fig. 79. Newtown

early town focused on the bridge, which was wooden until 1827,[12] with Broad Street as the principal axis. From Broad Street radiated a number of lesser streets at right-angles to it, with Llanfair chapel occupying the south-west corner below the river bank. Its remains can still be seen, but Newtown now has a newer church, St. David's, built in 1847, and the churchyard contains the tomb of the socialist, Robert Owen, who was born here in 1771. The Glansevern map provides the position of the old town hall which stood in the middle of Broad Street just opposite the Castle Vaults and Turner's Lane until being demolished in 1852. It was a brick-built structure measuring 21m. by 8m., and dates from the late 16th century, built on the site of the medieval town court-house.[13] Other than the remains of Llanfair which amount to a tower and a portion of the south aisle wall, Newtown contains no surviving medieval features. There are, however, some fine examples of late 17th- and early 18th-century domestic architecture, and *Checker's* inn in Broad Street dates from the early 1600s.[14]

1. *R.C.A.M.W.M., Mont.*, 161–2.
2. Anon, 'A Valuation for Tenths in the Diocese of St Asaph, *c.* 1253', *Mont. Coll.*, xxi (1897), 332.
3. *Cal. Ch. Rolls*, ii, 211.

4. Halr. MS. 1240, ff. 67-8; Williams, R., 'A Parochial Account of Newtown', *Mont. Coll.*, xxxii (1902), 188; *idem*, 'Early documents relating to Dolforwyn Castle, Newtown', *ibid.*, xxviii (1894), 147-8.

5. *Taxatio Ecclesiastica* (Rec. Comm.), 294.

6. Lewis, H., *et al.*, *Cywyddau Iolo Goch ac Eraill* (Cardiff, 1972), 76.

7. S.C. 6/1206/2.

8. *See* Williams, R., 'A Parochial Account of Newtown', *op. cit.*, 190. For an account of the town's foundation and development *see* Jones, E. V., *History of Newtown, 1221-1870*, 3rd revised edn., Newtown, 1970.

9. *Itinerary*, 12.

10. Horsfall-Turner, *Municipal History of Llanidloes*, 257.

11. Housed in the Glansevern Deposit Collection, National Library of Wales.

12. Lewis, *Topographical Dictionary, sub* Newtown.

13. Williams, R., 'Newtown: its ancient charter and Town Hall', *Mont. Coll.*, xii (1879), 92-3; *idem*, 'A Parochial Account of Newtown', *op. cit.*, 192, 195.

14. *R.C.A.M.W.M., Mont.*, 162.

OVERTON (Owrtyn), Clwyd (Flintshire)   SJ 373418

Overton lies within a few miles of the English border and is first mentioned in the Domesday Survey of 1086 when the manor is entered in the Cheshire *breve*.[1] Control of this marcher area changed hands frequently, however, and *c.* 1138 we find reference to the construction of the castle by Madog ap Maredudd, prince of Powys.[2] This was built on a cliff edge overlooking the Dee, but the site was eroded by the river[3] and by the 1530s Leland observed that only 'one part . . . yet remaineth the Residew is in the botom of Dee'.[4] This process continued throughout the following centuries, and the site and all remains have since been completely lost to the river.[5]

There is nothing to suggest that the building of the castle was accompanied by the laying out of any civilian settlement, and the indications are that Overton was a planted borough of the late 13th century. In 1279 a market was established within the manor,[6] and in 1286 Edward I granted it together with the whole of Maelor Saesneg to his queen, Eleanor, who two years earlier had commissioned the making of glass windows for 'the queen's chapel at Overton'.[7] The town appears gradually to have been taking shape, and in 1292 a royal charter created Overton a free borough and 56 taxpayers were recorded in that year.[8] Not all the burgages created were immediately taken up, however, for in June of the following year Reginald de Gray, the chief justice of Chester, was ordered to go to the borough and arrange for the remaining plots to be distributed, the recipients being given timber and land and exempted from the payments of dues for their first 10 years of residence.[9] Within two years, however, the town's development received a serious setback when it was badly ravaged and the mill destroyed during the revolt of Madog ap Llywelyn.[10]

The early borough was laid out in the area of St Mary's church which may have already been standing,[11] with the burgages lining the High Street, Wrexham Road, and the upper part of Salop Road, where vestiges of the former pattern can still be detected. There is also mention of plots in 'le Parsones rowe' in 1361,[12] but

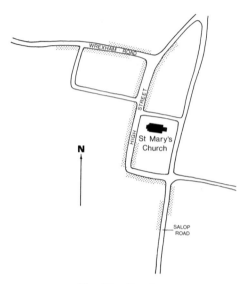

Fig. 80. Overton

these must also have been by the church, perhaps along the lane which runs south from the rectory. Overton does not appear to have been defended and there are no indications that the grant of murage received by the inhabitants in 1300 was ever carried out.[13] The failure to enclose the town must have been regretted after 1403 when Owain Glyndŵr put it to flames and virtually destroyed the entire vill, forcing it to be largely abandoned by the English inhabitants.[14] The event had important implications throughout the following centuries and the borough proved unable to recover its former extent. John Leland noted that 'the town . . . hath had burgesses but now there is not twenty houses',[15] an assessment which agrees with the evidence of muster rolls from the same period which put the number of males in Overton over the age of 16 at 26 in 1539, and 23 in 1543.[16]

1. *D.B.*, f. 264b.
2. Orderic Vitalis, *Hist. Eccles.*, xiii, 37; Lloyd, *History of Wales*, ii, 583–4.
3. *R.C.A.M.W.M., Flints.*, 111.
4. *Itinerary*, 67.
5. All traces had been lost by the 1830s (Lewis, *Topographical Dictionary, sub* Overton).
6. *Cal. Ch. Rolls*, ii, 213.
7. E 101/351/15.
8. *Cal. Ch. Rolls*, ii, 414; E 179/242/52.
9. *Cal. Cl. Rolls*, 1288–96, 285–6.
10. *Cal. Inq., Misc.*, 1307–49, No. 56; *Cal. Anct. Petitions*, 340–2.
11. On the discovery of a supposed Saxon stone coffin, *see* Howson, G. J., *Overton in Days Gone By* (Overton, 1883), 29–30.
12. *MSS. Relating to Wales*, iii, 752.
13. *Cal. Pat. Rolls*, 1292–1301, 505.
14. S.C. 6/775/1; Messham, J. E., 'The County of Flint and the Rebellion of Owen Glyndŵr', *op. cit.*, 14, 24.
15. *Itinerary, loc. cit.*
16. This evidence is discussed by Williams-Jones, K. (ed.), *The Merioneth Subsidy Roll of 1292/3*, li.

PAINSCASTLE (Llanbedr-Castell-Paen), Powys (Radnorshire)   SO 167464

Painscastle is situated in the south-east corner of the old county of Radnor, with the castle and adjoining houses lying in a vale above the northern bank of the Bach Howey stream. The place has no urban character now, and the majority of dwellings are farmhouses, but throughout the 13th and 14th centuries it was a moderately important borough. The settlement appears to have taken its name from Pain fitz John, who constructed the castle as part of the campaign to consolidate the position of the marcher lords. He appears attesting charters relating to the area in the 1120s, and the castle was probably thrown up in the same decade,[1] although there are no references to it until the 1180s.[2] It was rebuilt in 1191 by William de Braose and became known as *Castrum Matildis* or 'Castle Maud' after his wife. A Welsh force under Rhys ap Gruffudd captured the stronghold in 1196,[3] but it was subsequently regained by the English and rebuilt by Henry III in 1231, who used it as a base to direct campaigns against the Welsh.[4] The king stayed

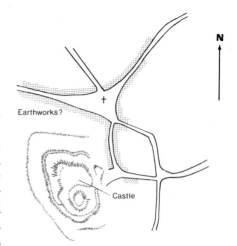

Fig. 81. Painscastle

here for part of that year[5] and it seems that the laying out of the borough was carried out during that period since there is no reference to any civil settlement before the mid-13th century. A weekly market on Tuesdays and an annual fair were granted to Robert de Toeni,[6] and by 1309 the borough contained 50 burgesses all paying the standard 1s. yearly rent.[7]

There is very little to record of the town's later history. The castle seems to have been abandoned at a comparatively early date, although it was re-fortified during the Glyndŵr revolt,[8] and Painscastle suffered the fate of similar small communities which had been created essentially as military bases. The virtual absence of later documentation is suggestive of decay, and the borough appears to have contracted, particularly to the east and west of the large triangular market-place where earthworks probably representing house-platforms can be seen, most noticeable immediately north of the castle. Originally the borough appears to have been laid out with a rectangular street-pattern similar to Caersws and Crickhowell, but the eastern limb beyond Newhouse Farm is now little more than a track.

By 1800 Painscastle had lost its weekly market through the competition of Hay, Builth, and Kington, and it has subsequently remained a very modest settlement.[9]

1. Round, J. H. (ed.), *Ancient Charters*, 8, 19.

2. Giraldus Cambrensis, *Opera*, i, 91, 95, 96.

3. *Brut y Tywysogion*, 76.

4. *Ibid.*, 101; *Ann. Margam*, 79. For a description of the castle *see R.C.A.M.W.M., Rads.*, 64.

5. *See Cal. Ch. Rolls*, i, 138–40.

6. *Ibid.*, ii, 479.

7. C 134/15/3.

8. Lloyd, *Owen Glendower*, 44.

9. Williams, J., *History of Radnorshire*, 254.

PEMBROKE (Penfro), Dyfed (Pembrokeshire)   SM 986014

The town is strikingly situated on a markedly elongated ridge of carboniferous limestone which extends into Milford Haven between two short, incised streams. This is a great, virtually impregnable, natural fortress, as John Leland realised in the 1530s when he noted 'Penbroke standith upon an arme of Milford, the wich about a mile beyond the towne creketh in so that it almost peninsulatith the toune that standith on a veri maine rokki ground'.[1]

Pembroke derives its name from the Welsh 'Pen' (head) and 'Bro' (district or region) which was originally applied to the surrounding area, 'Penfro' being one of the seven cantrefs of Dyfed.[2] Apart from the discovery of several Roman coins during restoration work on the castle in the 1880s,[3] however, there is nothing to suggest occupation of the town site prior to the arrival of the Normans in the late 11th century. The conquest of much of Dyfed in 1093 by Earl Roger of Shrewsbury opened the way for military and urban foundation at a variety of sites in south-west Wales and the Pembroke area was granted to his son, Arnulf de Montgomery.[4] A castle was constructed, a somewhat flimsy structure if Giraldus can be relied upon,[5] and it was entrusted to his chief follower, Gerald of Windsor, under whose direction the town began to take shape.[6] In 1098 Arnulf granted the church of St Nicholas 'within his castle of Pembroke' to the Norman abbey of St Martin, Séez, and soon after Monkton Priory was founded to the south of the castle.[7] Two years or more later the borough received its first charter from Henry I by which the king created a mayor, burgesses, and freemen, and gave them the power of government of the town and precincts and the control of all commercial activities.[8]

In 1138 the earldom of Pembroke was created a county palatine under Gilbert de Clare (Gilbert 'Strongbow') with the privilege of *jura regalia* and the town expanded with the growth of its administrative and commercial functions. A further contributory factor in this process was its ability to stand aloof during the Welsh wars of the 13th century, and it was never attacked, no doubt because of the sheer impregnability of the site.

The peninsula on which the town was built determined both its lay-out and extent. The castle was constructed at the western end with the borough running east, and the narrowness of the site afforded room for only one long street, appropriately called Main Street, which ran along the limestone ridge with the burgage plots on either side sloping down to the town walls and the water. As George Owen noted, it was 'without any cross streets'[9] and the few which exist today, such as New Way and Morgan's Way represent former burgages and are relatively recent. In 1324 there were 220 of these plots,[10] and in 1326–7 there were 238½,[11] and for the most part the burgage pattern is extremely well preserved. As for the walls themselves some sections are still standing while their complete former course is readily discernible from John Speed's map of 1610.[12] Leland also contributed to our knowledge of the subject when he observed that 'the toune is well waullid and hath iii gates by the est, west and north, of wich the est gate is fairest and strongest, having afore hit a compasid tour not rofid, in the entering whereof is a portcolys *ex solido ferro*'.[13] From the Mill Bridge the northern

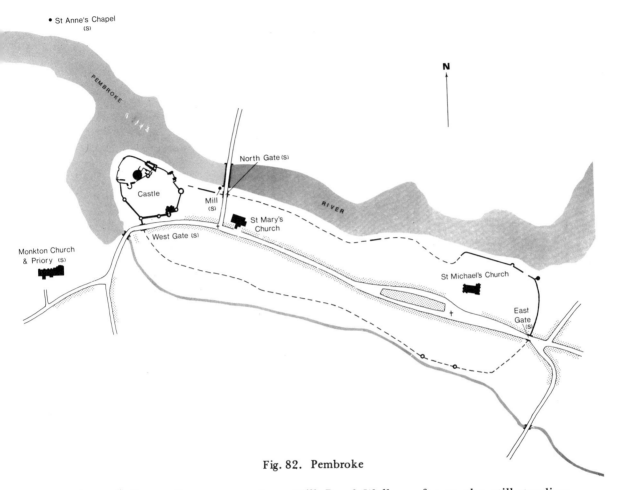

Fig. 82. Pembroke

section of the wall ran east along Mill Pond Walk as far as the still-standing Bernard's Tower, and then it veered south along Goose's Lane, where a second tower was located. From here the wall followed a westerly course as far as the castle, and some remains are still standing together with parts of two further towers in Rock Terrace. The southern stone wall of the castle bailey served as sufficient defence along Westgate Hill, and from here the wall continued along Castle Terrace and then turned sharply up Dark Lane to the bridge.

The positions of the three gates are indicated by Speed, with the North Gate situated at the bottom of Dark Lane at the junction with the Mill Bridge. The East Gate stood at the top of Goose's Lane in East End Square, and at the opposite end of the town stood the West Gate at the bottom of Westgate Hill. Portions of the latter have been incorporated into adjoining buildings, but all traces of the other gates disappeared in the 19th century. There is no documentary evidence for the erection of these defences, although Leland's observation that the East Gate was similar to that at Tenby may suggest a similar early-14th-century date.[14]

Within the walled area lie two churches, with St Mary's at the corner of Northgate Street probably the oldest. The present building dates from the late 12th or early 13th century, although there are some earlier remains, and it appears to have been the church of the early Norman town.[15] At the opposite end of the town stands St Michael's, erected in the second half of the 13th century. The present church was built in 1887, but its medieval predecessor with a central tower is shown by Speed. He also indicates two other religious houses beyond the walled town: St Anne's chapel on the north bank of the Pembroke River; and Monkton priory beyond the West Gate. Also known as the priory of St Nicholas, this was founded on a hill to the south of the castle by Arnulf de Montgomery, c. 1098, and it is traditionally regarded as having been built on the site of an earlier Celtic church. He granted it to Séez, but following the final seizure of the alien houses in 1414 the priory was made a dependency of St Albans, in whose possession it remained until the Dissolution. The church survived Henry VIII's measures, however, and was restored in 1882, but the domestic buildings fell into decay, and there are now few remains.[16]

On the south-eastern side of the churchyard stands a building known as 'The Old Hall', parts of which date from the 14th century, and which has been restored. It does not appear to have been connected with the priory and its purpose is unknown, although it may have been linked in some administrative capacity with the extra-mural settlement which developed here along Church and Bridgend Terraces.[17] Other features of early Pembroke include the town mill, which is shown by Speed to have stood by the bridge, and the old town hall, which appears in documents from the 16th century.[18] There were two market-places to house the Sunday market, and the two annual fairs,[19] at either end of Main Street by the Bridge Gate and St Michael's church.

Medieval Pembroke was a prosperous community with a viable commercial life, and its castle served as the administrative headquarters of the lordship. From the 14th-century burgage figures its population must have exceeded 1,000, and by the late 15th century the town had expanded beyond its walls with the appearance of suburbs by Monkton priory, beyond the East Gate, and across the river at the bridgehead.[20] By the end of the following century, however, although as Speed indicates these extra-mural settlements remained, the borough had experienced a serious decline. George Owen described it as 'very ruinous and much decayed'[21] and for Speed there were 'more houses without inhabitants than I saw in any one city throughout my journey'.[22] Unlike the majority of Welsh towns this decay cannot be linked with the Glyndŵr revolt since Pembroke was one of the few towns to remain untouched by the rebels. The decline of the borough's maritime trade was an important contributory factor, as also was the development of Haverfordwest which began to take away many of these commercial functions.[23] Since the Act of Union of 1536 Pembroke was no longer the *caput* of a wealthy earldom, and the castle was allowed to fall into decay. In 1648 both it and the town suffered during Cromwell's siege, and with the disappearance of both its military role and the trading privileges which had formerly afforded a monopoly to the burgesses, there remained few natural forces to sustain the community at its medieval level.[24]

In 1833 Samuel Lewis recorded that 'there are no particular manufactures carried on', although the town still serves 'in a great measure as a depot for the neighbouring districts'.[25] Pembroke had become and remains just a market town largely confined within the limited area of its own island site.

1. *Itinerary*, 115.
2. Clark, G. T., *The Earls, Earldom and Castle of Pembroke* (Tenby, 1800), 4; Lewis, *Topographical Dictionary*, sub Pembroke.
3. *See* Cobb, J. R., *Pembroke Castle*, Brecon, 1883.
4. Lloyd, *History of Wales*, ii, 401.
5. *Opera*, vi, 89. The castle was rebuilt by Gilbert de Clare, *c.* 1110, with the outer ward and circular keep added in the mid 13th century (*R.C.A.M.W.M., Pembs.*, 282-7; Taylor, A. J., 'Pembroke Castle', *Arch. Journ.*, cxix [1962], 343-4).
6. *Brut y Tywysogion*, 20, 28.
7. Knowles and Hadcock, *Medieval Religious Houses*, 73; Taylor, A. J., 'Monkton Priory', *Arch. Camb.*, xciii (1938), 299-300; Clark, G. T., *op. cit.*, 6-7.
8. The original charter has not survived, but details of the grant are recited in a confirmatory document of Henry II in 1154 (Ballard, *British Borough Charters*, 18; Owen, *Cal. Pembs. Records*, iii, 208-10).
9. *Description of Pembrokeshire*, ii, 557-8.
10. Owen, *Cal. Pembs. Records*, iii, 83.
11. *Ibid.*, 126-7.
12. *Atlas of Wales*, inter 101-2.
13. *Itinerary*, 115-6.
14. *Ibid.*, 117; Turner, *Town Defences*, 217-8.
15. Mathias, A. G. O., 'Church of St. Mary, Pembroke', *Arch. Camb.*, xciii (1938), 290-1.
16. Taylor, A. J., 'Monkton Priory', *ibid.*, 299-300; Thomas, W. G., 'Monkton Priory Church', *Arch. Journ.*, cxix (1962), 344-5.
17. *Ibid.*, 345.
18. Haverfordwest Corporation MS. 311; Howells, *Pembrokeshire Life*, 32.
19. Owen, *Cal. Pembs. Records*, iii, 209-10; Owen, *Description of Pembrokeshire*, i, 142-4. Bowen, however, stated that the market was on Saturdays (*Britannia Depicta*, 39).
20. An account of 1480-1 mentions burgages over the bridge together with a number beyond the East Gate (Owen, *Cal. Pembs. Records*, iii, 148-9).
21. *Description of Pembrokeshire*, iii, 359.
22. *Atlas of Wales*, 101.
23. The trade of the early town has been analysed by Sudbury, R. G., 'The Medieval Boroughs of Pembrokeshire', Univ. of Wales M.A. (1947), 169-74.
24. Leach, A., *History of the Civil War in Pembrokeshire* (London, 1937), 107, 191-207.
25. *Topographical Dictionary*, *loc. cit.*

PRESTATYN, Clwyd (Flintshire)   SJ 073833

Prestatyn lies on the North Wales coastline midway between the estuaries of the Dee and Clwyd. While the present town is essentially a modern development with a heavy dependence on the tourist industry, it had its medieval predecessor, albeit a small and short-lived settlement.

Very little is known of the early town and its origins, but there can be little doubt as to the antiquity of settlement in this area, with evidence from the Neolithic, Roman, and early-medieval periods. In 1933 an area of Roman occupation to the south-east of the town between St Chad's School and Llys Farm was discovered by F. Gilbert Smith and subsequent excavations revealed traces of defences and structural remains of several buildings, including a bath-house which indicated settlement from the closing years of the 1st century and well into the 3rd century. During the course of these excavations considerable evidence also came to light of prehistoric occupation with the discovery of nearly 100 artefacts, mainly Neolithic and later.[1]

Prestatyn is mentioned in the Domesday Survey of 1086 when this area of north-east Wales had fallen into Norman hands. The entry refers to the combined manor of Prestatyn and Meliden which contained 100 acres, a church, and a recorded population of 10, which suggests that the vill housed no more than 60 people.[2] We cannot be sure if the *caput* of the manor corresponded to an area of the present town, but in all probability the settlement lay in the area of the castle which was already standing before the compilation of the survey. The construction of the stronghold is sometimes ascribed to the early 11th century as the work of Llywelyn ap Seisyllt, then ruler of North Wales.[3] Very little is known of him, however, and it would seem more reasonable to associate it with Roger de Banastre in the 1160s. The latter is also said to have enlarged the town,[4] but in 1167 the castle was attacked and completely destroyed by Owain Gwynedd.[5] It was not rebuilt, and by 1279, when the site was the subject of a land dispute, it was stated that much of the fabric had disappeared, and the remainder was beyond repair.[6]

It seems likely that the Welsh attack of 1167 also succeeded in destroying the town since there are no further references to it for the remainder of the medieval period. This raises the fundamental problem of its location since the site of what was a comparatively small settlement cannot be determined, and neither can the church mentioned in the Domesday Survey be equated confidently with any of the present churches in the town or in Meliden. The oldest appears to be St Melyd's, and sections of 13th-century walling were observed during its rebuilding in 1884, and it is possible that the Domesday entry refers to an earlier building on the same site.[7] However, there may equally have been an early church by the castle which was also destroyed in 1167. It has also been suggested that the town has since been lost to the sea, a view which has also been put forward for Abergele. Edwards, the historian of Prestatyn, noted that 'as late as 1860 walls were to be seen at low water opposite the castle . . . it would seem very probable that the old town and church stood below the castle and Nant, on a site which is now covered by the sea'.[8] The opinion agrees with that of Samuel Lewis in 1833 who noted masonry remains on the north side of the castle beyond the railway line.[9]

1. Newstead, R., 'Roman Station at Prestatyn', *B.B.C.S.*, viii (1937), 98-9, 380-2; ix (1939), 285, 292-3; *Arch Camb.*, lxlii (1937), 208-32; lxliii (1938), 175-91; Daniels, C. M., 'A note on the Roman Bath-houses at Prestatyn and Tremadoc', *B.B.C.S.*, xxiii (1970), 187.

2. *D.B.*, f. 269a; Lloyd, *History of Wales*, i, 201.

3. Edwards, T., *Historical Guide to Prestatyn* (1905), 11; *R.C.A.M.W.M., Flints.*, 79.

4. *Rotuli Parliamentorum*, i, 2; *R.C.A.M.W.M., Flints.*, loc cit.

5. *Brut y Tywysogion* (Hergest version only), 149; Lloyd, *History of Wales*, ii, 520.

6. *Rot. Parl.*, loc. cit.

7. Edwards, *Prestatyn*, 26, 40.

8. *Ibid.*, 32.
9. *Topographical Dictionary, sub* Prestatyn.

PRESTEIGNE (Llanandras), Powys (Radnorshire)   SO 311645

Presteigne lies on the south bank of the River Lugg, which here acts as the boundary between Wales and England. As with many such border towns there is a tradition of early Anglo-Saxon settlement and the place-name itself is Old English, the original form being 'Presthemede' signifying 'a household of priests'.[1] Some details of the vill dating from 1128–39 appear in the Herefordshire Domesday of 1160–70,[2] but it was a small community which did not assume any urban characteristics until the middle years of the following century.

In 1225 William fitz Warin secured the grant of a weekly Wednesday market at Presteigne together with a yearly fair,[3] and by the end of the century the town had developed into a settlement of over seventy taxpayers[4], although the market day had in the meantime been changed to Saturdays.[5] There are numerous references to burgages, but there is no record of any grant of burghality. However, Presteigne was always considered to be a borough, though by prescription only. In its street-pattern there are indications that it was a planned town with two main streets: Broad Street leading south from the bridge, and the High Street running north-west at right angles to it. St Andrew's church is situated by the bridgehead and the building dates from the 14th century, although parts of the fabric are late Norman. It seems likely that the initial Saxon settlement grew up in this area.[6] With expansion in the 13th century burgages would have been laid out along Broad

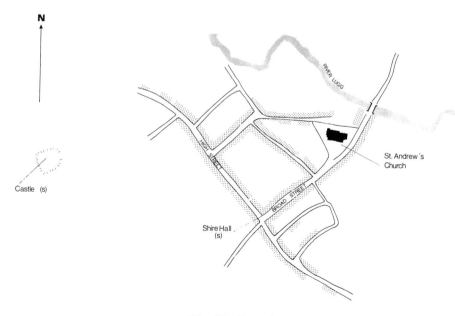

Fig. 83. Presteigne

Street, while others lined the track leading up to the castle which developed into the High Street.[7]

The castle itself lay to the west of the built-up area, but neither the date of its construction or the identity of its founder are known. It appears briefly in the records in 1262 when it was captured by Llywelyn apGruffudd,[88] but it subsequently disappears from notice and it was probably destroyed during the attack. An inquisition of 1337 refers to the 'Castelditch at Presthende', but the buildings appear to have been removed by that time[9] and most of the mound has since been levelled, the site being subsequently used as a recreation ground.

From the developing community which appears in 13th- and 14th-century records Presteigne declined significantly in the later Middle Ages. The abandonment of the castle and the withdrawal of the garrison must have played its part, but the major contributory cause was the devastation brought on the town and the surrounding countryside by the Glyndŵr rebels.[10] For much of the 15th century the place appears to have been reduced to the size of a village, and even the weekly market ceased to be held. In the latter part of the century, however, under the direction of Richard Martin, Bishop of St David's and a native of Presteigne, the town began to recover, and its commercial life, including the market was revived.[11] John Leland, writing in the 1530s, noted that it had become the chief town of Maelienydd,[12] while Camden observed what had been 'a very little village within the memorie of our grandfathers, is by the means of Richard Martin, Bishop of Saint Davids, growne now to be so great a mercate towne and faire withall, that at this day it dammereth and dimmeth the light in some sort of Radnor'.[13] John Speed endorsed both views in 1610 when he wrote that 'Prestatyn for beautious buildings is the best in this Shire, town of Commerce, wonderfully frequented, and that very lately'.[14] In the same year that Speed was praising the town, however, there was a serious outbreak of plague which was followed by further bouts in 1636 and 1637. Several hundred inhabitants died and the market had to be moved from the town for reasons of safety.[15] In 1681, just as the place was recovering, fire broke out, destroying the Free Grammar School, founded in 1565, and over seventy houses situated mainly in the High Street and St David's Street.[16] The catastrophe was followed by a busy period of rebuilding, and it is significant that while the present town still contains several late-17th- and early-18th-century buildings, little structural evidence survives from earlier periods except in the form of re-used timbers.[17]

1. Ekwall, E., *The Concise Oxford Dictionary of English Place-Names*, 4th edn. (Oxford, 1960), 373.

2. Galbraith, V. E., and Tait, J. (eds), *The Herefordshire Domesday*, Pipe Roll Soc., xxv (1947–8), 79; Howse, W. H., 'Presteigne in Domesday', *T.R.S.*, xxi (1951), 48–9.

3. Howse, W. H., 'Early Grant of a Weekly Market to Presteigne', *ibid.*, xxvi (1956), 43.

4. *Idem*, 'Some Early Presteigne Documents', *ibid.*, xxii (1952), 22–4.

5. *C.I.P.M.*, iv, No. 235, p. 160.

6. *R.C.A.M.W.M.*, *Rads.*, 136.

7. A 13th-century deed mentions burgages in 'Great Street', (Broad Street) and 'The King's Highway' which must have been the High Street which lies along the course of the old road to Hereford (Howse, W. H., 'Some Early Presteigne Documents', *loc. cit.*).

8. *Annales Cambriae*, 100.

9. *C.I.P.M.*, viii, No. 711, p. 502.

10. Howse, W. H., 'Some Early Presteigne Documents', *op. cit.*, 23; Rees, *South Wales and the March*, 277.

11. Williams, J., *History of Radnorshire*, 201; Lewis, *Topographical Dictionary*, *sub* Presteigne.

12. *Itinerary*, 10, 41.

13. *Britannia*, 623.

14. *Atlas of Wales*, 111.

15. Williams, J., *History of Radnorshire*, 197.

16. Howse, W. H., 'Presteigne's Great Fire of 1681', *T.R.S.*, xxv (1955), 17–19.

17. Brooksby, H., 'The Houses of Radnorshire, v, Town Houses', *ibid.*, xlii (1952), 39–54.

PWLLHELI, Gwynedd (Caernarfonshire) SH 376352

The medieval borough of Pwllheli, situated on the southern shore of the Llŷn peninsula, grew up and developed on similar lines to Nefyn on the opposite coast.[1] Both were initially manorial boroughs which grew up on the demesne lands of the princes of Gwynedd and the settlements were already well-established when Edward I began his policy of town foundation in North Wales. Pwllheli had emerged as the chief vill in the commot of Cafflogion and when the royal officials surveyed it in 1284 its commercial life was well established with the holding of two annual fairs and an occasional, but not regular, weekly market. As also with Nefyn the herring fishing was an important aspect of the town economy, but there were only 21 householders, less than half the figure for Nefyn, and the settlement was generally on a smaller scale.[2]

Immediately above the town stood the old church of St Bueno, pulled down in 1859 when St Peter's was built,[3] while to the east stands Henllys, which may well mark the site of the princely residence recorded by Edward I's officials who carried out sufficient repairs[4] for remains of the building to be still visible in the 1530s when John Leland visited the town.[5] Pwllheli was eventually granted full borough status by Edward the Black Prince in 1355,[6] but as T. Jones Pierce has observed the charter 'did little more than regularize prescriptive rights enjoyed by the Welsh community of the town'.[7]

The early settlement, with its associations with the sea and the fisheries of Cardigan Bay, developed close to the shoreline, but this has changed significantly since the medieval period. House plots were initially confined to the High Street which lay only 90m. from the shore, since large areas to the south and east, beyond Y Traeth (Sand Street) have subsequently been reclaimed. Some natural protection in this area—the town was not defended—was afforded by sand dunes, but the town lies only slightly above sea-level and was frequently liable to flooding.[8] Some dwellings also lined Stryd Penlan which led down to the old quay, while further east the former existence of a stronghold is suggested by the name Pen-y-Mownt. John Wood, in his plan of Pwllheli in 1834, records here the site of 'Cadlys' which suggests a camp or possibly a motte, but there is no documentary evidence, and the area has since been developed.

Despite being a Welsh town Pwllheli was not spared by the followers of Owain Glyndŵr. In 1408 no rents were forthcoming from the borough 'because of the

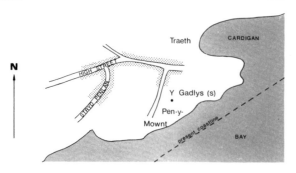

Fig. 84. Pwllheli

rebellion', while again in 1411 there was 'nothing . . . the entire township having been destroyed and laid waste'.[10] Within five years, however, there had been an influx of new inhabitants and there are signs that the community was beginning to revive, although progress was slow, and it was not until the middle years of the following century that Pwllheli had re-gained any real urban character.[11] By 1545 21 inhabitants were of sufficient social standing to be brought within the scope of special taxation,[12] and in 1566 the town was described as 'a port of haven . . . wherin are 36 householdes or cotages'.[12] The recovery continued for the remainder of the 16th century, and by the turn the population stood at over 300 hundred, with expansion both east and west of Y Gadlys and north along Kingshead Street.[14] The commerical core of the borough was also moving westwards to the area of Maes Square with the development of maritime trade and important local tanneries. Stryd Penlan was being further built up, and it is here that the oldest examples of domestic architecture, two 17th-century dwellings, can still be seen.[15]

1. This entry relies heavily on T. Jones Pierces's full study of early Pwllheli ('A Caernarvonshire Manorial Borough: Studies in the Medieval History of Pwllheli', *T.C.H.S.*, iii [1941], 9–32; iv (1942–3, 35–40; v [1944], 12–40, reprinted in *Medieval Welsh Society* [Cardiff, 1972], to which the references cited here apply).

2. *Ibid.*, 132–9; Lewis, *Medieval Boroughs of Snowdonia*, 7.

3. *R.C.A.M.W.M., Caerns.*, iii, 31; Jones Pierce, *op. cit.*, 191.

4. The work was carried out in 1306–7 (*idem*, 'Two Early Caernarvonshire Accounts', *B.B.C.S.*, v [1931], 151).

5. *Itinerary*, 88.

6. *Cal. Pat. Rolls*, 1381–5, 229 (*inspeximus* only). The full text is printed in Lewis, *Medieval Boroughs of Snowdonia*, 289–91.

7. *Medieval Welsh Society*, 152.

8. *Ibid.*, 128–30.

9. *A Plan of Pwllheli from an original survey*, Edinburgh, 1834.

10. S.C. 6/1175/7–9; T. Jones Pierce, *Medieval Welsh Society*, 156.

11. S.C. 6/1176/3; T. Jones Pierce, *Medieval Welsh Society*, *loc. cit.*

12. E 179/220/135.

13. Lewis, E. A. (ed.), *Welsh Port Books*, 308.

14. E 178/3380; T. Jones Pierce, *Medieval Welsh Society*, 161, 184.

15. Namely Penlan Fawr and Mathan House (*R.C.A.M.W.M., Caerns.*, iii, 32).

RAGLAN (Rhaglan), Gwent (Monmouthshire)   SO 404073

The town of Raglan lies at a point where the former Roman road from Gloucester and Monmouth to Usk crosses that from Chepstow to Abergavenny. The importance of the site, therefore, may suggest that settlement here was well established before

the Norman Conquest and certainly St Cadog's
church is a much older foundation since it was
originally dedicated to St David, who is said to have
established a monastery here.[1] Reliable evidence
is not forthcoming until the 11th century, however,
with the arrival of the Normans to the district under
the direction of William fitz Osbern, who bestowed
inter alia tithes of the vill of Raglan on the Norman
abbey of Cormeilles. He may also have been responsible for the construction of the initial motte-and-
bailey castle which appears to underlie the remains
of the impressive 15th-century structure which lies
to the north of the town.[2] The town was not a
planned settlement, and there is no record of any
borough charter, although the 68 holdings recorded
in 1354 were regarded as being burgages and the vill
as a *burgus*.[3]

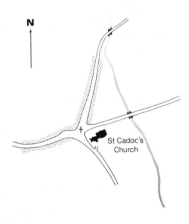

Fig. 85.   Raglan

Early Raglan centred on the church which Richard
de Clare granted to the monks of St Mary's priory
at Usk *c.* 1240[4] and which was rebuilt by the Bloets in the following century.[5]
The limits of the medieval town are difficult to determine as modern development
has removed all traces of any possible street-pattern existing to the west of Castle
Street. This area, however, may never have been built up; the market cross, the
focal point of the community, was located in Beaufort Square opposite the church,[6]
and it is likely that the 68 burgages lined the two highways, the High Street and
Castle Street, leading from it. The Ordnance Survey plan of 1880 confirms the
importance of the Square and shows that the principal areas were the High Street
and the lower part of Castle Street, with the remaining parts of the present town
then being open fields. The land to the north of the town between it and the
castle was not built upon and was mostly wooded and given over to fishponds, the
remains of which are still detectable.[7]

With a 14th-century population in the region of 250–300 Raglan was only a
modest town and did not experience any expansion when the new castle was built
in the following century. Indeed, it declined significantly, and by the 1530s Leland
could note that 'the town . . . ys bare'.[8] Whatever recovery was achieved in the
succeeding 100 years, moreover, received a further setback during the Civil War.
Raglan became the centre of royalist organisation in the area, and the castle was
garrisoned by the Earl of Worcester. Some additions were made to the castle itself
and further defences were provided by the construction of earthworks in the
surrounding area. It was besieged in 1646 by parliamentary troops under Sir Trefor
Williams of Llangibby and was taken on 19 August. Considerable destruction
followed, and the town did not escape, most of the houses being put to flames, and
the minor settlement shown on the map of 1880 suggests that a recovery was a
lengthy affair.[9] The modern Raglan retains the semi-rural atmosphere which must
have characterised its medieval counterpart.

1. Giraldus Cambrensis, *Opera*, iii, 386.

2. Taylor, A. J., *Raglan Castle*, H.M.S.O. Guide, 1950; Hogg and King, 'Masonry Castles', 120-1; Coxe, W., *Historical Tour through Monmouthshire*, 138; Clark, A., *Raglan Castle and the Civil War in Monmouthshire* (Chepstow, 1953), 1.

3. S.C. 11/970.

4. *MSS. relating to Wales*, iii, 660-2.

5. Bradney, *History of Monmouthshire*, ii, pt. i, 33.

6. *Ibid.*, 1.

7. Records of the siege of 1646 speaks of 'an area of meads between the town and castle' (below, note 9).

8. *Itinerary*, 45.

9. Phillips, J. R., *Memoirs of the Civil War in Wales and the Marches*, i, 368-74; Clark, *Raglan Castle and the Civil War in Monmouthshire, passim*. Bradney, writing in 1911, was of the opinion that 'the town or village . . . probably presents much the same appearance as for the last three or four hundred years' (*op. cit.*, 1).

RHAYADER (Rhaeadr Gwy), Powys (Radnorshire)   SN 970680

The small town of Rhayder lies on the east bank of the Wye and takes its name from the river which flows over a cataract immediately below the bridge. The regularity of the street-pattern which takes the form of two roads crossing at right-angles to each other suggests a planned settlement, and Rhayader was regarded as a borough, although by prescription only as there is no record of any charter.[1] In 1177 Rhys ap Gruffudd constructed the first castle which he placed on a ledge overlooking the Wye at a point where the river makes a sharp turn.[2] It was burnt in 1194,[3] but subsequently rebuilt, although there there is little to see now, and even much of the surrounding moat has disappeared through the efforts of the town council who used it as a refuse pit.[4] There is no mention of any civil settlement from this period, however, and the place is not specifically referred to as a town until 1304.[5] It appears as a borough in accounts of 1360[6] and 1371[7] and there were also markets and a fair held at this time, the market being usually on a Sunday as Speed observed in 1610—'Raihader Gowy . . . hath her Markets

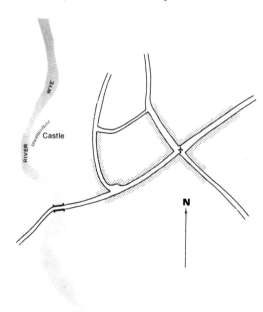

Fig. 86. Rhayader

there kept upon the Sabbath, which I there observed, and here note for an offence'.[8]

The medieval town was laid out to the east of the castle with the burgages lining the two principal streets which lead roughly north-south and east-west. The market-place stood at the junction and it was here that the town hall was also located until its demolition in 1922, although it dated only from 1762 and apparently had no predecessor.[9] Further west a second street leads north to St Clement's church which seems to lie beyond the area of the early settlement.

Rhayader appears to have been a defended town and the line of the ditch can still be traced following the outer limits of the property boundaries.[10] On the north side this would mean that the church stood beyond the enclosed area and was perhaps earlier than the foundation of the borough, like St Bridget's across the river. The latter is the parish church of Llansanffraid Cwmdeuddwr, and was formerly a grange of Strata Florida Abbey, a connection which led to the belief

Fig. 87. Rhayader
An early print of the old Market House

that Rhayader was the home of a Dominican friary.[11] Samuel Lewis actually went as far as to locate it near the bridge,[12] but there is no reliable evidence for the existence of such a house, and recent writers have rejected the claim.[13] Few other features of early Rhayder's topography are known, and no buildings of any great antiquity have survived; the oldest dates from the 17th century. The town mill stood below the castle on the east side and was fed by a stream which also served as a natural motte,[14] while across the Wye stood a wooden bridge which was not replaced with a stone structure until 1780.[15]

Like the majority of Welsh towns Rhayader suffered at the hands of the Glyndŵr rebels,[16] and it emerged as nothing more than a petty market centre, although during the reign of Henry VIII both the County Court and the Court of Great Sessions were held here until their transfer to Presteigne.[17] During the 18th century a small woollen industry was established and the town experienced some limited growth although in 1801 the population stood at only 400 living in 80 houses.

1. Williams, S. W., 'Rhayader and its Antiquities', *Mont. Coll.*, xxx (1897–8), 230.
2. *Brut y Tywysogion*, 72.
3. *Ibid.*, 75.
4. *R.C.A.M.W.M., Rads.*, 137.
5. *C.I.P.M.*, iv, 161.
6. S.C. 6/1209/4.
7. S.C. 6/1209/12.
8. *Atlas of Wales*, 111. Market day was subsequently changed to Wednesday (Bowen, *Britannia Depicta*, 7).
9. *R.C.A.M.W.M., Rads.*, 139; Williams, J., *History of Radnorshire*, 283.
10. *Ibid.*, 285; Williams, S. W., 'Rhayader and its Antiquities', *op. cit.*, 211.
11. *Ibid.*, 237.
12. *Topographical Dictionary, sub Rhaiadr.*
13. Easterling, V., 'The Friars in Wales', *Arch. Camb.*, 6th ser., xiv (1914), 350; Knowles and Hadcock, *Medieval Religious Houses*, 220.
14. Williams, S. W., 'Rhayader and its Antiquities', *op. cit.*, 219.
15. Williams, J., *History of Radnorshire*, 283; Bowen, *Britannia Depicta*, *loc. cit.*
16. Williams, J., *History of Radnorshire*, 283.
17. Williams, S. W., 'Rhayader and its Antiquities', *op. cit.*, 228.

RHUDDLAN, Clwd (Flintshire)   SJ 024779

Rhuddlan is situated near the mouth of the Afon Clwyd, and the settlement was founded at the nearest fording point to the sea and the highest point up-river reached by tidal waters. For both the historian and archaeologist this is potentially one of the most interesting urban sites in the north, if not in the whole of Wales. Recent excavations have revealed traces of early occupation from the Mesolithic through to the Romano-British period,[1] while in a border area much disputed by Celt and Saxon, organised settlement has a long and varied history. In 796 King Offa of Mercia, who had recently completed his famous dyke, gained control of the Welsh lordship of Tegeingl (Englefield), which included Rhuddlan, and in the same year an important battle is said to have been fought on the marsh of Morfa Rhuddlan (*bellum rudglann*).[2]

Throughout the following century Tegeingl appears to have remained in English hands, and in 921 the *Anglo-Saxon Chronicle* records the foundation of the *burh* of 'Cledemutha',[3] originally thought to have been somewhere near the mouth of the Cleddau, but on etymological grounds now considered to be a reference to 'the mouth of the Clwyd'.[4] The frequency of Scandinavian raids along this section of the coast, moreover, provides the reasoning for such a foundation,[5] and it seems likely that Rhuddlan's so-called Town Ditch, sections of which survive to the south and south-east of Twt Hill, enclosed the Anglo-Saxon *burh* and not its Norman successor as was once thought.[6] This is a formidable earthwork, probably originally of a ditch between two banks, with these two large sections remaining. The river was presumably incorporated into the defences on the west side. There are no traces of the northern line, although it was observed by Thomas Pennant in the 18th century running towards the moat of the Edwardian castle,[7] and recently

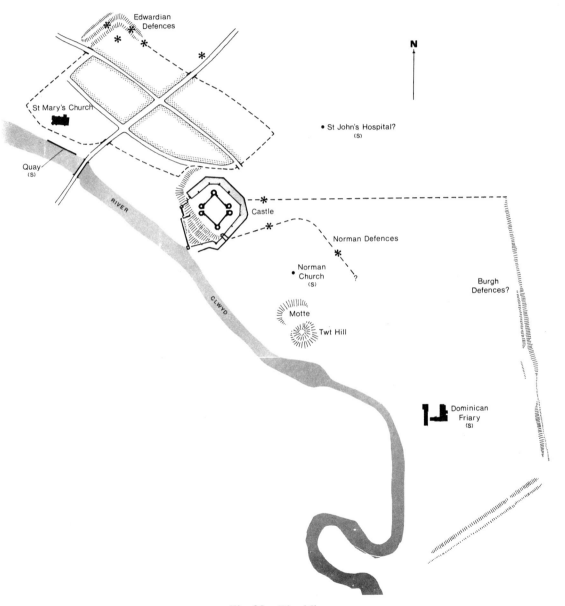

Fig. 88. Rhuddlan

sections have been revealed just south of Hylas Lane.[8] The problem with these defences is that they enclose too large an area to be in character with the small Norman borough mentioned in Domesday Book whose defences, in any case, have recently been revealed by excavation in the area of the Abbey Nurseries.[9] This demands a re-interpretation of the Town Ditch and in the light of present knowledge the only possible alternative points to a Saxon Provenance.

During the late 9th or early 10th centuries Tegeingl was regained by the Welsh, and in 1016 local ruler, Llywelyn ap Seisyllt, built a stronghold at Rhuddlan which he probably sited on Twt Hill. A small 'vill' may also have been founded, for in 1936 the remains of two Celtic crosses from this period were discovered built into a boundary wall of the vicarage.[10] It emerged as a royal seat of Gruffudd ap Llywelyn, and was attacked and destroyed by Harold Godwin in 1063,[11] but 10 years later a new castle was constructed under Norman direction by Robert, cousin of Hugh of Avranches, Earl of Chester, who appropriately adopted the styling of 'Rhuddlan'.[12] He also founded a small borough consisting of 18 burgesses, a mill, a church, and a mint, which appears in the Domesday Survey of 1086.[13] Robert's motte also appears to have been built on Twt or Bonc Hill, which is an impressive mound with a descent of some 20m. on the south side. Immediately to the north stood the church which was located in 1970 and excavations produced evidence of a graveyard together with two coins from the reign of William Rufus, dated c. 1096, which suggests that this was the church first mentioned in Domesday.[14] Sections of the borough defences have also been located in the area of the primary school and the Abbey Nurseries,[15] while the footpath which now runs from Hylas Lane to Twt Hill may well represent the line of one of the original streets as the church lies adjacent to it.

Throughout the following two centuries possession of Rhuddlan continued to alternate between English and Welsh, and the castle was frequently attacked and destroyed.[16] With the defeat of Llywelyn ap Gruffudd, however, the area finally fell to Edward I, and in 1277 he began to lay out at Rhuddlan a new castle-borough immediately to the north of the Norman town. Burgages were being allocated from 1278 to 1280,[17] and work began to divert the course of the Clwyd so that it washed the south-west corner of the castle and facilitated access to the sea.[18] In September 1278 the new borough received its royal charter which was based on the liberties of Hereford,[19] and by the end of 1280 work on the castle and town defences was largely completed.[20] It was Edward's intention to make Rhuddlan one of the most important towns in North Wales, and it was to that end in 1281 that he applied to the Pope for the transfer of the see of St Asaph to his new borough. The scheme came to nothing, however, due partly to a change in the papacy, but principally to the outbreak of Welsh discontent in 1282 which demanded the king's full attention.Rhuddlan itself was attacked, the church and the Dominican friary damaged, but eventual English victory presented Edward with Conwy and Caernarfon to which he turned his attention at the expense of this new foundation. As a result, the cathedral was never moved, the town defences, like those of Flint, were never reconstructed in stone, and the originally envisaged development failed to take place.

Fig. 89. Rhuddlan
An early-19th-century print showing the castle, St Mary's church, and the
old town quay

The borough itself was completed, however, and by 1292 housed 75 taxpayers.[22]
It followed a rectangular plan running north-south with the castle in the south-west
corner, and St Mary's church in the usual north-west corner. The whole was
defended on three sides by a bank and ditch with the river following its new cut
and a steep cliff providing sufficient natural defence on the western side. Remains
of the defences are still visible in the north-east corner of the borough and
excavations have revealed a broad, flat-bottomed ditch 2.4m. deep between two low
banks, the outer being nearly 17m. wide.[23] No traces were discovered of the
intended timber palisade and this agrees with the documentary evidence that it was
never erected.[24] On the south side the position of the defences is less clear; they may
have followed the line of Castle Street, or the builders may have incorporated the
older, possibly *burh* defences discovered beneath Hylas Lane. Within the walls the
burage plots were laid out along a rectilinear street-pattern with the High Street the
principal road running east–west and interesected by Gwindy, Church, Parliament,
and Castle Streets. An extent of 1428 shows that most of the streets have failed to
retain their original names: the High Street and Castle Street are mentioned; but the
others were then 'Peperstrete', 'Hardynstrete', 'Pyloristrete', and 'Briggestrete'.
The survey also mentions tenements 'upon le Ditch' and in 'le Oldtown' which
indicates the survival of settlement in the area of Twt Hill and the Norman church.[25]
The castle, defences and street-pattern constitute the chief feature of the medieval

town, but other aspects of its early topography are also known. St Mary's church remains in the north-west corner occupying the site which was probably originally earmarked for Edward's new cathedral. Sections of the original walling remain on the north and west sides, but considerable alterations were made in the late 15th century when the tower and a second nave were added, and the building underwent further substantial restoration in 1812 and 1870.[26] Nearby the bridge across the Clwyd also dates originally from the initial period of building, although it was reconstructed twice in the 14th century.[27] The present arched structure, though with a modern superstructure, bears the date 1595 and is said to have been the work of William Hughes, Bishop of St Asaph. Immediately above the bridge in the shadow of St Mary's stood the borough quay which served as the centre of Rhuddlan's maritime trade throughout the Middle Ages and continued in use until the 19th century.[28]

Little else of any antiquity remains within the enclosed area except for the fragment of masonry at the junction of the High Street and Parliament Street, known as 'The Wall'. It bears a commemorative stone which identifies it as the remains of the building where Edward I drew up the Statute of Rhuddlan in 1284, but the tradition is without historical foundation, and no part of the wall itself is older than the 16th century except for sections of carved freestone which were removed from the castle during its construction. Beyond the town walls stand two final features of interest, the remains of the Dominican friary at Abbey Farm[29] and the building known as Hendre on the east side of Prince's Road. The friary was in existence by the 1260s and was an important house, consisting at the time of its suppression of a church and cemetery, a hall with three chambers, two other chambers, a kitchen and a stable. Parts of the church were still standing in the late 18th century, but the only structural remains now amount to a fragment of the south cloister range incorporated into the farm buildings whose walls also contain a rich selection of monuments and memorial slabs. Hendre, situated 250m. north-east of the castle, may also have been a religious building. In 1278 Edward I had contributed towards the building of an almshouse at Rhuddlan, and later in 1284 Queen Eleanor contributed funds 'ad constructionem ecclesie sancti Johannis in villa Rodolani'.[30] Its site was clearly beyond the borough, but it cannot be as far away as 'Spital Cottage', to the east of Abbey Farm since the 1428 extent mentions land 'against le Spitele' in the delineation of burgages and associated holdings. In 1282 the hospice was assigned land for use as a graveyard[31] and graves have been periodically found in the fields adjoining Hendre along Dyserth Road,[32] but the site is to be excavated ahead of re-development, so a firm identification must away the archaeologist's trowel.

Rhuddlan, as has been pointed out, failed to live up to Edward I's grandiose expectations, and the later history of the borough is limited and largely uneventful except for the attack of Owain Glyndŵr. The borough was sacked in 1400, and in the following year it was said that the inhabitants were unable to pay their dues to the royal officials 'because the town had been completely burnt and totally destroyed by the rebels'.[33] Only 37 burgages are listed in the survey of 1428 (although it may be incomplete) against the 75 taxpayers recorded 130 years earlier. In the 16th century the development of lead mining in the surrounding districts contributed to the urban economy.[34] Additionally Rhuddlan continued to carry out a small seaborne trade, but by then it was a small settlement of no importance beyond its immediate locality.[35]

1. Miles, H., 'Excavations at Rhuddlan, 1969-71: Interim Report', *J.F.H.S.*, xxv (1971-2), 2-4.

2. *Annales Cambriae*, 11; Lloyd, *History of Wales*, i, 201-2.

3. Whitelock, D., *et al.* (eds.), *Anglo-Saxon Chronicle*, 68.

4. Wainwright, F. J., 'Cledemutha', *E.H.R.*, lxv (1950), 204-12.

5. Loyn, H., *The Vikings in Wales*, Dorothea Coke Memorial Lecture (Univ. of London, 1976), 10.

6. Taylor, A. J., *Rhuddlan Castle*, Official Guide (H.M.S.O., 1956), 15.

7. Rhys, J. (ed.), *Tours in Wales* (1883 edn.), ii, 117.

8. Miles, H., *op. cit.*, 4-5.

9. *Ibid.*, 2.

10. Hughes, H. H., 'A pre-Norman stone at Rhuddlan', *Arch Camb.*, xci (1936), 140-1; Nash-Williams, *Early Christian Monuments of Wales*, 127.

11. *Anglo-Saxon Chronicle*, 136; Taylor, *Rhuddlan Castle*, 3-4;

12. Orderic Vitalis, *Hist. Eccles.*, viii, 3; Lloyd, *History of Wales*, ii, 382.

13. *D.B.*, i, f. 269b.

14. Miles, H., *op. cit.*, 2, 6.

15. *Ibid.*, 2.

16. *Brut y Tywysogion*, 65, 86, 88.

17. *Cal. Welsh Rolls*, 165, 188; *Cal. Pat. Rolls*, 1272-81, 259, 366, 370.

18. *King's Works*, 319; Taylor, *Rhuddlan Castle*, 9.

19. *Cal. Ch. Rolls*, ii, 276-7.

20. For an account of the building of the castle *see King's Works*, 318-27; and Taylor, *Rhuddlan Castle*, 6-7.

21. For this episode and the documentation *see* Taylor, A. J., 'Rhuddlan Cathedral;: a "might-have been" of Flintshire history', *J.F.H.S.*, xv (1954-5), 43-51.

22. E 179/242/52.

23. Miles, H., *op. cit.*, 8.

24. The palisade intended for Rhuddlan was transferred for use at Caernarfon in June 1283 (*King's Works*, 323, 371).

25. Jones, A., 'A fifteenth-century document of Rhuddlan', *J. F. H. S.*, v. (1915), 45-90. During excavations in 1969-71 the remains of two 13th-century houses were discovered beyond the town walls on the Nursery site east of the castle (Miles, H., *op. cit.*, 5).

26. James, J. W., *Rhuddlan and its Church*, Rhuddlan, 1968.

27. S.C., 6/771/13; S.C. 6/774/4-6.

28. Taylor, *Rhuddlan Castle*, 10. The position of the quay is indicated on a drawing by Moses Griffith in 1782 (reproduced in James, J. W., *op. cit.*, 24).

29. Gumbley, W., 'The Dominican Priory of Ruhddlan', *J.F.H.S.*, v (1915), 34-5.

30. E 101/315/15; Taylor, *Rhuddlan Castle*, 11; *King's Works*, 319.

31. Haddan, A. W. and Stubbs, W., *Councils and Ecclesiastical Documents relating to Great Britain and Ireland* (Oxford, 1969), 540.

32. James, J. W., *op. cit.*, 14.

33. S.C. 6/775/1; Messham, 'The County of Flint and the Rebellion of Owen Glyndŵr', *op. cit.*, 13.

34. Rees, *Industry Before the Industrial Revolution*, 30, 41, 52.

35. Lewis, *Topographical Dictionary*, *sub* Rhuddlan.

RUTHIN (Rhuthun), Clwyd (Denbighshire)   SJ 125584

Ruthin lies at the southern end of the Vale of Clwyd with the site of the town occupying the summit of a low hill which rises abruptly from the river. The foundation of the borough dates from the Edwardian conquest, but settlement was already well established here before the English arrival. Traditionally Ruthin is considered to have been the administrative centre of the commot of Dyffryn Clwyd and there are good grounds for believing that a sizeable *tref* had developed in the area of the modern Well Street which was originally known as 'Welsh Street'. It has also been suggested that the later castle was constructed on or near the site of a Welsh stronghold known as 'the Red Fort'[1] but in the absence of any documentary evidence the view is no more than speculative.[2]

In 1247 Dyffryn Clwyd passed into English hands under the terms of the Treaty of Woodstock,[3] but was recovered by the Welsh under Llywelyn ap Gruffudd in 1256.[4] Edward I regained the territory in 1277 and granted it to Llywelyn's brother, Dafydd, and work on Ruthin Castle was started in the same year.[5] In 1282, however, Dafydd led a rebellion against the crown which proved abortive, and Dyffryn Clwyd was subsequently bestowed on Reginald de Grey, justiciar of Chester, who

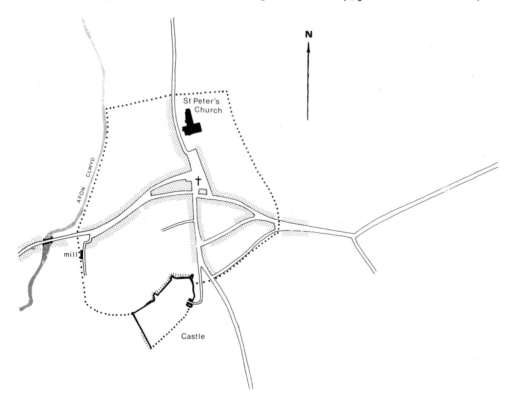

Fig. 90. Ruthin

had been instrumental in suppressing the revolt.[6] Reginald immediately set about the recommencement of work on the castle and began to lay out the borough which he centred on the existing Welsh community of Well Street. A survey of the town carried out in 1324 listed 100 burgages controlled by 70 burgesses of whom one-third were Welsh and noticeably concentrated in Well Street which indicates that the established community was not moved as happened at Llanfaes, but was simply reorganised along burghal lines.[7] The success of the borough can largely be attributed to the de Grey family, and by his charter of 1281-2 Reginald bestowed a variety of privileges which enhanced Ruthin's standing and economic superiority within the lordship.[8] During his lifetime the castle was largely completed[9] and he was also responsible for the foundation of St Peter's church which was rebuilt by his successor John de Grey in 1310 as a collegiate church with seven priests.[10] It stands at the north end of a long street leading from the castle gate, and the college buildings were in turn on the north side of the church and seem to have formed a quadrangle. Together they constituted a house of the order of Bonhommes but after the dissolution St Peter's was secularised, while the college buildings were obtained by Dr. Gabriel Goodman, dean of Westminster and a native of Ruthin, who converted them into Christ's hospital and further erected 12 almshouses nearby which can still be seen.[11] Reginald de Grey is also said to have founded a Carmelite priory at Ruthin which stood off St Peter's Square, the borough's market-place, but this is considered doubtful.[12]

In its plan the medieval town centred on St Peter's Square, which lies due north of the castle. In 1295 it was designated the permanent market-place and the borough stocks were also located here.[13] During the 15th century the court house was built in the Square and its cellars served as cells, while the remains of gallows still project from the wall of the building which now houses a bank. Nearby, in 1663, the town hall was erected using stone from the old collegiate church and the ground floor housed the meat market, although not without effect on the fabric as the hanging-up of carcasses was subsequently observed to be 'dangering the ruine of the Building'.[14] Nevertheless, the structure survived until 1863 when the present town hall was constructed off Market Street.

From this central square radiated the main streets of the borough which form an approximate north-south and east-west pattern with traces of the former burgages detectable off Clwyd Street and the west side of Castle Street. Curiously, however, no early attempt was made to defend this apparently prosperous borough, and there is no record of any town defences until Ruthin was sacked by Owain Glyndŵr in September 1400.[15] Most of the buildings were put to flames, and the burgesses were prompted to apply for an award of murage which was granted in 1407, 'because the town lies so open among the Welsh rebels'.[16] A ditch was consequently dug around the borough, but no traces of it remain, although a likely course can be suggested from the surviving property boundaries.[17] Natural protection was on the west side by the Clwyd, while the line of the northern section is indicated by the continuous stretch of boundaries which run past St Peter's church as far as School Road. On the east Wynnstay Road is the likely course of the defences, with a south-west turn at Well Street and a continuation as far as the

Fig. 91. The Town Hall, Ruthin

Built in 1663 and demolished 200 years later. The undercroft housed
the weekly meat market.

castle along Dog Lane, which is mentioned in the 1324 survey.[18] If the ditch was
also extended west of the castle it may have followed a straight line as far as the
river or more likely run north on the west side of Mill Street (where the original mill
still stands)[19] as far as Clwyd Street. According to Newcome in 1829 a section of
masonry defences could still be seen here, while he also mentions the demolition
30 years earlier of the Water Gate, Porth-y-Dwr, which led to the bridge.[20]

Despite the apparent severity of the Glyndŵr attack, Ruthin, unlike the majority
of similarly ravaged Welsh towns, was able to recover relatively quickly. The growth
of an important cloth industry centred on the borough proved to be the major
contributory factor, and Ruthin had its own guild of fullers and weavers.[21] By 1496
the burgage total had risen to 209, double the number recorded in 1324, and they
were held by only 90 burgesses, which points to the development of an urban
aristocracy.[22] The town's subsequent history is largely uneventful except for its
part in the Civil War when it was besieged twice by Parliamentary forces in 1644
and 1646.[23] When the borough finally fell the castle was pulled down, but it had
long ceased to play a part in the economic life of Ruthin, which remained 'the
greatest market town in all the Vale, full of inhabitants and well replenished with
buildings'.[24]

1. Taylor, A. J., 'Castle-building in Wales in the later thirteenth century', in Jope, E. M. (ed.),
Studies in Building History (London, 1961), 105; Lewis, *Topographical Dictionary, sub* Ruthin;

Jack, R. I., 'Welsh and English in the medieval lordship of Ruthin', *T.D.H.S.*, xviii (1969) 38.

2. Hogg and King, 'Early Castles', 119–20.

3. Lloyd, *History of Wales*, ii, 708; Robert, R. A. (ed.), *Ruthin Court Rolls* (temp. Edward I), Cymm. Rec. Soc., ii (London, 1893) vii.

4. Lloyd, *History of Wales*, ii, 717, 740.

5. *Littere Wallie*, 103; *King's Works*, 327.

6. *Cal. Welsh Rolls*, 243; Morris, *Welsh Wars*, 178. The text of Edward's grant to Reginald is in Roberts, *Ruthin Court Rolls*, 48.

7. Jack, R. I., 'Records of Denbighshire Lordships, ii; the Lordship of Dyffryn Clwyd in 1324', *T.D.H.S.*, xvii (1968), 13–18; *idem*, 'Welsh and English in the medieval lordship of Ruthin', *op. cit.*, 39.

8. The original grant is known only from an *inspeximus* of 1496 (Jack, R. I., 'The medieval charters of Ruthin borough', *ibid.*, xviii (1969), 16–22, and *idem*, 'The seigneurial charters of the Borough of Ruthin', *N.L.W.J.*, xvi (1969–79), 77–86.

9. For a description and account of the building of the castle *see R.C.A.M.W.M.*, *Denbs.*, 178–80, and *King's Works*, 327–9.

10. Knowles and Hadcock, *Medieval Religious Houses*, 203–4.

11. *R.C.A.M.W.M.*, *Denbs.*, 181.

12. Knowles and Hadcock, *Medieval Religious Houses*, 237.

13. Roberts, *Ruthin Court Rolls*, 48.

14. Tucker, N. (ed.), 'The Councell Booke of Ruthin, 1642–95', *T.D.H.S.*, x (1961), 39.

15. Lloyd, *Owen Glendower*, 31–2; Evans, B., 'Owain Glyndŵr's raid on Ruthin (1400)', *T.D.H.S.*, x (1961), 239–41. The surrounding area, and possibly the town, was ravaged again in 1402 (*Chron. Adam de Usk*, 239).

16. *Cal. Pat. Rolls*, 1405–8, 375; *Town Defences*, 218.

17. A late 15th-century rental records that the rent of half a burgage had been reduced 'because a *fossus* was made on that land in defence of the town of Ruthin in the time of the Welsh War' (S.C. 12/24/1; Jack, R. I., 'Welsh and English in the Medieval lordship of Ruthin', *op. cit.*, 37).

18. *Idem*, 'Records of Denbighshire Lordships, ii; the Lordship of Dyffryn Clwyd in 1324', *op. cit.*, 13–18.

19. The lower story of the building, which is now used as a shop, is of late 13th-century date which suggests that the mill was contemporary with the castle and the foundation of the borough (*R.C.A.M.W.M.*, *Denbs.*, 182).

20. Newcome, R., *An Account of the Town and Castle of Ruthin*, 2nd edn. (Ruthin, 1838), 24–5.

21. Jack, R. I., 'The cloth industry in medieval Ruthin', *T.D.H.S.*, xii (1963), 10–25.

22. *Idem*, 'The seigneurial charters of the Borough of Ruthin', *op. cit.*, 85.

23. Phillips, *Memoirs of the Civil War in Wales and the Marches*, i, 361–2.

24. Camden, *Britannia*, 676.

ST ASAPH (Llanelwy), Clwyd (Flintshire)   SJ 038744

St Asaph is situated in an area of low-lying land bounded on the east by the River Clwyd and on the west by the Afon Elwy, the proximity of the latter being responsible for the town's Welsh name of 'Llanelwy'. As it suggests, this is an ecclesiastical settlement, and the origins and early history of St Asaph begin with the foundation of the first 'cathedral', *c.* 560 A.D. by Kentigern, a native of Scotland who entrusted the new building to Asaph, himself a North Walian.[1] For the remainder of the Dark Ages the history of this community is obscure and like the monastery of Llantwit Major there are only occasional references to it until the arrival of the Normans.[2] In 1143 it became the centre of a new bishopric, which

Fig. 92. St Asaph

suggests that the traditions of the old church of Kentigern might have survived the preceding centuries, and both the cathedral and the church were subsequently rebuilt on a grander scale.

Of the medieval town itself very little is known. St Asaph was not granted borough status, and all the indications are that this was a small settlement overshadowed by its more prosperous neighbour to the north— Rhuddlan. It played a small role in the economic life of the area, however, and had its own fair,[3] but when the town was mapped by John Speed in 1610 it was still a small community entirely dominated by the cathedral.[4] From the plan it is clear that the present street-pattern was already well-established, and although not named, the High Street, Lower Street, the Gemig, and Denbigh Road are indicated. Speed shows less than 50 dwellings, however, with the only grouping of any note in the area of Lower Street, and most of the land to the north of the High Street was still open space. The cathedral and St Kentigern's church are marked, both of which had to be rebuilt after Glyndŵr's attack on the town in 1402,[5] and other features of the early topography include the old bridge, the mill, and the almshouse. The bridge across the Elwy at the end of the High Street was not built until 1630[6] and prior to that date the river was crossed by a wooden structure further north which, according to Speed, lay in the area of Llys-y-Felin. The river itself appears to have flowed closer to the town than at present, and the mill-stream washed the west side of the churchyard with the mill situated below at the west end of the High Street. Nearby, opposite the church, stand the almshouses which Bishop Barlow (1669–80) erected for 'eight poor widows', although the premises now house a restaurant.[7]

1. Lloyd, *History of Wales*, i, 166, 208, 242; Speed, *Atlas of Wales*, 121; Knowles and Hadcock, *Medieval Religious Houses*, 436.

2. Lloyd, *History of Wales*, ii, 455–6; Bax, P. B. I., *The Cathedral church of St. Asaph* (Bournemouth, 1896), 1–8; Thomas, D. R., *History of St Asaph*, 2nd edn., 3 vols. (Oswestry, 1908–13), 1–10.

3. *Cal. Anct. Corresp.*, 232.

4. *Atlas of Wales*, inter 121–2.

5. Lloyd, *Owen Glendower*, 125n; Bax, *op. cit.*, 73.

6. *R.C.A.M.W.M., Flints.*, 87.

7. Thomas, D. R., *op. cit.*, i, 387.

ST CLEARS (Sanclêr), Dyfed (Carmarthenshire)   SN 280154

The early history of St Clears is poorly documented and nothing is known about the construction of the castle or of the founder of the predominantly English borough which developed in its shadow. The fortification, a motte-and-bailey thrown up at the junction of the rivers Taf and Cynin, is first mentioned in 1188,[1] but on the evidence from nearby Laugharne and Carmarthen it was probably erected much earlier in the century and may correspond to the 'castle of Ystrad Cyngen' recorded in 1153.[2] It appears again in 1189[3] when it was sacked by the Welsh under Rhys ap Gruffudd, and was the target of fur-ther fighting in 1195 and 1215.[4] It does not appear to have been rebuilt in stone and was very likely abandoned later in the 13th cen-tury, although its outline has survived the centuries well. The remains of the motte rising to a height of 12m. can be seen on the east side of Bridge Street with the bailey leading southwards. There is an additional low bank outside it above the Cynin which appears to have been intended as a protection against flooding.

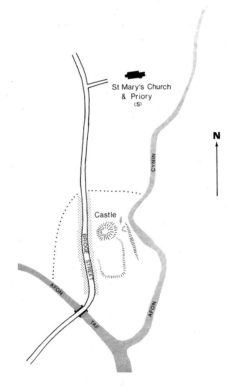

Fig. 93. St Clears

Almost contemporary with the building of the castle was the foundation of a Cluniac priory dependent on the French church of Saint Martin-des-Champs, Paris, which dates from the period 1147–84.[5] The priory church, dedicated to St Mary Magdalene, has since become the parish church of St Clears, but there are no remains of the con-ventual buildings which lay to the south. It was a small house with only two monks, notoriously corrupt,[6] and after its dissolution along with the other alien priories Henry VI granted it in 1446 to All Souls College, Oxford.[7] It seems likely that the beginnings of civil settlement also date from the late 12th century when a priory and castle would have appeared attractive to prospective tenants. There is no record of the town from this period, however, and the earliest known charter is dated as late as 1393,[8] but the 'bailiff of St Clears' is mentioned in 1282–88, when an organised settlement evidently existed.[9]

The main route to west Wales no longer passes through the historic part of St Clears, which today forms a declining suburb well away from the town's modern commercial core. No medieval population figures are known, but the borough was small and the burgages were confined to the area between the castle and church where some of the former plots are preserved off Bridge Street. This was at the principal area of the early town with the bridge across the Taf at its southern end and nearby, below Manardaf, the town quay which has since been demolished.[10] In its situation and plan St Clears accordingly has much in common with Newcastle Emlyn and both occupy peninsular sites of great natural strength. While there is no documentary or archaeological evidence for defences at either of them additional protection could easily have been provided by a bank and ditch across the peninsula.

   1. Giraldus Cambrensis, *Opera*, i, 59, 324; Lloyd, *History of Wales*, 576[n].
   2. *Brut y Tywysogion*, 58; Hogg and King, 'Early Castles', 120.
   3. *Brut y Tywysogion*, 73.
   4. *Ibid.*, 91.
   5. Knowles and Hadcock, *Medieval Religious Houses*, 97, 102; Thomas, D. A., 'St Clear's in the middle ages, 1100–1500', *Carmarthenshire Historian*, vi (1969), 66–8.
   6. *Cal. Anct. Corresp.*, 196.
   7. Lloyd, *History of Carmarthenshire*, i, 336.
   8. *Cal. Ch. Rolls*, v, 335.
   9. *Cal. Welsh Rolls*, 247, 279.
   10. Thomas, D. A., *op. cit.*, 63. The quay and the town's trading activities were frequently mentioned in presentments to the court-leet (Jones, T. I. J., 'The Court Leet Presentments of the Town, Borough, and Liberty of St. Clears, 1719–1889', *B.B.C.S.*, xiii [1950], 28–53).

ST DAVID'S (Tyddewi), Dyfed (Pembrokeshire)   SM 753253

St David's is situated in a sheltered position on the northern side of St Bride's Bay at what is the westernmost point in Wales. Although a cathedral city, the town itself is small and at no point in its history has its size been proportionate to the influence enjoyed by the impressive cathedral which dominates it. The origins of the ecclesiastical settlement are associated with the Celtic foundation of St David in the 6th century, but like similar foundations at St Asaph and Llantwit Major very little evidence from this early period has survived. The continued existence of the religious community is attested at various dates from the mid-7th century, when it was attacked and plundered by a succession of invaders, but nothing is known of any civilian settlement before the coming of the Normans.[1]

Some 320m. due west to the town lie the remains of a ring-and-bailey thrown up during the Norman period, either by William the Conqueror on his visit to the cathedral in 1081 or by one of the early bishops.[2] Its position beyond the later built-up area, however, does not suggest any settlement at this time, which is unlikely to have developed until after 1115 when Henry I granted a charter of privileges to St David's.[3] Five years later the Pope raised the international status of the cathedral by decreeing that two journeys to this shrine were the equivalent of one to St Peter's in Rome, and this would have led to the provisions of facilities for pilgrims and the beginning of commercial activity. Under the patronage of successive bishops, particularly Bishop Bek, the town grew steadily, receiving a grant of twice-weekly markets and two yearly fairs in November 1281.[4] By 1326 St David's had developed into a community of 130 burgesses, most of whom were Englishmen and was the economic centre of the district, even carrying out some maritime trade from nearby Porth Clais.[5]

Three centuries later, however, the picture had changed significantly and John Speed's plan of 1610[6] shows a mere 51 houses, and he adds pointedly that the city had 'few inhabitants and no more houses than are inserted in the draught'.[7] The original street-pattern has largely been preserved, however, and although there are few dwellings lining the courses Speed indicates Pit Street, Catherine Street, Goat Street, Nun Street, and the High Street. The surviving market cross is also marked, but there is no sign of the market house which stood nearby.[8] Nun Street, the main northern artery of the town, is said to derive its name from a nunnery which formerly stood there. Various attempts have been made to identify the building, without any degree of success, and, in fact, there is no supporting documentary evidence for its existence at all, the assumption resting solely on the street-name which was derived from the mother of St David, St Non, and not from the imaginary presence of a nunnery.[9]

There is definite evidence for another religious edifice within the area of the medieval town–Whitewell Hospice, which was founded by Bishop Bek (1280-93) to care for sick and infirm clergy and provide hospitality for pilgrims.[10] It functioned until *c.* 1377, when it was annexed to St Mary's College at St David's,[11] but remains of the buildings near the present *St Non's* hotel could still be seen early

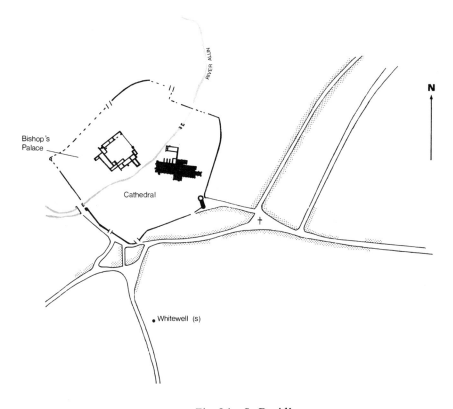

Fig. 94. St David's

in the 19th century.[12] The area is now given over to allotments, but pieces of loose masonry survive to indicate its site.

St David's, as Speed shows, was only a poor reflection of its medieval extent by the early 17th century. The majority of the former burgages lay desolate and decayed, and to Camden it was only 'a very small and poore Citie and hath nothing at all to make shew of'.[13] Surprisingly, despite being abandoned for several centuries, the burgage pattern has survived relatively intact, and the plots are most discernable off the High Street where Bryn Road clearly represents the original boundary line.

1. On this early period *see* Brut y Tywysogion, 3, 6, 9-12, 16-18, 20, and Ralegh-Radford, C. A., *The Bishop's Palace, St. David's*, Official Guide (H.M.S.O., 2nd edn., 1953), 5.

2. *Brut y Tywysogion*, 17; Lloyd, *History of Wales*, ii, 393-4; Nelson, *The Normans in South Wales*, 35.

3. The charter is known only from an *inspeximus* of Edward III in 1358 (*Cal. Pat. Rolls, 1358-61*, 7-8).

4. *Cal. Ch. Rolls*, ii, 258. A weekly market was already being held, however, and was worth 35s. 10d. in the previous year (E 352/73; Jones, F., 'Medieval records relating to the diocese of St. David's', *Journ. Hist. Soc. Church in Wales*, viii [1919-20], 83-8).

5. *Black Book*, xiii, 17-35.

6. *Atlas of Wales, inter* 101-2.

7. *Ibid.*, 101.

8. Manby, G. W., *History and Antiquities of the Parish of St. David* (London, 1801), 77.

9. On this and other early street-names *see* Green, F., 'Street Names of St. David's City', *West Wales Historical Records*, viii (1919-20), 83-8.

10. *Black Book*, 15.

11. Knowles and Hadcock, *Medieval Religious Houses*, 388.

12. *R.C.A.M.W.M., Pembs.*, 335.

13. *Britannia*, 653.

SKENFRITH (Ynysgynwraidd), Gwent (Monmouthshire)   SO 455203

Skenfrith is a small village situated on the west bank of the Monnow, commanding what was formerly one of the main routes from England into Wales. The site is dominated by the castle, and like Whitecastle and Grosmont (with which Skenfrith was traditionally associated, together forming the 'lordship of the three castles') its history is essentially that of the fortification. This commands an important bridge-point and is first mentioned in 1163,[1] although there are grounds for assuming that it dates back to the initial Norman advance into Wales and perhaps to the late 1070s.[2] During the tenure of Hubert de Burgh, who held Skenfrith for the greater part of the period 1201-39, the castle was rebuilt and enlarged, and the only subsequent addition of any significance was an extra tower on the west curtain walling erected in the 1260s.

Associated with the castle throughout the medieval period was a small town which grew up around St Bridget's church, although there is no indication that this was a planned settlement. Indeed, the natural advantages of the site and the importance of the bridgehead suggest an earlier phase of settlement and significantly, evidence of Roman ironworking has emerged during excavation of the castle.[3] Similarly, the dedication of the church (Welsh 'Ffraed') points to a

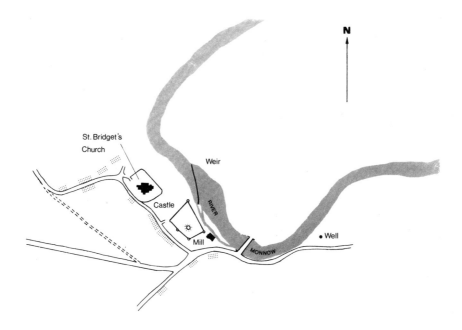

Fig. 95. Skenfrith

pre-Norman foundation and there is a St Ffraed's Well 450m. to the east. No doubt
further growth was prompted by the presence of the castle, and in 1219 Reginald
de Braose was clearing the surrounding woodland,[4] perhaps to accommodate new
burgages, but the absence of any charter or even a weekly market argues against
plantation.[5]

Today Skenfrith is only a slumbering village with a scattering of houses opposite
the castle, and beyond the church, and comparison with a tithe plan of Henry VIII's
reign shows the 16th-century picture to have been much the same.[6] There are
vestiges of burgages on the west side of the main street which runs past the castle
and church, and this may have been more densely built-up than at present. Other
likely areas of settlement lie beyond the castle gate by the river bank, and south of
the main street where the present footpath running through plots 635 and 638 is
shown on the tithe plan to have been an important road.

1. *Pipe Rolls*, 9 Hen. II, 7.

2. *See* Craster, O. E., *Skenfrith Castle*, Official Guide, H.M.S.O., 1970, and *idem*, 'Skenfrith
Castle: when it was built?', *Arch. Camb.*, cxvi (1967), 133–58.

3. *Archaelolgy in Wales*, x (1970), 26.

4. *Cal. Anct. Corresp.*, 8.

5. There was no weekly market within the entire manor (Rees, *Survey of the Duchy of
Lancaster Lordships in Wales, 1609-13*, 93).

6. In County Records Office.

SWANSEA (Abertawe), West Glamorgan   SS 656929

Swansea, traditionally regarded as the dominant town of the Gower peninsula, occupies a riverine site at the mouth of the Afon Tawe from which it derives its Welsh name.[1] The beginnings of settlement here appear to date from the 9th and 10th centuries, when the area was subject to Scandinavian raiding and colonisation as indicated by coastal place-names. That of Swansea itself (Sweyns-ey, 'Sweyn's island') was initially applied by the Norsemen to a small island between two arms of the river near its mouth, which was eventually removed in the mid-19th century during the development of the docks.[2] The settlement is unlikely to have amounted to more than a temporary trading station, however, with the later town a foundation *de novo* following the construction of military fortifications by the Normans in the early 12th century. By 1106, with the death of local ruler Hywel ap Goronwy, Henry de Newburgh was able to re-distribute the newly-acquired lands amongst his supporters and turn his attention to the foundation of a castle-borough which would serve as the *caput* of the lordship.[3]

Swansea's first castle, a motte-and-bailey, was in existence by 1116 when it was attacked and partly destroyed by Gruffudd ap Rhys.[4] It was erected on the site of the mound later known as the 'Old Castle' on the bank of the river immediately to the north of its successor, the work of William de Braose, *c.* 1300.[5] Excavations in 1913 on the site bounded by Worcester Place, Castle Bailey Street, and Welcome Lane revealed traces of both structures and also large numbers of skeletons,[6] probably from an early graveyard since the original church of Llangennydd may have occupied the site before being removed by Henry de Newburgh to the west of the peninsula.[7] Within a few years a town had developed to the north and east which received its first charter from Henry's successor, William de Newburgh, between 1153 and 1184.[8] Its early years were troubled times and the English community was frequently the target of Welsh unrest, as in 1215 when the castle was burnt by Rhys ap Gruffudd[9] and in 1287 when Rhys ap Maredudd

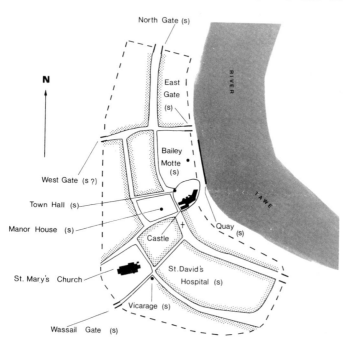

Fig. 96. Swansea

'wasted by fire the vill'.[10] Nevertheless, as administrative centre of the Gower and ideally suited for the development of commercial and maritime activities the borough proved able to survive, and in 1306 the burgesses secured confirmation of their rights and privileges from William de Braose.[11]

Until the early 19th century Swansea was confined to a cluster of houses at the mouth and along the bank of the Tawe, with the streets following the grain of the valley. There is sufficient evidence to indicate that the medieval borough was walled with defences constructed during the early years of the 14th century. Murage grants were received in 1317[12] and 1338[13] while the foundation charter to St David's hospital of 1332 indicates that they were then standing, since burgages were appropriated 'within the wall'.[14] Although no traces now remain, apart from a possible north-east corner incorporated into buildings in King's Lane, the actual course of the defences is now reasonably clear, although the plan devised in 1914 by Morgan needs revising in the light of later evidence. He regarded College Street, and its extension, Gower Street, as the line of the northern wall,[15] but it now seems more likely that the defences ran further north along Morris Lane (now King's Lane) and King's Street, with the North Gate at the junction.[16] At this point it would have turned southwards along the whole course of Orchard Street and the former Waterloo and Church Streets. There are no references to a gate on this west side, but it is highly improbable that such a length of defences would be without an access point, and the former presence of a washing-pool in Gower Street suggests that there was a gate at the end of College Street.

Further south the Wassail Gate stood at the junction of Church Street and Frog Street, and from here the wall continued almost to the river bank, although probably not along Salubrious Place as Morgan thought, but following the line of Rutland Street and Victoria Road. The South Gate stood at the end of Wind Street, while remains of the wall were found in nearby Quay Parade in 1926. At this point it veered to the north-west until eventually joining with the wall of the castle bailey at Castle Street. The defences do not appear to have followed the line of the Strand, which at first sight looks like a burgage boundary line, but rather followed a course nearer Wind Street, where remains of the wall were traced during the construction of the new post office. Finally, from the north-east corner of the castle bailey the remaining section ran north along the Strand until linking up with the North Gate. Some traces of the wall and a tower were discovered here in 1925, when two tenements were demolished midway between King's Lane and Welcome Street. Again, as on the west side, the exact position of the gate is a matter of conjecture, although there evidently was one since a survey of 1650 refers to houses 'on the East side, within the Gate'.[17] The most likely position would be at the end of the appropriately-named Welcome Street, which represented the northern limits of the bailey which in turn was reached by a gate known as 'Harold's Gate', situated at the end of Castle Bailey Street.[18]

The area enclosed by the medieval town walls thus formed an 'L'-shape with the castle occupying a roughly central position. The bailey lay to the north, though it had been abandoned as a defensive work by the late 14th century when Harold's Gate and the corner towers had been sold off. East of the castle stood the 'Plas'

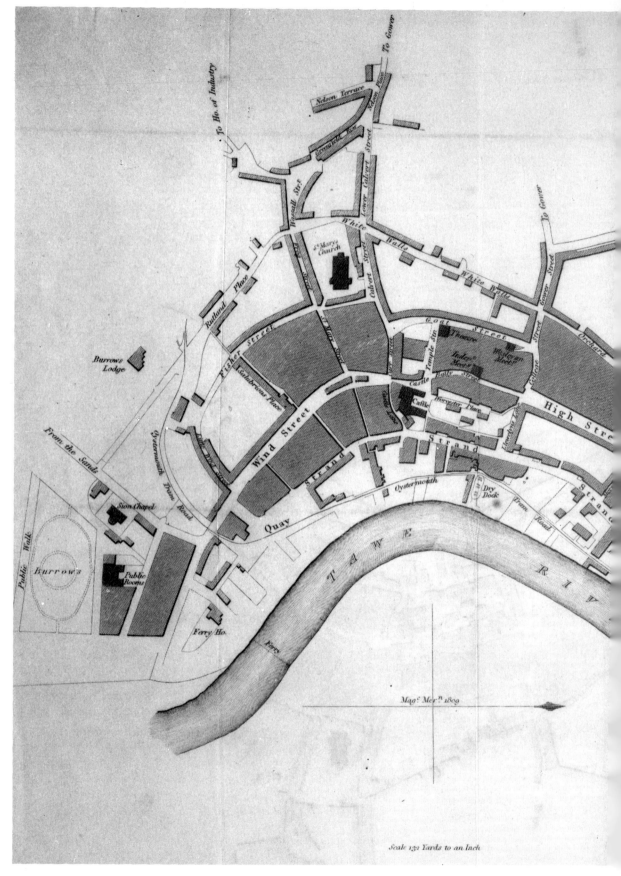

Fig. 97. Swansea in 1823.

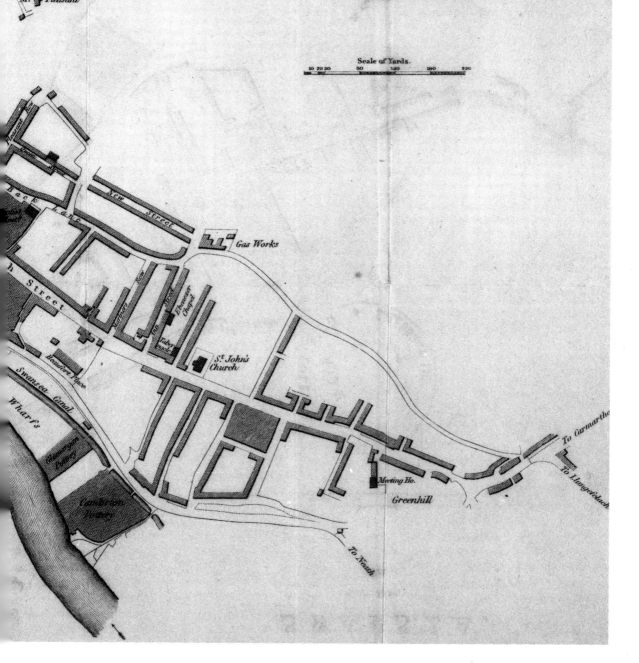

PLAN
OF
SWANSEA,

by Jno. EVANS.

1823.

Scale of Yards.

10 20 30   50   100   180   230

Mt. Pleasant

Pleasant How

Back Lane

New Street

Gas Works

Ebenezer Chapel

St. John's Church

Street

Beaudre Place

Swansea Canal

Wharfs

Glamorgan Pottery

Cambrian Pottery

Meeting Ho.

Greenhill

To Carmarthen

To Llangrdilach

To Neath

or 'Manor House' which occupied a site now given over to public gardens. During demolition of the building in 1870 a hoard of silver pennies dating from the reign of Edward I was discovered, although the 'Plas' is not thought to have been built before the late 14th century. Nearby, at the upper end of Castle Square, was the site of Swansea's weekly market, which continued to be an open-air affair until 1652, when the market house was built.[19] This building was erected midway between the modern Castle Street and Wind Street near the town hall, which occupied a site adjoining the north-west wall of the castle until its demolition in 1856 prior to the construction of the post office.[20]

Below the market-place and the commercial centre of the early town were several features of the borough's ecclesiastical life. The church of St Mary's remains, although much rebuilt, while the vicarage and tithe barn were located immediately opposite in the area of the modern Llanfair Buildings. To the east lay St David's hospital, founded by Henry Gower, Bishop of St David's, in 1332, and a section of the building was subsequently incorporated into the *Cross Keys* public house.[21] Beyond the walls lay two essential features of the early townscape, the medieval quay and the ferry. The latter, mentioned in William de Braose's charter of 1306, appears to have been of the rope and windlass type, and it operated across the Tawe just from outside the South Gate.[22] The same charter also made provision for the building and repairing of ships, and Swansea was a trading port of some significance from its earliest days. The area of the Strand was a busy one, and the remains of the town quay here were discovered at the rear of the castle during rebuilding in 1953.

The later history of Swansea is one of continued prosperity despite the damage caused by the Glyndŵr rebels, whose actions rendered the castle valueless, part of it subsequently being converted into a palace of the bishops of St David's.[23] The population of the borough in the mid-16th century has been estimated at nearly a thousand, increasing to about one thousand four hundred by 1631. The Assessment Rolls on which these calculations are based indicate the presence of a wealthy mercantile class living in properties such as the 'Great House' which stood beyond the North Gate.[24] Camden noted that the town was 'of great account'[25] while a survey conducted by Cromwell's officials in 1650 provides a valuable indication of Swansea's extent before it experienced the rapid expansion prompted by the development of the coal industry. The number of tenements in each street are listed, while the survey also indicates the size of the extra-mural settlement. Within the walls the principal streets were Castle Bailey Street (17), Wind Street (39), Fisher Street (12), Cross Street (11), Goat Street (17), and St Mary's Street (26). Also mentioned are Goat Street (2). 'East side within the Gate' (8), 'West side of the Market' (5), and Frog Street, representing a total of 143 dwellings. Seemingly located beyond the walls were a further 41 tenements with 17 'Above the Gate' and 12 each 'Without the gate' and on the 'East Side'.[26] As George Owen observed this was 'a pretie town and good'[27] and was already well-established as a prosperous port before the rapid industrialisation of the late 18th and 19th centuries transformed it into an extensive entrepôt and, ultimately, into a city.[28]

1. An early notice of the form 'Abertawe' is given by Giraldus Cambrensis (*Opera*, vi, 73). The area, and sometimes the castle, was also known to the Welsh as 'Seinhenydd' (Rees, W., 'Gower and the March of Wales', *Arch. Camb.*, cx [1961], 4).

2. Jones, W. H., *History of Swansea and Gower* (Carmarthen, 1920), 82-3.

3. Rees, *op. cit.*, 4.

4. *Brut y Tywysogion*, 40.

5. For an account of the castle and early excavations *see* Morgan, W. Ll., *The Castle of Swansea* (Devizes, 1914).

6. *Ibid.*, 384-5.

7. The church of Llangenydd is mentioned *temp* William I (*Liber Landavensis*, 551), and for the view that it was moved and its site appropriated for the castle *see* Jones, *History of Swansea*, 48-9, 129-30, and Morgan, *The Castle of Swansea*, vii.

8. Clark, *Cartae*, i, 136-8. A translation and discussion of the charter is in Jones, *History of Swansea*, 149-70.

9. *Brut y Tywysogion*, 9.

10. *Annales Cambriae*, 109; Griffiths, R. A., 'The Revolt of Rhys ap Maredudd', *op. cit.*, 129.

11. A translation and discussion of the charter is in Jones, *History of Swansea*, 292-317, and Robinson, W. R. B., 'Medieval Swansea', *Glam. County Hist.*, iii, 365-70.

12. *Cal. Pat. Rolls*, 1317-21, 59;

13. *Ibid.*, 1338-40, 6.

14. Wilson, J. B., 'The Hospital of the Blessed David, St. Mary Street, Swansea', *Arch. Camb.*, xliii (1888), 6-7.

15. *The Castle of Swansea*, 30, 37-9.

16. Much of Swansea's original street-pattern has been modified by redevelopment following extensive bombing during the Second World War. The following account of the town's defences is based largely on the evidence of the 1911 Ordnance Survey map where the present White Walls appears as Waterloo and Church Streets, St Mary's Square as Frog Street, Princess Way as Fisher Street, and Welcome Street as Welcome Lane.

17. *See below*, note 26.

18. Morgan, *The Castle of Swansea*, 30.

19. On this aspect of the town's history *see* Thomas, N. L., *The Story of Swansea's Markets*, Neath, 1966.

20. Morgan, *The Castle of Swansea*, 19, 44-5.

21. Wilson, J. B., *op. cit.*, 1-11.

22. Jones, *History of Swansea*, 310.

23. Morgan, *The Castle of Swansea*, 18.

24. Thomas, W. S. K., 'Tudor and Jacobean Swansea', *Morgannwg*, v (1961), 25-48.

25. *Britannia*, 646.

26. Francis, G. C., 'O. Cromwell's Survey of Gower, 1650', *Arch. Camb.*, Suppl. Vol., pt. i (1861), 21-30.

27. *Description of Pembrokeshire*, iii, 316.

28. City status was conferred on Swansea in 1969.

TALGARTH, Powys (Breconshire)   SO 154332

Talgarth is situated in the north-east corner of the former county of Breconshire and occupies an area of fairly level ground above the River Ennig. The position dominates the important Vale of Llynfi and its value was appreciated long before the Norman arrival since this is reputed to have been the chief royal residence of the kingdom of Brycheiniog.[1] Talgarth church is dedicated to St Gwen (now Gwendoline),[2] an offspring of Brychan, the legendary Dark Age ruler of the district, and there may have been a very early religious house on this site which lies at the

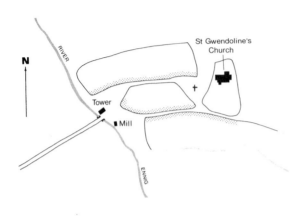

Fig. 98. Talgarth

eastern end of the old town. It was certainly well established in the late 11th or early 12th centuries when Bernard de Neufmarché granted it to his new priory at Brecon.[3]

From the early 14th century Talgarth was regarded as a borough and in 1309 there were 73 burgages in the town which also had its markets and fairs.[4] Its rights were prescriptive only, however, and there is no record of any charter or of foundation,[5] although it has the appearance of being a planned settlement. With the old town confined to the east bank of the Ennig the main streets run parallel and due west from the church with the familiar triangular market-place (since encroached upon) immediately beyond the church gates. To the south the house plots off the street known as The Bank run right down to the river, and vestiges of a burgage pattern can still be detected here, though this is no longer the case with the houses off the other main street, Back Lane. At its western end stands the old town mill, while nearby, dominating the bridge, is an unusual tower, now used as a private dwelling. It dates from the period 1250–1350 and appears to have been purely defensive since there is no suggestion of any other fortifications at Talgarth.[6] It was intended to guard the river crossing, and when this function was no longer required it housed the borough prison.[7]

1. Lloyd, *History of Wales*, i, 249, 272, ii, 397.

2. *See* Jones, T. T., 'The Daughters of Brychan', *Brycheiniog*, xvii (1976–7), 22. The church appears in Pope Nicholas's *Taxatio* of 1291 when it was valued at £18 (*Taxatio Ecclesastica P. Nicholai* [Rec. Comm.] , 273). The structure was rebuilt early in the 15th century (Jones, T., *History of Brecknock*, iii, 51).

3. Banks, R. W., 'Cartularium Prioratus S. Johannis Evang. de Brecon', *op. cit.,* 138; Roberts, G., 'Priory of St. John the Evangelist, Brecon', *ibid.,* v (1854), 22.

4. C 134/15/10.

5. Jones, T., *History of Brecknock*, iii, 39.

6. The design and function of the tower is discussed by Jones, S. R. and Smith, J. T., 'The Houses of Breconshire, iii, the Brecon District', *Brycheiniog,* xi (1965), 5–10, and King, D. J. C., 'The Castle of Breconshire', *op. cit.,* 83.

7. Leland, *Itinerary*, 108; Jones, T., *History of Brecknock*, iii, 42.

TEMPLETON, Dyfed (Pembrokeshire)   SN 113115

The village of Templeton is situated about two miles south of Narberth on the main road to Tenby. It takes its name from the society of Knights Templar who established a foundation there towards the end of the 12th century. The buildings lay in the area of St John's church at the bottom of the village, but the church is a modern structure unconnected with the Templars and any remains of their foundation have long since disappeared, and the house ceased functioning by 1312.[1] The origins of settlement here are vague and there is no record of any charter, although the tenements were regularly regarded as burgages. The presence of the priory would no doubt have attracted new tenants who could derive comfort from the existence, on the opposite side of the road, of the mound known as Sentence Castle. We do not know who built it, but this was probably the 'castle that was near Arberth' burnt by Gruffudd ap Rhys in 1116[2] and again attacked by the Welsh in 1215 and 1220.[3] The garrison appears then to have been withdrawn and military attention

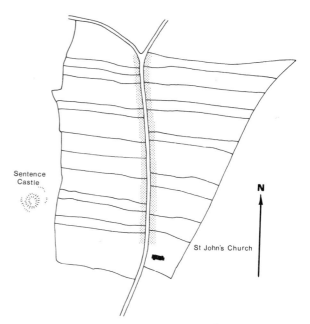

Fig. 99. Templeton

focussed on the new castle at Narberth, but a small civil population remained at Templeton. The 'villa Templariorum' is mentioned in 1283[4] and in the same year there were 'burgesses of the wind' (de vento') here each paying the statutory annual rent of 12d., and total rents of assize amounted to £7 9s. 4d.[5]

The present village lines the main road leading north from St John's church and there are no vestiges of any urban character. Farms are an integral part of the village. It has a very regular lay-out, however, and the plots at the rear of the properties probably represent former burgages, for the most part intact except for where the railway line cuts behind St John's church. The modern map shows some sign of coalescing, but these plots are remarkable for their length, being four to five times longer than the average burgage. Within the outer boundary, though, it is possible to detect another line on both sides of the road running some 50m. behind each property which appears to delineate the house plots and perhaps the remainder represents the arable lands attached to each burgage. In 1532–3 and 1545–6[6] there were 17 burgages at Templeton, so there is no reason to suppose that the early town occupied a greater area than that of the modern village.

1. Knowles and Hadcock, *Medieval Religious Houses*, 296; *R.C.A.M.W.M., Pembs.*, 296.

2. *Brut y Tywysogion*, 40.

3. *Ibid.*, 90, 111; Hogg and King, 'Early Castles', 117, 120

4. *Cal. Cl. Rolls*, 1279–88, 200.

5. C 133/32/7; Owen, *Cal. Pembs. Records*, ii, 75.

6. *Ibid.*, 99, 116.

TENBY (Dinbych-y-pysgod), Dyfed (Pembrokeshire)   SN 136005

'Tinby ys a walled towne hard on the Severn Se yn Penbrookeshire. There is a *sinus* [inlet or cove] and a peere made for shyppes, it 'stondith on a main rokke, but not veri hy, and the Severn Se so gulfeth in about hit, that at the ful se almost the thirde part of the toune is inclosid with water'.[1] These observations by John Leland made in the 1530s emphasise the principal features of the medieval town and of the site which encouraged the Normans to establish an early castle-borough here—its promontory position ideally suited for defence and the conduct of an efficient maritime trade. Indeed, these features appear to have been appreciated by a much earlier breed of colonists and chance finds within the area of the medieval town have produced evidence of Bronze Age and Romano-British occupation. The Welsh version of the place-name which emphasises the importance of the local fishing industry (Dinbych-y-pysgod—'Tenby of the fish') appears in the 9th century, while the Scandinavian raiders who were so active along this stretch of the Welsh coast may also have been attracted to the site.[2] Nevertheless, whatever the antiquity of settlement here, it is clear that the first substantial community was the work of the Normans, who began to establish bases in this area during the latter part of the 11th century. A castle was erected on rising ground at the very tip of the peninsula and the early borough centreing on St Mary's church was laid out to the west. The castle is not mentioned until 1153 when it was attacked by Maelgwyn ap Rhys ap Gruffudd,[3] but the church was granted to the Abbey of Sêez in 1100.[4] The example of Pembroke Castle, recorded *c.* 1093,[5] suggests that the first fortification at Tenby also dates from the late 11th century.

There is little indication of the extent of Norman Tenby since the early borough was sacked by the Welsh under Llywelyn ap Gruffudd in 1260 when the castle was also destroyed.[6] The medieval town as it has come down to us, therefore, is essentially that planned and built in the late 13th century by William de Valence who issued the first borough charter in the 1280s.[7] Under his direction the castle was rebuilt, while a new town was laid out on the western slopes which was further protected by stone walls. St Mary's was also rebuilt, although as parts of the present structure can be ascribed to the Norman period, the shell at least must have survived Llywelyn's attack.[8] Its central position together with the peculiar shape of the peninsula prevented William from achieving anything resembling a regular street-pattern except for Frog Street which runs parallel to the full length of the western wall. By the early 14th century Tenby had emerged as a prosperous borough with a sound economy based on the fishing industry and important trading links with Brittany, France, and Ireland.[9] In 1307 there were 241 burgages here[10] and by 1329–30 the figure had risen to 252[11] which suggests a population of about one thousand and five hundred. The town also had its weekly market on Wednesdays, and an annual fair,[12] but the focal point of the old town was the quay at the foot of the castle. The present pier incorporates part of the original structure, which was standing in the early 13th century when Warren de Monchensy built St Julian's chapel at the end of it.[13] The chapel was intended for use by seamen, and it remained *in situ* until 1842 when the pier was extended.[14]

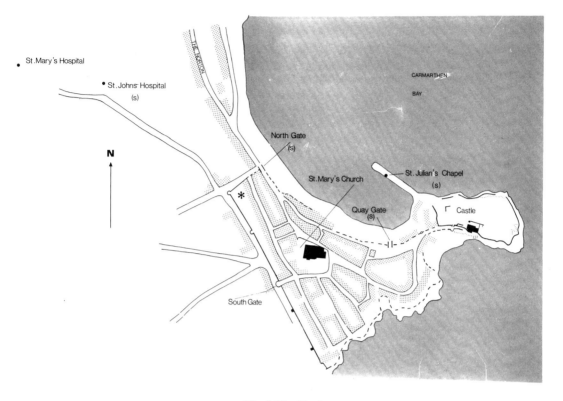

Fig. 100. Tenby

Of the walls which enclosed and protected the early town substantial sections remain, particularly on the west side. The town received a murage grant in 1328,[15] but it is probable that work had begun well before this and the initial course may even have been the work of de Valence. Extensive refortification was carried out in 1457 under the direction of Jasper Tudor when the dry moat, some 9m. wide, was cleaned out and the wall extended to the cliff edge.[16] There were further repairs at the time of the Spanish Armada.[17]

Until the second half of the 18th century Tenby's walls remained virtually complete and the three gates still survived. There are still substantial remains, principally along White Lion Street and South Parade, and it is possible to provide an accurate reconstruction of their entire course.[18] From the south-west tower on the south cliff the wall is intact along the course of St Florence Parade and South Parade. Four towers lie along this section, together with the sole surviving gate, the South Gate, at the end of St George's Street. At the junction of White Lion Street and South Parade the wall turns at right angles to run as far as the North Gate and the cliff. Much of this section survives except where it is bisected by Frog Street. The North or Carmarthen Gate was the most impressive of the three, and John Leland singled it out for comment when he observed that 'the gate that ledith to Cairmardin ward is the most semeliest, as circulid without with an embatelid but open rofid towr, after the fascion of the east gate of Penbroke'.[19] It was finally pulled down in 1781 and its site today is represented by the *Royal Lion* hotel.[20]

From the North Gate the wall continued as far as the cliff, although drainage excavations carried out in the 19th century revealed that the town ditch was not extended along this small section.[21] From the cliff the defences turned south-east and continued as far as the castle, but later re-development in this area has removed all traces of this stretch. A plan of Tenby in 1850 traces the wall on this side as running along the back of Belle Vue, then veering in to Crackwell Street, and following the cliff side of the street as far as the Quay Gate and the castle.[22] This all-important gate, demolished in 1811, stood to the west of St Julian's chapel. The southern cliff face of Tenby, between the castle and the *Imperial* hotel, was also defended, but remains are slight except for a surviving tower by Rock Terrace.

Although an unusually irregular shape, the walled town was sufficiently large to house all but a few of the 252 burgages recorded in 1329-30. For the most part the burgage pattern is still detectable, particularly off Frog Street and the High Street, the early town's main thoroughfares. Other than St Mary's church little else has survived from the medieval period, although the modern town does contain a feature of interest in the 'Tudor Merchant House' in Bridge Street. Known also as the 'Old House', this is the only fairly complete example of early domestic architecture within the town. The building, which was restored by the National Trust in 1939, dates from the early 16th century and once formed part of a larger complex which included portions of the houses on the north and south sides.[23] Another feature of the medieval topography was the 15th-century building known as 'the College' which stood immediately to the west of the church, where some sections of masonry remain. Its name is misleading since there is nothing to suggest that St Mary's was collegiate, and a more likely use was as a dwelling for chantry priests.[24]

With the bulk of the population housed within the walls there was little development outside except for the small suburb of the Norton which grew up beyond the North Gate. This extra-mural area contained two further interesting features associated with the medieval borough—the hospitals of St Mary and St John. No details are known about the foundation of the former which functioned until 1547 as a leper house.[25] The building lay to the north-west of the town near Heywood Lane where a section of the stone walling remains (SN 12780084). St John's hospital was founded by William de Valence in the late 13th century, and it also operated until its dissolution in 1547 when the site was leased to the Recorde family who built a dwelling there, now represented by Garden Cottage, near the railway viaduct (SN 12980081).[26] John Leland noted that the well of St John, which lay immediately to the east, was the only source of water for the town, there being no supply within the walled area.[27]

Unlike the vast majority of its fellow Welsh towns Tenby was not reduced to insignificance by the Glyndŵr rebels. With French help they attempted to take the town in 1405, but the siege was unsuccessful and the townsfolk gained relief by sea.[28] With its vital trading links with Ireland and the Continent the borough thrived and was able to sustain its 14th-century population level until the second half of the 17th century when the development of Narberth market led to a marked decline. Despite a royal order to suppress the activities at Narberth in 1676[29] the rival market reappeared and it was stated that 'the port and towne of Tenby is very near come to utter ruine and desolation; theire houses fallen down, the peere for preserving shiping in danger to fall into decay.[30] By 1670 the population had slumped to about eight hundred and fifty, and for the next 150 years there was no improvement with the 1810 census recording only 800 people in 210 houses. Yet by 1831 the figure had soared again to 2,100, with the growth of the tourist industry, and the effect of the twice-weekly steam packet from Bristol, and Tenby emerged as one of the principal Welsh resorts.

1. *Itinerary*, 61, 116.

2. Thomas, W., 'Tenby', *Arch. Journ.*, cxix (1962), 316; Lloyd, *History of Wales*, i, 265.

3. *Brut y Tywysogion*, 58; Lloyd, *History of Wales*, ii, 503.

4. Leach, A. L., 'Tenby town walls, church, the Old House and Museum', *Arch. Camb.*, xciii (1938), 279.

5. Taylor, A. J., 'Pembroke Castle', *Arch, Journ.*, cxix (1962), 343–4.

6. *Annales Cambriae*, 98.

7. Owen, *Cal. Pembs. Records*, iii, 221–2.

8. Leach, A. L., *op. cit.*, 279; Laws, E. and Edwards, E. H., *The Church Book of St. Mary the Virgin, Tenby* (Tenby, 1907), 3; Owen, *Cal. Pembs. Records*, i, 22.

9. Tenby's early trading activities have been investigated by Sudbury, 'The Medieval Boroughs of Pembrokeshire', Univ. of Wales M.A. (1948)., *op. cit.*, 174–82.

10. C 134/4/1; Owen, *Cal. Pembs. Records*, iii, 81.

11. C 131/9/1; Owen, *Cal. Pembs. Records*, iii, 119.

12. *Ibid.*, iii, 22–3; Owen, *Description of Pembrokeshire*, i, 135, 145.

13. *Ibid.*, 22; Allen, *Guide to Tenby* (Tenby, 1852), 19.

14. Leach, A. L., *Guide to Tenby* (Tenby, 1898), 37.

15. *Cal. Pat. Rolls*, 1327–30, 245; Owen, *Cal. Pembs. Records*, iii, 218–9.

16. *Ibid.*, iii, 234–6; Walker, R. F., 'Jasper Tudor and the town of Tenby', *N.L.W.J.*, xvi (1960–70), 1–22.

17. Smith, J. B., *Historical Sketch of Tenby* (Tenby, 1855), 26–7.

18. The following account owes much to the valuable series of sketches of Tenby and its defences as they appeared in Norris, C., *Etchings of Tenby*, London, 1812. For a more recent account *see* Turner, *Town Defences*, 218–24.

19. *Itinerary*, 116.

20. Leach, A. L., 'Tenby town walls', *op. cit.*, 278; Laws, E., 'Notes on the Fortifications of medieval Tenby', *Arch. Camb.*, 5th ser., xiii (1896), 182–3.

21. *Ibid.*, 277.

22. Reproduced in Thomas, W., *loc. cit.*

23. *Ibid.*, 324; Leach, A. L., 'Tenby Town Walls', *op. cit.*, 280.

24. Thomas W., *op. cit.*, 322. The building has also been linked with a supposed Carmelite friary within the town (Lewis, *Topographical Dictionary*, *sub* Tenby), but there is no evidence for such a foundation at Tenby and Lewis appears to have mistaken it for Denbigh (Dinbych) in North Wales (*R.C.A.M.W.M.*, *Pembs.*, 398; Knowles and Hadcock, *Medieval Religious Houses*, 237).

25. *Ibid.*, 397; *R.C.A.M.W.M.*, *Pembs.*, 398–400.

26. *Cal. Papal Letters*, i, 503–4; Laws and Edwards, *The Church Book of St. Mary the Virgin, Tenby*, 5.

27. *Itinerary*, 61.

28. Lloyd, *Owen Glendower*, 103.

29. For the documents relating to the dispute *see* Howells, *Pembrokeshire Life*, 48–52.

30. *Ibid.*, 48.

TREFILAN, Dyfed (Cardiganshire)   SN 549571

Trefilan lies in an overwhelmingly rural area midway between Tregaron and Newquay. Today it is little more than a hamlet consisting of only a few houses, a church, a school, and the remains of a motte, but the place appears in administrative records of the 13th and 14th centuries, when it was evidently more important. This was a Welsh vill which appears to date from the early 1200s when Maelgwyn ap Rhys built the castle which his son, Maelgwyn Fychan, completed in 1234.[1] The remains of the motte can still be seen opposite the school, but all traces of the bailey have disappeared. This was presumably the 'house of Trefilan' burnt by the English in 1282.[2] The absence of any later mention suggests that it was destroyed, though this was not true of the township. The 'reeve of Trefilan, 'is recorded at this time,[3] while the church was functioning in 1282.[4] In 1301-2 the inhabitants of the 'Welsh vill of Trefilan' are found paying 7s. 6d. annually for their lands, a figure which had increased to 11s. 2d. two years later, and they had their own mill which presumably lay beyond the church by the Nant Rhiw-afallen.[5]

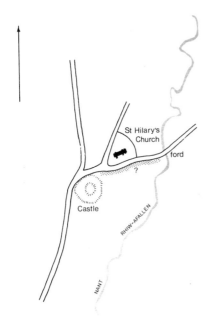

Nothing further is known of this settlement and there is little in the present village to indicate the extent of the medieval vill. By the late Middle Ages it had declined, and John Speed failed to include it on his map of Cardiganshire compiled in 1610.[6] The original church was demolished in 1810 when a smaller structure was erected on its site[7] and in all probability the early tenements lay within its immediate area where protection was also provided by the motte.

Fig. 101. Trefilan

1. *Brut y Tywysogion*, 103; *Annales Cambriae*, 81.
2. *Cal. Anct. Corresp.*, 131-2; Griffiths, R., 'The Revolt of Rhys ap Maredud', *op. cit.*, 125.
3. *Idem, The Principality of Wales in the Later Middle Ages*, 544.
4. *Cal. Ch. Rolls*, ii, 275.
5. Lewis, E. A., 'Chamberlain's Accounts for West Wales', *op. cit.*, 75-6; Rhys, M., *Ministers Accounts*, 76, 310-13, 377-80.
6. *Atlas of Wales, inter* 113-4.
7. Evans, G. E., *Cardinganshire and its Antiquities* (Aberystwyth, 1903), 246.

TREFNANT, Powys (Montgomeryshire)   SJ 185038

Trefnant is to be linked with Cefnllys, Knucklas and Castell-y-Bere as a further example of an attempt at town foundation which came to nothing. The circumstances of its creation centre on a dispute between the burgesses of Montgomery and Gruffudd ap Gwenwynwyn, the former claiming that Gruffudd's market at Welshpool was detrimental to their own commercial interests.[1] Accordingly, in August 1279, Edward I came to the rescue of the Montgomery burgesses by ordering that the Welshpool market be closed and by way of recompense Gruffudd was granted another on Mondays, plus two annual fairs at his manor of *Trevenant*.[2] In 1282, however, on reconsideration of the case, the king decided that the Montgomery allegations were unfounded and the Welshpool market was accordingly restored and that at Trefnant withdrawn.[3] This led to the decline of the new town, although the effect was not immediate; in 1292 there were 18 taxpayers paying 37s. 1¼d.,[4] but by 1332 the figure had fallen to 5s. 6d.[5]

No settlement of this name within the vicinity of Welshpool has survived the Middle Ages, although there are four instances of it as the name of a single dwelling or locality.[6] Since the locale had to be well beyond Welshpool to render the 1279 order effective, Trefnant in Castle Caereinion has the best claim.[7]

1. Davies, J. C., *The Welsh Assize Roll of 1277–84*, 148–54, 235–6.
2. *Cal. Ch. Rolls*, ii, 211. For the full text *see* Bridgeman, 'The Princes of Upper Powys', *op. cit.*, 128–9. *Cf. Cal. Welsh Rolls*, 179.
3. *Cal. Ch. Rolls*, ii, 263. For the text *see* Bridgeman, *op. cit.*, 129–30, and also *Cal. Anct. Corresp.*, 100–1.
4. E 179/242/52,
5. S.C. 6/1146/14.
6. Viz. in the parishes of Guilsfield and Alberbury, near Castle Caereinion, and in the manor of Teirtref (Jones, T. S. and Owen, R., 'A History of the Parish of Guilsfield', *Mont. Coll.*, xxxi [1900], 142).
7. Davies, J. C., 'Lordships and Manors in Montgomery', *ibid.*, xlix (1945), 133.

TREGARON, Dyfed (Cardiganshire)   SN 680598

Tregaron is a small market town occupying a central position within the former county of Cardiganshire.[1] The place takes its name from Caron, allegedly a 3rd-century Welsh ruler, to whom the church is dedicated. The origins of the settlement, in fact, appear to have been linked with this building which was sited on the east bank of the Afon Brennig, 'standin apon a rounde coppe of cast yerth'.[2] The dedication together with the two Dark Age inscribed stones which were formerly in the churchyard point to an early foundation,[3] and it is easy to envisage the subsequent appearance of dwellings in its vicinity. The church is recorded in 1284[4] while in 1290 Edward I granted the lordship of Caron to Geoffrey Clement.[5] Two years later he added the privileges of a weekly market on Tuesday and the right to hold two yearly fairs.[6] The Clement family continued to hold Tregaron until the mid-15th century,[7] and by the early 16th it had emerged as a sufficiently important market centre for Leland to call 'the chief toun of the lordship of Pennarth'.[8]

St Caron's church and the adjoining market square constitute the focal point of the town which was initially confined to the east bank of the river. The irregularity of the street-pattern is typical of the *treflan*, and there is nothing in the lay-out of the present town to suggest that the grants to Geoffrey Clement were

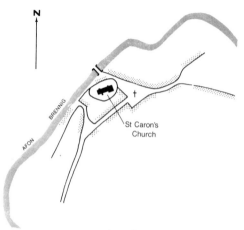

Fig. 102. Tregaron

accompanied by any extension or reorganisation of the settlement. The earliest plan
of Tregaron shows it to have been small with
a secondary grouping of cottages around the
town mill in the area now known as Pentref.[9]
With the development of the drovers' trade,
however, the period 1820–40 was one of
expansion and the town spread east, south and
across the Brennig, although its population
has continued to remain below one thousand.

1. For a general account of the town's history *see*
Rees, D. C., *Tregaron: Historical and Antiquarian*,
Llandysul, 1936. Also valuable is Jones, E., 'Tregaron:
the sociology of a market town in central Cards.,',
in Davies, E. and Rees. A., (eds.), *Welsh Rural Communities* (Cardiff, 1960), 67–117.
  2. Leland, *Itinerary*, 118.
  3. Williams, I. and Nash-Williams, V. E., 'Two Early Christian Stones from Tregaron,
Cardiganshire', *Arch. Camb.*, xci (1936), 15–19.
  4. *Cal. Ch. Rolls*, ii, 275.
  5. *Cal. Welsh Rolls*, 325; Ayloff, J., *Calendar of Ancient Charters* (London, 1774), 97, 100.
  6. *Cal. Ch. Rolls*, ii, 421.
  7. Rees, *Tregaron*, 12–15.
  8. *Itinerary*, 121.
  9. Lewis, W. J., *Illustrated History of Cardiganshire* (1970), *inter* 56–7. The growth of Tregaron
is discussed by Jones, E., *op. cit.*, 72–3, and Carter, *Towns of Wales*, 267–70.

TRELECH (Tryleg), Gwent (Monmouthshire)   SO 500055

Present-day Trelech is little more than a slumbering village lying midway between
Chepstow and Monmouth, but during the late 13th and 14th centuries this ranked
among the principal towns in Wales and outshone more familiar names like
Carmarthen, Abergavenny, and Swansea. It enjoyed the privileges of borough
status, although no charter has survived. and had its own market, and, for a while,
its motte-and-bailey castle.

Trelech—'the town of the stones'—derives its name from the three standing
stones situated just beyond the village by the Chepstow road. Known locally as
'Harold's Stones' they are said to commemorate the site of a battle between the
Welsh and Harold Godwinson, but they are obviously much older and point to a
Dark Age presence in the area. Whether there was any settlement here also in the
centuries before the founding of the medieval borough is a matter for conjecture,
and, it is hoped, excavations, since this prime site has yet to attract the attention
of archaeologists. The 'church of Trilecc' appears in the *Book of Llandaf* in a grant
which dates from the mid-8th century,[1] but the historian of Monmouthshire
considered this to be a reference to the church of Trelech Grange, 2½ miles to the
south and not to any predecessor of St Nicholas's within the later borough.[2]

Trelech's border position and the comparative evidence from other towns in Gwent point to the Norman period for the foundation of the town, although evidence is lacking before the 13th century. The motte, known as 'Twmp Turrett', is not mentioned before 1231,[3] and the first burgages appear in 1288 when the borough contained the substantial figure of 378 plots.[4] This seems to represent Trelech at its height, for eight years later 102 lay vacant, destroyed by fire during a Welsh attack.[5] The signs are that they were not reinhabited as the burgage figure was down to 271 in 1306, held by only 113 burgesses.[6] By 1314 it

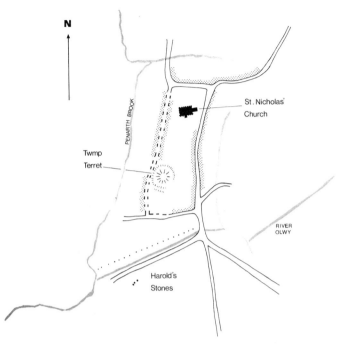

Fig. 103. Trelech

had fallen again to 265,[7] but this remained an impressive total and the place must have existed in striking contrast to the rural hamlet which occupies the site today.

Nevertheless, the modern settlement preserves the basic outline of the medieval borough which had all the appearances of a planned settlement. The site in its wider aspect is a small plateau bounded by the rivers Monnow and Usk, with Trelech laid out within a rectangular area shaped by the River Olwy to the south, the Penarth Brook on the west, and two lesser streams on the north and east. The motte occupies a central position within this area on the west side of the present highway, and there are still substantial remains, although agricultural activity has removed all indications of the bailey. There is nothing to suggest that there were ever any masonry defences here, and the motte had evidently been abandoned by 1306 when an inquisition refers to 'the site of an old castle'.[8] A hundred metres to the north on the same side of the road stands St Nicholas's church. This is a substantial building which dates from the 14th century, and its size is a valuable indication of Trelech's former extent and importance. The road which runs past it and through the village represents one of the original streets, although any traces of a flanking burgage pattern have long since disappeared. With nearly four hundred burgages to accommodate in the late 13th century, however, there were evidently others, and traces of a second street running parallel to the surviving road can be seen on the west side of the church and motte. This was noted by Bradney earlier in the century, who observed sections of paving and foundations.[9] In plots

Fig. 104. Trelech

Once one of the largest of the Anglo-Norman boroughs, the place is today only a slumbering village. The perimeter of the old town can be seen in the form of a rectangle, while the curve of the north-eastern defences is also detectable. The surviving motte is visible in the centre of this aerial view. In contrast to the accompanying town plan (Fig. 103), this view is from the north looking south.

0051, 9642 and 9334 house platforms lining its course remain visible. There may well have been other roads in this area, and two are suggested by field boundary lines which run east-west between the motte and the church. They lead from the main street at right-angles, and are parallel to each other with the distance between them sufficient to accommodate two rows of burgages.

Beyond this suggested street-pattern it is also possible to detect something of the defences which enclosed the medieval borough. These appear to have been in the form of a ditch and slight bank, perhaps topped with a timber palisade, which followed the rectangular course determined by the four streams. In plot 0024 remains of the southern line of the bank running east-west and parallel to the River Olwy can be seen.

The factors behind the decline of late-medieval Trelech have not been investigated although this is the most outstanding example of a decayed settlement in Wales. The withdrawal of the garrison must have played its part, and the town evidently suffered at the hands of the Welsh as witness the 120 burgages which lay burnt in 1296. Nevertheless, there were still 113 burgesses in 1306 and 265 plots in 1314 so other factors were involved. In 1369 Upper Gwent was ravaged by a serious outbreak of plague, and Trelech was badly hit with 48 burgages still vacant 40 years later.[10] It was far from the end of the borough, however, since in 1532 it was still valued at £8 1s. 5d.[11] It would appear to have declined gradually over a long period of time rather than drastically as a result of one or a series of calamities, and the process was still continuing in the 19th century: in 1861 29 houses remained, but by 1901 the number had fallen to 19 of which two stood uninhabited.[12]

1. *Liber Landavensis,* 199–200.
2. Bradney, *History of Monmouthshire,* ii, pt. 2, 150.
3. *Cal. Pat. Rolls,* 1225–32, 427.
4. S.C. 6/1247/21.
5. C 133/77/3; *C.I.P.M.,* iii, 245.
6. C 133/130; *C.I.P.M.,* iv, 326.
7. C 133/43; *C.I.P.M.,* v. 336.
8. Above, note 6.
9. *Op. cit.,* 130–1.
10. S.C. 6/928/19; Rees, *South Wales and the March,* 247.
11. *MSS. Relating to Wales,* iii, 605.
12. Bradney, *op. cit.,* 129.

TYWYN, Gwynedd (Merionethshire)   SH 588008

Tywyn, as its name suggests ('sandy place') is a coastal town which faces Cardigan Bay some five miles north of the Dyfi estuary. Unlike other medieval settlements in Merioneth, such as Bala and Harlech, this was not a planned town and its early development as a native religious and commercial centre affords greater similarities with Dolgellau and, beyond the county, St Asaph and Llantwit Major. The ecclesiastical origins date back to the mid-6th century when Cadfan, a monk from Bardsey, is said to have founded a monastery here which eventually emerged as the 'clas' or 'mother-church' of the surrounding district.[1] In 963 it

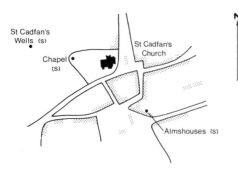

Fig. 105. Tywyn

was attacked by the Danes,[2] but recovered. The sources mention the name of an abbot in 1147,[3] while Giraldus visited the monastery 30 years later.[4] Parts of the present church of St Cadfan, notably the nave, aisles, and a section of the north transept, date from the 12th century, and it may well occupy the site of the original structure.[5] There are two early funerary stones here, one within the church and the other in the graveyard.[6] There was also a small chapel dedicated to St Cadfan at the north-eastern end of the churchyard which was demolished in the early 17th century, and the saint's holy well lies immediately to the north-west, where there is now a builder's yard.[7]

No date can be advanced for the appearance of the town, which is likely to have originated in a cluster of cottages in the shadow of the church. The 'villa de Tewyn in Merennyth' is recorded in 1283,[8] but 10 years later there were only nine taxpayers, and although there would also have been others exempt from payment, the total population was obviously small.[9] The town had a viable economic existence, however, with a market every Friday, and tolls in the late 13th century amounted to 13s. 4d. a year.[10]

There are no early plans of Tywyn, but there are good reasons for placing the medieval town in the area of St Cadfan's church and Corbett Square, which represents the early market-place. According to the Tithe Map of 1841, the area took the form of an elongated triangle with the apex on the western side at the junction of College Green and National Street, and the eastern area bounded by Maengwyn Street, Brook Street, and Frankwell Street.[11] Photographs from the late 19th century show a concentration of old cottages here, since demolished,[12] while there were also a number of almshouses at the junction of National Street and Frankwell Street, which were only recently removed. There are no indications of any defences and there is no evidence to suggest that the early town was ever enclosed by a bank and ditch.

In 1420 the 'villa de Towen' was valued at 60s., much of which derived from the market and fairs,[13] and the settlement itself was of little significance with few houses. As late as 1820 a traveller was able to note that 'as a town . . . it is hardly worthy of an appellation so lofty, and as for streets it has none merely lanes'.[14] The place remained small until the arrival of the railway and the development of the tourist industry which has seen the modern town expand westwards towards the sea and away from the church and the area of the early settlement.

1. Lloyd, *History of Wales*, i, 251-2.
2. *Brut y Tywysogion*, 8; *Brenhinedd Y Saesson*, 39; Lloyd, *History of Wales*, i, 351.
3. *Brenhinedd Y Saesson*, 153.
4. *Opera*, vi, 122.

5. *R.C.A.M.W.M., Mer.*, 170.

6. *Ibid.*, 171–4.

7. Jones, F., *The Holy Wells of Wales*, 191.

8. *Littere Wallie*, 192.

9. William-Jones, K., *The Merioneth Lay Subsidy Roll of 1292-3*, 30.

10. S.C. 11/789.

11. Housed in the Meirionnydd Record Office, Dolgellau.

12. *See* Edwards, J. C., *Guide to Towyn and Neighbourhood*, Tywyn, 1893.

13. *Rec. Caern.*, 276.

14. Thomas, H., 'Tywyn of a century and a half ago', *J.M.H.R.S.*, v (1967), 252.

USK (Brynbuga), Gwent (Monmouthshire)   SO 376008

The town lies on the east bank of the River Usk at a point where it is met by the lesser River Olway. The site is one of low-lying ground, liable to flooding, while to the north the land rises to a hill which has provided Usk with its Welsh name. As with Abergavenny and probably Monmouth the medieval town was preceded by Roman occupation and an intensive series of excavations have revealed the nature and extent of this early settlement—the *Burrium* of the Antonine Itinerary— and its relationship to the later borough. The first phase began *c.* A.D. 55 with the construction of a legionary fortress which was demolished about twenty years later when a smaller fort was built within its defences.[1] This in turn was abandoned towards the end of the 2nd century, but the site continued in use as an industrial and commercial settlement until the 4th century. Very little has come to light of any subsequent occupation here until the arrival of the Normans who erected a castle to the north of the Roman fortress. This is recorded in 1138,[2] but the structure is likely to have been earlier and contemporary with the foundation of the town which seems to have taken place a decade or two after the turn of the century.

Medieval Usk was a substantial place, but there are no indications of its size before the mid-13th century. The early town was probably confined to the area of the castle, which was strengthened in 1173,[3] with Twyn Square representing the central market-place.[4] No charter earlier than that granted by Edward II in 1324 has survived,[5] but Usk was evidently a borough well before this date and it contained 141 burgages in 1262.[6] Further work was carried out on the castle in the middle and late 13th century with the addition of three round towers,[7] and this seems to have been accompanied by the organised expansion of the civil settlement which had risen to 294 burgages by 1306,[8] and 296 in 1314.[9] Many of these plots were occupied only briefly, however, since the war against Llywelyn had resulted in the destruction of 180, while in 1314 a further 104 lay 'void and ruinous' through the poverty of their owners. Although in area it was clearly an extensive town the evidence suggests that the greater part of remained deserted beyond the 13th century.

The recent programme of Roman excavations has yielded valuable information on medieval Usk and in particular on the borough defences which enclosed a substantial area. These were marked by Coxe on his town map of 1801 as a bank and ditch on three sides with the river completing the circuit on the west.[10] Much of the section from Maryport Street to Four Ash Street, known as Clawdd Du, is

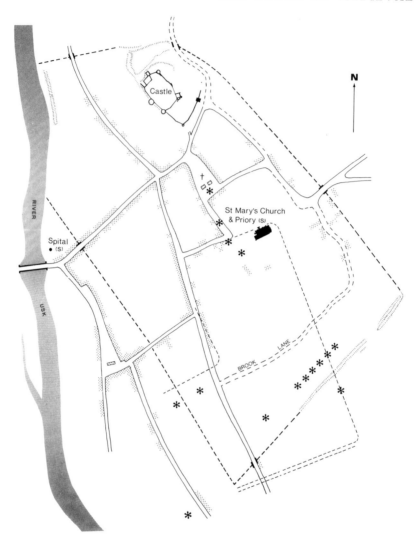

Fig. 106. Usk

still extant and it appears to have originally defended the Roman civil settlement which followed the abandonment of the two forts, and was then recut during the medieval period.[11] In 1974 excavations off Mill Street exposed a large ditch which was part of the western defences and indicated that the river did not constitute the sole protection on this side as Coxe's plan suggests.[12] The line of this ditch, however, does correspond to a continuous boundary line which Coxe shows running parallel to Mill Street and then across Old Market Street and on to Bridge Street, following a course parallel to New Market Street.

From Coxe's map there would appear to have been four gates leading out of the town: the North Gate at the top of Porthycarne Street ('Porth'-gate) by

Fig. 107. The Priory, Usk

A Benedictine nunnery founded in the early 13th century. The rear of the
building is still used as a private dwelling.

Fig. 108. The Gatehouse, Usk Priory

Plas-newydd; the West Gate, near the bridge; the South Gate, at the bottom of Maryport Street, where the name again seems to incorporate the Welsh 'porth'; and, finally, the East Gate at the end of Four Ash Street where the town mill was also located. Occupying a central position within this enclosed area was St Mary's church and the Benedictine priory founded by Richard de Clare. On architectural grounds the church may date from the mid-11th century, although the priory, a house for nuns, was not founded until c. 1236.[13] Much of the building remains, the east wing being still inhabited, while the gatehouse leading to the grounds is also in good repair. Another feature of the medieval town was the 'hospitalis de Usk' recorded in 1322 and dissolved in 1536.[14] The building stood on the north side of Bridge Street just by the bridge and beyond the town defences, although all traces have long since been removed.

The destruction wrought by the Welsh in the early 1280s meant that much of the defended area must have remained vacant throughout the Middle Ages, and indeed right up to the beginning of the present century. Some attempt to revitalise the borough may have been made in the 14th century, but in 1402 and 1405 it was attacked again by Owain Glyndŵr and put to flames.[15] A century later the antiquary, John Leland, noted the remains of the castle, but added that 'the town by semeth not bene of any renown'.[16] His successor, Camden, was equally unimpressed, adding that Usk could 'show nothing but the ruins of a large and strong castle'.[17] From Coxe's map it is evident that much of the inter-mural area had been abandoned and given over to agricultural use as also happened with Chepstow and New Radnor. The lines of former streets are now only represented by footpaths and field boundaries such as Book Lane in the south-east corner of the town. A survey of 1630 records 19 burgages here, although by 1670 the number had fallen to 11,[18] and by 1801 there were only a few houses at its eastern end. House foundations lining this lane were observed by Bradney,[19] while excavations at the western end in 1973 exposed the remains of two 14th-century dwellings.[20] From being an important street Book Lane had declined to a track by Coxe's time, while today it is the smallest of footpaths.

A similar fate has befallen streets in the south-western part of the old borough. Coxe indicates that Baron Street, which leads south from New Market Street, continued right down to the southern defences, but the lower section has since disappeared and is represented only by field boundaries. Excavations off the lower part of Maryport Street on the site of the cattle market also produced evidence of medieval occupation, although this area is also shown as uninhabited in 1801.[21] Recent development has seen Usk gradually regaining many of these abandoned areas, although the south-eastern section of the old town remains essentially farmland.

1. Manning, W. H., *Archaeology in Wales*, vii–xliii (1962-73) and *Current Archaeology*, vi (1978), 71-7. *See also* Boon, G. C., 'Remarks on Roman Usk', *Mon. Antiq.*, i (1962), 28-33.

2. Ordericus Vitalis, *Hist. Eccles.*, v, 110. For a recent discussion of the castle *see* Knight, J. K., 'Usk Castle and its Affinities', in Apted, M. R., Gilyard-Beer, R. and Saunders, A. D. (eds.), *Ancient Monuments and their Interpretations*: Essays presented to A. J. Taylor (London, 1977), 139–54.

3. *Pipe Roll*, 20 Hen. II, 22.

4. The original market-place was subsequently abandoned in favour of a site at the junction of Old and New Market Streets. The move had taken place by 1598 and a central market house was built *c.* 1620, which was demolished in 1834 (Bradney, *History of Monmouthshire*, iii, pt. i, 12, 23).

5. The charter survives in an *inspeximus* by Edward III in 1359 (*Cal. Ch. Rolls*, v. 164; Clark, *Cartae*, iv, 1303–5).

6. S.C. 6/1202/1.

7. Knight, 'Usk Castle', *op. cit.*, 141–7.

8. C 133/130.

9. C 134/43; *C.I.P.M.*, iii, 2. The inquisition is published in full in Bradney, *op. cit.*, 2–4.

10. *Historical Tour through Monmouthshire*, 123.

11. *Archaeology in Wales*, xii (1972), 27; xv (1975), 50.

12. *Ibid.*, 49.

13. *Mon. Angl.*, iv, 591; Cowley, *Monastic Order in South Wales*, 38.

14. *Cal. Ch. Rolls*, iii, 449; Clark, *Cartae*, iii, 1100; Knowles and Hadcock, *Medieval Religious Houses*, 400.

15. *Chron. Adam de Usk*, 247, 282; Lloyd, *Owen Glendower*, 54, 96–7.

16. *Itinerary*, 44.

17. *Britannia*, 635.

18. The surveys of 1630 and 1670 are most accessible in Bradney, *op. cit.*, 23–33, and Clark, J. H., *Usk, Past and Present* (Usk, undated), 211–24.

19. *Op. cit.*, 12.

20. *Archaeology in Wales*, ix (1969), 22.

21. *Ibid.*, viii (1968), 18; xiii (1973), 42.

WELSHPOOL (Y Trallwng), Powys (Montgomeryshire)   SJ 224075

Welshpool lies only two miles from Offa's Dyke, the historic boundary between Wales and England, and like many of the Powys towns it came into being as a deliberate attempt on the part of local ruler, Gruffudd ap Gwenwynwyn, to emulate the more prosperous boroughs like Hereford across the border.[1] The chosen site for the venture was the entrance to the deep valley of the Lledan, and although open to the Severn valley on the east side natural protection was afforded by the Golfa moorland on the west side. Although essentially a planned town of the mid-13th century, it is nevertheless important to note that the site may have a much longer settlement history dating back to the late Roman period. During the building of a new Smithfield in 1959 a phase of 2nd-century occupation was unearthed with the discovery of a number of Romano-British objects, and several Roman coins have also come to light from the area of the town and its immediate environs.[2] Early literary sources also state that the 6th-century St Cynfelyn founded a church at Welshpool, and that his brother, Llywelyn, did likewise.[3] Indeed, the site of this early religious house has been traditionally identified as that of the 'Old Church' which stood at the corner of Salop Road and Mill Lane (formerly Clerk's Lane). Distinct from the borough church of St Mary's this building was erected in 1587, but was destroyed by fire in 1659, although masonry remains were still visible in the late 19th century. An adjoining graveyard is indicated by the regular discovery

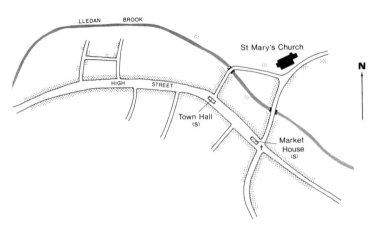

Fig. 109. Welshpool

of human remains nearby.[4] No attempt has been made to date these finds, but they may represent interments associated with a predecessor of the 'Old Church' since St Mary's had its own graveyard attached.

Whatever the nature and extent of any Dark Age settlement at Welshpool the 13th-century borough was a planned town which owed little to an existing community. The latter, in fact, may have been in the area of the motte-and-bailey castle recorded in 1196, and whose remains can be seen half a mile to the east of the medieval borough.[5] The fortification was abandoned in the second half of the 13th century when Powys Castle was built[6] and the foundation charter to the Welshpool burgesses may be as early as 1241-45.[7] Provision was made for a weekly market,[8] temporarily moved to Trefnant in 1278 after complaints from the Montgomery burgesses that it was damaging their commercial activities, but subsequently restored,[9] and by 1292 'La Pole', as the town was then known, had emerged as a sizeable borough of 106 taxpayers.[10] The early years of the following century were a period of sustained growth, and from a burgess total of 173 recorded in 1309,[11] the figure had risen to 225 by 1322.[12]

In its lay-out the early town was fashioned along a distinct linear pattern with the principal thoroughfare, High Street, following the line of the Lledan Brook. Curiously St Mary's church lies on the north side of the brook, although it may be significant that this area is called 'Welshe towne' on Humphrey Bleaze's town map of 1629. Could it be that St Mary's and not the 'Old Church' represents the site of the early Celtic church?[13] Bleaze's map provides much other valuable information on medieval Welshpool and shows several since-vanished topographical features.[14] Prominently marked to the south of the town is 'The Poole' which gave the town its name. Now an insignificant pond in the enclosure of Powys Castle this was formerly a more extensive sheet of water, as Leland noted in the 1530s: 'The Walsche Poole, a market toune, taketh name of a poole therby, meatly large and plentiful of fische'.[15] Leland, in fact, was one of the first writers to refer to the borough as 'Welshpool' rather than 'Pool' which name had served the town and castle for centuries, the qualification being necessary to distinguish it from the expanding English port of Poole in Dorset. Along the line of the High Street, Bleaze indicates the built-up areas and names the lesser streets, although many of these no longer retain their original form.[16] The market cross is shown *in situ* at

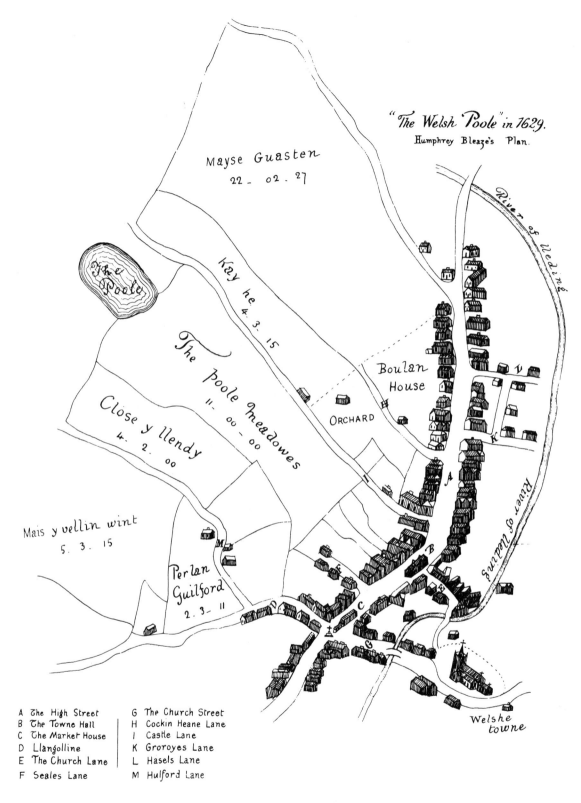

"The Welsh Poole" in 1629.
Humphrey Bleaze's Plan.

A The High Street
B The Towne Hall
C The Market House
D Llangolline
E The Church Lane
F Seales Lane
G The Church Street
H Cockin Heane Lane
I Castle Lane
K Groroyes Lane
L Hasels Lane
M Hulford Lane

Fig. 110. Welshpool in 1629

An early plan of the borough by Humphrey Bleaze. As its single street
suggests this was a planned settlement, the work of Gruffudd ap Gwenwynwyn in the mid-13th century. Bleaze's map shows the Town, Hall,
Market House and Town Cross *in situ*.

east end of the High Street, where it joins Church Street, while nearby Bleaze marked the market house which was demolished in 1761. Also in the middle of the High Street, but further west at the junction with Hall Street, was the old town hall, which stood until 1873 when a successor was built nearby. One building omitted from this map was the *Old Pack-Horse* inn, which was a timber-framed building dating from the mid-16th century. It stood off Mount Street, near St Winifride's Roman Catholic church (SJ 220075) until the site was cleared in 1958.[17]

Apart from delineating several lost features of early Welshpool, Humphrey Bleaze's map is additionally valuable in that it shows that the town was not seriously affected by the forces which reduced many thriving 14th-century boroughs to insignificance by the 16th century. It would be unwise to count the number of individual houses shown, but the importance of the plan is that it shows the full length of the High Street as developed with the beginnings of growth eastwards along Severn Street, and southwards along Berriew Street. Despite the ravages of Glyndŵr,[18] then, Welshpool remained a sizeable community with an important commercial existence based on the market and its three yearly fairs. In later years this existing function was to attract large-scale investment from textile manufacturers, and during the late 18th and early 19th centuries the development of the flannel industry saw the old borough expand well beyond its medieval confines.

1. On the general history of the town *see* Jones, M. C. 'Welshpool', *Mont. Coll.*, vii (1874), 267-352; xii (1879), 309-56; xiii (1880), 191-286; xiv (1881), 161-236; xv (1882), 249-360, and Owen R., 'Welshpool and Powys-land; a history of the Town and Borough of Welshpool and surrounding District', *ibid.*, xxix (1896), 161-288.

2. Boon, G. C., 'Roman Antiquities at Welshpool', *Antiq., Journ.*, xli (1961), 13-31.

3. Lloyd, *History of Wales*, i, 248.

4. Owen, R., *op. cit.*, 188; Jones, M. C., *op. cit.*, xiii (1881), 269-70 where a drawing of the remains is attached; Davies, R., *Welshpool Sixty Years Ago* (Welshpool, 1954), 65.

5. *Brut y Tywysogion*, 76.

6. Hogg and King, 'Masonry Castles', 119.

7. For the text and a translation of this and an additional charter of 1406 *see* Jones, M. C., 'The Feudal Barons of Powys', *Mont. Coll.*, i (1868), 302-12. For the dating cited here, which is earlier than usually ascribed, *see* the discussions by Morgan, R., 'The foundation of the Borough of Welshpool', *ibid.*, lxv (1977), 9.

8. The market is recorded in 1252 when market day was changed from Friday to Monday (*Cal. Cl. Rolls*, 1251-3, 142).

9. For the documentation *see above sub* 'Trefnant'.

10. E 179/242/54.

11. C 134/10/16. The text of the inquisition appears in full in Bridgeman, 'The Princes of Upper Powys', *op. cit.*, 152-62, with the Welshpool entry on p. 153.

12. S.C. 6/1146/52.

13. On the church *see* Millward, W. J. N., 'St Mary's Church, Welshpool', *Mont. Coll.*, xliv (1936), 129-38.

14. A reproduction of the map also appears in Jones, M. C., 'Welshpool', *ibid.*, xiii (1880), *inter* 242-3.

15. *Itinerary*, 41.

16. For a discussion of the old street-names and their modern equivalents *see* Jones, M. C., *op. cit.* (1880), 241-2;

17. Hague, D. B., 'The Old Pack-horse Inn, Welshpool', *ibid.*, lv (1958), 125-7.

18. Lloyd, *Glendower*, 32, 44.

WISTON (Cas-wis), Dyfed (Pembrokeshire)   SN 022181

Wiston is situated in an overwhelmingly rural area some four miles north-east of Haverfordwest. Today the place is little more than a collection of farms grouped around the Norman church of St Mary's, and the impressive remains of a motte-and-bailey, but this was formerly a market town as well as a borough, though purely by prescription. The castle,[1] the *caput* of the lordship of Deugleddyf, was the work of a Fleming named Wizo, whose name became incorporated in that of the stronghold and the borough. The castle and church are first documented in the period 1115-47,[2] but Wizo had died before 1130,[3] which suggests that the motte, and in all probability St Mary's, was built in the early years of the century when the town was also laid out.[4] In 1220 the castle was destroyed by the Welsh under Llywelyn ab Iorwerth, and the sources add that the 'town' was also burned.[5] The castle does not appear to have been refortified, and very little is known of the subsequent history of the borough. By George Owen's day the weekly market had been discontinued,[6] although a yearly fair remained, and Lewis noted that it was still being held in 1833.[7] No community of any note appears to have survived beyond the medieval period, although Wiston was able to retain its burghal status and the privileges which went with it; in 1710 we find the mayor and burgesses petitioning the House of Commons and emphasising that their town was 'an ancient borough by prescription and hath divers franchises and privileges belonging thereunto'.[8]

1. For a description of the castle, which has a stone keep, *see* King, D. J. C., 'Wiston Castle', *Arch. Journ.*, cxix (1962), 326-8.
2. *Ecclesiam castelli Wystsonis de Dugledin* (Hart, W. H., *Historia et Cartularium Monasterii Sancti Petri Gloucestriae* (R.S.), i, (1863), 265; *Brut y Tywysogion*, 55-6.
3. Lloyd, *History of Wales*, ii, 425.
4. *R.C.A.M.W.M.*, *Pembs.*, 418.
5. *Brut y Tywysogion*, 97; *Brenhinedd Y Saesson*, 223; *Cal. Anct. Corresp.*, 4.
6. *Description of Pembrokeshire*, i, 142.
7. *Topographical Dictionary*, *sub* Wiston.
8. Bronwydd MS., 1674; Howells, *Pembrokeshire Life*, 56-7.

WREXHAM (Wrecsam), Clwyd (Denbighshire)   SJ 336502

Although Wrexham was not made a chartered borough until 1857 the town has a long history and it has traditionally occupied an important position in the urban hierarchy of north-east Wales. Situated in an area where control frequently alternated between English and Welsh, the initial settlement, like that of Rhuddlan, may well have been Saxon with early forms of the place-name such as *Wryghtlesham* (1317) indicating that 'ham' or settlement of *Wryht*, either a personal name or that of a craft.[1] For two centuries following the Domesday Survey Wrexham formed part of the lordship of Maelor which remained largely in Welsh hands except for periodic spells of English control.[2] It was probably during one of these periods that the castle 'de Wristlesha', recorded in 1161,[3] was built, but its location was probably at Erddig and it played little part in the development of the early town which was focussed on the church of St Giles overlooking the River Gwenfro. The foundation is mentioned in 1220 when half the rectorial income was granted to Valle Crucis abbey, but it was probably much older than this and appears to have originated as a private chapel built by some local Welsh lord on his demesne.[4] Twenty years earlier Valle Crucis had also been granted lands in Wrexham which came to form the manor of Wrexham Abbott with the remainder constituting the manor of Wrexham Regis, and since their boundary line ran through the early town Wrexham for much of its history was in the curious position of being governed through two manorial courts.[5]

As part of the marcher lordship of Bromfield and Yale Wrexham was included in the first survey of the lands carried out in 1315.[6] The findings revealed an established community which had its own markets, valued at £17 a year, its courts, a mill, and the list of inhabitants showed that a wide variety of trades were being carried out there. In all there were 52 tenements held by 44 tenants, and since all but eight were Welsh the early development of Wrexham appears to have owed little to the English conquest. The weekly market was originally held on a Sunday, but in 1331 (the year after the collapse of the church belfry was considered a sufficiently noteworthy event to attract the attention of the *Brut's* chronicler) the *Brut* records a change to Thursday.[7] The town received a grant of privileges in April 1380 from Richard fitz Alan II, lord of Bromfield and Yale, but in reality the award was little more than a confirmation of existing rights whose formalisation added to Wrexham's curious administrative position. Although never rising above the rank of 'villa mercatoria' Wrexham's features closely resembled those of the minor Welsh boroughs.[8]

Throughout the medieval period Wrexham was an important commercial centre, and John Leland noted that it was 'the only market towne of Walsch Maylor'.[9] The early development of iron and coal mining in the surrounding area did much to prevent the marked decline which many towns experienced in the 15th century, and as well as a viable tanning industry there were also 'sum merchauntes and bokeler makers'.[10] Although there is insufficient evidence for an estimate of the early population the extent and many of the features of the medieval town are known. The initial growth was to the north of St Giles's church where the original street-pattern appears to have survived with little modification. The first tenements began at Town Hill which led into the High Street, the town's principal thoroughfare, and from here two streets run due north: Chester Street and Hope/Queen Street, to form a large rectangle bounded on the north by Lambpit Street.[11] At the corner of Hope Street and Town Hill stood the town hall with the market cross located directly in front of it. The building is first mentioned in 1562, but it was apparently then of considerable age, although it was not rebuilt until a century later after the old hall, together with a quarter of the town, was destroyed by fire in 1643.[12] Its successor, as John Wood's map of 1833 indicates, protruded a long way into the street and in 1939 it succumbed to the pressures of modern traffic and had to be demolished.[13]

With the exception of the Abbott's Mill mentioned in the extent of 1315 and situated near the present Brewery Place,[14] there was little development on the

south bank of the Gwenfro
which, until much of its
course was culverted in
1881, flowed through the
middle of what is now
Brook Street and was
crossed by bridges at the
bottom of Pentre'r Felin
and Vicarage Hill. The latter
takes its name from the
old vicarage which was still
standing during the early
17th century. By this date
Wrexham also had its first
grammar school, which had
been founded in 1603 by
Alderman Valentine
Broughton of Chester. The
first buildings lay south of
Lambpit Street, and in
1800 they were demolished
and replaced by a larger
structure which was pur-
chased by the Corporation
in 1883 and transformed
into the guildhall.[15] The
endowment of Wrexham
Grammar School reflects
the growing importance of

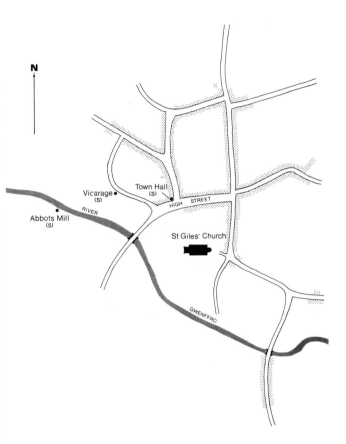

Fig. 111. Wrexham

the town in the early 17th century which is also illustrated by the appearance of
several impressive *plasau*, town houses of the local gentry. Among these were
'Plas Gwern', the home of the Salusburys,[16] and 'The Mount', which lay off the
south side of Mount Street near the river. The latter was demolished in the early
1890s,[17] together with what was probably the most impressive of these gentry
seats, 'Brynyffynnon', which stood near the junction of Regent Street and Hill
Street.[18] The appearance of these buildings on the townscape were indicative of
Wrexham's growing stature, and with a viable economic life centring now on
two weekly markets,[19] brewing, tanning, and iron-making, the foundations for later
industrial growth were already well established.

1. Charles, B. G., *Non-Celtic Place-Names in Wales* (London, 1938), 207; Melville Richards,
in Nicolaisen, W. (ed.), *The Names of Towns and Cities in Britain* (London, 1970), 196.
2. Dodd, A. H. (ed.), *History of Wrexham* (Wrexham, 1957), 17.
3. *Pipe Roll*, 8 Hen. II, 20.
4. For a discussion of this view *see* Dodd, *op. cit.*, 20–1, and on the structural history,
Arch. Journ., xciv (1937), 313–4.

5. Palmer, A. N., *History of the Town of Wrexham* (Wrexham, 1893), 2.

6. Ellis, T. P. (ed.), *The First Extent of Bromfield and Yale, A.D., 1315,* Cymm. Rec. Ser., xi (London, 1924), 47–57.

7. *Brut y Tywysogion,* 126.

8. Evans, B., 'A Grant of Privileges to Wrexham (1380)', *B.B.C.S.,* xix (1962), 42–7.

9. *Itinerary,* 60.

10. *Ibid.,* 70; Palmer, *History of Wrexham,* 9–11.

11. On the street-names *see* Lerry, G. C., 'The Street-Names of Wrexham', *T.D.H.S.,* xv (1966), 169–85. The eastern part of the town was mapped in 1767 (Clwyd Rec. Offices, D/GW/661).

12. Palmer, *History of Wrexham,* 10, 39–44; Lerry, *op. cit.,* 169.

13. *Ibid.,* 169. Wood's map is reproduced in Dodd, *op. cit. inter* 98–9.

14. Ellis, *Extent of Bromfield and Yale,* 57; Pratt, D., 'The Medieval Water-mills of Wrexham', *T.D.H.S.,* xiii (1964), 26.

15. Palmer, *History of Wrexham,* 105–11; Dodd, *op. cit.,* 270.

16. *Ibid.,* 41; Palmer, *History of Wrexham,* 155–6.

17. *Ibid.,* 148; Dodd, *op. cit.,* 220.

18. Palmer, *History of Wrexham,* 58–63.

19. The medieval Thursday market was supplemented with another on Mondays (Bowen, *Britannia Depicta,* 266; Pratt, D., 'Wrexham's Medieval Market', *T.D.H.S.,* xv [1966], 8–14).

INDEX

Because the major part of this book takes the form of an alphabetical gazetteer the index does not include individual towns except those which do not figure in this study.

273

LIST OF SUBSCRIBERS

G. R. Airth
Dr. J. R. Alban
Leslie Alcock
Afan Ab Alun
Dr. R. Penry Ambler
A. Th. Arber-Cooke
M. St. H. Armitstead
Michael A. Aston, BA, FSA
Katherine Barker
D. H. Bartlett
D. A. Bartley, BA
Julia M. Beeden
Stephen H. Beun
Gareth A. Bevan
J. M. H. Bevan
Martin Biddle
Edward Biffin, MA
Stephen H. Billson
C. J. Bond
George C. Boon
John Bosanko
H. Brooksby, FSA
Rev. Roger L. Brown
Edward Cooper Bryan, LLB
John R. Bulmer
M. T. Burdett-Jones
T. Duncan Cameron, FRICS
Dr. A. J. P. Campbell
Alan Carter
Professor Harold Carter
Ian Caruana
A. O. Chater
Dr. R. C. Chivers
H. B. Clarke
Clwyd Library Service
Clwyd-Powys Archaeological Trust
Michael Collins
Anna Cooper
T. L. Cooper
George Prothro Coulter
O. Cowburn
Rev. Canon James Cunnane
Professor Clyde Curry Smith
Cynon Valley Borough Libraries
Alun G. Davies, CBE
D. Garfield Davies, FRCS
D. Wheway Davies, OBE, FIFE
Dr. Edward J. J. Davies
Gillian P. Davies
Joan Davies
J. Barry Davies
Rev. Maldwyn A. Davies
Michael Glanmor Davies
Morgan Lyle Davies
Mrs. Norma E. Davies
O. Talog Davies
Miss P. M. Davies, MA (Oxon),
  MA (Wales)
R. J. Davies
R. R. Davies
P. E. Davis
Rev. M. C. Donaldson
Mrs. Joan Downes-Evans
Dyserth Field Club
M. R. Eddy
Allen Edwards

Trefor Edwards
Mary Ellis
Dr. Ann Ellison
A. Weston Evans, JP, LLB
C. J. Evans, CPM, AIL
D. H. Evans
Evan M. P. Evans, BSc
H. John Evans
J. A. H. Evans
J. M. Evans
J. Wynford Evans
S. Ungoed Evans
Michael Eyers
P. J. Fasham
Eric Finney
M. J. Fisher
Hon. Mrs. Fisher-Hoch
Miss H. A. Formby
E. J. K. Francis
Alan C. Fraser
Dr. K. Gammon
Charles John Gittins
Sir William Gladstone, Bt.
Robin E. Glasscock
Glasgow University Library
Mrs. D. Goodman
Mr. & Mrs. E. J. Grainger
Frank Robert Green
His Honour Judge Bruce
  Griffiths, QC
Colin Griffiths
D. B. Griffiths, MS, FRCS
Mrs. Mair Wynn Griffiths
N. A. Griffiths
T. D. Groves
K. Lloyd Gruffydd
R. Geraint Gruffydd
Dr. G. H. Guest
Hikki Haines-Kälin
G. H. Hammersley
Dr. David J. Harris
D. W. Harris
R. Gwilym Harris
Alan H. Hart
Tom Hassall
Dr. N. J. Higham
Michael B. Hill, ALA
Dr. Malcolm J. Hockaday
Robert J. S. Hodgkinson
Rod Hough, BA
Peter Howell-Williams
D. G. Lloyd Hughes
D. R. Hughes
Dr. Goronwy Alun Hughes
Richard Hughes
T. Wesley Hughes
Kathleen A. Humphreys
Professor R. Ian Jack
E. L. James
Mr. & Mrs. N. A. James
W. E. James
Mr. & Mrs. T. G. John
Dr. Alun H. Jones
Dr. Arthur M. Jones
Daffydd Morris Jones
Elizabeth Jones

Dr. E. D. Jones
Emyr Wyn Jones
Mrs. Grace Alwyn Jones
Dr. Glynne R. Jones
Professor G. R. J. Jones
Gwenllian V. Jones
Megan Eileen Jones
Megan Price Jones
Merfyn O. Jones
M. Rhys Jones
Neil Dickerson Jones
O. Rocyn Jones
Philip Henry Jones
Tegwyn Jones
D. W. Jones-Williams
J. V. Joyce
Eleanor Kelsall
Lord Kenyon
Geoffrey E. Kilfoil, MA
P. W. King
C. H. Knowles
Mrs. I. M. Lambot
James Lawson
D. R. Lewis
Edward William Lewis
Dr. & Mrs. G. E. D. Lewis
Glyn Meredith Lewis
Lewis John Daniel Lewis
Richard Philip Lewis
Herbert Johnes Lloyd-Johnes,
  OBE, TD, LLD, FSA
Julian E. Lloyd
Nesta Lloyd
Thomas O. S. Lloyd
Professor Henry Loyn
Mrs. Isabel F. McGraghan, ATD
Dr. Joanna Martin
S. N. Mastoris
A. G. Mein
Colin J. N. Merrony
Julian Mitchell
Donald Moore
D. Morgan
Howard Morgan
John Morgan
Richard Morgan
T. Edgar H. Morgan
Dafydd Albert Morris
Ieuan Gwyn Morris
Jan Morris
Susan Jacqueline Morris
Dr. Richard Muir
Julian Munby
National Museum of Wales
C. W. Newman
Keith Nurse
J. D. Owen
John G. Owen
M. G. Owen
G. R. Pack
Stuart R. Paltridge
A. K. Parker
R. H. Parry
Edward Parry-Jones MD, MS,
  FRCOG
John C. Pentney

Martin Petchey
Anthony Powell
R. F. Peter Powell
Derrick Pratt
R. H. C. Pugh
P. D. Randall, MRTPI
J. E. Raw-Rees, DFC, JP, DL
Henry Rees
Iorwerth Rees, DipLH
Trefor I. Rees
Dr. Una Rees
Ceredig Phillips Rhys
Joyce E. Richards
Dr. J. M. Richards
Lt. Col. G. G. Roach
Doris Olwen Roberts
Enid Roberts
John Benson Roberts
John Lewis Roberts
Dr. David M. Robinson
Dr. Warwick Rodwell, FSA
Mr. & Mrs. J. B. Rowlands
G. K. Russell
J. G. T. Rutherford
Peter Sheppard
J. G. T. Sheringham

Shrewsbury School Library
J. B. Sidebotham, CMG, MA
D. W. Smith
Ceinwen A. Snowdon
S. C. Stanford
J. A. Stratton
Swansea Museum
R. E. Takel, MSc, FRICS, MCIT
Tim Tatton-Brown
T. J. Taylor
Dr. Ceinwen H. Thomas
E. Hugh Thomas
George C. Thomas
Harry Mainwaring Thomas
R. A. S. Thomas
M. W. Thompson
Nonn Trangmar
Margaret Trigg
Professor D. Gordon Tucker
D. J. Turner
Dr. John R. T. Turner
University College, Cardiff,
 Dept. of Extra-Mural Studies
Piers Vitebsky, MA, PhD
D. A. Walker

T. Mervyn Ll. Walters, MBE
Richard G. Waters
His Honour Judge Watkin
 Powell
Nia M. Watkin Powell
Dr. J. R. S. Webb
Max W. Wheeler
Dr. Eurwyn Wiliam
Rev. Dr. David H. Williams, FSA
Dr. David L. Williams
Elvira Williams
Gwyneth A. Williams
Dr. G. Aled Williams
Henry Williams
Howard F. Williams
J. G. Williams
John Williams
R. B. M. Williams
Robert C. Williams
Rhodri W. M. Williams
Dr. T. C. Williams
L. S. Willmore
Andrew J. Wilson
Jane D. D. Wood
Michael V. Wynne